The Role of Financial Stability in EU Law and Policy

European Monographs Series Set

VOLUME 101

Editor

Prof. Andrea Biondi is Professor of European Law and Director of the Centre of European Law at King's College London

Introduction & Contents/Subjects

As the process of European integration assumes an increasingly complex character, the EU legal system continues to undergo sweeping changes. The European Monographs series offers a voice to thoughtful, knowledgeable, cutting edge legal commentary on the now unlimited field of European law. Its emphasis on focal and topical issues makes the series an invaluable tool for scholars, practitioners, and policymakers specializing or simply interested in EU law.

Objective

The aim is to publish innovative work appealing to academics and practitioners alike. The result is an original and ongoing library of detailed analyses, theories, commentaries, practical guides, and proposals, each of which furthers the cause of meaningful European integration. Cumulatively, the series may be regarded as a 'work in progress' engaged in building a sharply defined representation of law in Europe.

Readership

Academics and practitioners dealing with EU law.

The titles published in this series are listed at the end of this volume.

The Role of Financial Stability in EU Law and Policy

Gianni Lo Schiavo

Wolters Kluwer

Published by:
Kluwer Law International B.V.
PO Box 316
2400 AH Alphen aan den Rijn
The Netherlands
Website: www.wklawbusiness.com

Sold and distributed in North, Central and South America by:
Wolters Kluwer Legal & Regulatory U.S.
7201 McKinney Circle
Frederick, MD 21704
United States of America
Email: customer.service@wolterskluwer.com

Sold and distributed in all other countries by:
Turpin Distribution Services Ltd
Stratton Business Park
Pegasus Drive, Biggleswade
Bedfordshire SG18 8TQ
United Kingdom
Email: kluwerlaw@turpin-distribution.com

FSC
MIX
FSC® C103993

Printed on acid-free paper.

ISBN 978-90-411-8230-2

e-Book: ISBN 978-90-411-8613-3
web-PDF: ISBN 978-90-411-8612-6

Printed in the United Kingdom.

Ai miei genitori ed a Eleni

'Per aspera sic itur ad astra'
(Senex, Hercules furens, Act II, v. 437)

Table of Contents

Foreword

The financial crisis, which started to unfold in 2007, has had a major impact on the political, economic and social shape of Europe. It is often not emphasised enough that it has also re-shaped the evolution of European law. That is the contribution of this pioneering book by Gianni Lo Schiavo to European legal scholarship. It depicts a Copernican revolution in European law: the shift from market integration to financial stability as the justification for the law of the single financial market.

Until the financial crisis and within the framework of the Treaty, the sole purpose of the law of the single financial market was achieving market integration. It aimed essentially at removing national obstacles to the freedom to provide financial services. This created a contradiction between market integration and financial stability, for two main reasons. First, since regulatory competences remained national, financial stability could only be achieved by constraining the activities of financial institutions and markets within national borders. For example, at the limit, imposing capital controls could be a financial stability measure. In turn, this would contradict market integration and is prohibited by the Treaty. Second, only national fiscal sovereignty could provide the backstop for addressing financial crises. The fiscal capacity of the state was the last resort for containing financial instability, including through the bailout of banking institutions as it happened during the crisis. Since there was no European fiscal capacity, financial stability could not be ensured across national borders despite market integration.

Over time, the outcome was that the single financial market steadily expanded but without a European framework for financial stability. All the financial stability functions remained national: the monitoring of the financial system; the supervision of financial institutions and markets; the provision of lender of last resort (LOLR) facilities; the insurance of deposits; the winding down of financial institutions. Even the creation of the single currency did not change this outcome, with the ECB given the limited task to contribute to the smooth conduct of national policies on prudential supervision and financial stability. It was widely assumed that national competences, together with spontaneous cooperation between national authorities, would suffice to contain systemic risk. This would enable further market integration without transferring financial stability competences to the European level or impinging on national fiscal sovereignty. In other words, Member States would be able to share the benefits of market integration without sharing any of its potential risks and related costs.

This proved an illusion. When the crisis erupted, the contradiction between market integration and financial stability came to the fore. There were no European institutions, rules or instruments to prevent or manage the crisis in the single financial market. Member States rescued their domestic institutions with public funds and ring-fenced their markets. The liabilities of these institutions became the liabilities of the Member States that came to their rescue, later contributing to the sovereign debt crisis. The previous dominance of market integration over financial stability in the single financial market was inverted: national financial stability prevailed and led to a retrenchment in European market integration.

This is where the book of Gianni Lo Schiavo starts. It analyses whether financial stability has become a new justification for European law. As well argued throughout the book, the legal and institutional developments in European law since 2008 have been remarkable. They include the introduction of the European Systemic Risk Board as a macro-prudential body; the creation of new supervisory agencies; the transfer of banking supervision and resolution to the Single Supervisory Mechanism (SSM) and the Single Resolution Mechanism, respectively, as the two pillars of the Banking Union; the reform of economic governance, including the Treaty on Stability, Coordination and Governance (TSCG); the establishment of the European Financial Stability Facility (EFSF) and European Stability Mechanism as backstops for the stability of individual Member States; and a new approach to European financial regulation based on a single rulebook and 'total harmonisation'.

These developments are quite diverse, but there is a common denominator between them, which corresponds to the title of the book: the pursuance of 'stability'. This required at every step a balancing act in law between achieving stability and market integration, while respecting national fiscal sovereignty. As highlighted in the book, there was a plethora of legal solutions. Some were found within the boundaries of the Treaty, which remained unchanged. For example, the harmonisation clause of Article 114 of the Treaty, which provided the legal basis for all market integration measures before the crisis, had also to provide the basis for a large part of the financial stability initiatives since the crisis, including more recently the Single Resolution Mechanism. Other solutions were found outside the Treaty, notably on the basis of intergovernmental agreements. There were several judicial challenges along the way at the Court and national constitutional courts, which reaffirmed, by turns, the primacy of the Treaty and of national sovereignty.

Ultimately, the evolution of European law itself was re-shaped by these developments, as concluded by Gianni Lo Schiavo. While stability was initially justified for safeguarding market integration, it became a constitutional requirement for wider European integration, towards a 'Stability Union' where not only the benefits but also the risks of integration are shared.

Frankfurt, 1 September 2016
Pedro Gustavo Teixeira
Director-General Secretariat
European Central Bank

List of Abbreviations

A.G.	Advocate General
AT1	Additional Tier 1
BCBS	Basel Committee on Banking Supervision
BIS	Bank for International Settlements
BoE	Bank of England
BoP	Balance of Payments
BRRD	Bank Recovery and Resolution Directive
CCI	Convergence and Competitiveness Instrument
CEBS	Committee on European Banking Supervisors
CET	Common Equity Tier
CMU	Capital Markets Union
COM	European Commission
CPI	Consumer Price Index
CRD	Capital Requirements Directive
CRR	Capital Requirements Regulation
DG	European Commission Directorate-General
DGS	Deposit Guarantee Scheme
EBA	European Banking Authority
EBU	European Banking Union
ECB	European Central Bank
ECJ	European Court of Justice
ECMH	Efficient Capital Market Hypothesis
EDIS	European Deposit Insurance Scheme

EDP	Excessive Deficit Procedure
EDRF	European Debt Redemption Fund
EFSF	European Financial Stability Facility
EFSI	European Fund for Strategic Investments
EFSM	European Financial Stabilisation Mechanism
EIB	European Investment Bank
EIOPA	European Insurance and Occupational Pensions Authority
EIP	Excessive Imbalance Procedure
ELA	Emergency Liquidity Assistance
ELTIF	European Long Term Investment Fund
EMU	Economic and Monetary Union
ENISA	European Network and Information Security Agency
ESAs	European Supervisory Authorities
ESCB	European System of Central Banks
ESFS	European System of Financial Supervisors
ESM	European Stability Mechanism
ESMA	European Securities and Market Authority
ESMT	European Stability Mechanism Treaty
ESRB	European Systemic Risk Board
EU	European Union
EUR	Euro
EUSEF	European Social Entrepreneurship Fund
EuVECA	European Venture Capital Fund
FCA	Financial Conduct Authority
FPC	Financial Policy Committee
FISMA	Financial Stability, Financial Services and Capital Markets Union
FRS	Federal Reserve System
FSA	Financial Services Authority
FSAP	Financial Sector Assessment Program
FSA Plan	Financial Services Action Plan
FSB	Financial Stability Board
FSF	Financial Stability Forum
FSOC	Financial Stability Oversight Council
GDP	Gross Domestic Product

GFSR	Global Financial Stability Report
G-SIB	Global-Systemically Important Banks
HM	Her Majesty
IFA	International Financial Architecture
IMF	International Monetary Fund
IRB	Internal Risk Based
IT	Information Technology
JST	Joint Supervisory Team
LCR	Liquidity Coverage Ratio
LOLR	Lender of Last Resort
LTRO	Long(er) Term Refinancing Operations
MIP	Macroeconomic Imbalance Procedure
MoU	Memorandum of Understanding
MREL	Minimum Requirements for Eligible Liabilities
MTO	Medium-Term Budgetary Objective
NCA	National Competent Authority
NCB	National Central Bank
NRA	National Resolution Authority
NSFR	Net Stable Funding Ratio
OJ	Official Journal
OMTs	Outright Monetary Transactions
PMSF	Primary Market Support Facility
PRA	Prudential Regulation Authority
PSPP	Public Sector Purchase Programme
QE	Quantitative Easing
RQM	Reverse Qualified Majority
RWA	Risk Weighted Assets
SGP	Stability and Growth Pact
SIFIs	Systemically Important Financial Institutions
SMEs	Small and Medium Enterprises
SMSF	Secondary Market Support Facility
SRB	Single Resolution Board
SREP	Supervisory Review and Evaluation Process

SRF	Single Resolution Fund
SRM	Single Resolution Mechanism
SSB	Standard Setting Body
SSM	Single Supervisory Mechanism
SSR	Short Selling Regulation
TEU	Treaty on the European Union
TFEU	Treaty on the Functioning of the European Union
TLAC	Total Loss Absorbing Capacity
TLTROs	Targeted Longer-Term Refinancing Operations
TSCG	Treaty on Stability, Coordination and Governance
UK	United Kingdom
UN	United Nations
US	United States
WFO	World Financial Organisation

Acknowledgements

This book is the revised version of my Ph.D. that was successfully defended at King's College Law School in 2016[1]. Writing a book is very challenging without the appropriate motivation and inspiration. The journey of thinking, researching, developing arguments, writing and refining a book is a unique experience that requires a lot more than one would normally need in life. My interest in the EU law and policy responses to the financial crisis dates back to my years in Bruges and Brussels. During those years, I have developed a true passion for EU law that I have kept and will keep forever. The possibility to join King's College with a project on the EU law response to the financial crisis has strengthened my interest for EU law and policy by allowing me to deepen my research interests in the field.

I would first like to thank my Ph.D. supervisors, Professor Alex Türk and Dr Michael Schillig as they have done a great job in constantly following me and in providing insightful and critical comments throughout these years. Furthermore, I would like to thank Professor Jean-Victor Louis and Professor Mads Andenas for having accepted to be my Ph.D. examiners and for their invaluable suggestions to improve the Ph.D. thesis and to turn it into a book.

This book would not have been possible without two professors that have been crucial in my life. Professor Mario Pilade Chiti and Professor Giuseppe Conte have done more than I could think it would be possible in encouraging me to develop my ideas and tell me always what the good choice to take was.

In the course of these years, I have had the privilege to engage in many parallel works and experiences. Joining the European Central Bank (ECB) in 2014 as a pioneer in European banking supervision and being a 'founder' of the European Banking Union (EBU) have made my dream of working for Europe come true. In this context, I wish to acknowledge Pedro Gustavo Teixeira, Petra Senkovic and Georg Gruber as well as my colleagues and friends at the Supervisory Board Secretariat of the ECB for their essential contributions in making me a fervent ECB official. Other people have also contributed to this book by generously offering to discuss some ideas or parts of my

1. The views expressed in this book are purely personal and they are in no way intended to represent those of the ECB or its SB Secretariat. All errors and omissions remain my own.

work with me. In particular, I would like to thank, among others, Professor Andrea Biondi (whom I thank also for having accepted the Ph.D. in the European Monograph Series), Professor Edoardo Chiti, Professor Federico Fabbrini, Professor Vassilis Hatzopoulos, Professor Massimo Merola, Professor Aurelio Pappalardo and Professor Takis Tridimas for having found their time to discuss and be engaged in my researches and interests at various occasions.

I also thank my dearest friends all over Europe for having always kept me in the real world during my research journey and for having provided me with constant motivation and interests in life.

Above all, I really want to thank my parents, Giancarlo and Paola, Eleni and my brother, Marco. My family and Eleni have given everything to me and never asked for anything in return. Your unconditional support, incommensurate patience, fervent strength, constant inspiration and unlimited belief in me make you special persons to me.

CHAPTER 1

General Introduction

No civilization (...) would ever have been possible without a framework of stability, to provide the wherein for the flux of change. Foremost among the stabilizing factors, more enduring than customs, manners and traditions, are the legal systems that regulate our life in the world and our daily affairs with each other. ... The variety of such systems is great, both in time and in space, but they all have one thing in common – the thing that justifies us in using the same word for phenomena as different as the Roman *lex*, the Greek nomos, the Hebrew *torah* – and this is that they were designed to ensure stability.[1]

§1.01 OBJECTIVE

This book consists of a study into the concept of financial stability, and in particular into the normative instruments taken to boost financial stability in the European Union (EU) law and policy. In general terms, research in the field of financial stability has been carried out in the context of economics and finance.[2] Limited attention has been given to what the meaning and implications of financial stability are for the

1. Hannah Arendt, *Civil Disobedience*, Crisis of the Republic 64 (Penguin Books Harcourt Brace & Company 1969).
2. In the vast body of literature in the field of financial stability in other social sciences disciplines *see*: Andrew Crockett, *The Theory and Practice of Financial Stability*, 203 Essays in International Finance 2 (1997); Garry J. Schinasi, *Defining Financial Stability*, 04/187 IMF Working Paper (2004); Garry J. Schinasi, *Safeguarding Financial Stability Theory and Practice*, 77–134 (IMF 2005). For attempts to quantify (model) the different properties of financial stability, *see* Oriol Aspachs, et al., *Searching for a Metric for Financial Stability*, 167 Special Paper LSE Financial Markets Group (2006); William Allen, Geoffrey Wood, *Defining and Achieving Financial Stability*, 2 Journal of Financial Stability 152–172 (2006); Charles Goodhart & Dimitrios Tsomocos, *Analysis of Financial Stability*, 173 LSE Financial Markets Group Special Paper (2007); David Bieri, *Financial Stability, the Basel Process and the New Geography of Regulation*, 2 Cambridge Journal of Regions, Economy and Society 303 (2009); Blaise Gadanecz & Kaushik Jayaram, *Measures of Financial Stability – A Review* 31 IFC Bulletin 365 (2010).

shaping of Europe in the last two decades from a legal perspective. Attention has been focused rather on the role and concept of financial stability in other political sciences.[3]

The EU has not – yet – directly recognised the role of financial stability as a legal principle or as one of the EU objectives, nor has EU primary or secondary law. The only reference to 'stability of the financial system' can be found in Article 127(5) Treaty on the Functioning of the European Union (TFEU) indicating that the European Central Bank (ECB), as a non-basic European System of Central Banks (ESCB) task, shall *contribute* to the stability of the financial system.[4] While there is limited reference to the concept of financial stability in EU primary law, its importance to shape policies in the Union has been progressively recognised in recent attempts to avoid the collapse of the financial system and sovereign defaults in Europe. As held by Tuori and Tuori, the 'crisis has replaced price stability with financial stability as the overriding objective which European economic policies (...) are expected to serve'.[5]

As a consequence of the financial and euro crisis, the recent European efforts to reform economic governance[6] and regulate financial institutions[7] have been analysed from various aspects in the law. The predominant literature analyses the fact that the financial and sovereign crisis has reshaped the rules from the perspective of constitutional, administrative or financial law, but it engages only partially with a critical assessment of whether Europe has evolved because of the need to achieve financial stability and has not yet appraised in details what this entails.[8] Most authors tend to approach financial stability as a disputed concept that, as an objective, does not seem to add as much to the discourse on how to improve recovery or growth in Europe. In this sense, many authors conclude that financial stability is a difficult and evasive concept that does not have legal implications apart from the importance of being a general policy objective or an undetermined policy driver.[9]

Given the absence of well-established legal literature on the topic, this book takes into account the difficulties in defining financial stability in legal terms as well as in

3. Mads Andenas & Iris Chiu, *The Foundations and Future of Financial Regulation* 27 (Routledge 2014).
4. Art. 127 TFEU is the key Treaty provision on the tasks of the ESCB. Art. 127(5) TFEU states that 'The ESCB shall *contribute* to the smooth conduct of policies pursued by the competent authorities relating to the prudential supervision of credit institutions and *the stability of the financial system*.' (emphasis added). For further discussion on this provision *see* Chapter 3 section §3.02[B][1][i].
5. Kaarlo Tuori & Klaus Tuori, *The Eurozone Crisis. A Constitutional Analysis*, 183 (Cambridge University Press 2014).
6. Among other recent general studies on the recent EMU reforms, *see*: Tuori, Touri, *supra* n. 5; Alicia Hinarejos, *The Euro Crisis from a Constitutional Perspective* (Oxford University Press 2015); Federico Fabbrini, *Economic Governance: Comparative Paradoxes. Constitutional Challenges* (Oxford University Press 2016); Rosa Lastra, *International Financial and Monetary Law* (Oxford University Press 2015).
7. On the recent EU banking and financial law reforms *see* Niamh Moloney, *EU Securities and Financial Markets Regulation* (Oxford University Press 2014); Danny Busch & Guido Ferrarini (eds), *European Banking Union* (Oxford University Press 2015).
8. Tuori, Tuori, *supra* n. 5, 183; Kern Alexander, *European Banking Union: A Legal and Institutional Analysis of the Single Supervisory Mechanism and the Single Resolution Mechanism*, 40 European Law Review 154–187 (2015).
9. Howard Davies & David Green, *Banking on the Future. The Fall and Rise of Central Banking*, 61 (Oxford University Press 2010).

providing the legal boundaries of what financial stability entails for European polity. In light of the theoretical difficulties of a commonly accepted definition of financial stability in Europe, this study approaches these challenges by subsuming financial stability into the theory of public goods and by developing the argument that financial stability bears the attributes of a 'public good' in Europe.[10]

Against this background, financial stability is approached as a holistic concept. A better understanding of the current policy-making and regulatory efforts to shape what has been termed a 'risk-sharing' Union[11] is developed. Hence, the two main theoretical questions of this study are: first, whether and to what extent financial stability is a new *foundational* and *supranational* 'public good' objective in the European legal order shaping EU law and policy; and, second, what the normative instruments for such development in the EU legal order are.[12]

Under the pressing impact of the credit and sovereign crisis as well as the increasing interconnection and integration of the EU internal market, a comprehensive approach to the concept of financial stability appears necessary. As put by Moloney, a great part of the:

> [EU crisis-related] reform agenda is designed to ensure that financial institutions internalise the risks and costs of their activities and that financial stability is thereby promoted.[13]

This opens the question of what the role of financial stability in EU law and policy is. A first assessment of financial stability reveals that it is a disputed concept as there is no commonly accepted ground to determine whether it constitutes either an objective, or a value or a principle. The key aspect in qualifying a concept as an objective is to consider it as a target towards which the use of available resources or instruments is aimed. This study contends that financial stability has acquired the role of supranational and foundational objective in EU law and policy.

The terms *foundational* and *supranational* are both essentials to characterise financial stability. Objectives in EU law and policy are intended to be goals towards which the set of rules or the system are aimed to. It is argued that there are two categories of objectives in Europe: *foundational* and policy objectives. While the latter are those having a normative dimension delimited to certain areas of the law (competition, environment, free movement), the former are intended to establish the existential normative basis of a given legal order.

In the EU legal system, foundational objectives are those indicated in Article 3 Treaty on the European Union (TEU). These are: the promotion of peace, the Union's values and the well-being of its peoples; the creation of an internal market without frontiers through market integration; free and undistorted competition; sustainable development; balanced economic growth and price stability; a highly competitive social market economy, aiming at full employment and social progress. Following the

10. For the theory of 'public good', *see* Chapter 2 section §2.02.
11. Edoardo Chiti & Pedro Gustavo Teixeira, *The Constitutional Implications of the European Responses to the Financial and Public Debt Crisis*, 50 Common Market Law Review 685 (2013).
12. For the main theoretical questions of this study, *see* Chapter 3 section §3.02.
13. Moloney, *supra* n. 7, 5–6.

above distinction, the objectives in Article 3 TEU are intended to be foundational objectives of the EU legal system, and, hence those that have a normative structural function for the whole EU legal and political order. While not being included in Article 3 TEU, which was reformed before the eruption of the financial crisis in Europe with the Treaty of Lisbon, this book contends that financial stability is a new *foundational* objective of EU law establishing the existential basis of the European system, together with the objectives enlisted in Article 3 TEU.

For the purpose of this research, financial stability has also the characteristics of a *supranational* objective as it has a predominately European nature. The supranational dimension is a consequence of the limitation of sovereignty of Member States and the transfer of tasks and powers to the EU institutions in specific fields.[14] Therefore, the exercise of tasks and powers to attain financial stability may take place at the supranational level by EU institutions and beyond the sovereign powers of the nation states.

Together with financial stability, other concepts of stability have been developed before or in the context of the financial crisis. Monetary stability[15] is the most closely related concept to the development of a financial stability policy. It refers to the need to have an appropriate control of monetary policy to be preserved both as an external value and as an internal value. However, the financial crisis has shown that monetary stability is not sufficient to provide a comprehensive normative response to prevent and manage (systemic) risks and shocks in Europe. Similarly, fiscal stability may overlap with financial stability.[16] In broad terms, fiscal stability aims to realise regulation, supervision and enforcement of government spending and taxation. However, it does not provide a satisfactory supranational answer as the EU lacks fiscal powers and resources to attain fiscal stability.[17]

As a second research question, the book submits that the supranational objective of financial stability is founded on normative instruments to create a financially 'stable' Union. As it will be argued throughout this study, in the context of the regulatory response to the financial crisis, there are some normative instruments essential to attain financial stability in Europe. A clear or comprehensive list of normative instruments to boost the objective of financial stability in EU law and policy has not been developed at present. Hence, this book contends that there are certain supranational normative instruments making financial stability a foundational objective in EU law and policy.

Futhermore, this study intends to answer the lack of understanding on the concept of financial stability by determining what the essential areas to achieve such financially 'stable' Union are.

14. *See* Case 6/64, *Costa v. E.N.E.L.* ECLI:EU:C:1964:66.
15. *See* Claus Zimmermann, *The Concept of Monetary Sovereignty Revisited*, 25 (Cambridge University Press 2013).
16. *See* Federico Lupo Pasini, *Economic Stability and Economic Governance in the Euro Area: What the European Crisis Can Teach on the Limits of Economic Integration*, 16 Journal of International Economic Law 221 (2013).
17. *See* Chapter 4 section §4.05[B] for limitations on fiscal capacity at the EU level.

First, the creation of an economic governance model for Member States finances entails the development of a supranational economic surveillance model over Member States budgetary and fiscal decisions. Second, the shaping of a constitutional system of financial assistance mechanisms for distressed Member States is needed in order to safeguard the stability of their finances, but, most importantly, the stability of the Union as a whole. Third, a resilient banking market requires supranational prudential requirements for banks and a supranational regulatory structure protecting investors, depositors and consumers. Fourth, there shall be a centralised supranational level of prudential supervision ensuring the exercise of supervisory tasks at the centre by European institutions or authorities and avoiding supervisory fragmentation in the internal market. Finally, a harmonised and centralised system of banking resolution and a single system of deposit insurance in the euro area at the supranational level are required in order to guarantee that appropriate losses are suffered by private parties by way of burden-sharing, and that European depositors receive an appropriate level of compensation if necessary.

The absence of a clear understanding on financial stability, revealed also in the existing legal literature, requires that the conceptual underpinnings of financial stability *in* Europe and *for* Europe are determined. Therefore, this book constructs a general normative framework on financial stability built on certain supranational normative instruments, which are able to prevent and manage (systemic) risks and shocks.

§1.02 FOCUS OF THE RESEARCH

The book aims to assess in details the major institutional and substantive reforms to address the financial crisis by looking at them through the lens of financial stability as their overarching foundational objective. The research will address the renewed Economic and Monetary Union (EMU) by looking at the major reforms of economic governance, by assessing the creation of stability mechanisms for sovereigns and by appraising the new European framework for banking regulation, supervision and resolution.

Since the outbreak of the European financial crisis, EU institutions and Member States have engaged in major efforts to repair the architecture of the EMU. The main political narratives that prevailed in Europe since 2009 have been two. First, Europe has witnessed a deterioration of the European economy that found its roots in the negligent fiscal behaviour of several Member States. Second, the irresponsible lending and investment policies followed in the banking sector have caused considerable problems to the business structures and creditworthiness of the banking sector in Europe.

As a result, the EU institutions unequivocally followed an interpretation of the financial crisis as a problem of sovereign debt and of the banking sector and have reformed the set-up of EMU accordingly. This has brought to institutional and substantial reform of the originally construed EMU constitution architecture developed in the Maastricht Treaty.

While setting up an essentially federal framework on monetary affairs, establishing a common currency and empowering the ECB to maintain 'price stability',[18] the Maastricht Treaty of 1992[19] developed, in fiscal and economic affairs, a loose economic policy coordination, nationally centred fiscal discipline and unlimited faith in the capacity of the markets to align governmental fiscal misalignments. Furthermore, financial markets remained nationally centred and heavily reliant on national regulation and supervision.

The constitutional architecture of EMU that has recently emerged from the responses to the financial crisis in Europe, on the contrary, is based on three new main components based on the objective of financial stability as this book shows. First, the EMU has evolved into a highly structured surveillance framework with budgetary constraints and a highly complex system of coordination of economic and budgetary policies.

Second, the EMU has endowed with new instruments of financial stabilisation, aimed at providing financial assistance to Member States in financial difficulties and preventing contagious effects from sovereigns' or banks' defaults in the EMU together with duties for the Member States (especially those receiving financial support) to implement reforms to their economies as a condition for financial assistance.

Third, the EMU has provided a clear mandate for the establishment of the European Banking Union (EBU) as a new framework of supranational regulation, supervision and resolution of credit institutions in Europe, introducing supranational powers for the EU institutions and agencies to set supranational policies and control over the banking sector. This is made of an institutional dimension with the conferral of supervisory powers to the ECB and the conferral of delegated powers to EU agencies (European Banking Authority (EBA) and the Single Resolution Board (SRB)) as well as a substantial reformulation of the rules on banking and the creation of a new single rulebook composed of hard law and soft law instruments. An important focus of the research is therefore on substantive and institutional aspects related to banking as the main area where efforts have been taken to stabilise banking markets and to create a more resilient framework for credit institutions in Europe.

In conclusion, reforms in the area of coordination of economic and budgetary policies, sovereign financial stabilisation and banking regulation, with steps taken towards economic, banking (and fiscal) union have profoundly affected the architecture of the EMU in light of the objective of financial stability. In particular, the research will approach the EBU as a major reform to strengthen financial stability with the creation of a supranational system for banking regulation, supervision and resolution.

18. *See* Arts 119(2) and 127(1) TFEU on the ESCB primary objective of price stability and the exercise of the monetary policy task for the Members whose currency is the euro. For an economics analysis of monetary policy in the euro area, *see* Paul De Grauwe, *Economics of Monetary Union* (Oxford University Press 2014).
19. For detailed accounts of the history and progressive development of the EMU in the Maastricht Treaty *see*, e.g., Francis Snyder, *EMU – Integration and Differentiation: Metaphor for European Union* in Paul Craig & Grainne De Búrca (eds), *The Evolution of EU Law*, 687 (Oxford University Press 2011); Charles Proctor, *Mann on the Legal Aspect of Money*, 681–724 (Oxford University Press 2013); Lastra, *supra* n. 6, Chapter 6.

The main achievements of the EBU have allowed the reinforcement of the banking system by developing a supranational approach in the assessment of banks. This justifies extensive focus on the EBU rather than on other financial law reforms. In particular, the efforts to improve the EMU have been accompanied by major institutional reforms that have (re-)designed the role of banking supervisors and resolution authorities in Europe. These have enhanced the supranational dimension of financial stability as a foundational objective in EU law and policy.

§1.03 BOUNDARIES OF THE RESEARCH

Financial stability as a supranational foundational objective can be clearly seen in the development of the reformed EMU as well as in regulation, supervision and resolution of credit institutions in Europe. However, some preliminary remarks regarding the limits of the present book are required.

First, it has not been possible to reconstruct all the phases of the global financial crisis, to refer to the extensive literature on it and to look at the main responses to achieve financial stability at the international, regional and national levels.[20] This study cannot discuss general debates on the financial crisis or take into account other social science areas that have analysed the financial crisis in Europe. Its objective is rather to set a theoretical framework for financial stability as a supranational foundational objective in EU law and policy and examine how it has been driving supranational reforms for the surveillance of Member State finances, financial stabilisation mechanisms and the regulation and supervision of credit institutions in Europe.

Second, space and time restraints render an in-depth analysis of all the regulatory response to the financial crisis in Europe and a detailed assessment of the institutional and substantive initiatives by the EU to strengthen financial stability impossible. In the last eight years, the EU has promoted important initiatives in the field of financial regulation. Strong efforts have been taken to improve the regulation, supervision and resolution of financial market institutions other than credit institutions,[21] financial

20. For official reports on the global financial crisis, *see* Jacques de Larosière (chaired, *Report of the High Level Group on Financial Supervision in the EU* (Brussels 2009) (de Larosière Report); United Nations Conference on Trade and Development (UNCTAD), *The Global Economic Crisis, Systemic Failures and Multilateral Remedies* (2009), available at http://unctad.org/en/Docs/gds20091_en.pdf (accessed 31 December 2016); Financial Crisis Enquiry Commission, *The Financial Crisis Enquiry Report: Final Report of the National Commission on the Causes of the Financial and Economic Crisis in the United States* (January 2011) http://fcic.gov/report (accessed 31 December 2016). For books and papers on the financial crisis, *see* Rosa Lastra & Geoffrey Wood, *The Crisis of 2007– 09: Nature, Causes, and Reactions*, 13 Journal of International Economic Law 531 (2010); Larry Allen, *The Global Economic Crisis: A Chronology* (Reaktion Books 2013); Tony Ciro, *The Global Financial Crisis* (Ashgate 2016); Timothy Geitner, *Stress Test: Reflections on Financial Crisis* (Broadway Books 2014); Adrian Buckley, *Financial Crisis: Causes, Context and Consequences* (Financial Times/ Prentice Hall 2011); Anat Admati & Martin Hellwig, *The Bankers' New Clothes* (Princeton University Press 2013); Carmen Reinhart & Kenneth Rogoff, *From Financial Crash to Debt Crisis*, 101 American Economic Review 1676 (2011); Emilios Avgouleas, *Governance of Global Financial Markets*, 89–156 (Cambridge University Press 2012).
21. *See* Regulation (EU) No 600/2014 of the European Parliament and of the Council of 15 May 2014 on markets in financial instruments and amending Regulation (EU) No 648/2012, OJ L 173,

market infrastructures,[22] modernisation of prospectus rules,[23] payment systems[24] as well as the promotion of measures to address shadow banking markets in Europe.[25] Furthermore, noteworthy initiatives have been taken to supervise credit-rating agencies at the supranational level, in particular by conferring direct supervisory powers to European Securities and Market Authority (ESMA).[26]

Third, from a theoretical perspective, the study cannot engage in the wider theoretical debate of whether the European economic constitution has changed because of the financial crisis.[27] This would require detailed constitutional analysis, which would go beyond the purpose of the research question of this book, by assessing supranational constitutionalism and evaluating in details other areas of EU law and policy such as the four freedoms, the changing nature of European constitutionalism and the relationship between the rules on the internal market and those on competition.[28]

Following also the main priorities of the Five President Report of 2015,[29] this book focuses on the renewed EMU and the newly established EBU as the key reforms to achieve supranational financial stability in Europe. EU institutions are primarily concerned with further reforms to the economic governance framework, the completion of a truly EBU and the creation of a primordial fiscal and budgetary union with the ultimate purpose of strengthening financial stability in Europe. This is shown by the considerable efforts placed on discussions regarding the future of the economic governance framework and the completion of the EMU.

To sum up, in light of the objective of financial stability, the book focuses on the main institutional and substantial changes that have reformed the EMU or have promoted the establishment of the EBU such as the creation of intergovernmental frameworks for financial assistance to sovereigns or the conferral of prudential supervisory powers to the ECB.

12.6.2014 (MiFIR) and Directive 2014/65/EU of the European Parliament and of the Council of 15 May 2014 on markets in financial instruments and amending Directive 2002/92/EC and Directive 2011/61/EU, OJ L 173, 12.6.2014 (MiFIDII).

22. *See* Regulation (EU) No 648/2012 of the European Parliament and of the Council of 4 July 2012 on OTC derivatives, central counterparties and trade repositories, OJ L 201, 27.7.2012.
23. *See* Proposal for a Regulation on the prospectus to be published when securities are offered to the public or admitted to trading, COM(2015)583 final, 30.11.2015.
24. *See* Regulation (EU) No 260/2012 of the European Parliament and of the Council of 14 March 2012 establishing technical and business requirements for credit transfers and direct debits in euro and amending Regulation (EC) No 924/2009, OJ L 94, 30.3.2012.
25. *See* European Commission, Communication on Shadow Banking – Addressing New Sources of Risk in the Financial Sector, COM (2013)0614.
26. *See* Andenas, Chiu, *supra* n. 3, 135.
27. Tuori, Tuori *supra* n. 5, 13; Tony Prosser, *The Economic Constitution*, 7 (Oxford University Press 2014).
28. *See* e.g., Julio Baquero Cruz, *Between Competition and Free Movement. The Economic Constitutional Law of the European Community* (Hart Publishing 2002); Wolf Sauter & Harm Schepel, *State and Market in European Union Law. The Public and Private Spheres of the Internal Market before the EU Courts*, 1–21 (Cambridge University Press 2009).
29. Five Presidents' Report, 22 June 2015 at http://ec.europa.eu/priorities/economic-monetary-union/docs/5-presidents-report_en.pdf (accessed 31 December 2016).

§1.04 STRUCTURE

The approach taken in this study is intended to provide a new and original reading on financial stability in EU law and policy from a supranational perspective. The book is structured as follows.

Chapter 2 presents the historical, theoretical broader background to the concept of financial stability. It looks at financial stability by assessing it from the social sciences perspectives (history, finance and economics) and by focussing on its role in the context of the theory of public goods. It then examines financial stability at national levels – United States (US) and United Kingdom (UK) – and international level by arguing to what extent financial stability is a recognised objective under the International Financial Architecture (IFA).

Chapter 3 introduces the disputed concept of financial stability from an EU law and policy perspective. It argues that financial stability is a supranational foundational objective aimed at establishing a normative environment in Europe where the EU machinery, powers and resources are capable of preventing and managing (systemic) risks and shocks. For these purposes, the chapter distinguishes financial stability from other stability concepts emerged before and during the financial crisis in Europe (e.g., price stability, monetary stability, stability of the euro area as a whole). To support these findings, it indicates what the main normative instruments for financial stability in Europe are and reflects upon them to ascertain to what extent they are desirable to attain supranational financial stability.

Chapter 4 evaluates how the surveillance model in the new European economic governance has changed throughout the financial crisis. The adoption of EU law measures as well as intergovernmental agreements between Member States have created a new system for economic governance. However, it is demonstrated that the appropriate level of financial stability for economic governance surveillance is far from being achieved. This is because there are still considerable open questions as to the nature of the new European economic surveillance model as well as political difficulties to achieve supranational substantive and institutional arrangements in European economic governance.

Chapter 5 analyses the progressive establishment of permanent financial stability mechanisms for sovereigns in Europe. The aim of the chapter is to contribute to the understanding of what the current limits of financial stability mechanisms intended to safeguard the stability of the Union as whole are and, at the same time, to provide legitimate alternatives to the absence of automatic fiscal transfers or sovereign debt supranational arrangements in EU law and policy.

Chapter 6 looks into the main aspects of banking regulation in Europe by focussing on the creation of a resilient banking regulation framework. The analysis is twofold. The first is institutional and the second is substantive. The institutional part looks at the current institutional framework for the adoption of EU rules in the banking sector. The substantive part assesses the recent regulatory reform intended to create a 'single rulebook' for banks and identifies what is still missing or should be improved in European banking regulation.

Chapter 7 examines the current aspects of banking supervision and assesses to what extent this is achieved with the recent European reforms. Most of the chapter will examine the new framework of the Single Supervisory Mechanism (SSM) as the clearest example of a regulatory supranational answer to attain supranational financial stability in Europe by empowering the ECB with supervisory tasks. Furthermore, it will assess the new ECB substantive powers in banking supervision as a clear case of supranational financial stability powers.

Chapter 8 assesses the emerging supranational framework of banking resolution. The analysis is twofold. First, it evaluates substantively to what extent the new Banking Recovery and Resolution Directive frames new resolution powers and whether these are sufficiently strong to attain supranational financial stability. Second, it examines the Single Resolution Mechanism (SRM) as the new institutional reform for the resolution of credit institutions at the supranational level to safeguard supranational financial stability.

CHAPTER 2

Financial Stability in Context

§2.01 INTRODUCTION

This chapter aims to provide a background reconstruction of the term 'financial stability' as a disputed concept that has emerged during the financial crisis as well as to frame 'financial stability' at the national and international contexts. This analysis attempts to illustrate the difficulties encountered in defining in a proper way the term 'financial stability' in social sciences disciplines due to the lack of clarity on its perception, especially from the legal perspective. At the national and international level, the emergence of a theory of global public goods provides the starting point of the debate on financial stability. This is because financial stability can be seen as one – if not currently the main – national and global public goods that has arisen after the outbreak of the global financial crisis. This will be reflected at the European level in the following chapter.

As held in the general introduction to this study, financial stability is difficult to define in legal terms. The need to achieve global financial stability can be seen as the driving source for reconstructing the IFA.[1] Important reforms have restructured the international financial order and have been prompted by a renewed importance of the objective of global financial stability. While the IFA has been partially strengthened with a renewed interest on financial stability, institutional and substantive weaknesses remain in the global financial order.

The chapter is structured as follows. After a brief review to the underlying theory of global public goods and financial stability as a major public good in social sciences literature (section §2.02), the chapter will examine the role of financial stability at the national level with a brief analysis in the US and UK systems (section §2.03). Then it

1. *See* Mario Giovanoli, *The International Monetary and Financial Architecture – Some Institutional Aspects* in Thomas Cottier, Rosa Lastra, Christian Tietje (eds), *The Rule of Law in Monetary Affairs*, 45 (Cambridge University Press 2015).

will approach the main scholarly reviews on the role of financial stability as a global public good by distinguishing the main interpretations as to its bearing (section §2.04). Finally, it will look at and assess what the main role of financial stability is in the international economic order by focussing on the major changes that have taken place to restructure the IFA (section §2.05).

§2.02 THE THEORY OF PUBLIC GOODS

The starting point of the analysis of financial stability, and of this book, is the identification of the theory of 'global public goods'. The first economic scholar to theorise the notion of public goods is the Nobel Prize Paul Samuelson who in his famous essay on public expenditure provided a definition of public goods at the national level. He argued that:

> collective consumption goods are those that all enjoy in common in the sense that each individual's consumption of such a good leads to no subtraction from any other individual's consumption of that good.[2]

This model shows that some goods in society are of a collective consumption nature and, thus, cannot be subtracted from individual's consumption in society.[3] This makes it possible to consider some goods as 'public' in a sense that all society can enjoy them.

The model developed by Samuelson has been increasingly followed in subsequent literature.[4] Musgrave argued that public goods are also 'non-excludable' in their benefits.[5] In other words, public goods cannot be excluded from being the object of consumption in society. Public goods share some characteristics with each other. It emerges that public goods have two main characteristics: they are non-rival, thus they are equally enjoyed by the society; they are non-excludable, thus they cannot be eliminated from the society. Hence, two criteria identify public goods: non-rivalry and non-excludability.

While the notion of public goods in public economics or political economy was limited to the national sphere of the notion of public good, Inge Kaul et al. elaborated a theory that extrapolated the notion of public good from the national to the global sphere.[6] This study set out the theoretical underpinnings to the elaboration of the concept of *global* public good to provide action at global level to strengthen international cooperation. The institutional 'appetite' for a definition and a general theory on global public goods was developed in 2002 when an international task force for the determination of global public goods was established during the 2002

2. Paul Samuelson, *The Pure Theory of Public Expenditure*, 36 Review of Economics and Statistics 387 (1954).
3. *Oxford Dictionary of Economics*, 305–306 (Oxford University Press 2009).
4. *See* Richard Cornes & Todd Sandler, *The Theory of Externalities, Public Goods and Club Goods*, 10 (Cambridge University Press 1996).
5. Richard Musgrave, *Public Goods*, in Cary Brown, Robert Solow (eds), *Paul Samuelson and Modern Economic Theory*, 141 (McGraw-Hill 1983).
6. *See* Inge Kaul, Isabelle Grunberg, Marc Stern (eds), *Global Public Goods: International Cooperation in the 21st Century*, 9 (Oxford University Press 1999).

Johannesburg World Summit on Sustainable Development. In 2006, the International Task Force on Global Public Goods elaborated a definition to the term 'global public goods' as:

> issues that are broadly conceived as important to the international community that for the most part cannot or will not be adequately addressed by individual countries acting alone and that are defined through broad international consensus or a legitimate process of decision-making.[7]

This definition proves to be essential to define and develop a sound interpretation of the role of global public goods as a broadly accepted concept in the international community.

Global public goods are thus those goods that are non-rivalrous and non-excludable at the international level. The absence of any of these two features makes public goods either common goods or club goods. Common goods are those goods that are non-excludable but rivalrous, while club goods are non-rivalrous but excludable.[8] The non-rivalrous criterion signifies that one entity's consumption of the good does not affect the amount available to others. This means that consumption does not lead to depletion of the good for the others while there is no need to reproduce the good for every single entity. The non-excludable criterion means that once the good has been achieved, nobody can be excluded from enjoying it. This means that everyone can enjoy it and cannot be prevented from its consumption. As examples of global public goods, the following may be considered: natural commons, such as a clean environment, climate stability, biodiversity and the ozone shield; human-made commons, such as transnational infrastructures (the Internet) or international standards (peace); global policy objectives or outcomes: peace, security, international monetary stability and financial stability.

Before assessing the international dimension of financial stability as a global public good, financial stability as a national public good needs to be examined.

§2.03 FINANCIAL STABILITY AS A NATIONAL PUBLIC GOOD: THE US AND UK EXPERIENCE

This section briefly looks at the role of financial stability at the national level by examining its recognition at the US and UK level before and after the financial crisis. It serves to demonstrate that financial stability has developed as a national public good dimension, which can be then transposed to the international and regional levels.

In the US, since 1913, the Federal Reserve is responsible for the conduct of monetary policy. The Federal Reserve Act was adopted to address banking panics and crisis, and it empowered the Federal Reserve System (FRS) 'to furnish an elastic currency, to afford means of rediscounting commercial paper, to establish a more

7. International Task Force on Global Public Goods, *Meeting Global Challenges: International Cooperation in the National Interest*, 13 (Final Report, 2006).
8. *See* Annamaria Viterbo, *International Economic Law and Monetary Measures*, 14 (Edward Elgar 2012).

effective supervision of banking in the United States, and for other purposes'. The famous 2010 Dodd-Frank Wall Street Reform and Consumer Protection Act[9] enhanced the Fed's surveillance powers and imposed new constraints on risk-taking in the financial sector, all aimed at reducing the probability of the type of financial market turmoil experienced during the recent crisis.[10] The Act's main objective is to address the issues of financial stability and systemic risk and to prevent further bailouts of the financial system at taxpayers' expense.[11] The Act established a new federal regulator, the Financial Stability Oversight Council (FSOC), and expands the responsibilities and powers of the Board of Governors of the FRS. The FSOC consists of ten voting members and five non-voting members in an advisory role.[12] The FSOC[13] is charged with identifying risks to the financial stability of the US caused by large interconnected bank holding companies or non-bank financial companies, enhancing market discipline, and responding to emerging threats to the stability of the US financial system.[14]

Also the UK has witnessed an important reform on financial stability during the financial crisis. The term 'financial stability' has been first used at the institutional level in a document published by the Bank of England (BoE) in 1994.[15] This was named financial stability report and was consequently published at regular intervals by the main central banks. Therefore, the UK has been the first country to recognise financial stability as a primary concern in institutional policy. In response to the financial crisis, the UK Financial Services Act 2012[16] replaced the tripartite regime consisting of the BoE, the Financial Services Authority (FSA), and Her Majesty (HM) Treasury sharing regulatory responsibilities.[17] The new framework concentrates major responsibilities for financial market supervision in the BoE and replaces the FSA's integrated model of supervision with a 'twin peaks' model. The primary objective of the reform is to strengthen fundamentally the supervisory system by promoting the role of financial stability and the safety and soundness of supervised entities. Importantly, the Financial Services Act has amended the BoE Act 1998 by clearly stating that the BoE shall protect and enhance financial stability.[18] The FSA is broken down into the Prudential Regulation Authority (PRA) and the Financial Conduct Authority (FCA). The PRA, as a subsidiary of the BoE,[19] is responsible for micro-prudential regulation of

9. H.R. 4173 Pub. L. No 111- 203, 124 Stat. 1376 (2010).
10. An almost final version of the 2010 Dodd-Frank Act almost took this step, stating that '[t]he Board of Governors shall identify, measure, monitor, and mitigate risks to the financial stability of the United States.'
11. Dodd-Frank Act, Preamble.
12. *See* further Emilios Avgouleas, *Governance of Global Financial Markets*, 272 (Cambridge University Press 2012).
13. Dodd- Frank Act, §111.
14. Dodd- Frank Act, §§112–115 (12 USC §§5322–5325).
15. William Allen & Geoffrey Wood, *Defining and Achieving Financial Stability*, 2 Journal of Financial Stability 152 (2006).
16. Financial Services Act 2012 at http://www.legislation.gov.uk/ukpga/2012/21/contents/enacted (accessed 31 December 2016).
17. *See* Eliahu Ellinger, Eva Lomnicka & Richard Hare, *Ellinger's Modern Banking Law*, 28, 33 (Oxford University Press 2011).
18. Financial Services Act (2012), 2.
19. *Ibid.*, 6.

deposit-taking institutions and certain investment firms. The FCA, as the renamed FSA, is responsible for conduct of business and supervision of non-PRA regulated firms. At the same time, the Financial Policy Committee (FPC) is situated within the BoE and acts as a macro-prudential regulator. Its role is to identify, monitor and take action to remove/ reduce systemic risk with a view to protecting and enhancing the resilience of the UK financial system.[20]

In sum, following the global financial crisis, the mandate for financial stability has been strengthened at the national level and, in particular, in national central banking or agency frameworks. This has taken place both with the recognition of direct or indirect mandates of financial stability to established public bodies or with the creation of special bodies, agencies, institutions concerned with financial stability (i.e., the FSOC in US and the FPC in UK). The term 'financial stability' is used directly or indirectly by central banks or agency statutes as an objective they need to pursue and promote. At the same time, the term 'financial stability' has acquired an essential function also in the global and regional reform agenda.[21] Therefore, the analysis moves to the role of financial stability as a global public good at the international level.

§2.04 THE EMERGENCE OF FINANCIAL STABILITY AS A PROMINENT 'GLOBAL' PUBLIC GOOD

This part aims to address the theoretical problem of defining financial stability as a global public good in the international legal order, especially because of its indeterminacy. This is shown by the evolving predominance that financial stability has acquired as an international public good in literature.

In the context of the debate on public goods, Quintyn and Taylor suggested that the financial sector plays a special and unique role in an economy, and that as a result, 'the achievement of *financial stability* (...) is now generally considered a *public good*'.[22] Bieri argued that:

> [F]inancial stability carries all the textbook hallmarks of a public good: first, it is nonrival, [s]econd, financial stability is nonexcludable ... [l]astly, individual agents cannot actively withdraw themselves from the influence of financial stability.[23]

Stiglitz et al. offered arguably the clearest picture on the role of financial stability as a global public good 'ensuring global financial stability to support economic stability'.[24] This clearly indicates that financial stability has a major role in the international agenda. Therefore, in the context of the theory of 'global' public goods,

---

20. *Ibid.*, s. 4, inserting s. 9B and 9C into the Bank of England Act 1998.
21. Joel Trachtman, *The International Law of Financial Crisis: Spillovers, Subsidiarity, Fragmentation and Cooperation*, 13 Journal of International Economic Law 719 (2010).
22. Marc Quintyn & Michael Taylor, *Regulatory and Supervisory Independence and Financial Stability*, 8 IMF WP/02/46 (2002) (original emphasis).
23. David Bieri, *Regulation and Financial Stability in the Age of Turbulence*, in Robert Kob (ed.), *Lessons from the Financial Crisis*, 327 (John Wiley 2010).
24. Joseph Stiglitz (chaired), *Report of the Commission of Experts of the President of the United Nations General Assembly on Reforms of the International Monetary and Financial System*, 51 (UN 2009).

financial stability shares the two main characteristics of public goods. Financial stability is non-rivalrous in a sense that the consumption of financial stability by one actor does not subtract it from the same consumption that other actors in the same system and is non-excludable in a sense that financial stability is a common pool source that cannot be taken away from any actor. Financial stability has progressively acquired the role of a global public good as it bears the main characteristics of being non-rivalrous and non-excludable. With the outbreak of the financial crisis, financial stability has been placed at the centre of the international reforms and has acquired a prominent role in the global public good debate. Many contributions have assessed the importance of public goods in the international legal order with particular emphasis on the role of financial stability. In sum, financial stability can well be conceptualised under the theory of global public goods. However, the difficulties to define it as a general concept need to be assessed.

[A] Defining Financial Stability as a Global Public Good

Defining the role or the content of financial stability is a very difficult task. The concept is inherently disputed, and different perspectives and theories give it a different meaning. Central banks have hardly attempted to define what they mean by financial stability. Goodhart held that there is 'no good way to define, or to give a quantitative measurement to, financial stability'.[25] Financial stability and its components are contested expressions especially in legal terms, while the recent financial crisis has restated the importance of global financial stability.

As shown earlier, the financial crisis has generated amendments to the statutes of central banks or creation of statutory agencies or bodies to recognise the topical role of financial stability.[26] In 2011 a Bank for International Settlements (BIS) study paper summarised the main existing operational definitions of financial stability as developed at the international and academic level by framing the debate into five different categories.[27] The definitions provided in the BIS study are grouped in five categories: those defining financial stability in terms of preconditions; the absence of financial instability (negative definition); the smooth functioning of key elements of the financial system (positive definition); definitions in the sense of robustness to shocks; and definitions as smooth functioning and robustness to shocks. Against this background, it is argued that there are three main theoretical strands of definitions of financial stability.

A first strand identifies financial stability as a positively performing condition of the economy. In this sense, Schinasi defined financial stability in economic terms as when a:

25. Charles Goodhart, *Myths about the Lender of Last Resort*, Financial Market Group LSE (1999) at http://econpapers.repec.org/scripts/redir.pf?u = http%3A%2F%2Fwww.lse.ac.uk%2Ffmg%2Fdocuments%2FspecialPapers%2F1990s%2Fsp120.pdf;h = repec:fmg:fmgsps:sp120 (accessed 31 December 2016).
26. *Ibid.*, 5.
27. Bank of International Settlement, *Central Bank Governance and Financial Stability*, 32 Report by a Study Group (May 2011).

> financial system (...) is capable of facilitating (...) the performance of an economy, and of dissipating financial imbalances that arise endogenously or as a result of significant adverse and unanticipated events.[28]

This approach, which is only one of those offered by Schinasi, shows that financial stability is defined as a capacity of the financial system to perform well and to withstand shocks. However, the lack of a reference to an effective benchmark makes it difficult to attain financial stability in practice.

A second strand considers financial stability in the negative as the 'absence' of financial instability or financial crises. Crockett has considered financial stability as the absence of financial stability arguing that this is a situation in which:

> economic performance is potentially impaired by fluctuations in the price of financial assets, or in the ability of financial intermediaries to meet their contractual obligations.[29]

Similarly, it has been suggested that financial instability refers to 'the conditions in financial markets that harm, or threaten to harm, an economy's performance through their impact on the working of the financial system'.[30] It appears that the predominant economic literature considers financial stability as a negative concept given the substantial difficulties in developing policy-making indications on how to improve financial stability. However, a negative definition creates uncertainties regarding the benchmark level of intervention required for determining when financial instability ceases. Moreover, it may have a meaning that is merely economic or political and not legal as such. It may also be deprived of any valuable meaning and thus be undetermined.

A third strand of definitions considers financial stability as a conditional responsiveness of the financial system to mitigate mainly or absorb risks or shocks. Padoa-Schioppa argued that financial stability is:

> [a] condition where the financial system is able to withstand shocks without giving way to cumulative processes which impair the allocation of savings to investment opportunities and the processing of payment in the economy.[31]

Similarly, Allen and Wood sustained that financial stability is the ability of the financial system to absorb financial shocks.[32] According to Schinasi et al., financial stability may be considered as a 'situation in which the financial system is capable of: (1) allocating resources efficiently between activities and across time; (2) assessing and managing financial risks, and (3) absorbing shocks'.[33] In this sense, Schinasi has

28. Garry Schinasi, *Defining Financial Stability*, 8 IMF WP/04/187 (2004).
29. David Crockett, *The theory and practice of financial stability*, 532 De Economist (1996) (original emphasis).
30. John Chant *et al.*, *Essays on Financial Stability*, 3 Bank of Canada Technical Report (2003).
31. Tommaso Padoa-Schioppa, *Central Banks and Financial Stability: Exploring a Land in Between*, ECB Policy Paper Introductory Paper (2002) at https://www.ecb.europa.eu/events/pdf/conferences/tps.pdf (last accessed 31 December 2016).
32. Allen, Wood *supra* n. 15, 155.
33. Aerdt Houben, Jan Kakes & Garry Schinasi, *Toward a Framework for Safeguarding Financial Stability*, 11 IMF WP/04/101 (2004).

provided the most convincing positive and comprehensive definition of financial stability by stating that it is:

> a situation in which the financial system is capable of satisfactorily performing its three key functions simultaneously. First, the financial system is efficiently and smoothly facilitating the intertemporal allocation of resources from savers to investors and the allocation of economic resources generally. Second, forward-looking financial risks are being assessed and priced reasonably accurately and are being relatively well managed. Third, the financial system is in such condition that it can comfortably if not smoothly absorb financial and real economic surprises and shocks.[34]

Schinasi's definition is wide and very comprehensive, and it has the merits of capturing the main positive aspects to the achievement of financial stability. Hence, this third strand of definitions appears to be valuable in clarifying that financial stability shall primarily aim for, i.e., the prevention and management of risks and shocks in the financial system.

Overall, the above literature review suggests that financial stability should be considered as a 'global' public good objective, whose pursuit is attained where the financial system capable of preventing and managing financial risks or shocks. This construction mainly follows the third strand of the above-mentioned literature strands as it defines financial stability in positive terms and gives it a substantive meaning. Neither the first nor the second strands are satisfactory as they are insufficiently clear in indicating *what* financial stability is. The first strand is preoccupied with a situation where financial stability contributes to the good performance of the economy, but does not provide for a specific benchmark to determine what is needed to achieve financial stability. The second strand stresses the lack of financial stability as the main benchmark to reach financial stability. They are both unsatisfactory, as they do not purport to look to the constituent components of financial stability in a given framework.

On the contrary, the third strand focuses on the existence of a system capable to prevent, mitigate or absorb risks or shocks. In this context, the link of financial stability to risks or shocks is essential to structure financial stability as a 'global' public good objective. The proposed reading suggests that the financial system be in a situation of financial stability where instruments for the prevention and management of risks or shocks are in place.[35]

While the above literature analysis is quite developed, the nature of financial stability remains highly disputed and contested in legal scholarship, most prominently because financial stability remains an evolving and expansive normative concept and legal benchmarks are difficult to determine. Furthermore, a major difficulty lies in framing financial stability as a concept having a determinable legal dimension. What is

---

34. Garry Schinasi, *Safeguarding Financial Stability: Theory and Practice*, 82 (International Monetary Fund 2006).
35. *See* the development of a definition of financial stability in EU law and policy in Chapter 3 section §3.02[B].

a legal framework that promotes financial stability? What are the main components of a legal definition of financial stability? Osterloo and De Haan argued that there is 'no unambiguous definition of financial stability or systemic risk, and that generally the responsibility is not explicitly formulated in laws (...)'.[36] Lastra contended that financial stability in Europe is an evolving concept orientating the functioning of the European financial architecture and comprises a variety of elements.[37] Andenas and Chiu recently affirmed that financial stability is a malleable concept that can operate at different levels and could justify different policy choices.[38] Legal scholarship denounces certain difficulties in giving a role and in defining financial stability. Notwithstanding the difficulties to define financial stability, the next subsection develops on the main components of the definitions of financial stability promoted by the third strand of economics literature.

[B] The Main Components of Financial Stability as a Global Public Good

The third strand identified above, and substantially followed in this book, shows that financial stability as a general concept having the nature of objective is characterised by two main components. [39] These are: (a) a financial system; (b) ability to withstand risks and shocks. They will also be analysed when assessing financial stability at the European level.

[1] Financial System

Determining the scope of the term, 'financial system' is essential to understand financial stability. Financial system usually comprises individual financial institutions, the banking system, the financial system or the economy as a whole (national, regional, global). As argued by Anabtawi and Schwarcz in order to qualify as a system, an entity must be composed of interconnected elements that, in a combined fashion, have a function distinct from those of these elements individually.[40] The system's behaviour is dependent on the state of each element and the interactions between them. Therefore, the system behaviour may be addressed by altering the behaviour of any of its elements or their interconnections.[41]

Given the general nature of financial stability, the financial system comprises all the different actors that play an essential role in the economy, although with different importance. However, special focus for the definition of financial stability shall be

36. Sander Osterloo & Jakob De Haan, *Central Banks and Financial Stability: A Survey Journal of Financial Stability*, 1 Journal of Financial Stability 257 (2004).
37. Rosa Lastra, *International Financial and Monetary Law*, 126 (Oxford University Press 2015).
38. Mads Andenas & Iris Chiu, *Financial Stability and Legal Integration in Financial Regulation*, 38 European Law Review 343–344 (2013).
39. For discussion on the general components of financial stability in Europe, *see* Chapter 3 section §3.02[B].
40. Iman Anabtawi & Steven Schwarcz, *Regulating Ex Post: How Law Can Address the Inevitability of Financial Failure*, 92 Texas Law Review 75, 78 (2013).
41. *Ibid.*, 80.

given to the banking system and sovereigns as these are essential players in the financial system. This is because the former are essential intermediaries in the structure of the economy while the latter are indispensable public structures for the economy as a whole.

[2] Ability to Prevent and Manage Risks and Shocks

Risks and shocks are considered as factors that could deviate from the expected outcome.[42] In other words, they are state of affairs that can negatively change the prospect given at the certain point in time. Risks and shocks are therefore the main concern to financial stability as they are the main drivers to generate *in*-stability of a given financial system. Among other types of risks and shocks, 'systemic' risk has acquired substantial relevance in the general framework of financial stability. This is generally intended as a situation that posits to the collapse of the general economy. While the term 'systemic risk' is used quite widely among policy makers and regulators, systemic risk is difficult to qualify and quantify in legal terms. Schwarz defines systemic risk as:

> the risk that (i) an economic shock such as market or institutional failure triggers (through a panic or otherwise) either (X) the failure of a chain of markets or institutions or (Y) a chain of significant losses to financial institutions, (ii) resulting in increases in the cost of capital or decreases in its availability, often evidenced by substantial financial-market price volatility.[43]

This definition encapsulates the main objectives of systemic risk by identifying both the failure of the markets and the consequential production of losses that endanger the capital markets. At the institutional level, the International Monetary Fund (IMF) has provided a wide definition to systemic risk:

> as a risk of disruption to financial services that (1) is caused by an impairment of all or parts of the financial system and (2) has the potential to have a serious adverse effect on economic activity.[44]

This concept shows that systemic risk is composed of two elements. First, some (or all) financial services are temporarily unavailable or their provision is substantially impaired. Second, such impairment shall have repercussion over the general economy, in particular on the real economy. Interestingly, Lastra stressed that systemic risk would be incomplete without a reference to the transmission mechanisms as the channels of propagation of a crisis.[45] These mechanisms may take the form of four inter-related channels: the inter-bank, inter-institution, inter-instrument channel; (2) the payment systems channel; (3) the information channel; and (4) the psychological

42. *Ibid.*, 99.
43. Steven Schwarcz, *Systemic Risk*, 97 Georgetown Law Journal 204 (2008).
44. IMF, *Systemic Risk and the Redesign of Financial Regulation*, 10 (2010) at https://www.imf.org/external/pubs/ft/gfsr/2010/01/pdf/chap2.pdf (accessed 31 December 2016).
45. Rosa Lastra, *Systemic Risk, SIFIs and Financial Stability*, 11 Capital Markets Law Journal 201 (2011).

channel.[46] This analysis shows a wide recognition of the need to prevent and mitigate systemic risk as a major cause of financial *in*-stability.

While these components are important to define financial stability, it is difficult to argue that financial stability has the nature of a foundational objective with tangible and enforceable instruments at the international level. This is precisely because '*the ability to withstand*' risks and shocks is not evident at the international level. While financial stability has been recognised as a global public good, the soft law nature of the IFA as well as the lack of a strong institutional design to prevent, manage and absorb risks and shocks do not make it possible to recognise a truly foundational role of financial stability at the international level. In fact, the IFA lacks normative instruments to achieve international financial stability.

Conversely, as it will be shown in the next chapter of this book, these difficulties are easier to tackle at the European level by proposing a new supranational dimension to financial stability as a foundational objective in EU law and policy. This is mainly because of the normative instruments to achieve financial stability that exist in EU law and policy. However, before moving to the next chapter, it is essential to assess the limitations of the existing international dimension of financial stability as a global public good.

§2.05 THE OBJECTIVE OF FINANCIAL STABILITY AT THE INTERNATIONAL LEVEL: TOWARDS A NEW INTERNATIONAL FINANCIAL ORDER? A CRITICAL VIEW

After looking at the intricacies of defining financial stability, this part assesses the impact of the recent normative reforms of the IFA in the pursuit of global financial stability.[47].

Before the global financial crisis, policy-makers established a new order for the financial sector, the IFA, especially after the 1997 East Asian financial crisis. The 1997 East Asian crisis led to the convening of the first edition of the Group of Twenty Finance Ministers and Central Bank Governors (G-20) as well as of the Financial Stability Forum (FSF).[48] As put by Crockett, the IFA encompasses:

> [t]he rules, the guidelines and the arrangements governing international financial relations as well as various institutions, entities and bodies through which such rules, guidelines and other arrangements are developed, monitored and enforced.[49]

46. *Ibid.*, 202.
47. For scholarly contributions on the IFA, *see*, among others, Lastra, *supra* n. 37, 499–554; Giovanoli, *supra* n. 1, 45; Mario Giovanoli, *The International Financial Architecture and Its Reform after the Global Crisis*, in Mario Giovanoli, Diego Devos (eds) *International Monetary and Financial Law: The Global Crisis*, 3–39 (Oxford University Press 2010); Avgouleas, *supra* n. 12, 185–212; Claus Zimmermann, *The Concept of Monetary Sovereignty Revisited*, 192 and following (Cambridge University Press 2013).
48. *See* Douglas Arner, *Financial Stability, Economic Growth and the Role of Law*, 51–88 (Cambridge University Press 2007).
49. *See* David Crockett, *Lessons from the Asian Crisis* in Joseph Bisignano, William Hunter, George Kaufman (eds), *Global Financial Crises*, 7–15 (Springer 2000).

The effects of the global financial crisis have had some implications on the theory of global public goods. The global financial crisis has reshaped the dimension and the context of international financial stability by positing it at the centre of attention of policy-makers and arguably by improving the structure of IFA, which was exclusively based on Standard Setting Bodies (SSBs).[50] Without assessing in details the status of the IFA and the proposals for further reforms at the international level, which would go beyond the scope of this book, this final section shows the efforts to strengthen the international dimension of financial stability. Four major reforms have reshaped the IFA and have reframed the debate on the role of global financial stability. The main reforms can be summarised as follows: the G-20 has acquired a central role in promoting global financial reforms;[51] the FSF has been re-structured into the Financial Stability Board (FSB); the Basel Committee of Banking Supervision (BCBS) has promoted new standards; and the IMF has gained a seminal role in administering financial surveillance.[52]

[A] The Role and Achievements of the G-20 for Global Financial Stability

The G-20 has acquired a leading role for the restructuring of IFA. The leaders of the world's biggest economies embarked on an intensified horizontal and intergovernmental cooperation process rather than following vertical or institutional venues.

The G-20 is defined as the 'premier forum for international cooperation on the most important issues of the global and financial agenda'.[53] This is a forum composed of finance ministers and central bank governors of the world's major economies, which runs in parallel to those of the leaders of the G-20 countries. The G-20 forum was chosen rather than G-7, G-8 or G-10 fora as representing better the worldwide dimension of problems related to global financial stability.

The G-20 has the main objectives of: (1) policy coordination between its members in order to achieve global economic stability sustainable growth; (2) promoting financial regulations that reduce risks and prevent future financial crises; (3) modernising the IFA.[54]

At present, the G-20[55] represents 90% of gross domestic product (GDP), 80% of global trade and two-thirds of the world population.[56] The role of the G-20 has been essential in the context of the financial crisis. The G-20 meetings were held for the

50. For analysis of SSB in international law, *see* Chris Brummer, *Soft Law and the Global Financial System*, 119 and following (Cambridge University Press 2015).
51. G-20, *Declaration on the Summit of Financial Markets and the World Economy*, 14–15 November 2008, point 9.
52. *See* Zimmermann *supra* n. 47, 211–225.
53. G-20, website: www.g20.org (accessed 31 December 2016).
54. *Ibid.*
55. The following nineteen states plus the European Union (EU) are members of the G-20: Argentina, Australia, Brazil, Canada, China, France, Germany, India, Indonesia, Italy, Japan, Mexico, Russia, Saudi Arabia, South Africa, South Korea, Turkey, the UK and the US. Spain attends the G-20 leaders summits as an invitee.
56. G-20, website: www.g20.org (accessed 31 October 2016).

purposes of restoring global financial stability already in 2008 with the first G-20 meetings in Washington in November 2008.

The role and activities of the G-20 are *par excellence* an example of international soft law. This is because the G-20 declarations are not international treaties, but are international soft law measures. In terms of effectiveness, the G-20 relies essentially on peer pressure as the declarations open the way for further commitments to harmonise policies on regulation or supervision. Furthermore, G-20 declarations express a commitment by its membership to follow formal initiatives in other multilateral organisations, such as the IMF, or in regional organisations.

Following the global financial crisis, the G-20 has launched important initiatives to foster global financial stability. These show that the G-20 has played a key role in promoting reforms to increase the global dimension of financial stability. Already in the G-20 Washington summit in November 2008, the G-20 leaders agreed on five principles for the reform of financial markets: strengthening transparency and accountability, enhancing sound regulation, promoting integrity in financial markets, reinforcing international cooperation and reforming international financial institutions.[57] In the London Summit of April 2009, the G-20 leaders decided to put forward commitments to strengthen the financial system and to reform the FSB.[58] A number of subsequent G-20 meetings reiterated the efforts to restructure the international financial system and prompted the input for reforms to strengthen global financial stability.[59] Most recently, in November 2015, the G-20 Antalya meeting highlighted that 'as a key step towards ending too-big-to-fail, [the G-20 has] finalized the common international standard on total-loss-absorbing-capacity (TLAC) for global systemically important banks'.[60] At the same time, it denounced 'the continued delay in implementing the IMF quota and governance reforms agreed in 2010'.[61] Hence, the G-20 members suggested the need to progress with the adoption of a loss-absorption mechanism, the TLCA, and to review the IMF's 2010 Quanta and Governance Reform.

From the analysis above, it can be concluded that the G-20 has been an essential international body to prompt action against the global financial crisis and reinforce global financial stability.[62] This is for three main reasons. First, the G-20 has been actively involved in discussing measures to strengthen financial stability at the global level by promoting the initiatives undertaken by other international institutions and players. Second, the G-20 is a body representing the highest political personalities in economic and monetary matters allowing the use of peer pressure to come with internationally agreed solutions to strengthen global financial stability. Third, the G-20

57. G-20, *Declaration on the Summit on Financial Markets and World Economy*, 15 November 2008.
58. G-20, *Declaration on Strengthening the Financial System*, 2 April 2009.
59. Zimmermann *supra* n. 47, 198.
60. G-20 Finance Ministers and Central Bank Governors, *Communiqué*, 24 July 2016, para. 9 at http://www.g20.utoronto.ca/2016/160724-finance.html (accessed 31 December 2016). For an analysis of TLAC and MREL in Europe *see* Chapter 8 section §8.05[B].
61. G-20 Finance Ministers and Central Bank Governors, *Communiqué*, 15–16 November 2015, para. 17.
62. Giovanoli, *supra* n. 1, 47.

appears as the political originator of international initiatives to be implemented at regional and national levels.

[B] The Establishment and Legal Strengths of the FSB for Global Financial Stability

Following the suggestions of the G-20 Washington Summit in November 2008, the pre-crisis existing FSB[63] has been transformed into the FSB. The main objective of the FSF was to coordinate the work of the various international financial SSBs that have emerged worldwide since the creation of Basel Committee on Banking Supervision (BCBS) in 1974. Among the most prominent tasks of the FSF was the compilation of a comprehensive Compendium of Standards to provide a 'common reference work for the various standards and codes of good practice that are internationally accepted as relevant to sound, stable and properly functioning financial systems'.[64]

The financial crisis has promoted a change in the name, role and tasks of the FSF. At the G-20 Washington Summit in November 2008, G-20 leaders called for a significant extension of the FSF's membership, notably to emerging economies. Then, in the G-20 Pittsburgh Summit in September 2009, the Charter for a new FSB was adopted. The FSB's main tasks are, among others, to: assess vulnerabilities affecting the financial system and identify and oversee action needed to address them; promote coordination and information exchange among authorities responsible for financial stability; monitor and advise on market developments and their implications for regulatory policy; advise on and monitor best practice in meeting regulatory standards; manage contingency planning for cross-border crisis management, particularly with respect to systemically important firms.[65] The FSB's Charter, as amended in June 2012, gives two additional tasks to the FSB. First, the FSB is given the additional task to

> promote and help coordinate the alignment of the activities of the SSBs to address any overlaps or gaps and clarify demarcations in light of changes in national and regional regulatory structures relating to prudential and systemic risk, market integrity and investor and consumer protection, infrastructure, as well as accounting and auditing.[66]

Second, it allows the FSB to 'address regulatory gaps that pose *risk to financial stability*, develop or coordinate development of standards and principles, in collaboration with the SSBs and others, as warranted, in areas which do not fall within the

63. The FSF was created by the G-7 finance ministers and central bank governors at the Bonn meeting in February 1999. On the FSF *see* further Mario Giovanoli, *A New Architecture for the Global Financial Market: Legal Aspects of International Financial Standard Setting* in Mario Giovanoli (ed.), *International Monetary Law: Issues for the New Millennium*, 25–26 (Oxford University Press 2000).
64. *Ibid.*, 27.
65. *See* FSB, *FSB Charter*, Art. 2(1) at http://www.fsb.org/wp-content/uploads/FSB-Charter-with-revised-Annex-FINAL.pdf (accessed 31 December 2016).
66. *Ibid.*, Art. 2(2).

functional domain of another international standard setting body, or on issues that have cross-sectoral implications'.[67]

Overall, the establishment of the FSB with both a significantly broadened mandate and a more inclusive membership should be viewed as the key achievement of the G-20 summits and of global financial stability. There are a number of advantages in the reinforced role of the FSB. The FSB is more inclusive and representative as compared to the predecessor. Its membership includes now representatives from the major economies under a Chairmanship. Hence, the FSB appears to be a legitimate body in the way it is shaped and on it conducts its activities. However, it remains clear that the FSB is not an international organisation and lacks legal personality under international law. At the same time, the fact that international institutions, such as the IMF and the World Bank, as well as regional institutions, such as the ECB, have their seats in the FSF shows that the FSB is a key player in the pursuit of global financial stability. The FSB is therefore a legitimate body that adopts and catalogues international standard setting measures. For instance, the update of the Compendium of Standards contributes to highlight the main standards accepted by the international community for the sound, stable and well-functioning financial systems at the international, regional and national levels.[68] Furthermore, in November 2015, the FSB published principled standards such as 'Principles on loss-absorbing and recapitalization capacity for Global-Systemically Important Banks (G-SIBs) in Resolution' and a 'Total Loss-absorbing Capacity (TLAC) Term Sheet'.[69] However, while it has been argued that the FSB constitutes an important improvement as compared with the FSF, it still shows considerable limitations, especially because of its lack of enforceable and institutional powers.[70]

[C] The BCBS and Its Soft Law Role for Global Financial Stability

The BCBS is one of the key actors in IFA for global financial stability.[71] The importance of the BCBS lies in its function of SSB in the field of banking regulation and supervision.

The BCBS was originally established under the framework of the BIS in 1974.[72] The BCBS is now provided with a Charter detailing its objectives and tasks. Most importantly, the BCBS Charter states that:

---

67. *Ibid.*, Art. 2(3), emphasis added.
68. Lastra, *supra* n. 37, 509.
69. On the TLAC, *see* http://www.fsb.org/2015/11/total-loss-absorbing-capacity-tlac-principles-and-term-sheet/ (accessed 31 December 2016).
70. Avgouleas, *supra* n. 12, 208–209.
71. The focus of this book on banking regulation and supervision and not on other areas of financial law justifies the assessment of the BCBS. Other sectorial standard-setters are the Committee on Payment and Settlement Systems (CPSS), the Committee on the Global Financial System (CGFS), the International Accounting Standards Board (IASB), the International Association of Insurance Supervisors (IAIS), and the International Organization of Securities Commissions (IOSCO).
72. On the history, role and activities of the BCBS, *see*, among others, Charles Goodhart, *The Basel Committee on Banking Supervision. A History of the early years 1974–1997* (Cambridge University Press 2011); Brummer, *supra* n. 50, 77; Lastra, *supra* n. 37, 505.

> The BCBS is the primary global standard-setter for the prudential regulation of banks and provides a forum for cooperation on banking supervisory matters. Its mandate is to strengthen the regulation, supervision and practices of banks worldwide with the purpose of *enhancing financial stability*.[73]

While being an informal body that does not adopt legally binding decisions, the Basel Committee has exerted the role of the international SSB *par excellence* in banking regulation and supervision. The BCBS adopts prudential standards for the prudential regulation and supervision of banks to be implemented in BCBS members and followed by internationally active banks.[74]

The BCBS has been the main promoter of principles for effective prudential supervision. In fact, in the 2012 version of the Core Principles of Banking Supervision, the BCBS stresses the core aspects for a sound banking system. First, there is the need for greater intensity and resources to deal effectively with systemically important banks.[75] Second, they highlight the importance of applying a system-wide, macro-perspective to the micro-prudential supervision of banks to assist in identifying and analysing systemic risk and taking pre-emptive action to address it.[76] Furthermore, the Core Principles reveal the increasing focus on effective crisis management, recovery and resolution measures in reducing both the probability and the impact of a bank failure.[77] Finally, they require good corporate governance,[78] as well as appropriate disclosure and transparency policies.[79]

In the last two decades, the BCBS has played an essential role especially in agreeing stringent supervisory standards for cross-border credit institutions. Bank prudential requirements accords have undergone three phases in which Basel negotiations led to the adoption of three standard agreements: Basel I Capital Accord (Basel I) in 1988, Basel II in 2004 and Basel III in 2010. With Basel III, the Basel Committee has reformed its capital adequacy standards and has introduced a new supervisory framework to regulate liquidity adequacy and suggested the introduction of a global leverage ratio. Furthermore, the Basel Committee has issued standards to improve governance and risk management in the banking sector. Therefore, the adoption of a Basel III standard-setting round has been an important driver for financial stability, in particular to solve the under-capitalisation of banks. The Basel III standards have driven two main reforms to deal with the financial crisis and the pursuit of global financial stability.[80] First, there has been a noteworthy development of macro-prudential supervision at the international level. In particular, the strengthening of the Basel standards are intended to allow banks to withstand financial stress by addressing exposure of banks to economic cycles, bubbles and other macro-economic events.

73. BCBS, *BCBS Charter*, Mandate (emphasis added).
74. *Ibid.* See also BCBS standards, guidelines and sound practices.
75. BCBS, *Core Principles for Effective Banking Supervision*, September 2012 www.bis.org/publ/bcbs230.pdf (accessed 31 December 2016).
76. *Ibid.*, 5.
77. *Ibid.*, 6--7.
78. *Ibid.*, Core Principle 14.
79. *Ibid.*, Core Principle 28.
80. *See* further Avgouleas, *supra* n. 12, 266–272.

Second, Basel standard reforms have led to an increase of capital levels for banks. In particular, the introduction of liquidity and leverage ratios as well as important risk management standards have boosted the level of stability of cross-border financial institutions.

Overall, the BCBS is an essential international standard setter in banking regulation and supervision. Three main reasons place it as a main player in pursuit of global financial stability. First, it sets standards as a soft law measures to be followed at the regional and national levels. Second, its wide membership allows discussions and negotiations concerning the instruments for more stable banking sector. Third, the BCBS exerts an important influence in the promotion of rules that serve to strengthen prudential supervision especially of G-SIB.

[D] The IMF and Its Renewed Role for Global Financial Stability

The IMF is a fully-fledged international institution established by the IMF Agreement with the Bretton Woods Agreement in 1944.[81] Before the financial crisis, the IMF exercised surveillance predominantly over the international monetary system and the exchange rates policies of its membership. The global financial crisis has strengthened some IMF functions for the benefit of global financial stability. The G-20 suggested that the IMF plays a leading role in the global financial architecture for financial stability.[82] In particular, the IMF has strengthened its surveillance function under Article IV of the Agreement.[83] This provision of the IMF Agreement states that one of the key functions of the IMF is to 'oversee the international monetary system in order to ensure its effective operation'.[84] The same Article establishes that the IMF:

> [s]hall exercise firm surveillance over the exchange rate policies of members, and shall adopt specific principles for the guidance of all members with respect to those policies.[85]

Article IV of the IMF Agreement frames the multilateral and the bilateral IMF surveillance system.[86]

As regards the multilateral surveillance system, the IMF adopts the Global Financial Stability Report (GFSR),[87] a semi-annual report on global financial stability. As provided in the 2016 GFSR, the IMF analyses key risks facing the global financial

81. IMF, *IMF Agreement* at http://www.imf.org/External/Pubs/FT/AA/ (last accessed 31 December 2016). The role, tasks and functioning of the IMF go beyond the scope of this monograph. On the IMF in general *see* further Lastra, *supra* n. 37, 429–498; Matthias Herdegen, *Principles of International Economic Law*, Ch. XXXIX (Oxford University Press 2016); Viterbo, *supra* n. 8, 67.
82. *See* G-20, *Declaration of the Summit on Financial Markets and the World Economy*, 2008 para. 9.
83. The IMF has also played an important role in financial assistance measures to EU Member States. For an analysis of financial assistance instruments by the IMF to the EU Member States, *see* Chapter 5 section §5.02.
84. IMF Agreement, Art. IV s. b.
85. *Ibid.*
86. Sean Hagan, *Enhancing the IMF's Regulatory Authority*, 13 Journal of International Economic Law 955 (2010).
87. For the latest editions of the GFSR, *see* the IMF's *website* at http://www.imf.org/external/pubs/ft/gfsr/index.htm (accessed 31 December 2016).

system. As outlined in the 2016 GFSR, 'In normal times, the report seeks to play a role in preventing crises by highlighting policies that may mitigate systemic risks, thereby contributing to global financial stability and the sustained economic growth of the IMF's member countries.' Therefore, the GFSR is a multilateral surveillance instrument to analyse global financial stability and to show the main risks that may jeopardise global financial stability.

As part of its bilateral tasks, the IMF has restructured its bilateral financial sector surveillance function by providing a more enforceable financial surveillance role in assessing the financial conditions of its members than in the past. In particular, the IMF role for global financial stability under Article IV of the IMF Agreement has been considerably strengthened through a review of the Financial Sector Assessment Program (FSAP).[88] This is analysed in more details.

The FSAP,[89] which is a comprehensive in-depth analysis of a country's financial sector, was created in 1999. The IMF is in charge of conducting financial sector assessments in advanced as well as low-income and emerging market countries. The focus of FSAP assessments is always twofold: 'to gauge the stability of the financial sector and to assess its potential contribution to growth and development'.[90] In September 2009, the IMF Executive Board reviewed the experience with the FSAP over the first ten years of its existence and discussed options for strengthening the programme in light of the financial crisis. The existing FSAP at the time showed several weaknesses, notably the fact that liquidity risks and cross-border or cross-market linkages were underappreciated as sources of risk and that recommendations were not clear and country-specific enough.[91] This led to an improvement of the mechanism's analytical tools and assessment methodologies. As further explained by the Fund:

> To assess the stability of the financial sector, FSAP teams examine the resilience of the banking and other non bank financial sectors; conduct stress tests and analyze systemic risks including linkages among banks and nonbanks and domestic and cross border spillovers; examine microprudential and macroprudential frameworks; review the quality of bank, and non bank supervision, and financial market infrastructure oversight against accepted international standards; and evaluate the ability of central banks, regulators and supervisors, policymakers, and backstops and financial safety nets to respond effectively in case of systemic stress.[92]

Furthermore, the FSAP serves:

> [t]o assess the development aspects of the financial sector, FSAPs examine the development needs in terms of institutions, markets, infrastructure, and inclusiveness; quality of the legal framework and of payments and settlements system; identify obstacles to the competitiveness and efficiency of the sector; topics

88. *See* IMF, *Financial Sector Assessment Program website* at http://www.imf.org/external/np/exr/facts/fsap.htm (last accessed 31 December 2016).
89. *See* Zimmermann, *supra* n. 47, 214–220.
90. IMF, *The Financial Sector Assessment Program (FSAP) (Factsheet)* at http://www.imf.org/external/np/exr/facts/fsap.htm (accessed 31 December 2016).
91. *Ibid.*
92. *Ibid.*

relating to financial inclusion and retail payments; and examine its contribution to economic growth and development.[93]

Most recently, after having established the FSAP as a mandatory exercise under Article IV consultations for some jurisdictions, the IMF has expanded the list of members subject to the FSAP to twenty-nine jurisdictions in 2013. In 2014, the IMF has further reviewed the FSAP reform and highlighted the need to focus the FSAP assessments on systemic risk and on the use of an expanded set of tools to track weaknesses in the financial sector.

Overall, the IMF, especially through its FSAP has played a primary role in the context of the financial crisis for the pursuit of global financial stability. The FSAP clearly shows that the main concern of this surveillance exercise is global financial stability by assessments of the financial sectors of FSAP jurisdictions. Furthermore, the FSAP proves to be an instrument aiming to track risks that may arise in the financial system as a whole of an IMF member. Therefore, the review of the FSAP in the context of the Article IV surveillance has been an important IMF reform to conduct financial stability assessments, especially for systemically important financial sector jurisdictions.

[E] Is the New IFA Pursuing Global Financial Stability as a Truly Global Public Good? A Critique

From the reconstruction of the main reforms to the IFA, it can be concluded that the global financial crisis has reshaped the international financial system by taking into account the 'global' public good dimension of financial stability, albeit only to a certain extent. This final subsection shows that the major reforms in strengthening the IFA have not been sufficient to make financial stability a foundational 'public good' objective at the international level. This is because the IFA lacks strong normative instruments to make financial stability a truly prescriptive objective at the international level.

While the analysis has demonstrated that international policy-makers have promoted financial stability as a global public good, it remains clear that the international efforts to restructure international economic law so far under the influence of the objective of financial stability have not been as effective as expected.[94] This is because the international system does not provide for truly normative and enforceable instruments capable of effectively preventing and managing (systemic) risks or shocks that policy-makers and market players should follow. In other words, the limits of the IFA are detectable in the lack of strong instruments to pursue financial stability at the international level. At the same time, the difficulties in establishing legally binding instruments for global financial stability in an international community composed of very different economic powers pursuing policy interests remain a major constraint to the future improvements of the IFA.

93. *Ibid.*
94. *See Ibid.*, 435–457.

The main normative limitations arising from the current international economic law system are highlighted. First, the reform of the global financial system has not conferred hard law powers to international institutions and bodies in the pursuit of global financial stability. The international bodies and institutions exercise functions mainly limited to soft law, standard setting or reporting instruments such as surveillance reports that are incapable of effectively pursuing global financial stability. The IFA is still based on soft law measures that have limited effects at the regional or national levels. Second, the supervision of financial market players, banks, securities and insurance is not sufficiently integrated at the international level. This is due to the different players and jurisdictions existing at international level and to the lack of consensus on the creation of a strong body or institution with the task of the regulation, supervision and resolution of systemically important financial institutions (SIFIs). Third, micro-prudential and macro-prudential supervision are not exercised in the same manner and with a strong degree of powers at the international level. The most important role is that of the SSB (the Basel Committee for banking supervision) for micro-prudential supervision as well as that of the IMF surveillance procedure in macro-prudential supervision. However, there is still not a truly international authority supervising financial markets. Fourth, the level of prudential regulation and supervision is still scattered at the international level, and there is no clearly visible hierarchical structure to conduct prudential supervision. Fifth, the functions of Lender of Last Resort (LOLR) or of rescue of financial institutions or sovereigns do not exist at the international level. On the one hand, the functions of central banks differ profoundly around the world and their mandates are not spelt out in a uniform way. On the other hand, there are no international frameworks for the resolution of cross-border SIFIs or for the restructuring of sovereign debts. Finally, the institutional relationship between the different global actors for financial stability, the FSB and the IMF in particular, remains uncertain. There is no specific mandate for any of the global financial bodies or institutions to exercise financial stability policy.

Overall, the assessment shows that the crisis-related reform efforts have placed a great emphasis on financial stability as a global public good. However, such efforts have not been sufficient to develop a sufficiently strong international legal framework for the attainment of international financial stability and establishing a fully-fledged international governance system for the pursuit of financial stability. In the wake of the global financial crisis, the international community has embarked in many reform projects based on long-term perspectives. Some authors have elaborated normative proposals to address partially or entirely the limitations to the IFA.[95] These span from the reinforcement of the FSB to the creation of new or reformed international supervisory and resolution tools such as the FSAP. However, at present the objective of financial stability as a global public good has not yet gone in the direction of an international binding agreement to create a World Financial Organisation (WFO) charged with the adoption of binding legal rules on all aspects of financial regulation

95. For an analysis on the conferral of hard law powers to the IFA, *see* Avgouleas, *supra* n. 12, 433–434 and Bin Gu, Tong Liu, *Enforcing International Financial Regulatory Reforms*, 17 Journal of International Economic Law 139 (2014).

and day-to-day supervision at macro- and micro-prudential level.[96] To the extent that the creation of stability-enhancing international frameworks replacing domestic and regional regulatory regimes is pursued via soft law standards and informal policy coordination bodies, the international framework of financial stability will not be capable of truly attaining the objective of international financial stability.

§2.06 CONCLUSION

This chapter has opened the debate on the role and function of financial stability. First, the chapter has adopted as a starting point the theory of public goods to argue that financial stability has the characteristics of the public goods. This is an important aspect regarding the debate on financial stability as it reveals where the roots of financial stability as a non-legal concept. The chapter then showed that the US and the UK have placed great attention to place financial stability at the centre of their regulatory and supervisory policy-making in the context of the global financial crisis.

Then, identifying financial stability as a global public good has allowed a literature review on this disputed concept. The assessment has revealed the difficulties in achieving a univocal and comprehensive understanding of the term 'financial stability'. In particular, the chapter has focussed on the definition of financial stability developed in other social sciences to demonstrate that financial stability is much more than an 'empty shell'. On such basis, the chapter has elaborated a working definition of financial stability as a global public good based on the components of the financial system and the ability of such system to prevent and manage risks and shocks.

This has justified then an assessment of the main reforms at the international level to boost financial stability. The global financial crisis has triggered major restructurings of the IFA that have strengthened the role of financial stability at the international level. Four main players have emerged as the main components of the reorganised IFA for the pursuit of global financial stability: the G-20 as the self-appointed political body of the world economy initiating reforms for global financial stability; the FSB with its expanded mandate and membership as the 'supervisor' of global financial stability; the BCBS as an international standard setter for banking regulation and supervision; the IMF as a renewed international organisation promoting global surveillance over risks in global financial stability.

However, the approach in restructuring the IFA reveals that financial stability at the international level does not have in substance the character of a foundational objective with strong normative instruments for its fulfilment. The means through which the international community has restructured the IFA as well as the soft law initiatives to strengthen global financial stability show that international policy-makers have not yet promoted strong normative instruments for the pursuit of global financial stability. Therefore, the absence of truly effective and enforceable normative tools for financial stability at the international level makes it difficult to consider financial stability as a truly enforceable objective at the international level. International

96. Lastra, *supra* n. 37, 547–553.

policy-makers and institutions cannot truly attain and enforce global financial stability, as international hard law instruments lack at present. Conversely, in the following chapter of this book, it will be argued how financial stability has emerged in EU law and policy as a foundational objective having certain normative instruments. Therefore, the analysis moves to the next chapter that will propose a definition of financial stability in EU law and policy and determine its normative instruments.

CHAPTER 3

Financial Stability as a New Supranational Foundational Objective in EU Law and Policy

§3.01 INTRODUCTION

This chapter aims to provide a critical reconstruction of the term 'financial stability' as a foundational supranational objective in EU law and policy. This analysis attempts to illustrate the difficulties encountered in defining in a proper way the term 'financial stability' in EU due to the lack of clarity on its understanding and perception, especially from the legal perspective. It will attempt to elaborate on the concept of financial stability as a new foundational objective in EU law and policy. As argued by existing scholarly studies, the term 'stability' itself may refer to many concepts - economic stability, monetary stability, fiscal stability, stability of the euro area as a whole - that can be associated with the word 'stability' and apply in different areas and contexts.

The chapter will highlight that *financial* stability needs to be seen as a new foundational objective in EU law and policy as it captures the crisis-related efforts made so far to strengthen the legal framework of the EMU and to reform the supranational level of financial regulation and supervision. As held in the previous chapter to this study, financial stability is difficult to define in legal terms. Differently from the international level, this chapter contends that financial stability, encapsulating a normative concept, is framed in the European context as a foundational supranational objective having the nature of a European public good, which endeavours to prevent, absorb and manage risks and shocks in EU law and policy. This is possible through normative instruments aiming to attain supranational financial stability.

The chapter is structured as follows. It first looks at the challenging contours of the term 'financial stability' from a conceptual perspective (§3.02). In particular, it focuses on the main different concepts of stability that have arisen before or during the financial crisis in Europe (§3.02.[A]). The same section discusses the definition of financial stability in EU law and policy (§3.02.[B]). Then, it assesses to what extent it has become a supranational foundational objective of EU law and policy (§3.02.[C]). The chapter proceeds then with an assessment of the main challenges (§3.02.[D]) and benefits (§3.02.[E]) of framing financial stability as a foundational objective in EU law and policy. Furthermore, the chapter sets out the normative instruments to achieve supranational financial stability in EU law and policy, i.e. supranational regulation, supervision/surveillance, burden-sharing, rescue measures and LOLR functions (§3.03). Before extensive analysis in subsequent chapters of the book, it introduces the two main areas of such development: the EMU and the EBU (§3.04). The last section concludes (§3.05).

§3.02 FINANCIAL STABILITY IN EU LAW AND POLICY: IN SEARCH OF A ROLE

The purpose of this part is to construct financial stability as a foundational and supranational objective in EU law and policy. It assesses the main concepts of stability elaborated in the European context (section [A]) and focuses on the role of financial stability as a foundational objective at the European level (section [B]). Then, it examines the need to conceive financial stability as a supranational objective (section [C]). Finally, it looks at the challenges and benefits of framing financial stability as a foundational objective in EU law (sections [D] and [E]).

[A] The Financial Crisis and the Many Concepts of Stability in the EU

The financial crisis has had an enormous impact in Europe. It has been held that 'the financial crisis rapidly became hydra-headed, spawning interconnected banking, market and fiscal crises'.[1] This statement shows the seriousness of the financial crisis in Europe that has led to unprecedented waves of reforms. According to the ordo-liberal school, the European economic constitution has provided a European constitutional framework based on integration policies and price stability.[2] However, this has not been sufficient to provide a general framework for supranational stability. The inadequacies of the pre-crisis EU framework contributed to national support measures to banking institutions and to consequential burden-sharing measures. At the same time, the deepening of public rescue measures to credit institutions has led to

1. Niamh Moloney, *EU Securities and Financial Markets Regulation*, 30 (Oxford University Press 2014).
2. Kaarlo Tuori & Klaus Tuori, *The Eurozone Crisis. A Constitutional Analysis*, 57 (Cambridge University Press 2014). For a thorough account of the change to the European economic constitution during the financial crisis, *see* Edoardo Chiti & Pedro Gustavo Teixeira, *The Constitutional Implications of the European Responses to the Financial and Public Debt Crisis*, 50 Common Market Law Review 698 (2013).

increasing sovereign indebtedness.[3] The costs of banking rescues in some Member States combined with the creation of a vicious circle between credit institutions and sovereigns have turned the EU financial crisis into a euro-area sovereign debt crisis. The banking crisis and public rescues led to high pressures and contagion effects especially in euro area Member States. This forced the EU to adopt a series of exceptional and unprecedented measures to address pressures both on banking markets and on economic and fiscal sustainability. Without going into the details of the impact of the financial crisis in Europe,[4] the financial crisis has revealed the failure of the national frameworks to address banking market structures as well as economic and fiscal sustainability.

Against this background, the need to achieve *stability* has played an increasingly important role in the EU reform agenda. The financial crisis has generated a substantial rethinking on the role of supranational powers, financial regulation and institutional functions in Europe.[5] This has led to a renewed focus on the many concepts of stability as economic stability, monetary stability, price stability, fiscal stability, stability of the euro area as a whole. Their role in EU law and policy is assessed below.

[1] Economic Stability

Economic stability can be considered as being of paramount importance to frame the discussion on the concept of stability in Europe. In macro-economic terms, economic stability refers to the absence of excessive fluctuations in the macro-economics.[6] As indicated by the IMF the promotion of global:

> economic stability is partly a matter of avoiding economic and financial crises, large swings in economic activity, high inflation, and excessive volatility in exchange rates and financial markets. Instability can increase uncertainty, discourage investment, impede economic growth, and hurt living standards.[7]

This means that economic stability aims at avoiding primarily financial and economic crisis and economic shocks that may put at risk financial markets. Scholarship argued that economic stability is an objective that is:

> achieved through a combination of policies in monetary, fiscal, and financial fields, which, through various means, aim at ensuring the smooth functioning of an economy and preventing the occurrence of an economic crisis.[8]

---

3. *See* European Commission, *European Financial Stability and Integration Report*, April 2015, 12–14. *See also* ECB, *Report on Financial Integration in Europe*, April 2015, 5.
4. *See* Jacques de Larosière, *High Level Report of the Group on Financial Supervision in the EU*, 13 (2009).
5. *Ibid.*
6. *See* IMF, *How the IMF Promotes Global Economic Stability* http://www.imf.org/External/np/exr/facts/globstab.htm (accessed 31 December 2016).
7. *Ibid.*
8. Federico Lupo Pasini, *Economic Stability and Economic Governance in the Euro Area: What the European Crisis Can Teach on the Limits of Economic Integration*, 16 Journal of International Economic Law 235 (2013).

This reading of economic stability can be seen in the European framework. In fact, in the context of the EU, one of the founding objectives indicated in the Treaties is 'the strengthening and the convergence of [Member States] economies'[9] which shall take place on the basis of 'balanced economic growth'.[10] This means that the pursuit of economic stability serving the objective of economic growth is one of the main objectives in Europe.

However, at a closer look, economic stability is a purely economic concept, lacks a legal meaning and does not indicate the main necessary normative instruments for its attainment. This remains problematic. It is submitted that the purely economic dimension of economic stability makes it hard to transpose it into a truly legal perspective. In particular, economic stability can be hardly used to justify legal reforms or normative instruments and to drive policy makers at the European level as it appears too vague and general.

[2] Monetary Stability

A concept of stability that can be linked to economic stability is that of monetary stability. The term 'monetary stability' is well developed in literature and is usually considered as being the main target of monetary and interest rate policies conducted by central banks.[11] Lastra argues that monetary stability can be defined in positive terms as:

> [t]he maintenance of the internal value of money (i.e. price stability) as well as of the external value of the currency (i.e., the stability of the currency vis-à-vis other currencies, which is, in turn, influenced by the choice of exchange rate mechanisms).[12]

This means that monetary stability is a general objective of monetary policy conducted by central banks which has both an internal dimension for the stability of the system as such and an external dimension for the stability of the system vis-à-vis other currencies. Gianviti criticised the dual nature of monetary stability and argued that the objectives of price stability and exchange rate may conflict in the medium- to long-term.[13] This means that internal and external objectives for monetary stability may not be achieved at the same time and that one of the two needs to be prioritised.

For the purposes of this analysis, monetary stability as a policy objective driving central banking activities cannot be considered as a foundational concept to provide adequate responses to the financial crisis in EU law and policy. Monetary stability is an

9. TEU, Preamble.
10. TEU, Art. 3(3).
11. Claus Zimmermann, *The Concept of Monetary Sovereignty Revisited*, 25–26 (Cambridge University Press 2013).
12. Rosa Lastra, *International Financial and Monetary Law*, 56 (Oxford University Press 2015).
13. François Gianviti, *The Objectives of Central Banks* in Mario Giovanoli, Diego Devos (eds), *International Monetary and Financial Law. The Global Crisis*, 473 (Oxford University Press 2010).

established concept in literature. However, its role is limited to the monetary dimension and, differently from financial stability, cannot be transposed into broader areas of policy reforms and law-making having an impact on financial regulation or supervision. This makes monetary stability an insufficient legal and policy objective to drive reform responses at European level and can only be considered as an objective with a limited normative meaning.

[3] Price Stability

The dual dimension of monetary stability can generate frictions in the overall objective of stability. This requires the analysis of price stability. The importance of price stability is considered of primary importance in the conduct of monetary policy in the European Sytem of Central Banks (ESCB). In the context of a monetary stability policy, price stability constitutes an essential component, especially in the ESCB.

Price stability is, usually, defined as the stability of domestic prices.[14] This means that the stability of prices is the essential component of monetary stability. As argued by Gianviti, the term 'price' is generally understood as to indicate the consumer price index (CPI).[15] Hence, prices of consumer goods and services are usually taken into account when calculating prices increases. On the contrary, asset prices are not usually included in the definition of price stability. This is because a definition of asset prices is complex in nature and is reflected in a wide set of variables that change faster than consumer prices.

The concept of price stability is the only one that has a specific consideration in the European Treaties. Following the negotiations of the Maastricht Treaty, the term 'price stability' is considered in the European Treaties as one of the main objectives of the Union[16] and constitutes the primary objective of the single monetary policy and exchange rate policy in the EMU.[17] Price stability constitutes the primary objective of the EMU monetary policy, whereas the support of the general economic policies in the Union is only considered as the secondary objective of the monetary policy.[18] The single monetary policy established in the Maastricht Treaty has been anchored to the term 'price stability'. This resulted from the stability culture of the German Bundesbank which supported the case for an independent ECB with price stability as the primary objective.[19]

The term 'price stability' is defined more specifically in Protocol 13 to the Treaties on the convergence criteria. Under Article 1 of the said Protocol, the criterion of price stability:

14. *Ibid.*, 449.
15. *Ibid.*, 469.
16. TEU, Art. 3(3).
17. TFEU, Art. 119(1).
18. *See* Art. 119(1) TFEU.
19. *See* Paul de Grauwe, *The Economics of Monetary Union*, 150–153 (Oxford University Press 2014).

> shall mean that a Member State has a price performance that is sustainable and an average rate of inflation, observed over a period of one year before the examination, that does not exceed by more than 1 ½ percentage points that of, at most, the three best performing Member States in terms of price stability.

The ECB has identified the inflation target as the most important criterion to determine price stability as it has stated that, in pursuit of price stability, it aims to maintain inflation targets below but close to 2% over the medium term.[20] This objective is based on a quantitative-targeted inflation ceiling. A more detailed assessment of price stability and its implementation by the ECB during the financial crisis is provided below.

[a] Price Stability and the ECB: The General Legal Framework

This first section aims to describe briefly the role of the ECB in the EMU. Scholarship has already identified much of the existing and complex institutional framework of the EMU and the relevant distribution of competences and powers in the ESCB.[21] This part briefly summarises the most important issues on the establishment of the supranational monetary competence under EU law.

The creation of the ESCB was agreed upon in the Maastricht Treaty in 1993 whereby the EMU was established in three subsequent phases. As of 1999, the ECB is the European institution which conducts monetary policy for the Member States whose currency is the euro.[22] Together with the National Central Banks (NCBs), it constitutes the ESCB.[23] The ESCB is governed by the ESCB Statute, agreed in the Maastricht Treaty negotiations, which lays down the rules on the ESCB structure and functioning. Pursuant to the ESCB Statute, the ESCB defines and implements the basic and non-basic tasks of the ECB and the NCBs.

Traditionally, the functions of the ESCB, and consequently those of the ECB, are divided into basic and non-basic tasks. Many scholars have provided legal interpretations on the nature and tasks of the ESCB.[24] The formulation and implementation of monetary policy is the most important basic task of the ESCB. The exercise of the monetary policy functions amounts to the conduct of monetary policy instruments to achieve the ESCB primary objective, namely price stability.[25] In this framework, the definition and implementation of monetary policy for the euro area Member States represents the core responsibility of the ECB. For such purpose, the ESCB Statute indicates that the ECB and the NCB possess a number of instruments to conduct monetary policy operations. In particular, the use of open market operations is an

20. ECB, *Monetary policy webpage* at http://www.ecb.europa.eu/mopo/html/index.en.html (accessed 31 December 2016).
21. *See* Francis Snyder, *EMU-Integration and Differentiation: Metaphor for European Union* in Paul Craig, Grainne de Búrca (eds), *The Evolution of EU Law*, 687 (Oxford University Press 2011); Charles Proctor, *Mann on Legal Aspects of Money*, 728–731 (Oxford University Press 2012).
22. Art. 282 TFEU.
23. Protocol n. 4 on the Statute of the European system of central banks and of the European Central Bank (hereinafter the 'ESCB Statute') C326/230, Art. 1.
24. Rosa Lastra & Jean-Victor Louis, *European Economic and Monetary Union: History, Trends and Prospects*, Yearbook of European Law 134 (2013).
25. *See* de Grauwe, *supra* n. 19, 153 (Oxford University Press 2014).

essential instrument for the conduct of monetary policy as they implement monetary policy in practice. Article 18 ESCB Statute indicates that the ECB and the NCB may:

> [o]perate in the financial markets by buying and selling outright (spot and forward) or under repurchase agreement and by lending or borrowing claims and marketable instruments, whether in euro or other currencies, as well as precious metals; conduct credit operations with credit institutions and other market participants, with lending being based on adequate collateral.[26]

In general terms, this provision allows the ECB to exercise open market and credit operations with considerable marge of manoeuvre in order to manage liquidity in the markets and signal the stance of monetary policy. The monetary policy functions are mainly regulated in the 2011 Guidelines on the conduct of monetary policy in the ESCB.[27] This is an essential document to understand how ESCB open market and credit operations work. While the ECB authorises monetary policy operations at the central level, the actual implementation normally takes place at the level of NCB in a decentralised fashion.[28]

[b] The Main Unconventional ECB Monetary Policy Instruments for the Pursuit of Price Stability

While the preceding section briefly looked at the basic objective of the ESCB, price stability, this section analyses the exercise of ECB unconventional policy instruments intended to pursue price stability under the Treaty framework. These instruments have been used in order to generate liquidity in the markets and achieve the objective of price stability in the context of the financial crisis in Europe.

The Use of (Much) Longer-Term Refinancing Operations

Longer-Term Refinancing Operations LTROs are ECB open market operations consisting in refinancing ESCB counterparties in a longer term.[29] This is a well-used liquidity provoking monetary policy instrument. In particular, as of December 2011, the ECB Governing Council conducted two LTROs with a maturity of thirty-six months and the option of early repayment after one year.[30] In autumn 2014, the ECB launched a series of targeted longer-term refinancing operations (TLTROs) aimed at improving bank

26. ESCB Statute, Art. 18.
27. ECB, Guideline (EU) 2015/510 of the ECB of 19 December 2014 on the implementation of the Eurosystem monetary policy framework (ECB/2014/60) (hereinafter 'Guideline').
28. *See* René Smits, *The European Central Bank*, 264–274 (Kluwer Law International 1997).
29. *See* ECB, *ECB announces details of refinancing operations with settlement from 19 January to 12 April 2011*, ECB Website, 2 December 2010 at http://www.ecb.europa.eu/press/pr/date/2010/html/pr101202_1.en.html (accessed 31 December 2016).
30. ECB, *ECB announces measures to support bank lending and money market activity*, Press release, ECB Website, 8 December 2011 at http://www.ecb.int/press/pr/date/2011/html/pr111208_1.en.html (accessed 31 December 2016).

lending to the euro area non-financial private sector.[31] These operations had a great success among credit institutions, especially in the euro area periphery. The impact of this liquidity-provoking measure allowed financial institutions to buy sovereign bonds, resulting in a significant drop in their interest rate. As submitted by Lastra and Louis, the 'provision of liquidity to financial institutions was useful in a period of paralysis of the interbank financing'.[32]

Easing Collateral Requirements for Open Market Operations

The ECB open market operations are conducted with respect to the principle of 'adequate collateral'.[33] The presence of collaterals is an essential instrument to guarantee that, in the case of solvency problems for the counterparty in an open market operation measures, some assets stand ready to fulfil the outstanding credit. The easing of collateral requirements for open market operations is a noteworthy policy measure exercised by the ECB throughout the financial crisis.[34]

Outright Monetary Transactions

While the preceding policy measures were important to generate liquidity to financial institutions, the announcement of Outright Monetary Transactions (OMTs) in August 2012 has been the key measure to calm down financial markets. Outright transactions are one of the instruments of monetary policy of the Eurosystem. According to the ECB Guideline on monetary policy, the 'outright open market transactions' refer to operations 'whereby the Eurosystem buys or sells eligible assets outright on the market'.[35] The recurrence of the financial crisis forced the ECB to move forward in terms of intervention and, as famously held by the ECB President Mario Draghi, 'do whatever it takes to preserve the euro'.[36] In August 2012, the ECB Governing Council announced its new bond purchase programme as an explicit monetary purchase instrument. The legal basis of this OMT programme is Article 18(1) of the ESCB Statute (the same used for the ECB open market operation measures) and the ECB Guideline on monetary policy where it is stated that the ECB may conduct outright transactions. The ECB published the technical features for the adoption of the ECB outright purchase in September 2012.[37] These provide for conditionality, coverage, creditor treatment, sterilisation and transparency.[38]

31. ECB, *ECB announces monetary policy measures to enhance the functioning of the monetary policy transmission mechanism*, ECB Website, 5 June 2014 https://www.ecb.europa.eu/press/pr/date/2014/html/pr140605_2.en.html (accessed 31 December 2016).
32. Lastra, Louis, *supra* n. 24, 93.
33. *See* ESCB Statute, Art. 18.
34. Decision of ECB of 14 December 2011 ([2011] OJ L341) on additional temporary measures relating to the Eurosystem refinancing operations and eligibility of collateral.
35. ECB Guideline, Art. 2(72).
36. Mario Draghi, *Speech*, Global Investment Conference in London, 26 July 2012.
37. ECB, *Technical features of Outright Monetary Transactions*, Press Release ECB Website, 6 September 2012 http://www.ecb.europa.eu/press/pr/date/2012/html/pr120906_1.en.html (accessed 31 December 2016).
38. *Ibid.*

The objective of the OMT programme is to safeguard the monetary policy transmission mechanism in all countries of the euro area, to preserve the singleness of the ECB's monetary policy and to address severe distortions in government bond markets that originate from fears on the part of investors about the reversibility of the euro.[39]

The *Gauweiler*[40] judgment has been an essential test case for the viability of price stability instruments, and in particular the legal feasibility of the OMTs, in line with the monetary financing prohibition under Article 123 TFEU. The European Court of Justice (ECJ) has endorsed the interpretation of the OMT programme as being strictly within the mandate of price stability of the ECB. The *Gauweiler* judgment, delivered on 16 June 2015, has been an essential test case to legitimise the OMT programme, and – more generally – unconventional monetary measures, of the ECB. This case has demonstrated that the ECB can adopt unconventional monetary policies grounded on the objective of price stability.

The substantial part of the ECJ judgment is split between an assessment of the OMT under the provisions on the monetary policy competence and powers (in particular Articles 119 and 127 TFEU as well as Articles 17–24 of the ESCB Statute) and under Article 123 TFEU. Paragraphs 46–65 of the judgment analyse in depth the delimitation of monetary policy based on price stability. After stressing the importance of the objectives of any single monetary policy measure, the ECJ held that the OMT is intended to safeguarding an appropriate transmission of monetary policy. In particular, the ECJ argues that, whenever a disruption to the transmission mechanisms of monetary policy takes place, monetary policy instruments allow the possibility to address such disruptions by preserving the ESCB's ability to guarantee price stability. The ECJ held that both the possible indirect effects of such measures on the stability of the euro area as a whole and the wide array of monetary policy instruments under Article 18 ESCB Statute allow the ECB to adopt such programmes. Following a reference to the selectivity of the OMT programme, the ECJ stressed that the programme is intended to 'rectify the disruption to the monetary policy transmission mechanism caused by the specific situation of government bonds issued by certain Member States'.[41] This allowed the ECJ to submit that, while the OMT might have indirect effects on economic policy, it is strictly within the confines of the monetary policy framework provided in primary law.[42] Therefore, OMT interventions are justified as in cases when there are disruptions of the monetary policy transmission mechanism or the singleness of monetary policy.[43]

Public Sector Purchase Programme

The outcome of the *Gauweiler* case has reinforced the legitimacy of the Public Sector Purchase Programme (PSPP). The PSPP was launched in the first half of 2015 as an

39. *See* Tuori, Tuori *supra* n. 2, 104.
40. Case C-62/14 *Peter Gauweiler and others* ECLI:EU:C:2015:400.
41. *Ibid.*, para. 55.
42. *Ibid.*, para. 61.
43. *Ibid.*, para. 62.

unprecedented Quantitative Easing (QE) programme for the euro area. The ECB does not have the mandate to carry out structural reforms or restructure sovereign or private debt. However, the ECB can still engage in purchases of corporate and public bonds or securities in financial markets with the aim to raise the credibility of the ECB's inflation target, asset prices, lowering real interest rates and strengthen household, corporate and bank balance sheets. As legitimised in *Gauweiler*, outright purchases of sovereign bonds in secondary markets are compliant with Article 123 TFEU and have their legal basis in Article 18 ESCB Statute.

On 22 January 2015, the Governing Council approved the PSPP to revamp the interest rate in order to reach price stability of interest targets below but close to 2%. The PSPP was adopted by an ECB decision in March 2015,[44] was launched in March 2015 and is currently ongoing. It may be even longer if the ECB considers that the inflation is still low.

The main features of the PSPP are as follows. First, the PSPP comprises the purchase of government bonds in secondary markets in monthly purchases.[45] The ECB and the NCB accept the same (*pari passu*) treatment as private investors as regards the marketable debt securities.[46] Second, the PSPP provides for the purchase of international and national public sector instruments.[47] Third, the PSPP is shared between the ECB and the NCB. This means that the NCBs, in proportions reflecting their respective shares in the ECB's capital key, and the ECB purchase and are liable on the outright eligible marketable debt securities from eligible counterparties on the secondary markets.

In conclusion, the PSPP is a massive monetary policy operation in the euro area aiming to fulfil the price stability mandate. The programme is unprecedented in the ECB monetary policy and the key ECB monetary policy measure to reach the inflation target for price stability purposes.[48]

[c] Assessment

The analysis of price stability has revealed that this is the main objective of the ESCB in the conduct of monetary policy in the EMU. The recent ECB unconventional monetary policy measures have been taken to guarantee the transmission of the monetary policy across the euro area and to attain the quantitative objective of inflation targets below but close to 2% over the medium term.

The relationship between price stability and financial stability shows that they are different in nature and are separate objectives in EU law and policy. While price

---

44. *See* ECB, Decision (EU) 2015/774 of the European Central Bank of 4 March 2015 on a secondary markets public sector asset purchase programme (ECB/2015/10). *See also* ECB, *More details on the public sector purchase programme (PSPP) – Questions & answers* at http://www.ecb.europa.eu/mopo/implement/omt/html/pspp-qa.en.html (accessed 31 December 2016).
45. *See* ECB, *ECB announces expanded asset purchase programme*, 22 January 2015 https://www.ecb.europa.eu/press/pr/date/2015/html/pr150122_1.en.html (accessed 31 December 2016).
46. ECB, Decision ECB/2015/774, Recital 8.
47. *Ibid.*, Art. 6(1).
48. Claire Jones, *Mario Draghi's Bond-Buying Plan Outstrips Expectations*, Financial Times 22 January 2015 https://www.ft.com/content/8f215db8-a256-11e4-9630-00144feab7de (accessed 31 December 2016).

stability is anchored in the Treaty provisions to ensure the exercise of monetary policy by the ESCB, financial stability is broad in nature, applies to the financial system in general and is nowhere defined in EU primary law.

There are two arguments that justify the construction of financial stability as a foundational objective in EU law and policy as a different objective in comparison with price stability. First, the clear definition and the consideration of price stability as a quantifiable objective limit the scope of action for policy-makers to the central banking task of the conduct of monetary policy. The ESCB's primary objective in monetary policy is to reach the quantitative value of inflation targets below but close to 2% over the medium term. Differently from financial stability, price stability is framed in the definition and implementation of monetary policy in the ESCB. Second, the clear and exclusive institutional mandate for the achievement of price stability, as only the ESCB is in charge of attaining price stability, makes price stability less functional than financial stability to achieve the overall stability of the European financial system. The financial crisis has not impacted the ESCB mandate to pursue price stability with the objective of attaining 2% of inflation. In January 2016, Draghi affirmed that there are:

> no limits to how far [the ECB is] willing to deploy [its] instruments within [its] mandate to achieve [its] objective of a rate of inflation which is below but close to 2%.[49]

At the same time, as put by an ECB Executive Board Member,

> preserving financial stability is truly a Herculean task. [The ECB] aim must be to make the whole financial system stronger and more resilient. So it's a logical step for [the ECB] to target all the measures at [ECB] disposal towards realising this objective. But the ECB's primary objective is still to maintain price stability in the medium term.[50]

This suggests that while price stability is the primary objective of the ECB, financial stability has a broad(er) role in the economy and can be achieved with various instruments. In sum, while acknowledging that the word *stability* is used for both financial stability and price stability, the former is broad in role, scope and nature while the latter is framed in the single monetary policy of the ESCB.

[4] Fiscal Stability

Another emerging context of stability is that of fiscal stability. Fiscal stability presupposes the power to control economic choices over budgets, tax, welfare, labour, external financing, and other macro-economic policies in order to exercise public functions and respect fiscal discipline.[51] The main instruments for fiscal stability are

49. Mario Draghi, *Introductory Statement to the Press Conference (with Q&A)*, 21 January 2016 at https://www.ecb.europa.eu/press/pressconf/2016/html/is160121.en.html (accessed 31 December 2016).
50. Sabine Lautenschläger, *Low Inflation as a Challenge for Monetary Policy and Financial Stability?*, ECB Press Release, 7 July 2014 at http://www.ecb.europa.eu/press/key/date/2014/html/sp140707.en.html (accessed 31 December 2016).
51. *See*, similarly, Lupo Pasini *supra* n. 8, 235.

the preparation and management of budgets as well as the formulation and imposition of taxes, labour and other economic policies. This means that fiscal stability depends mainly on the existence of tools that are capable of maintaining fiscal discipline, avoiding sovereign default and perform public functions.

The EU does not yet have an autonomous supranational power to raise general taxation and to decide on public spending in the Member States. This is shown by two main examples. In the EU Treaties, rudimentary forms of supranational budget control are provided in the economic policy. Title VIII, Chapter 1 of the TFEU envisages the application of an economic framework for fiscal surveillance between Member States to have sound finances and to avoid excessive deficits. However, this Treaty Chapter does not create a fiscal framework for supranational control over national finances or taxation and does not set fiscal stability as one of the main objectives of EU law and policy. The fact that economic policy is considered to be an area where Member States shall 'coordinate' each other (Article 5(1) TFEU) excludes that the EU can exercise supranational fiscal competences over Member States.[52] Furthermore, the TFEU limits instruments for fiscal stability between the EU and Member States and between Member States. Article 125 TFEU provides for the no-bail out clause which prohibits Member States or the EU to be liable or assume the commitments of other Member States.[53] Similarly, Article 123 TFEU prohibits:

> [o]verdraft facilities or any other type of credit facility with the European Central Bank or with the central banks of the Member States (...) in favour of (...) Member States shall be prohibited, as shall the purchase directly from them by the European Central Bank or national central banks of debt instruments.

The content of Article 123 TFEU has been specified in a Council Regulation by stating that Article 123 TFEU should not be circumvented by secondary market operations.[54] While it has been questioned that secondary market purchases are a disguised way to finance government by improving the fiscal position of Member States,[55] the reading of Article 123 TFEU only suggests that the monetary financing prohibition applies for primary markets as a way to ensure fiscal discipline.

The no-bailout clause and the monetary financing prohibition have been introduced to the benefit of sovereign fiscal discipline. Both Articles 123 and 125 TFEU are ensured to maintain fiscal discipline of individual Member States, but they are not meant to set out fiscal stability as a primary objective in EU law and policy. In other words, these two provisions have been included to keep fiscal discipline in the EU as a matter of national concern and to avoid financial support or joint and several liability between Member States or the EU. Moreover, the financial crisis in Europe has strengthened fiscal discipline of the Member States. To overcome fiscal prolificacy and

52. *See* the discussion on the nature of Art.5 TFEU in Chapter 4 section §4.02.
53. For further analysis of Art. 125 TFEU *see* Chapter 5 section §5.05[A][2].
54. Council Regulation (EC) No 3603/93 of 13 December 1993 specifying definitions for the application of the prohibitions referred to in Arts 104 and 104b (1) of the Treaty, OJ L 332[1993] Recital 7.
55. Thomas Beukers, *The New ECB and Its Relationship with the Member States of the Euro Area: Between Central Bank Independence and Central Bank Intervention*, 50 Common Market Law Review 1605–1606 (2013).

sovereign financial distress, crisis-related measures in Europe have reinforced fiscal stability of Member States by adopting and implementing the Treaty on Stability, Coordination and Governance (TSCG), and adopting EU secondary law framework to strengthen fiscal surveillance, and creating EU and intergovernmental financial assistance mechanisms.[56]

Whilst this analysis suggests that fiscal stability is intrinsically connected to financial stability as the former is beneficial to the latter as unsound fiscal policies may jeopardise financial stability, this does not mean that fiscal stability is a foundational objective in EU law and policy. It cannot be argued that fiscal stability has a foundational role in Europe as there is no supranational fiscal framework allowing EU institutions or agencies to raise pan-European taxes, to manage public spending in Europe and to adopt national government budgets. While attempts to create a truly European fiscal framework have been suggested, there is still not a supranational fiscal stability framework in EU law and policy. Fiscally sound sovereign finances are instrumental to achieve financial stability in EU law and policy. However, differently from financial stability, fiscal stability does not have the role of supranational objective in EU law and policy.

[5] Stability of the Euro Area as a Whole

Stability of the euro area as a whole is an emerging crisis-related concept of stability. The expression is now enshrined in the Treaty under Article 136(3) TFEU as from the entry into force of Council Decision 199/2011.[57] According to this new paragraph, Member States are allowed to 'establish a stability mechanism to be activated if indispensable to safeguard the stability of the euro area as a whole'.[58] The same stability expression is also used in the Preamble to the TSCG where it is indicated that the:

> need for governments to maintain sound and sustainable public finances and to prevent the general government deficit to becoming excessive is of essential importance to safeguard the stability of the euro area as a whole.[59]

Moreover, the European Stability Mechanism Treaty (ESMT) provides for financial assistance to sovereigns and is aimed to the stability of the euro as a whole. Also the ECJ case law has recognised the importance of euro area as a whole. The *Pringle* judgment stressed the importance of the stability of the euro area as a whole and of its Member States as indicated in the ESMT and supported the argument that the main objective of the European Stability Mechanism (ESM) is precisely 'to support the stability of the euro'.[60] Stability of the euro area as a whole was also mentioned in the

56. *See* Chapter 4 for the developments in economic governance and Chapter 5 for the creation of stability mechanisms for sovereigns.
57. European Council Decision 2011/199/EU [2011] OJ L91.
58. *See also* Chapter 5 section §5.04[A].
59. TSCG, Preamble.
60. Case C-370/12 *Thomas Pringle v. Government of Ireland, Ireland and The Attorney General* ECLI:EU:C:2012:756, para. 93. On *Pringle see* Chapter 5 section §5.04[C].

Gauweiler case where the ECJ stated that 'the ESM's intervention is intended to safeguard the stability of the euro area'.[61] These judicial references highlight that the concept of stability of the euro area as a whole is of seminal importance. It could be considered as an objective that shall make it possible for the euro area to exist and to avoid the break up of the euro area. The stability of the euro area indirectly requires that the conditions for monetary transmission, credibility of the single currency and reliability of finances are guaranteed.

While this concept is an interesting novelty in the financial crisis-related framework, it is argued that it is not a central concept as financial stability in EU law and policy. This is for two main reasons. First, the stability of the euro area as a whole is deprived of content as it does not indicate *what* is necessary to achieve such stability and what its scope is. In other words, there is no direct or indirect reference as to what the attainment of the stability of the euro area entails and appears to be a vague concept. Second, its nature is limited to the stability of the euro area Member States neglecting the fact that the EU is composed of other Member States that do not share the same currency, but are still part of the internal market. These arguments suggest that the stability of the euro area as a whole cannot have the same implications of financial stability as the former remains vague and limited in nature. This concludes the assessment of the various concepts of stability in Europe. The analysis moves to examining financial stability.

[B] The Role of Financial Stability in EU Law and Policy: Towards a New Foundational Objective

While the previous sections looked at other concepts of stability as developed in Europe, this section focusses on the seminal role of financial stability at the European level. The term 'financial stability' is used to express a wide range of aspects in the EU law and policy, and its nature can be interpreted in various ways. For the purpose of this book, it is argued that financial stability has acquired the role of a foundational objective in EU law and policy.

In order to amount to a foundational objective,[62] an objective must be central (i.e. it must form the basis of a given framework regardless of other objectives) and have an essential function in a given framework (i.e., it must drive what regulators and policy-makers pursue in the given framework). Against this background, this section examines as from where the foundational nature of financial stability comes (subsection [1]) and proposes a definition to make financial stability a foundational objective in EU law and policy (subsection [2]).

[1] Where Does Financial Stability in EU Law and Policy Come From?

As demonstrated in the previous chapter, the concept of financial stability suffers from a degree of indeterminacy as a guideline for policy-makers and as a legal standard: How

61. Case C-62/14 *Peter Gauweiler and others*, para. 64.
62. *See also* Chapter 1 section §1.01.

should EU law and policy be driven by financial stability, and how is financial stability achieved? Given its indeterminacy, it is no surprise that the concept of financial stability had limited attention before the financial crisis. At this stage, it is therefore necessary to assess financial stability in EU primary law and evaluate to what extent financial stability has developed beyond EU primary law.

[a] Financial Stability in EU Primary Law

In primary EU law, the only explicit reference to financial stability is contained in Article 127(5) TFEU. Among the tasks of the ECB as enshrined in the Treaty, Article 127(5) TFEU contains the only textual reference in the EU Treaties to the contribution of the ECB to financial stability as a non-basic ESCB task.[63] The Treaty provision states that:

> [t]he ESCB shall contribute to the smooth conduct of policies pursued by the competent authorities relating to the prudential supervision of credit institutions and the stability of the financial system.[64]

Non-basic ESCB tasks are scattered throughout the Treaty provisions and consist of some unrelated functions that are conducted by the ESCB.[65] The ECB task in Article 127(5) TFEU is considered as a non-basic task, i.e. a task that is not considered as one that shall drive the main activities of the ECB, but that should be pursued by the ECB together with the basic tasks.[66] Also Article 3.3 of the ESCB Statute states that the ESCB shall contribute to the smooth conduct of policies pursued by the competent authorities relating to the prudential supervision of financial institutions and the stability of the financial system. This provision echoes Article 127(5) TFEU. Article 25(1) of the ESCB Statute specifies in this regard that the ECB may offer advice to and be consulted by the Council, the Commission and relevant national authorities on legislation on these issues.

However, there is no clear indication of what the main instruments to contribute to the stability of the financial system are. This requires a brief analysis of the negotiations that brought to the adoption of Article 127(5) TFEU. During the Maastricht Treaty negotiations, there were strong oppositions on the part of some Member States to qualify prudential supervision and the stability of the financial system as a basic task of the ESCB.[67] A draft Statute of the ESCB and ECB, prepared by the Committee of Central Bank Governors, initially gave the ESCB a greater responsibility for financial stability and listed it among its 'basic' tasks instead of placing it in a separate indent. Similarly, the draft ESCB Statute envisaged also prudential supervision and stability of the financial system among the basic tasks of the ESCB. Several Member States opposed this proposal, and the final Treaty text did not include stability of the financial

63. *See also* Chapter 1 section §1.01.
64. Art. 127(5) TFEU.
65. Lastra, Louis *supra* n. 24, 137–139.
66. *Ibid.*
67. Lastra, *supra* n. 12, 221–222.

system in the basic tasks of the ESCB.[68] Rather, the outcome of the Treaty negotiation process ended up framing prudential supervision and stability of the financial system as non-basic ESCB tasks. This left open the question to know what powers the ECB could exercise to 'contribute' to the stability of the financial system.[69]

Article 127(5) TFEU is not the only provision referring to a certain concept of stability beyond price stability in the Treaties. In establishing the ESM as an intergovernmental institutions providing financial assistance to Member States in the euro in financial distress, the European Council decided to include a new third paragraph to Article 136 TFEU.[70] The creation of the ESM Treaty was accompanied by a Treaty revision procedure to amend Article 136 TFEU. On 16 December 2010, the Belgian Government submitted a proposal for the review of Article 136 TFEU, pursuant to Article 48(6) TEU, with a view to add a paragraph 3 to that article. Council Decision 199/2011 was adopted on 25 March 2011.[71] Accordingly, the European Council decision added a new paragraph to Article 136 TFEU according to which:

> [t]he Member States whose currency is the euro may establish a stability mechanism to be activated if indispensable to safeguard the *stability of the euro area as a whole*. The granting of any required financial assistance under the mechanism will be made subject to strict conditionality.[72]

After ratification in the Member States, the amendment to the Treaty entered into force on 1 January 2013. This provision therefore refers to the above-mentioned concept of stability of the euro area as a whole. While this provision explicitly mentions the term 'stability', its value has been rightly considered as being declaratory in nature as also the ECJ held in *Pringle*.[73] This means that Article 136(3) TFEU does not add any substantial dimension to financial stability in EU primary law.

Against the lack of clear textual references in EU primary law, it is submitted that financial stability is an autonomous objective as compared to other objectives of stability in Europe.[74] The concept of financial stability is far more reaching than the limited reference to the 'stability of the financial system' as established in Article 127(5) TFEU or the declaratory paragraph in Article 136(3) TFEU. The objective of financial stability has a wider and more general scope than the one indicated in Article 127(5) TFEU. The Treaty provision suggests that the ECB merely contributes to financial stability in Europe. However, as also argued by Gianviti, central banks are

68. *See* Art. 3 of the Draft Statute of the ESCB and ECB (Europe Documents, No 1669/1670, 8 December 1990). For further analysis of this draft *see* René Smits, *supra* n. 28, 336–338. *See also* Rosa Lastra, *The Governance Structure for Financial Regulation and Supervision in Europe*, 10 Columbia Journal of European Law 56 (2003).
69. Dirk Schoenmaker, *Central Banks Role in Financial Stability*, in Gerard Caprio (ed.), *Safeguarding Global Financial Stability: Political, Social, Cultural and Economic Theories and Models*, 272 (Elsevier 2013).
70. On the role of the ESM as a financial stability tool *see* further Chapter 5 section §5.05.
71. European Council, Decision of 25 March 2011 amending Article 136 of the Treaty on the Functioning of the European Union with regard to a stability mechanism for Member States whose currency is the euro 2011/199/EU [2011] OJ L91.
72. emphasis added.
73. *See* Case C-370/12, *Pringle*, paras 184–185.
74. For the other objectives of stability *see supra* section §3.02[A].

important, but not the exclusive entities responsible for financial stability.[75] In Europe, this suggests that the ECB is an important, but not the exclusive entity responsible for financial stability in Europe. There are many players acting to achieve financial stability in Europe. Therefore, it seems that financial stability has certain implications going beyond EU primary law. These are discussed in the next section.

[b] Financial Stability Beyond EU Primary Law

At this stage, it seems important to examine whether a definition of financial stability can be developed by looking at how financial stability is considered in EU policy-making. The financial crisis has showed that financial stability has a foundational role in EU law and policy going beyond the EU Treaty provisions. This is clear in many legal and policy acts adopted by EU institutions, agencies and bodies.

The de Larosière Report of 2009 indicated that the financial crisis has created the conditions to restore financial stability.[76] Recent EU regulations and directives reinforcing the EMU and establishing the EBU place great importance to the term 'financial stability' as a main driver for reform. However, they fail to define financial stability. Four examples show these trends. First, the Two Pack is composed of Regulation 472/2013 and addresses economic and budgetary surveillance of Member States in the euro area experiencing or threatened with serious difficulties with respect to their *financial stability.*[77] Second, the Capital Requirements Regulation (CRR) states in Recital 7 that '[the] Regulation should, inter alia, contain the prudential requirements for institutions that relate strictly to the functioning of banking and financial services markets and are meant to *ensure the financial stability* of the operators on those markets (...)'.[78] Third, the SSM Regulation clearly highlights in its Recital that '(...) Coordination between supervisors is vital but the crisis has shown that mere coordination is not enough, in particular in the context of a single currency. In order to *preserve financial stability in the Union* and increase the positive effects of market integration on growth and welfare, integration of supervisory responsibilities should therefore be enhanced (...)'.[79] Finally, EBA Regulation makes reference to the objective of financial stability where it is stated that EBA's tasks purpose and tasks comprise the

75. *See* Gianviti, *supra* n. 13, 475.
76. de Larosière, *supra* n. 4, 13, 33, 38.
77. Regulation (EU) No 472/2013 of the European Parliament and of the Council of 21 May 2013 on the strengthening of economic and budgetary surveillance of Member States in the euro area experiencing or threatened with serious difficulties with respect to their financial stability, OJ L 140, 27.5.2013, pp. 1–10 (emphasis added).
78. Regulation (EU) No 575/2013 of the European Parliament and of the Council of 26 June 2013 on prudential requirements for credit institutions and investment firms and amending Regulation (EU) No 648/2012, OJ L 176, 27.6.2013, Recital 7 (emphasis added).
79. Council Regulation (EU) No 1024/2013 of 15 October 2013 conferring specific tasks on the European Central Bank concerning policies relating to the prudential supervision of credit institutions [2013] OJ L 287, Recital 5 (emphasis added).

attainment of financial stability necessary for financial integration.[80] This succinct overview demonstrates that financial stability is at the centre of attention of EU institutional players as a key objective in policy-making in recent European initiatives. At the same time, the content of financial stability remains undefined.

At institutional level, there seems to be recently more appetite to define financial stability at the European level. The ECB, in a broad and systemic approach, defines financial instability as the prevalence of a financial system that is unable to ensure, in a lasting way and without major disruptions, an efficient allocation of savings to investment opportunities.[81] The ECB in its financial stability web page states that:

> [f]inancial stability is a state whereby the build-up of systemic risk is prevented. Systemic risk can best be described as the risk that the provision of necessary financial products and services by the financial system will be impaired to a point where economic growth and welfare may be materially affected.[82]

This definition identifies a wide notion of stability. However, it anchors the benchmark of financial stability to one source of risk, systemic risk, as a risk of impairment of the necessary financial products and services in the financial system. The ECB then states that three main situations generate systemic risks:

> an endogenous build-up of financial imbalances, possibly associated with a booming financial cycle; large aggregate shocks hitting the economy or the financial system; contagion effects across markets, intermediaries or infrastructures.[83]

An ECB Executive Board member has reiterated that financial (in)stability is linked to the materialisation of systemic risk which generates a situation of impairment of the financial markets inducing losses in the real economy.[84] This shows that the ECB predominantly interprets financial stability as a state of prevention of systemic risks and seems to follow a negative definition stance centred on the absence of systemic risks.

The Commission has also developed certain policy stances on financial stability. Apart from various references to financial stability in its proposals for regulations and directives in the financial sector, the EU Commission has been considering financial stability as a general objective in its recent policy-making. A number of factors demonstrate this. First, the Juncker Commission has placed great emphasis on

80. Regulation (EU) No 1093/2010 of the European Parliament and of the Council of 24 November 2010 establishing a European Supervisory Authority (European Banking Authority), amending Decision No 716/2009/EC and repealing Commission Decision 2009/78/EC [2010] OJ L331, Recital 17.
81. Otmar Issing, *Monetary and Financial Stability: Is There a Trade-Off?* (2003) at http://www.ecb.int/press/key/date/2003/html/sp030329.en.html (accessed 31 December 2016).
82. ECB, *What is financial stability?*, ECB website at http://www.ecb.europa.eu/pub/fsr/html/index.en.html (accessed 31 December 2016).
83. *Ibid.*
84. *See* Vito Constançio, *The Role of the Banking Union in Achieving Financial Stability*, 26 November 2014 at https://www.ecb.europa.eu/press/key/date/2014/html/sp141126.en.html (accessed 31 December 2016).

financial stability as shown by the creation of the new Commission Directorate on Financial Stability, Financial Services and Capital Markets Union (DG FISMA). Second, since 2009, the Commission has started publishing Annual Reports on financial stability and integration. For instance, in the 2014 Report, the Commission placed a great importance on financial stability as an objective to be achieved through 'aggregate measures of financial stress and indicators pointing toward a normalisation of markets in terms of liquidity, risk aversion, volatility or perception of sovereign strength'.[85] Together with market integration, the Commission puts financial stability as the main objective to be achieved to restore growth and confidence in Europe. This is also confirmed in the recent proposal on European Deposit Insurance Scheme (EDIS) where the Commission recognises that 'the overall objective of financial stability (...) underpins the economic and monetary policy of the Union'.[86]

The recognition of financial stability as a foundational objective is traceable also in the recent crisis-related ECJ case law. In the *Pringle* case, while assessing the no-bail out clause under Article 125 TFEU, the ECJ affirmed that the said provision 'contributes at Union level to the attainment of a higher objective, namely maintaining the *financial stability* of the monetary union'.[87] This suggests that the no-bailout clause serves to ensure financial stability in the monetary union. Also in the *UK v. European Parliament and Council (ESMA)* case, the ECJ observed that the measure to allow an EU agency to prohibit or impose conditions on the entry of a person into short selling is driven by 'the pursuit of the objective of *financial stability* within the Union'.[88] Even more interestingly, the *Gauweiler* A.G. opinion refers to the mandate of achieving financial stability as an essential objective in the EMU by equating financial stability to the objective of price stability.[89] The A.G. opinion indicates that financial stability has a primary role of an objective that shall be considered as 'inviolable by the institutions and the Member States'.[90] Also the recent *Ledra Advertising* case recognises the essential role of ensuring the *stability* of the banking system as a general objective in the EU.[91]

However, in this emerging case law, the ECJ has not provided further clarifications as to the meaning or the scope of financial stability as an overarching objective in EU law and policy. These explicit references to financial stability provided in the texts the ECJ cases show that the ECJ is conscious of the objective of financial stability, although it reveals certain difficulties in defining its nature.

Although EU primary law does not make explicit references to the role of financial stability as an essential EU objective, this section has shown that EU institutions and agencies have progressively recognised financial stability as an objective in Europe. EU institutions and EU agencies consider financial stability as a key concept in EU law and

---

85. European Commission, *European Financial Stability and Integration Report*, 12 (2014).
86. Commission, Proposal for a Regulation of the European Parliament and of the Council amending Regulation (EU) 806/2014 in order to establish a European Deposit Insurance Scheme COM/2015/0586 final – 2015/0270, section 1.3.
87. *Pringle*, para. 135 (emphasis added).
88. Case C-270/12 *United Kingdom of Great Britain and Northern Ireland v. European Parliament and Council of the European Union* (ESMA case) ECLI:EU:C:2014:18, para. 85 (emphasis added).
89. A.G. opinion, Case C-62/14 *Gauweiler and others* ECLI:EU:C:2015:7, paras 215 and 219.
90. *Ibid.*
91. Case C-8/15 P *Ledra Advertising v. Commission and ECB* ECLI:EU:C:2016:701, para. 74.

policy. However, EU institutions and agencies show different approaches in their recognition of financial stability. Furthermore, they do not seem to specify whether financial stability has an explicit autonomous role in EU law and policy and to what extent it contains certain normative instruments. The next section suggests that, under the impact of the financial crisis, financial stability shall be attributed a new foundational role in EU law and policy and elaborates a definition on it.

[2] Financial Stability as a Foundational Objective in EU Law and Policy: Building a Definition and Assessing Its Essential Components

As submitted in Chapter 1,[92] the 'foundational' nature of financial stability makes it possible to place it as one of the central and overriding objectives in the EU law and policy. This book contends that the new European framework for regulation, supervision/surveillance and burden-sharing is driven by the objective of financial stability.[93] In other words, the increasing importance of financial stability in EU law and policy, which has also been recognised by EU institutions and agencies, suggests that financial stability has become foundational in nature as it is central and essential in the European framework.

To date legal scholars have argued that, as a policy-making benchmark, financial stability has only been partially achieved at the European level.[94] Many different definitions have been advocated in the economics literature for financial stability in Europe.[95] In legal literature on EU law, Lastra and Louis argue that financial stability is a task shared between the national and the European level as well as between different European institutions, authorities and bodies at the European level.[96] Borger, while discussing solidarity in Europe, stresses that European economic policy, which has been predominantly focused on budgetary prudence and price stability, now takes also financial stability into account.[97] However, Andenas and Chiu argue that:

> (t)he understanding of financial stability/instability is (...) made difficult (...) because value judgments need to be made as to the tolerance of levels of financial stability or instability.[98]

While acknowledging the difficulties in adopting a definition to financial stability, Lastra claims that this concept has acquired a central importance to the reform debate at the global and European level.[99] However, no clear definition of this expression in legal terms can be seen. Legal literature on financial stability still has not developed an elaborate definition of it.

---

92. *See* Chapter 1 section §1.01.
93. For the normative instruments for financial stability, *see infra* section §3.03.
94. *See* Mads Andenas & Iris Chiu, *The Foundations and Future of Financial Regulation*, 53–54 (Routledge 2014).
95. *See* de Grauwe, *supra* n. 19, 166–169.
96. Lastra, Louis *supra* n. 24, 139.
97. Vestert Borger, *How the Debt Crisis Exposes the Development of Solidarity in the Euro Area*, 9 European Constitutional Law Review 16 (2013).
98. Andenas, Chiu, *supra* n. 94, 28.
99. Lastra, *supra* n. 12, 128–129.

Notwithstanding these conceptual difficulties, Tuori and Tuori have attempted to provide a definition of financial stability in legal terms by stating that:

> financial stability refers to a situation where the distinct parts of the financial system are able to perform their functions without major disruptions in the financial system or the economy in general.[100]

They convincingly argue that financial stability is an 'overriding' economic objective at the centre of the constitutional mutation of the European economic constitution as a consequence of the financial crisis in Europe.[101] However, their approach does not explore further on what is needed to avoid major disruptions to financial stability and does not elaborate on the normative instruments to achieve such objective.

These scholarly references to the legal nature of financial stability indicate that a definition to financial stability in EU law and policy is conceivable. They argue that financial stability is an objective and show the wide nature of financial stability. However, they do not address the question of determining what is essential for financial stability nor do they provide normative instruments for its attainment.

Having reviewed the main scholarly contributions on financial stability in Europe, a normative definition of financial stability in EU law and policy is developed as follows. For the purpose of this study:

> financial stability in Europe is a supranational foundational objective, having the nature of public good, as a result of which Europe is in a generalized and lasting state of economic growth and welfare as the main normative instruments of the European financial system - supranational regulation, supervision/surveillance, burden-sharing mechanisms and last-resort or rescue measures - are able to prevent and manage risks or shocks.

This definition encapsulates what the essential components of financial stability as a normative objective in EU law and policy are. Furthermore, it includes the normative instruments for its attainment. This definition is based on the establishment of a normative environment capable of preventing and managing risks and shocks as well as on recognizing financial stability as a public good in Europe as outlined above.[102] While some aspects of this definition – the normative instruments to financial stability – will be dealt with below,[103] some assessment is provided as to the two most important elements of the proposed definition of financial stability: 'risks or shocks' and 'European financial system'.

[a] Risks and Shocks

Risks and shocks are essential components in the definition of financial stability as they constitute the benchmark notions against which normative instruments are needed to

---

100. Tuori, Tuori *supra* n. 2, 58.
101. *Ibid.*, 183–184.
102. *See* Chapter 2 section §2.04 for some definitions of financial stability elaborated in other social sciences fields.
103. *See* infra section §3.03 for the normative instruments of the definition.

pursue financial stability.[104] *Systemic* risk has acquired a peculiar role in EU law as the EU legislator has defined it. The European Systemic Risk Board (ESRB) Regulation states that systemic risk as the 'risk of disruption in the financial system with the potential to have serious negative consequences for the internal market and the real economy'.[105] This definition captures the context of risk in the financial system well, but also appears to be limited in scope as it refers to the macro-prudential dimension of risk prevention and management while not considering the micro-prudential dimension of financial stability as well as the consequences that other forms of risks may have for financial stability.

Various types of risks are directly mentioned in European legal acts such as credit, legal, operational or model risks. The existence of various risks or shocks suggests that there are many forms of *financial* risks and shocks primarily associated with a state of affairs negatively affected (e.g., capital, liquidity, credit situation) or by the nature of the risk or shock (e.g. exogenous, systemic). EU law and policy has embraced a general recognition of risks and shocks in its regulatory instruments. For instance, macro-economic adjustment programmes for Member States under the Two Pack are intended to reduce the risks of contagion to the euro area as a whole.[106] Furthermore, risks reduction measures are an essential paradigm in the prudential evaluation of financial firms. Capital requirements for banks are based on the assessment of their risk profiles and determine the bank resilience. The Basel Committee,[107] whose standards have been substantially implemented in EU law, has developed a non-exhaustive list of risks of banks.[108] This important list comprises: – credit risk, including counterparty credit risk: the risk that a borrower will partially default on his obligation to repay the loan or to pay interest; – liquidity risk: the risk inherent in all maturity transformation processes of being unable to satisfy (short-term) cash flow needs; – market risk, including interest rate risk and foreign exchange rate risk: the risks of losses from changes in market prices; – concentration risk: the risk of loss resulting from being overly exposed to a single counterparty or several counterparties belonging to a group, to borrowers / counterparties in the same geographic region, industry, etc., or to a particular class of assets, etc.; – country risk, including sovereign risk: the risk of loss caused by events in a foreign country; – transfer risk: the risk that a borrower will not make debt service payments in a foreign currency because of his inability to obtain the pertinent currency; – operational risk: the risk of loss resulting from inadequate or failed internal processes, people (fraud) and systems (Information Technology (IT) systems) or external events, including legal risk; –

104. *See* Andenas, Chiu, *supra* n. 94, 30. *See* already the analysis of risk in Chapter 2 section §2.04[B][2].
105. Regulation (EU) 1092/2010 of 24 November 2010 on European Union macro-prudential supervision of the financial system and establishing a European Systemic Risk Board [2010] OJ L331/1, Art. 2.
106. *See* Chapter 4 section §4.03[A][3] for the analysis of the Two Pack.
107. On the Basel Committee on Banking Supervision *see* Chapter 2 section §2.05[C].
108. Basel Committee on Banking Supervision, *Core Principles for Effective Banking Supervision* (2012), Principles 17–25. *See* further Peter Mülbert, *Managing Risk in the Financial System*, in Niamh Moloney, Eilís Ferran, Jennifer Payne (eds), *The Oxford Handbook of Financial Regulation*, 369–370 (Oxford University Press 2015).

reputational risk: risk arising from negative perception on the part of other market participants. Risk is also considered as a key element in the Capital Requirements Directive (CRD) as part of the corporate governance of credit institutions, such as for the assessment of senior management of credit institutions, risk committees and risk management.[109]

In the context of the definition of financial stability, the assessment of risks can be applied both to sovereigns and financial institutions in Europe. As to the former, sovereigns, thus the Member States of the EU, may pose (systemic) risks if they get over-indebted and are not able to offer sufficient guarantees as to their debt repayments. This arises from the assessment of sovereign fiscal sustainability and market access as well as of the sovereign inability to pay as a threat to stability.[110] As to financial institutions, and in particular banks, financial regulation on minimum requirements and compliance with certain ratios play a major role to avoid or limit risks. Some indicators capture risks of individual banks or banking groups.[111] These indicators include the size of a bank's balance sheet, the complexity of its structure and its interconnectedness with other financial institutions and markets.[112] These three elements suggest the following: the size of a bank is a general element which captures systemic risk; the complexity of the individual banking structure creates a lack of transparency to assess the impact and nature of a crisis; the interconnectedness may generate spillover effects to other banks and to the real economy. Therefore, different forms of risks as well as the size, complexity and interconnectedness of certain players play a clear role in contributing to risks faced in the financial system.

Shock is the alternative component as part of the proposed definition of financial stability. Shock is defined in economics as 'an unexpected and unpredictable event that has a positive or a negative effect on the economy'.[113] Not all shocks jeopardise financial stability, but only those that have repercussions at the level of the European financial system. This suggests that the objective of financial stability purports to establish a normative environment where shocks as 'unexpected and unpredictable changes to the conditions of the economy' are successfully prevented and managed.

Risks and shocks are general terms essential to define what financial stability is. They aim at determining the most important component against which the normative instruments for financial stability serve their normative function. This moves the analysis to the second key component of the definition: the European financial system.

[b] European Financial System

The expression 'European financial system' delineates the material, territorial and subjective scope of financial stability and its normative instruments. This term is wide

109. *Ibid.*, 372.
110. IMF, *Sovereign Debt Restructuring – Recent Developments and Implications for the Fund's Legal and Policy Framework*, 9–10 (2013).
111. *See* Basel Committee on Banking Supervision, *Global Systemically Important Banks: Assessment Methodology and the Additional Loss Absorbency Requirement*, paras 15–25 (2011).
112. *Ibid.*
113. *Oxford Dictionary of Economics* (Oxford University Press 2009).

in nature as it may refer to financial institutions including credit institutions, non-financial institutions having a systemic importance and sovereigns. The term 'system' refers to a framework composed of interconnected elements that, in combination, have a function distinct from those of these elements individually.[114] In other words, a system is a general framework that is constructed of components necessary for the attainment of an objective. While system is a vague term, 'financial' has an essential role in defining financial stability. Allen and Wood have stated that 'financial stability (...) shall apply to financial institutions, non-financial companies and sovereign nations'.[115] Following this broad scope, it is submitted that financial stability as a foundational objective shall apply to a European financial system composed of both the market operators (financial and non-financial institutions) and sovereigns (Member States). This is because both market operators and sovereigns may exert risks and shocks that may hinder the attainment of financial stability. At the same time, while other market players may have an essential role in the financial system, such as central counterparties or payment systems, these are not considered as being essential for the expression 'European financial system'. This is mainly because they have not an intermediation function between the financial system and the economy. Rather, for the purpose of this study, the main market operators that may most effectively affect the attainment of financial stability as a foundational objective in Europe are credit institutions and sovereigns.

Credit institutions are essential in the European financial system. Also the ECJ recognized the central role of credit institutions in the economy. As recently held by the ECJ in *Ledra Advertising* '[b]anks and credit institutions are an essential source of funding for businesses that are active in the various markets. In addition, the banks are often interconnected and certain of their number operate internationally'.[116] Credit institutions are special entities in nature performing special functions in the economy for mainly four reasons. First, credit institutions are the most important intermediaries between lending and borrowing in the economy. Credit institutions are financial intermediaries that primarily reallocate resources from entities with surplus funds to entities with funding needs.[117] This is because credit institutions channel the transmission of funds, and they play the role in the economy of financial intermediaries by transforming short-term supply of funds from their depositors into long-term lending to their borrowers.[118] Second, they also mobilise capital via payment and settlement systems. Third, credit institutions are the link between monetary policy and the real economy.[119] They are counterparties to central bank refinancing operations and get

114. *See* Iman Anabtawi & Steven Schwarcz, *Regulating Ex Post: How Law Can Address the Inevitability of Financial Failure*, 92 Texas Law Review 75, 78 (2013).
115. William Allen & Geoffrey Wood, *Defining and Achieving Financial Stability*, 2 Journal of Financial Stability 154 (2006).
116. Case C-8/15P *Ledra Advertising v. Commission and ECB*, para. 72.
117. On the financial intermediation theory *see* Jordi Canals, *Universal Banking. International Comparisons and Theoretical Perspectives*, 28 (Clarendon Press 1997); Tommaso Padoa-Schioppa, *Regulating Finance: Balancing Freedom and Risk*, 13 (Oxford University Press 2004).
118. Mathias Dewatripont & Jean Tirole, *The Prudential Regulation of Banks*, 104 (MIT Press 1994).
119. *See* Padoa-Schioppa *supra* n. 117, 46.

access to liquidity from the central banks. Fourth, they are exposed to high vulnerabilities as they are the main financial intermediaries both in the financial system and from the financial system to the real economy. Vulnerabilities may materialise by a loss of confidence in the financial system and may generate runs by depositors and wholesale lenders. In sum, regulators and policy-makers treat credit institutions as being subject to a special treatment mainly because they perform special functions in the economy and they are subject to vulnerabilities that may jeopardise the financial system and eventually the real economy.

Sovereigns are the second essential constituent of the European financial system. They are, by definition, central public bodies carrying out public and administrative functions and services. Sovereigns carry out activities that require financing and public spending. There are two main ways to compensate public spending. First, sovereigns have the sovereign power to raise and collect taxes. Second, they finance their budgets issuing financial instruments and indebting themselves in order to carry out public function activities. Sovereigns shall respect some level of fiscal discipline in order not to increase their debt and jeopardise their fiscal sustainability. Should a sovereign not being capable of financing itself in the financial markets, this would generate sovereign default affecting the pursuit of financial stability.

In sum, the definition of European financial system encompasses the underperformance and vulnerabilities of credit institutions as special entities as well as the sovereign inability to pay back debts and its fiscal sustainability. This leads the discussion to assess why financial stability shall be considered as a *supranational* foundational objective in EU law and policy.

[C] The Supranational Dimension of Financial Stability in Europe

This section addresses the question as to why the need to achieve financial stability shall have a *supranational* rather than a national character in Europe. This suggests that, differently from the international level, the supranational level can well achieve financial stability. The section looks at the dual aims of addressing national inadequacies (subsection [1]) and correcting market failures (subsection [2]).

[1] Addressing National Inadequacy

As the financial crisis has demonstrated so far, purely national responses to the achievement of financial stability have questioned the very idea of the European integration project. The high degree of integration in financial markets and the single currency in the euro area suggest that a purely national dimension for the attainment of financial stability is not and shall not be a desirable option. At the same time, the increasing indebtedness of national public finances, mainly caused by public interventions to sustain the national banking sector and by the structural difficulties in fiscal sustainability, has exacerbated national responses to the financial crisis. Among others, these developments provided for the creation of a malicious nexus between sovereigns and financial institutions showing that a purely national response to address financial stability is not desirable.

As this study will show in subsequent chapters, a purely national response alone cannot achieve financial stability. In an interconnected and integrated market based on cross-border activities, sovereigns or national bodies cannot resolve these problems alone.[120] This is for a number of reasons. First, the financial involvement of sovereigns to solve problems related to financial markets has generated a huge amount of public resources spent or committed that have progressively deteriorated public finances. During the financial crisis, public intervention in the form of State aids to credit institutions deteriorated the sustainability of public finances, particularly in the euro area, increased the indirect costs paid by taxpayers to sustain financial institutions and has generated a vicious circle between the sovereign and the banking sector.[121] Resort to State aid measures has been a de facto solution in the absence of a supranational regime to deal with financial (and in particular banking) crises.

Second, during the financial crisis, Member States have adopted national regulatory measures. Such measures have generated ring-fencing and protectionist policies that cannot adequately and sufficiently protect against risks and shocks to the economy of the European internal market. Purely national responses in addressing risks that may destabilise the economy in a single Member State are not efficient to withstand the possible consequences of instable financial markets. Member States' economy, as a fraction of a regional internal market, cannot alone provide sufficient responses to the stability problems affecting the whole Europe and the internal market.

Third, the State is necessarily pursuing national interests which may conflict with the wider European institutions' objective of reaching an 'ever closer Union'. The pursuit of national interest stands in contrast with the need to address State inadequacies through supranational solutions. The adoption of national measures to resolve issues related to financial stability may also generate disruption to the objectives of the EU, namely market integration and undistorted competition.

Fourth, the creation of a supranational currency in the euro area and the related impossibility to devaluate a currency at the national level suggest that national responses are by definition inadequate. This is because the role of a currency managed at the national level allows national banking authorities to act independently of any supranational decision on the matter. The single monetary policy in the euro area does not allow a national answer to ensure the stability of the financial system.

At the same time, while the national level has been ineffective in achieving financial stability in Europe, a new phenomenon has also generated a new trend of intergovernmental instruments. Intergovernmentalism refers to the use of international agreements in the development of certain policies. As it will be argued in subsequent chapters of this book, Member States have made use of international agreements to regulate certain aspects of financial stability such as the creation of a fund for financial assistance to sovereigns, the ESM, or the adoption of reinforced rules for economic surveillance, through the TSCG. These developments may question the

120. *See contra* Andenas, Chiu, *supra* n. 94, 53–54.
121. On the analysis of state aid and credit institutions *see* Chapter 8 section §8.02[B].

real effectiveness of a supranational response to achieve financial stability. Such development cannot be analysed further. [122] Suffice it to say that intergovernmental means are seen as a necessity-driven phenomenon justified by the absence of unanimous agreements to develop EU rules or by the absence of legal basis in EU law and policy. Therefore, it is argued that intergovernmentalism plays a supporting role to the strengthening of financial stability at the European level.

Overall, these reflections suggest that a *supranational* response to the attainment of financial stability in Europe is the desirable solution. This justifies that financial stability shall be achieved in Europe to the extent that supranational frameworks and powers exist for such purpose.

[2] Correcting (Banking) Market Failures

The correction of market failures is the second major argument suggesting that financial stability shall be supranational in nature. Financial markets do not always work properly, and this means that market failures may arise. Francis Bator was the first one to develop the market failures theory in economics.[123] The theory of market failures has demonstrated that financial markets alone are not always able to allocate financial resources in an optimal way. The presence of intermediaries, and specifically credit institutions, contributes to the creation of market failures, which can, in turn, distort equilibrium in financial markets.[124] As this study demonstrates, the reinforcement of supranational regulation and supervision in banking markets is an essential component to achieve financial stability in EU law and policy.[125] This is because banks as financial intermediaries in the financial system may produce important market failures that, as argued in this book, can be only solved at the supranational level.

A regulatory response to market failures in a supranational fashion is justified for a number of reasons. First, as the saver/consumer does not have the same level of information of intermediaries/banks, the financial markets generate information asymmetries.[126] Second, intermediaries (i.e., credit institutions) engage in risky activities without an appropriate assessment of risks on the part of the initial saver/consumer placing resources with an intermediary. These activities may deteriorate the financial markets and generate undue costs for other parties. Third, risky and speculative activities may lead to bank group failures that would need to be addressed at cross-border level. However, traditional national insolvency measures should not apply to individual banks as they do for other firms. The too-big-to-fail doctrine requires that distressed big credit institutions are not subject to traditional insolvency proceedings due to the essential role that such credit institutions have in the economy. Fourth, individual banking failures may have spillover effects to other banks or

122. *See* in this context Chiti, Teixeira *supra* n. 2, 689.
123. Francis Bator, *The Anatomy of Market Failure*, 72 Quarterly Journal of Economics 351 (1958).
124. Moloney *supra* n. 1, 4.
125. *See* infra section §3.03[A].
126. *See* Larisa Dragomir, *European Prudential Banking Regulation and Supervision: The Legal Dimension*, 44 (Routledge 2008).

financial institutions, hence creating a domino effect.[127] Fifth, individual or collective banking failures require public intervention, may affect the real economy and may create the conditions for (systemic) risks in the entire economy.

Against this background, the response to market failures may take place following two main theories on the role of regulatory intervention: the public interest approach and the private interest approach.[128] The former considers that public power is able to act efficiently to correct market failures and has the correct incentives to intervene.[129] The latter argues that regulation and supervision is merely a response to demands by private interest groups.[130] While it is not possible to address in details the above theories, this study follows the public-interest approach by assessing to what extent market failures may be avoided at the supranational level. The high degree of European economic and market integration shows that a supranational response to address such market failures is inevitable.[131] The public interest approach suggests that it is essential that public supranational powers are exercised to guide financial markets in pursuing financial stability, and that an appropriate supranational answer to address market failures is provided. This is possible through robust public regulatory measures, adequate supervision and appropriate burden-sharing arrangements aimed at achieving financial stability. Rather than leaving market powers free to decide how to conduct their activities, there is a need to supervise public and private market forces to limit or avoid market failures.

Overall, this section suggests that a European *supranational* public interest approach is the key approach to address market failures in Europe, especially because market failures may have cross-border effects and a supranational impact that individual States are not able to address. The next section examines the main challenges and benefits of considering financial stability as a foundational objective in EU law and policy.

[D] The Main Challenges to Financial Stability as a Foundational Objective in EU Law and Policy

The argument that financial stability should be seen as foundational objective of EU law and policy can be subject to critical challenges intending to downsize its relevance or importance. This section aims to examine such challenges and provide an answer to them.

127. *See also* Case C-8/15 P *Ledra Advertising v. Commission and ECB*, para. 72.
128. *See* James Barth, Gerard Caprio & Ross Levine, *Rethinking Bank Regulation. Till Angels Govern*, 22 (Cambridge University Press 2006).
129. *Ibid.*
130. *Ibid.*
131. *See infra* section §3.03 for the instruments of supranational regulation and supervi sion/surveillance.

[1] The Challenge of Definition

It remains uncontested that financial stability has a very controversial benchmark definition in social sciences.[132] The lack of a clear and quantifiable benchmark definition does not contribute to identify an appropriate role for the achievement of *sufficient* financial stability in Europe. Furthermore, the problems in providing a definition to financial stability make it difficult to understand what the main components of financial stability are. As demonstrated earlier, it is possible to define financial stability by developing a normative system to the prevention and management of risks or shocks in the European financial system. The lack of a benchmark definition remains a major difficulty in developing a theory of financial stability. Nonetheless, it is argued that both a wide legal definition and a foundational dimension of financial stability in EU law and policy make it possible to set a benchmark definition to the term. By selecting credit institutions and sovereigns as the main focus of the European financial system, financial stability can be linked to specific entities having a key role to understand financial stability. Therefore, these links make it possible to give financial stability a specific definition.

[2] The Challenge of Instrumental and Purposive Uncertainty

In the previous sections, it has been argued that financial stability is a new foundational objective in Europe. This interpretation makes it difficult to have an instrumental or purposive certainty as to its achievement. In other words, it is not possible to say when financial stability is achieved. Rather, there is a structural difficulty in finding clear and straightforward instruments that may contribute to the ultimate achievement of financial stability. Furthermore, financial stability does not give any indications of what the main instruments and objectives for financial stability are. EU primary law does not explicitly refer to the role of financial stability and the lack of clear instruments and objectives to achieve financial stability adds complications to theorise financial stability as a foundational objective of EU law and policy. However, as it will be demonstrated below, placing financial stability in a specific framework derived from certain normative instruments attributed to a number of supranational players and within a specific normative framework may solve these instrumental and purposive uncertainties.[133] Moreover, financial stability is not necessarily an achievable foundational objective, but can be considered as an instrumental objective towards which a given system needs to look for. This is also the case of other foundational objectives in EU law and policy such as a sustainable development or full employment.

---

132. *See* Chapter 2 section §2.04 for the different theories in economics on financial stability.
133. *See infra* section §3.03[A], [B].

[3] The Challenge of Temporal Uncertainty

Together with the instrumental and purposive uncertainty, the lack of temporal certainty is a further challenge to make financial stability a foundational objective in EU law and policy. Financial stability cannot be verified within a specific timeframe or achieved in a given time. This suggests that the absence of indicators as to when financial stability is achieved may create a challenge to its role. In economic terms, temporal uncertainty is related to the different fluctuations driving economic cycles in modern economies and the fact that an appropriate benchmark for financial stability may be achieved neither in normal nor in crisis times. The different fluctuations in aggregate production, trade and services within an economic cycle impact the objective of financial stability as they drive conservative or proactive policy choices to attain financial stability. The four Schumpeterian economic cycles (expansion, crisis, recession and recovery) support the argument that it is difficult to determine when *actual* financial stability is achieved at a given point in time.[134] In simple words, it is difficult to state whether financial stability is achieved at a given point in time. However, framing financial stability as a public good objective makes it as a benchmark term that shall be normatively pursued regardless of whether or when it may be achieved. This suggests that temporal uncertainty does not jeopardise the attainment of financial stability.

[4] The Challenge of Financial Stability Versus Other Objectives in Financial Regulation

The relationship between financial stability and other objectives in the European financial system: efficient markets, investor protection and market integrity is a key challenge.

Efficient markets: Financial stability as a foundational objective in EU law and policy may contrast with the need to ensure efficient markets. Market efficiency would allow an efficient allocation of resources and a certain degree of regulatory or market competition based on a certain level of flexibility that could contrast the need to ensure financial stability in a regional normative framework such as Europe. A supranational normative framework based on financial stability may generate uncertainties as to whether an efficient market perspective or a purely free competition perspective may be more beneficial to Europe. Against this challenge, it is contended that the theoretical foundations on European market integration were erroneous without an appropriate consideration to financial stability. Thus far, the 'Efficient Capital Market Hypothesis' (ECMH) has been one of the main dogmas of the EU project before the financial crisis.[135] This hypothesis argues that markets provide at any time all the available information on a financial asset into its price.[136] In other words, markets work

134. *See* Joseph Schumpeter, *Capitalism, Socialism and Democracy*, 82–85 (Harper 1975).
135. Eugene Fama, *Foundations of Finance: Portfolio Decisions and Securities Prices*, 5 (Basic Books 1977).
136. André Prüm, *The European Union Crisis Responses and the Efficient Capital Markets Hypothesis*, 60 Columbia Journal of European Law 2 (2014).

efficiently even without any degree of public intervention as the principles and rules governing a given financial system are driven by an efficient capital market.[137] The financial crisis has shown that the ECMH was based on the wrong assumption that markets would efficiently work without any public interest intervention. On the contrary, the need to prevent intense market reactions and to reduce or minimise (systemic) risks suggests that a new normative framework should be developed in Europe. As this study will demonstrate, there was an erroneous assumption that the pre-crisis financial market rules and loose fiscal coordination measures in the EMU would work well without due attention to the supranational dimension of financial stability. Therefore, the need to ensure financial stability shall drive EMU governance and financial market reforms.

Overall, the argument that financial stability conflicts with an efficient market perspective shall be discarded as financial stability aims to supersede the idea that markets can work well without any public regulatory intervention aimed at addressing vulnerabilities and risks.

Investor Protection: Another key objective in the European financial system is investor protection. The outbreak of the financial crisis has also prompted a new regulatory wave to strengthen investor protection. While being a relatively recent phenomenon, investor protection has been perceived as important element in the regulation of European financial markets. Investors have usually been identified as wholesale investors and retail investors. The former include sophisticated entities, corporations, institutional investors and collective investment vehicles. The latter are mainly consumers. As argued by Andenas and Chiu, '[t]he notion of investor protection is now infused with wider financial stability concerns.'[138] The consideration of investor protection is essential in financial regulation and in the conduct of financial activities. Investor protection is considered as being the key principle in allowing the proper functioning of financial markets. This is framed as an objective aiming at the defensive protection of the vulnerable investor against sophisticated market participants.[139] Given the prominence of investor protection, it is essential to understand what the relationship between financial stability and investor protection is. As argued in this book, financial stability has acquired a prominent role in Europe. On the contrary, investor protection remains a sectorial objective in financial regulation. It is questioned whether the existence of a strong objective of financial stability in Europe may conflict with the need to ensure an adequate protection of investors. However, it would be wrong to consider investor protection as conflicting with financial stability. Rather, they seem to be consistent objectives. The nature of investor protection as a sectorial objective contributes to financial stability to the extent that it prevents risks and ensures that market failures are limited through disclosure and transparency requirements in the financial sector.

137. *Ibid.*, 3.
138. Andenas, Chiu, *supra* n. 94, 136.
139. Niamh Moloney, *How to Protect Investors* 46 (Cambridge University Press 2010).

Overall, investor protection is a key objective in financial markets which does not conflict with the foundational objective of financial stability. Rather, given its different nature, investor protection may contribute to the attainment of financial stability.

Market integrity: Finally, some attention should be given also to the relationship between financial stability and market integrity. This is usually intended as the absence of money laundering, insider trading and illegal capital flows, and is commonly regarded as contributing not only to increased global security but also to increased financial stability. The EU has increasingly protected market integrity by reinforcing the regulatory regime against market abuses and manipulations in financial services. Similar to investor protection, there seems to be a link between the objective of market integrity and financial stability by considering that the former is beneficial to financial stability to the extent that it fosters the respect of rules. At the same time, market integrity remains a sectorial objective as compared to the foundational role of financial stability.

[5] The Challenge of Financial Stability in the Euro Area and in the EU

The relationship between financial stability in the EU and in the euro area as a block of nineteen Member States pursuing a more advanced level of integration is a further challenge to supranational financial stability as a foundational objective for the Union as a whole.[140] The EU Treaties recognise to a certain extent a set of rules applying only to the euro area such as the exclusive competence of monetary policy for the Member States having adopted the euro[141] or the TFEU articles related to measures that may reinforce the economic policy framework only for the euro area Member States.[142] The ESM and the Two Pack crisis-related reforms apply only to euro area. Similarly, the creation of the EBU clearly shows that integration in the euro area Member States is more advanced than outside the euro area in the field of banking supervision and resolution.[143] The different degree of integration in the euro area as compared to the non-euro area shows that a different level of supranational financial stability may be reached in EU law and policy as part of the recent reforms to strengthen the EMU.

As argued by Hinarejos, there is a growing impression that different interests and immediate priorities drive the euro and the non-euro Member States, together with a need for prompt and at times politically sensitive action.[144] This has arguably created a greater fragmentation of EU integration.[145] The question is whether fragmentation between euro area and non-euro area may apply also to the concept of financial

140. *See* in general on the idea of a two-speed Europe, Jean-Claude Piris, *The Future of Europe. Towards a Two-Speed EU?*, 61 (Cambridge University Press 2011).
141. Art. 4 TFEU.
142. Art. 136 TFEU.
143. *See* Chapter 7 section §7.04[F] and Chapter 8 section §8.03[B][2] on close cooperation arrangements and the relationship between euro area and non-euro area in the EBU.
144. Alicia Hinarejos, *The Euro Area Crisis in Constitutional Perspective*, 104 (Oxford University Press 2015).
145. *See* Jean-Claude Piris, *The Lisbon Treaty: A Legal and Political Analysis*, 63 (Cambridge University Press 2010).

stability as a supranational objective in the EU. The creation of institutional and substantive frameworks for financial stability in EU law and policy applying only to euro area Member States is undisputed. This is especially because the euro area crisis has exacerbated the need of supranational reforms for Member States which have adopted the same currency. Financial stability as a supranational objective in EU law and policy has been pursued more effectively for the euro area Member States. This may put at risks the understanding of financial stability in the euro area and outside the euro area.

While noting the above challenge, financial stability is an objective in nature which has acquired a supranational dimension. The distinction between euro area and non-euro area Member States does not put into question that argument, as it is clear that financial stability is not contested in the non-euro area Member States as a guiding objective of reform to the European financial system. Indeed the instruments for attainment of financial stability may differ for the non-euro area Member States such as having a single supervisory or resolution authorities in the euro area.

However, the central role of financial stability in EU law and policy does not differ on the basis of participation to the single currency. Moreover, the existence of rules applying throughout all the EU – the CRR as a directly applicable law in all Member States, the EU single rulebook for credit institutions – as well as close cooperation mechanisms to participate in the EBU make it possible to argue that a similar degree of supranational financial stability may also be achieved by the non-euro area Member States.

[E] The Main Benefits of Financial Stability as a Foundational Objective in EU Law and Policy

While the preceding section examined the main challenges on financial stability as a foundational objective in EU law and policy, this section analyses its main benefits.

[1] The Benefit of Promoting Economic Growth in Europe

The foundational objective of financial stability is primarily important to attain economic growth in Europe. As Samuelson assumed, there is a widespread assumption that the reach of financial stability is in itself a fundamental proxy to reach a desirable level of economic growth.[146] However, it remains difficult to align economic growth to a specific criterion. Is it the overall increase of the market value of the goods and services produced in the economy? Is it GDP levels? Is it debt ratio to GDP? Is it merely the absence of financial crises? In general terms, it may be said that financial stability aims to achieve a level of economic growth independently from a specific criterion linked to it or to its normative instruments. The purpose of financial stability is, thus,

146. *See* Paul Samuelson, *The Pure Theory of Public Expenditure*, 36 Review of Economics and Statistics 387 (1954).

to allocate resources to their most productive use. Economic growth is the axiomatic consequence arising from the reach of financial stability.

[2] The Benefit of Producing Efficient Markets and Contributing to Generalised Welfare

Although the previous section argued that attaining financial stability might question flexibility of financial markets, there is also the counterargument that the normative objective of financial stability contributes to the attainment of efficient markets by framing the normative context to allocate resources to the markets. It is submitted that the objective of financial stability is the key to establish efficient markets in order to attain Pareto-efficiency situation in which nobody can be made better off without making someone else worse off.[147] While in reality the efficient market paradigm is almost impossible to reach, the Kaldor-Hicks criteria acknowledge the limitations of Pareto optimality and refer to compensation between losers and gains in the economy to attain efficiency in the market.[148] By offsetting the losses and gains in the economy for the sake of efficiency, the Kaldor-Hicks criteria support the argument that financial stability serves as a foundational objective to increase market efficiency.

At the same time, generalised welfare is another benefit arising from financial stability. Welfare can be defined as the minimal level of well-being and social support for individuals. Although not directly related to the reach of generalised welfare, framing a supranational normative framework for financial stability purports to increase the general level of welfare in Europe by allowing an appropriate allocation of financial and non-financial resources that can ultimately be transposed to the real economy and to individuals.

Financial stability, as a foundational objective in EU law and policy, does not purport to introduce static measures whose presence is deemed rigid to regulate and supervise markets. Rather, as argued above, it serves to provide a normative benchmark for mitigating, reducing or absorbing (systemic) risks or stocks. Such benchmark cannot be ignored in the post-financial crisis era and serves to guide policy-making in Europe. The practical relevance of this in various fields will be assessed in subsequent chapters of this study.

[3] The Benefit of Addressing Too-Big-to-Fail, Moral Hazard and Free-Riding

The development of a supranational dimension of financial stability in Europe has further, the benefit of addressing the too-big-to-fail problem, moral hazard and free-riding. These are issues that have arisen in the context of the financial crisis in Europe, and that indicate that a robust institutional and substantive framework shall exist in order to avoid negative repercussions in Europe.

147. *See* Wilfredo Pareto, *Cours d'Economie Politique*, 420, 436 (Rouges 1896).
148. *See* John Hicks, *The Foundations of Welfare Economics*, 49 The Economic Journal 696 (1939).

The need to address the 'too-big-to-fail' issue has come to the attention of the regulators in the context of the financial crisis in Europe. The 'too-big-to-fail' notion is usually meant as an implicit public guarantee against failures according to which a big entity, usually a credit institution whose balance sheet is more than the home country GDP, will be rescued at the taxpayers expenses through public money and be subject to deposit insurance. In other words, some big entities and groups benefit from a 'regulatory protection', as they are too big to fail. This is true in particular in the context of cross-border activities of big financial institutions representing a threat to global financial stability. The too-big-to-fail issue is linked to other related concepts.[149] The too-interconnected-to-fail means that an entity is so interconnected with the rest of the financial system that its failure may trigger risks and shocks to other institutions. The too-complex-to-fail notion refers to the complexity of an entity whose activities and links to the financial system as a whole cannot be understood. The too-many-to-fail means that an entity is part of a group of similar institutions that are all vulnerable to similar risks or shocks and whose failure would generate massive risks and shocks. Supranational financial stability as an objective should aim at preventing and managing risks and shocks which can be generated by the above notions and limit their impact by avoiding market failures.[150]

Financial stability as a supranational objective aiming to prevent and manage risks and shocks addresses also moral hazard. This is a notion similar to the too-big-to-fail one. In economic terms, Krugman defines moral hazard as 'any situation in which one person makes the decision about how much risk to take, while someone else bears the cost if things go badly'.[151] This definition takes into account the policy rationale according to which there is a risk that the institution benefiting from a measure taken by someone else might be willing to engage in a full-of-risk strategy that might make financial crisis more likely in the future. Moral hazard is thus a perverse phenomenon that allows some institutions to benefit from the support they will have from public authorities or other entities in cases of crisis. Similar to the too-big-to-fail issue, the role of financial stability in addressing moral hazard through robust normative instruments is beneficial to let market operators pay the costs of their full-of-risk strategies.

Also free-riding is a problem associated with public goods, and thus financial stability. As defined in economic terms by Baumol, the free-rider problem occurs when those who benefit from resources, goods or services do not pay for them, which results in an under-provision of those goods or services.[152] The pursuit of financial stability as a public good in Europe may result in positive externalities that may not be well compensated for those that have not been subject to burden-sharing measures. The

149. Rosa Lastra & Geoffrey Wood, *The Crisis of 2007–09: Nature, Causes, and Reactions*, 13 Journal of International Economic Law 539 (2010).

150. *See* Emilios Avgouleas, *Governance of Global Financial Markets*, 118 (Cambridge University Press 2012).

151. Paul Krugman, *The Return of Depression Economics and the Crisis of 2008*, 63 (Norton Company Limited 2009).

152. *See* William Baumol, *Welfare Economics and the Theory of the State* (Harvard University Press 1952).

beneficiaries of these measures could be induced to take advantage within the framework. In practice, sovereigns and market operators that have benefitted from external interventions may be induced not to produce financial stability gains and generate risks and shocks. Thus, these entities may take the advantage of financial stability measures and benefit from that without contributing themselves to the achievement of financial stability. This necessitates policy-making solutions aimed to provide benefits as well as burden-sharing arrangements to sovereigns and market operators and avoid that they take undue advantages. The free-riding problem may be solved by letting free-riding private or public parties pay the costs of their free-riding activities. This is possible through *ex ante* regulation and surveillance/supervision intended to prevent free-riding through conditional public intervention or burden-sharing measures to pay the cost of free-riding.

In sum, the existence of a supranational financial stability as a foundational objective in Europe aims to reduce the 'too-big-to-fail' phenomenon and to address moral hazard by establishing a framework preventing and managing risk- or shock-based policies by regulatory interventions in the market. Free-riding is subsequently reduced if such framework is in place. A strongly supranational dimension of financial stability reduces further risks and shocks that public resources are used to rescue too-big-to-fail entities, entities generating moral hazard or free-riding market operators and sovereigns. This opens the question of understanding what the normative instruments to attain financial stability are.

Having completed the analysis of the main benefits of financial stability as a foundational objective in EU law and policy, the chapter now turns to the supranational normative instruments to achieve financial stability as a key component in the definition of such concept.

§3.03 THE NORMATIVE INSTRUMENTS FOR SUPRANATIONAL FINANCIAL STABILITY IN EU LAW AND POLICY

After having analysed the main challenges and benefits of financial stability as a foundational supranational objective in EU law and policy, this section attempts to look at what the main normative instruments for financial stability in Europe are. This part identifies the main instruments that should drive regulators and policy makers at the supranational level and constitute essential components of the definition of financial stability proposed in this book.

The purpose of this part is not to list a static and autonomous set of normative instruments, but rather to set normative instruments building a supranational system to achieve financial stability in EU law and policy and to give legitimacy to the definition of financial stability. From a conceptual perspective, these normative instruments are part of the proposed definition of financial stability in EU law and policy. At the same time, while these instruments are normatively framed to prevent and/or manage risks or shocks, some of them are stand-alone concepts developed in EU law and policy.

It seems important to emphasise that the definition of financial stability[153] comprises normative instruments that are not normative in the sense that they only set binding legal rules whose breaches may be enforceable. They are normative in the sense that EU policy-makers - EU institutions, agencies, bodies - exercising powers in the field of EU law and policy (or even outside) shall take into account in order to attain a sufficient degree of legitimacy to supranational financial stability. *A contrario*, they serve as a means not to endanger financial stability as a foundational objective in EU law and policy. Hence, they are normative as they confer *legitimacy* to the definition of financial stability developed in this study.

The normative instruments of financial stability in Europe are diverse in nature, and it is difficult to come up with an exhaustive list of norms and rules for supranational financial stability in Europe. This is especially because the concept of financial stability in Europe is difficult to define in legal terms and because *supranational* financial stability is to a certain extent bound to the international and national dimensions of financial stability.[154] Notwithstanding these limitations, this section argues that certain normative instruments may still be identified based on the constituent component of financial stability as an objective intended to prevent and manage risks or shocks. In particular, the existence and use of these normative instruments are essential to strengthen the 'public good' dimension of financial stability as they set out the main instruments to reinforce the non-excludability and non-rivalry of financial stability as a 'public good'.[155] First, the exercise of these instruments at supranational level makes it possible to attain financial stability in all jurisdictions and, hence, make the objective non-rivalrous. Second, the supranational exercise of these instruments allows Member States to benefit from financial stability and, hence, make the objective non-excludable.

Other normative instruments, which are important in the context of EU law and policy such as regulatory competition[156] or informal instruments for coordination,[157] are deemed not to be sufficient to set the frame for the foundational supranational objective of financial stability in EU law and policy. This is because they are nationally centred or based on soft law, and they do not have the same normative implications that the selected normative instruments have for the prevention and management of risks or shocks in Europe at the supranational level. In other words, they are not capable of attaining a truly supranational dimension to financial stability, as they do

153. *See supra* section §3.02[B][2] for the definition of financial stability for the purpose of this study.
154. *See* Lastra, Louis *supra* n. 24, 139.
155. *See* Chapter 2 section §2.02 for the characteristics of public goods.
156. Regulatory competition, which cannot be examined further in this book, is defined as 'process whereby legal rules are selected and de-selected through competition between decentralised, rule-making entities'. *See*, further, Simon Deakin, *Legal Diversity and Regulatory Competition: Which Model for Europe?*, 12 European Law Journal 441 (2006); Barbara Gabor, *Regulatory Competition in the Internal Market*, 1 (Edward Elgar 2013).
157. Coordination and in particular Open Method of Coordination (OMC) is considered as being an exclusively soft law framework based on transparency, peer pressure and deliberation. *See* Paul Craig, *EU Administrative Law*, 182 (Oxford University Press 2012).

not aim to make financial stability entirely non-rivalrous and non-excludable objective as well as a supranational public good in Europe.

With that said, it appears possible to identify two main 'pillars' on normative instruments for supranational financial stability in Europe: (i) preventive; and (ii) management normative instruments for risks or shocks. This distinction reflects the moment in which the instrument plays its role. They are divided into *ex ante* and *ex post* instruments to prevent (supranational regulation and supervision/surveillance) and to manage (burden-sharing arrangements, rescue and last resort measures) risks or shocks. As Figure 3.1 and this section show, normative instruments for the attainment of financial stability are identifiable in the new measures to reinforce the EMU as well as to establish the EBU. The practical importance of these two frameworks will be examined in details in the subsequent chapters of this book.

Figure 3.1 The Normative Instruments of Supranational Financial Stability in EU Law and Policy

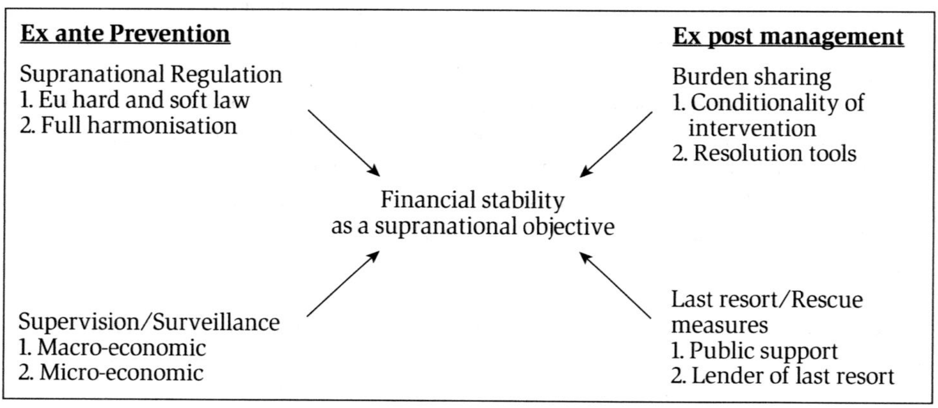

This section is structured in two parts. The first part looks at the *ex ante* prevention instruments for supranational financial stability (section [A]) and identifies the two instruments of supranational regulation and supervision/surveillance. The second section provides for the *ex post* management financial stability instruments (section [B]) and looks at the burden-sharing measures and last resort/rescue measures.

[A] The *Ex Ante* Prevention Instruments for Financial Stability

This first section looks at the *ex ante* prevention instruments for financial stability. As argued earlier, financial stability shall be achieved with normative instruments conferring normative legitimacy to supranational financial stability. These instruments are driven by the precautionary principle according to which it is better to set a framework preventing and anticipating any risks or shocks that may arise.[158] This includes a cost/benefit analysis to prevent risks and shocks. In this vein, it is essential that normative instruments aim to achieve financial stability from an *ex ante* perspective before high(er) risks and/or shocks arise in Europe. This part looks at supranational regulation and supervision/surveillance as the main preventive instruments to attain supranational financial stability.

[1] Supranational Regulation: The Power to Regulate in the EU

Regulation constitutes the first normative instrument for financial stability in EU law and policy. Black defines regulation as 'the sustained and focused attempt to alter the behaviour of others in order to address a collective issue or attain an identified end'.[159] This definition considers regulation as a normative effort to change the behaviour of other entities to address a collective problem or to achieve a purpose. The nature of regulation refers to the basic and inherent features of the rules.[160] In other words, regulation within the objective of financial stability can be considered as the normative power to adopt a set of rules having the force of law the scope of which is to regulate within their specific field of competence market forces as well as prevent and manage risks and shocks. This interpretation supports the argument that regulation, in general terms, is a preventive means for financial stability law-making.

Before entering into the specificities of EU supranational regulation, it is essential to clarify succinctly what the two main theories on regulation are and to specify that regulation, as a normative component, be considered as supranational in nature. First, the theory of regulation distinguishes between public regulation and self-regulation. Public regulation is the form of public authority intervention reducing the impact of a market participant's failure on a system as a whole. Instead, self-regulation is achieved with private market discipline, i.e., when market participants seek to minimise the negative impact of one participant on the others.[161] In this study, regulation is meant as public regulation.[162] Second, as detailed above, regulation shall be seen in its supranational dimension because of the national inadequacies of the Member States to address coherently and successfully financial stability in Europe.[163]

With the above clarifications, it is possible to assess supranational regulation as a normative component of financial stability in EU law and policy. A theoretical framework for EU supranational regulation comprises three main aspects. First, it is necessary to identify who regulates in Europe, i.e., who the European regulators are. These are intended to be the supranational institutions, bodies or agencies producing

158. On the precautionary principle in EU law *see* Craig, *supra* n. 157, 642.
159. Julia Black, *Constructing and Contesting Legitimacy and Accountability in Polycentric Regulatory Regimes* 2 Regulation & Governance 139 (2008).
160. Julia Black, *Paradoxes and Failures: 'New Governance' Techniques and the Financial Crisis*, 75 Modern Law Review 1037 (2012).
161. *See* Andenas, Chiu, *supra* n. 94, 85–86.
162. *See supra* section §3.02[C][2] for an analysis of the public and private interest approach.
163. *See supra* section §3.02[C][1] for the national inadequacy argument to provide financial stability in Europe.

regulation within a specific framework. In EU law and policy, regulators are provided in primary and secondary law. EU primary law indicates that the EU is a system based on a repartition of powers between institutions as long as the EU is given competence on the matter.[164] In this context, regulation can be adopted so long as the EU possesses competences and is attributed powers enshrined in the Treaties under the principle of conferral of power. Furthermore, the system of institutional balance provides that law-making powers be conferred to EU institutions in light of the principle of division of powers and by dividing power among EU institutions, organs and agencies.[165] As long as the powers are not conferred to the EU, Member States retain the powers to adopt regulation in their reserved domains.[166] In the international sphere, this means that in their domain of reserved sovereignty Member States may conclude international treaties among themselves in accordance with the principle of freedom to conclude treaties while respecting EU law and sincere cooperation.[167] Second, it is important to determine to what extent supranational regulation can be adopted. As held earlier, the EU operates on the basis of the conferred powers granted in the Treaties to the EU and its institutions by the Member States. The EU can adopt supranational legal acts only so long as it possesses the required powers and uses the appropriate legal bases. In this sense, EU regulators shall respect the principles of subsidiarity and proportionality[168] and adopt legal acts that have the sound legal basis. Third, it needs to be determined who the addressees of regulation are i.e., the entities towards which regulation is intended to apply. Regulation can be of general application or the addressees may be Member States or private entities - natural or legal persons.

As it will be analysed in details in the subsequent chapters of this study, two paradigms constitute the essence of regulation as the supranational normative instrument for financial stability in EU law and policy: hard/soft law distinction and harmonisation.

[a] Hard Law Versus Soft Law

Supranational EU regulation can be hard law and soft law.[169] Hard law is meant to be binding law upon the addressees or to have a general binding and enforceable nature. Hard law sources for regulation are indicated in primary law and secondary EU law. The EU Treaties contain the necessary provisions for the adoption of hard law rules. In particular, legal bases serve as the legal 'justification' for the adoption of hard law measures. Article 288 TFEU provides for the list of binding EU acts: regulations, directives and decisions. The Treaty of Lisbon clarified the power to adopt legislative

164. *See* Art. 5(1) TEU and the system of EU competences in Arts 2–6 TFEU.
165. Art. 13(2) TEU.
166. Art. 4(1) TEU.
167. Art. 4(3) TEU. *See also Pringle* as discussed in Chapter 5 section §5.04[C].
168. *See* Protocol on the application of the Principles of Subsidiarity and Proportionality, OJ C310/207.
169. Other forms of regulation such as self-regulation are outside the scope of the analysis as they are deemed not to be essential normative instruments for supranational financial stability.

act under the ordinary or special legislative procedures. Furthermore, EU institutions can adopt legislative and non-legislative acts.[170] This constitutes a procedural difference clarifying the way in which an act is adopted under EU law.

In the context of the development of supranational financial stability in Europe, regulation is composed of both legislative and non-legislative EU acts. The former are directives, regulations and decisions adopted following a legislative procedure while the latter are regulations and decisions adopted in the form of delegated or implementing acts. Directives and regulations adopted under a legislative procedure are the main instruments to adopt EU secondary law and policy. The main difference between directives, on the one hand, and regulations and decisions, on the other, is the need for directives to be transposed into national law while regulations and decisions are directly applicable to the addresses and in national legal systems. The use of regulations or decisions has a strong impact as a means of supranational regulation. This is because regulations and decisions are directly applicable and do not require, as a rule, any implementing measures by the Member States.[171] EU regulations and decisions are directly enforceable and applicable. The binding force of these acts at the supranational level strongly supports the supranational dimension of financial stability in EU law and policy.

Conversely, the use of directives is by definition an expression of limited intervention of supranational regulation. This is because directives are binding 'as to the result to be achieved' but leave the Member States the choice of 'form and methods'. Therefore, whilst directives bring about the necessary changes in national laws, they respect as far as possible the national legal systems, with their own conceptions, terminology and peculiarities and they have direct effect only under certain circumstances. The distinction between the CRR and the CRD is a clear example in this sense.[172] The CRR contains rules directly applicable in Member States while the CRD requires the implementation into national law of supranational provisions in banking matters. An open problem on the use of EU directives is that determining the scope of their implementation at the national law may be unclear.

The Lisbon Treaty has introduced also the categories of delegated and implementing acts in the forms of regulations and decisions.[173] These acts are adopted when a delegation from the European legislators – the European Parliament and the Council – has taken place or when implementing aspects of a general act are to be adopted.

Differently from hard law, soft law acts, adopted by EU institutions, agencies and organs, are different instruments for supranational regulation. EU institutions, agencies and organs have adopted a vast number of soft law instruments in the form of opinions, recommendations, guidelines or communications in order to support and complement EU hard law measures. Soft law measures have played an increasingly

170. On the concept of legislative and non-legislative act, *see* Jürgen Bast, *New Categories of Acts after the Lisbon Reform: Dynamics of Parlamentarization in EU Law*, 49 Common Market Law Review 885 (2012).
171. Nonetheless, it is still possible that regulations contain options for Member States.
172. *See* Chapter 6 section §6.03[C] for assessment of the CRR/CRDIV.
173. Arts 290 and 291 TFEU. *See* Paul Craig, *Delegated Acts, Implementing Acts and the New Comitology Regulation*, 36 European Law Review 671 (2011).

important role as normative instruments for regulation in EU law and policy. They represent an important alternative to hard law regulation in the internal market. Soft law has been defined as:

> [r]ules of conduct that are laid down in instruments which have not been attributed legally binding force as such, but nevertheless may have certain (indirect) legal effects, and that are aimed at and may produce practical effects.[174]

In EU law, Article 288 TFEU indicates that recommendations and opinions are soft law measures. There are, however, other 'instruments' such as guidelines, technical standards, resolutions, statements and policies that are equally considered as EU soft law tool. The financial crisis has shown the developing importance of soft law measures, especially as part of renewed efforts to adopt EU supranational regulation. There are two major examples of such development in EU law and policy. First, EU institutions and agencies have increasingly relied on the adoption of soft law measures to regulate the internal market. This is particularly the case of the European System of Financial Supervisors (ESFS) that adopts soft law measures to address important aspects of financial markets.[175] Second, the role of soft law is in place also in the context of the EMU where EU institutions have adopted or may adopt soft law measures such as recommendations and opinions to address concerns regarding Member States' economic policy measures.

[b] Full Harmonisation as a Tool of Supranational Regulation

Harmonisation is an essential tool in EU law and policy that shows to what extent supranational regulation develops as a normative instrument for supranational financial stability. Harmonisation is a typical feature of the EU integration process and it consists in replacing the multiple and divergent national rules with a single EU rule.[176] This is justified when a specific market failure needs to be corrected beyond the national borders and in order to generate welfare.[177]

The desired level of harmonisation in EU law and policy has been subject to extensive scholarship.[178] Harmonisation has been considered both in the negative and in the positive sense.[179] Negative harmonisation relates to the interpretation given by the ECJ as a way to shape the internal market and to remove trade barriers between Member States. This is achieved by judicial interpretation favourable to the free

174. Linda Senden, *Soft Law in European Community Law*, 112 (Hart Publishing 2004).
175. *See* Eilis Ferran & Kern Alexander, *Can Soft Law Bodies Be Effective? The Special Case of the European Systemic Risk Board*, 35 European Law Review 751 (2010).
176. Catherine Barnard, *The Substantive Law of the EU*, 558 (Oxford University Press 2016).
177. Moloney *supra* n. 1, 19.
178. *See*, among others, Piet Slot, *Harmonisation*, 21 European Law Review 378 (1996); Stephen Weatherill, *The Limits of Legislative Harmonisation Ten Years After Tobacco Advertising: How the Court's Case Law Has Become a 'Drafting Guide'*, 12 German Law Journal 827 (2011); Jukka Snell, *The Internal Market and the Philosophies of Market Integration* in Catherine Barnard, Steve Peers (eds), *European Union Law*, 315 (Oxford University Press 2014).
179. *See* Isidora Maletic, *The Law and Policy of Harmonisation in Europe's Internal Market*, 7 (Edward Elgar 2013).

movement rules in the EU Treaties. Conversely, positive harmonisation refers to the introduction of supranational legal acts for the establishment and integration of the EU internal market. In EU law, positive harmonisation can take place by making use of the EU Treaty provisions under Articles 114 and 115 TFEU. These allow the adoption of EU supranational rules for the harmonisation of the internal market. In particular, Article 114 TFEU enables the EU to adopt legislative measures for the effective establishment and functioning of the internal market. In the case of positive harmonisation, various types of harmonisation techniques have developed. The level of positive harmonisation varies from a minimum level to a full degree of harmonisation in a specific sector. The different degrees of harmonisation that may be applied to the European financial system reveal that such process exerts an important influence in centralising rules in Europe.

In particular, the distinction between maximum and minimum harmonisation is relevant. Maximum harmonisation is defined as the technique to adopt EU supranational measures that, ideally, leave no more options or discretions to Member States or their competent authorities at the national level. Differently, minimum harmonisation provides for a minimum set of supranational EU rules allowing Member States to adopt more stringent, detailed and differentiated measures at the national level. Harmonisation plays an essential role in the European financial system in order to make uniform rules and to hedge against financial risks in an integrated manner. In the EU, financial markets have historically developed following a minimum harmonisation approach. More recently and following the financial crisis in Europe, regulatory efforts have shown that EU regulators have followed the maximum harmonisation paradigm to regulate financial markets.

While minimum harmonisation is a technique used in cases where there is no common agreement for the adoption of a supranational legal norm and allows for national flexibilities, it is submitted that only maximum harmonisation can 'maximise' supranational financial stability. Given the important developments in the EMU and the EBU, minimum harmonisation does not seem the appropriate instrument in areas at the heart of the European integration process.[180] The attainment of financial stability as a supranational objective can only be validly pursued if EU supranational rules exist and no differential approach is adopted at the national level. Divergent rules at the national level regarding various aspects still reveal an uneven treatment. Differential national approaches may also generate excessive regional specificities that could distort the principle of equal treatment at the supranational level.

The case of maximum harmonisation is clear in the banking sector. The creation of a single rulebook in banking shows that harmonisation is a central aspect of the new banking regulatory space. The CRR/CRD package contains, among others, rules on capital, liquidity, large exposures and corporate governance that are intended to apply in all Member States as regards the conduct of prudential activities of credit institutions in the internal market. However, especially the provisions contained in the CRDIV are

180. Michael Dougan, *Minimum Harmonisation and the Internal Market*, 37 Common Market Law Review 860 (2000).

subject to different degrees of harmonisation that jeopardise the creation of a supranational level-playing field for supranational EU regulation. Similarly, the Bank Recovery and Resolution Directive (BRRD), the Deposit Guarantee Scheme (DGS) directive apply a minimum harmonisation paradigm in resolution and deposit guarantees at European level. This indicates that the absence of maximum harmonisation on all banking rules in the context of the EU single rulebook remains problematic. Supranational legal instruments still contain many exceptions and provisions allowing for national discretions in banking regulation. Member States are still free to adopt exceptions or more stringent rules that may jeopardise the objective of harmonisation as a tool for supranational regulation. This is usually the consequence of a minimum harmonisation approach through the adoption of EU directives, which may also lead to cases of gold-plating. Recently, the ECB has adopted a regulation harmonising certain options and discretions in EU law – the CRR – and applied by competent authorities on prudential requirements for credit institutions.[181] This effort reveals that, in the exercise of supranational tasks and powers, rules shall be uniformly applied in a given framework.

In sum, harmonisation is an essential paradigm for supranational financial stability in Europe that derives from the power to regulate the internal market in a supranational fashion. Maximum harmonisation has four main advantages. First, it creates legal certainty on the rules to apply in a specific case by adopting a European supranational approach to the regulation of rules. Second, it generates integration as it aims to create rules that are applicable in the internal market alike while avoiding the risks of fragmentation or unnecessary regulatory competition. Third, it orientates the behaviours of the regulated entities by establishing common supranational rules in the internal market. This serves to have clarity as to the application of the rules in a specific case. Fourth, it creates the conditions for supranational enforcement and compliance of a set of rules at the European level. Harmonisation can achieve supranational financial stability so long as it does not provide for national discretions and flexibilities that may jeopardise its objective. The current EU regulatory framework still shows some areas where, also in cases of EU regulations, national discretions and flexibilities are present and generate fragmentation.

[2] Supervision/Surveillance

Supervision/surveillance is the second preventive normative instrument for supranational financial stability in Europe. The term refers to the exercise of monitoring and control of the addressees of the rules adopted through regulation. In Europe, literature argues that the nature of supervision/surveillance remains contested as its distinction

181. *See* Regulation (EU) 2016/445 of the ECB of 14 March 2016 on the exercise of options and discretions available in Union law (ECB/2016/4), OJ L 78, 24.3.2016.

from regulation is not clearly spelled out.[182] Some argue that regulation and supervision are part of the same process.[183] Others stress that regulation and supervision are intertwined with each other but are different in nature.[184] For the purpose of this book, it is argued that surveillance/supervision plays an autonomous function from regulation. Furthermore, the words 'supervision' and 'surveillance' are different: the former relates to constant monitoring and control while the latter has a softer connotation and refers to close observation. This is clear in distinguishing between the ECB supervision over credit institutions in the EBU and the Commission surveillance over Member States' economic policies in economic governance.

Four elements characterise supervision/surveillance: who, how and whom to supervise. The first question relates to the identification of the desirable supervisor. Supervisor shall possess the powers to exercise control or at least close observation over supervised entities. In Europe, the power to supervise varies according to the type of supervision. In certain sectors, supranational supervision has been conferred to EU institutions or agencies. For instance, the ECB is the supervisor of significant credit institutions in the euro area, or the ESMA supervises credit rating agencies in the EU. Second, the means of supervision refers to the nature of supervision and powers that a supervisor may exercise. These are usually indicated in the founding acts of the supervisor and may have different forms: the supervision on the exercise of activities, day-to-day supervision, the application of administrative penalties or sanctions, instructions and recommendations to national supervisors or to the addressees. At the European level, supervision over entities is conferred to EU institutions or agencies to different degrees depending on the nature of supervision or the type of powers. The addressees of supervision/surveillance can potentially be every entity operating in the internal market framework. The supervisees are usually market players – an undertaking, an industry operator, a company – which operate in a specific framework or can also be directly the Member States as the surveilled entities.

The creation of supranational supervision/surveillance frameworks is essential for supranational financial stability. Supervision/surveillance generates legal certainty by providing the appropriate supervision over the supervisees/surveilled entity. Furthermore, robust supervision/surveillance allows respect of the rules and the application of regulation by the addressees uniformly in a given system. Moreover, supranational supervision/surveillance guarantees an approach that is not biased by national politics and influence. At this stage, it is important to differentiate the supervision/surveillance models in Europe between a macro- and a micro-economic paradigm.

182. Eddy Wymeersch, *The Future of Financial Regulation and Supervision in Europe*, 42 Common Market Law Review 987–988 (2005).
183. *See* Eilis Ferran, *Understanding the New Institutional Architecture of EU Financial Market Supervision* in Eddy Wymeersch, Klaus Hopt, Guido Ferrarini (eds), *Financial Regulation and Supervision. A Post-Crisis Analysis*, 140 (Oxford University Press 2012).
184. *See* Lastra *supra* n. 12, 112, 117.

[a] *Macro-Economic Supervision/Surveillance*

The level of macro-economic supervision refers to the analysis of trends and imbalances in the financial system as a whole with specific attention to systemic risk. In the context of this book, it is argued that the need to conduct macro-economic supervision/surveillance applies both to the supervision of sovereigns in Europe and to the supervision of the financial system as a whole. This is because shocks and risks affecting sovereigns in Europe have repercussions that are systemically relevant in the macro-dimension.

The debate on the role of macro-economic supervision has developed only as of the financial crisis. While the macro-economic dimension of surveillance of Member State finances has been loosely provided in the Maastricht Treaty Chapter on economic policy, there has been no real effort to develop a macro-prudential system to assess the financial system as a whole. In 2001, the ECB identified macro-prudential supervision as:

> all activities aimed at monitoring the exposure to systemic risk and at identifying potential threats to stability arising from macroeconomic or financial market developments, and from market infrastructures.[185]

While the ECB stressed the role for macro-prudential supervision, Europe did not provide for an institutional system for macro-prudential supervision of financial institutions before the financial crisis. This problem has been partially solved in the post-crisis environment. The development of a macro-economic framework for surveillance/supervision has been elaborated both for Member State finances and for the financial system as a whole. As regards Member State finances, new constitutional reforms, which will be discussed in subsequent chapters of this book, have restructured the loose economic policy control established in the Maastricht Treaty. In particular, the European Semester, the Six Pack, the Two Pack and the TSCG go in the direction of strengthening the Maastricht supranational macro-economic surveillance framework. At the same time, the supranational dimension of macro-economic supervision/surveillance over Member States is not particularly strong in a normal scenario, as the EU institutions do not possess, at present, powers to dismiss national budgets or to impose tax collection on behalf of the Member States. However, a situation of stronger macro-economic supervision/surveillance exists in the context of Member States subject to macro-economic adjustment programmes. EU institutions can play a considerable role in macro-economic supervision/surveillance vis-à-vis Member States in financial difficulties.

As regards the financial system as a whole, some important reforms to strengthen supranational macro-prudential supervision have taken place. The de Larosière Report

185. ECB, *The Role of Central Banks in Prudential Supervision* (2001) at https://www.ecb.europa.eu/pub/pdf/other/prudentialsupcbrole_en.pdf 3 (accessed 31 December 2016). *See also* ECB, *Financial Stability Review* 136 (2014).

stressed the absence of macro-prudential supervision in Europe.[186] The follow-up reforms brought to the creation of the ESRB which, as a general mandate:

> shall be responsible for the macro-prudential supervision of the financial system within the Union in order to contribute to the prevention or mitigation of systemic risks to financial stability in the Union (...).[187]

However, the absence of legal personality and of legally binding powers does not entirely solve the problem of a lack of strong supranational macro-prudential supervisor in Europe.[188] At the same time, the ECB has been conferred also some macro-prudential powers in the SSM which may be exercised at supranational level.[189] This has recently suggested further reflections at the supranational level to reinforce the macro-economic supervision/surveillance over the financial system.[190] This is justified by the need to monitor the resilience of the macro-economic system against systemic risks and strengthen the supranational powers to address such risks.

In sum, the macro-economic supervision/surveillance dimension is related to the control of the financial system with an analysis of the main trends affecting the economy as a whole. This is based on the exercise of powers to prevent systemic shocks or risks affecting financial stability. At present, the level of supranational macro-economic supervision/surveillance is still underdeveloped in the debate on supranational financial stability in Europe. Nonetheless, it can be concluded that macro-economic supervision/surveillance is progressively acquiring a supranational dimension.

[b] Micro-Economic Supervision/Surveillance

The micro-economic paradigm refers to the micro-prudential supervision over single market operators or single entities. Already in 2001, the ECB identified micro-prudential supervision as including:

> all on and off-site surveillance of the safety and soundness of individual institutions, aiming in particular at the protection of depositors and other retail creditors.[191]

The financial crisis has revealed the micro-economic dimension as a new field of supranational developments. The micro-economic dimension is predominantly identified as the micro-prudential supervision of financial market operators. In this sense, the 2014 ECB Financial Stability Report identified the focus of micro-prudential supervision in the safeguard individual financial institutions from idiosyncratic risks

186. de Larosière *supra* n. 4, 39–40.
187. Regulation 1092/2010, Art. 3(1).
188. Andenas, Chiu, *supra* n. 94, 441.
189. *See* Chapter 7 for the role of the ECB as the new prudential supervisor in the SSM.
190. *See* European Commission, *Review of the EU macro-prudential policy framework*, 2016 Consultation document at http://ec.europa.eu/finance/consultations/2016/macroprudential-framework/docs/consultation-document_en.pdf (last accessed 31 December 2016).
191. ECB, *The Role of Central Banks in Prudential Supervision*, 3.

and in their prevention from taking too much risk.[192] The most common form of supervision is that of the Commission which ensures the application of EU law through its role as the guardian of the Treaties.[193] For instance, this supervision is exercised by controlling the correct implementation of EU law in the Member States or through cartel or merger control.

The de Larosière Report stressed that the level of micro-prudential supervision was not sufficiently stringent at European level before the financial crisis in Europe mainly for a lack of coordination between supervisors and resources.[194] The proposal to upgrade the system of micro-prudential supervision was put forward with the establishment of European Supervisory Authorities (ESAs) in the banking, the securities and the occupational pension sectors. However, this reform did not reconfigure the supranational micro-economic paradigm as the day-to-day supervision of financial markets and financial institutions remained at the national level.[195] More recently, the risks in financial stability have promoted an important reconfiguration on the role of central banking in conducting micro-prudential supervision. The ECB has been conferred the unprecedented powers to supervise credit institutions in the SSM as from 2014.[196] Before the financial crisis, Padoa-Schioppa was the strongest advocate in support of supranational micro-prudential supervision.[197] Similarly, Schoenmaker called for the exercise of prudential supervision at the supranational level and has developed the 'financial trilemma'. He showed that the objectives of stable financial system, integrated financial markets and national financial supervision are inconsistent in nature.[198] This suggested the need for supranational micro-prudential supervisory arrangements that have now been implemented in the SSM reform. This reform, as part of the EBU, shows that micro-prudential supervision of credit institutions has acquired central importance in the debate on supranational financial stability. The analysis here has shown that supranational micro-economic supervision/surveillance has gained importance in the recent years. The micro-level of supervision plays a strong role in avoiding individual risks and shocks that can jeopardise supranational financial stability.

[B] The *Ex Post* Management Instruments for Financial Stability

The absence of financial stability raises problems. This is because there may be a situation in which financial crises generate risks or shocks that may lead to the collapse of the entire system. Therefore, normative instruments allowing the financial system as a whole to react in a positive way to strong shocks or to risks are essential. For this

192. ECB, *Financial Stability Review* 136 (2014).
193. Art. 17(1) TEU.
194. *See* de Larosière, *supra* n. 4, 41.
195. Donato Masciandaro & Marc Quintyn, *Regulating the Regulators: The Changing Face of Financial Supervision Architectures before and after the Crisis*, 6 European Company Law 191–192 (2009).
196. *See* Chapter 7 for the analysis of the SSM.
197. Tommaso Padoa-Schioppa, *EMU and Banking Supervision*, 2 International Finance 307 (1999).
198. Dirk Schoenmaker, *Financial Supervision: From National to European?*, Financial and Monetary Studies 10 (2003).

purpose, a second group of normative instruments for supranational financial stability are those intended to provide a regulatory solution after a situation of shocks and risks materialises and is able to jeopardise the attainment of financial stability. These are *ex post* measures typically intended to counteract the negative effects that the absence of financial stability might have for Europe. These are burden-sharing arrangements (subsection [1]) and last resort/rescue measures (subsection [2]).

[1] Burden-Sharing Arrangements

Burden-sharing is the main instrument to manage *ex post* risks and shocks to (re-)achieve supranational financial stability in Europe. Burden-sharing arrangements are mechanisms whereby the costs to provide a public good such as supranational financial stability are shared between different stakeholders, also taking into account their past behaviours.[199] Burden-sharing is thus an essential instrument to force the involvement of entities in the increase of shocks and risks or, in other words, to allow other entities to 'pay the costs' of financial in-stability. In a nutshell, burden-sharing is aimed to allocate the burden of failures among the players responsible for such failures.

At present, it seems that there is no regulatory definition of burden-sharing in EU law and policy. The 2013 Banking Communication of the EU Commission on State aid to banks highlights that a certain level of loss-absorption measures in the form of burden-sharing by those who invested in a bank needs to be made before State aid is granted.[200] In the recent *Kotnik* judgment,[201] the ECJ had the opportunity to establish what the purpose of burden-sharing measures is. The judgment, which will be analysed in a subsequent chapter,[202] states that burden-sharing measures are 'measures (…) to restore the financial position of credit institutions and to overcome their capital shortfall, [whose purpose] is to preserve or re-establish the financial situation of a credit institution'.[203] Hence, according to the ECJ, burden-sharing measures are intended to restore the situation of a financially viable institution. In legal terms, the function of burden-sharing is to provide a framework whereby losses arising from a failure are allocated among different stakeholders through some collective procedures.[204]

Against this background, three questions arise: what type of burden-sharing measures exist, who may contribute to burden-sharing measures and whether a specific form of burden-sharing is necessary for supranational financial stability in Europe. As regards the nature of burden-sharing measures, these may be conceived as public and/or private solutions. Public solutions provide for the use of statutory rules

199. *See* Seraina Grünewald, *The Resolution of Cross-Border Banking Crises in the European Union*, 52 (Kluwer Law International 2014).
200. Communication from the Commission on the application, from 1 August 2013, of State aid rules to support measures in favour of banks in the context of the financial crisis ('Banking Communication'), 2013/C 216/01, paras 15 and 16.
201. Case C-526/14 *Kotnik and Others* ECLI:EU:C:2016:570.
202. *See* Chapter 8 section §8.02[B].
203. Case C-526/14 *Kotnik*, para. 108.
204. Grünewald, *supra* n. 199, 52.

or public funds to allow burden-sharing. Allocation of burden-sharing may take place exclusively with private resources or in conjunction with public solutions. The existence of a framework for conditional state support measures, the new regulatory framework of the BRRD and the Single Resolution Mechanism (SRM) as well as the new DGS Directive set some rules on burden-sharing. These are intended to solve crises that may have an impact for financial stability in Europe by the use of regulatory instruments to allocate and absorb market failures and losses among stakeholders, such as imposing restructuring measures or applying resolution tools or providing financing arrangements.

The second question is the identification of who may contribute to burden-sharing measures. Based on the type of intervention there may be three situations. First, there may be a completely internalised burden-sharing measure that is exclusively affecting the entity as being the primary cause of shocks and risks jeopardising financial stability. This is what should optimally happen in the context of crisis affecting individual market operators or sovereigns. Internalising completely the costs may result in affecting also other entities such as shareholders and creditors as being those having invested in the entity. Second, there may be the situation in which other entities of private or public nature contribute together with the entity having caused shocks and risks jeopardising financial stability. This is what usually would happen in the case where internalised costs are coupled with resolution financing measures or the use of DGSs or even with public contributions. These external interventions are usually accompanied with conditionality of intervention such as restructuring measures imposed on the entity having caused risks or shocks affecting financial stability. Third, there may be a situation in which only other entities contribute to the risks and shocks that have been caused by the entity at stake. This intervention usually takes the form of loans, credit lines or recapitalisation made by private or public entities. This is a case imposing a strong degree of conditionality of intervention and which strongly affects the entity having caused shocks or risks jeopardising financial stability. For instance, the macro-economic adjustment programmes require that the beneficiary Member State implements burden-sharing measures such as cutting public costs or raising taxes.

Third, despite the developing nature of burden-sharing arrangements in Europe, the question remains whether supranational financial stability in Europe requires a particular form of burden-sharing. It is difficult to ascertain the specific relationship between burden-sharing and financial stability. This is because burden-sharing may take place with recourse to the principle of conditionality in intervention and/or with mechanisms that let the entity pay internally the costs of losses, while also other entities may have to pay certain costs. In this situation, burden-sharing shall be fully and primarily suffered by the entity itself and, only if a viable solution is not possible, other private sources should intervene. The role of publicly funded external sources shall be limited to the minimum possible and be adopted only in special circumstances and with adequate burden-sharing measures. This suggests that the preferable option for the treatment of burden-sharing is a fully internalised solution with no involvement of publicly funded resources. Nevertheless, such approach is less viable for sovereigns where the risk of default, especially in a single currency, may require the intervention of external public sources to support an ailing Member State. Similarly, public sources may still be used by Member States to support ailing institutions in accordance with the State aid regime in Europe.[205]

Overall, the development of burden-sharing arrangements is an essential *ex post* management instrument to attain supranational financial stability. Burden-sharing entails the need to let the entity responsible for risks or shocks pay its own costs. However, burden-sharing arrangements are still at an early stage of development in Europe. The too-big-to-fail doctrine and the need to avoid sovereign restructuring suggest that burden-sharing measures can still be limited or compensated by external sources, especially public funding. In perspective, the normative instruments of supranational regulation and supervision/surveillance should avoid at any costs the use of burden-sharing measures.

[2] Last Resort/Rescue Measures

The use of last resort or rescue measures towards public or private supervised/surveilled entities is the *ultima ratio* normative instrument for supranational financial stability. Last resort/rescue mechanisms can be identified in frameworks for the bailout of public or private entities. As held in the previous section, last resort/rescue measures are not necessarily stand-alone measures, but they can be combined with burden-sharing measures, especially when there are different ways to manage *ex post* shocks and risks to attain supranational financial stability.

The power to rescue has traditionally been exercised by national public authorities. In particular, there are two main players for rescue. The former are the Member States which may decide to make use of their public finances to save entities in distress through State aids.[206] The latter are international institutions, in particular the IMF, and now the ESM, which are given the power to provide loans to its members in order to safeguard the sovereigns' credit liability.[207] The nature of the power to rescue consists in the use of funds to finance entities. Rescue measures usually take the form of loans or credit lines or guarantees. The addressees of rescue powers may consist in both public and private entities. A particular category of rescue measures is represented by the LOLR function which can be used in particular circumstances, i.e., when it is not possible to use any other measures and the LOLR is the last resort source of funding to rescue an entity.

The existence of rescue mechanisms was an until-recently neglected normative component of financial stability. The financial crisis has demonstrated that rescue measures are important for three main reasons. First, they establish safety nets that are essential for the conduct of activities in a normal situation. Second, they confer

205. *See* Chapter 8 section §8.02[B] for an analysis of the State aid regime in the banking sector.
206. *See Ibid.*
207. *See* Chapter 5 section §5.04 for an analysis of the ESM as the intergovernmental euro area 'sovereign fund'.

confidence to the market, individuals and the public powers as they allow, albeit as an *ultima ratio*, financial stability to be safeguarded. Third, they allow some market forces to be saved without generating excessive panic, bank runs or further systemic risks. Until recently, purely national or international responses were the main rescue instruments in Europe. This is because traditionally EU primary law does not include a specific competence or certain powers to rescue entities. Rather it provides for limitations to rescue/resolve entities as provided in Articles 123 and 125 TFEU.

The financial crisis has witnessed that Europe, and in particular the euro area, lacks a clear institutional mandate for European rescue measures or LOLR function.[208] Following the sovereign debt crisis, a new supranational role as LOLR and some new structural rules on rescue measures have been developed.[209] This is in particular the case of instruments aimed to support illiquid but solvent credit institutions to be financed[210] or to provide primary market or secondary market facilities to sovereigns.[211] Two European institutional players come into question.

First, it could be argued that the ECB may be considered as de facto LOLR in the euro area in the pursuit of supranational financial stability. This role could be exercised through Emergency Liquidity Assistance (ELA) to financial institutions or through OMTs to sovereigns. While there is no direct reference in the Treaties to a role that the ECB should play as LOLR, one non-basic task of the ECB suggests that the ECB may acquire a de facto role of LOLR in Europe in crisis times: the contributing role in stability of the financial system.[212] This means that the interventionist role of the ECB may be in the direction of an extensive interpretation of this non-basic task of the ECB.[213] This could also be the case for ELAs or OMTs. However, the current ECB stance is that ELA remains a national task[214] and that the OMTs is a monetary policy instrument firmly grounded on the ECB price stability mandate as also confirmed in the *Gauweiler* judgment.[215]

Second, together with the ECB having an LOLR, the creation of a supranational fiscal backstop for market operators and sovereigns to complete the EBU indicates that also the ESM could play a major role as LOLR. This is because the ESM is already a fund for the financial assistance of euro area Member States in financial difficulties. Moreover, the explicit conferral to the ESM of the role as fiscal backstop in the EBU would reinforce the supranational dimension of an LOLR in Europe. This aspect would need to be clarified in future.[216]

---

208. On the debate on LOLR, *see* Lastra *supra* n. 12, 113–124 and doctrine quoted therein.
209. *See also* Mads Andenas, *Harmonising and Regulating Financial Markets*, in Mads Andenas, Camilla Andersens (eds), *Theory and Practice of Harmonisation*, 22 (Edward Elgar 2011).
210. *See* Armin Steinbach, *The Lender of Last Resort in the Eurozone*, 53 Common Market Law Review 361 (2016).
211. ESM Treaty, Arts 17 and 18.
212. Art. 127(5) TFEU.
213. Willem Buiter & Ebrahim Rahbari, *The European Central Bank as Lender of Last Resort for Sovereigns in the Eurozone*, 50 Journal of Common Market Studies 32–33 (2012).
214. *See* ECB website, ELA page at https://www.ecb.europa.eu/mopo/ela/html/index.en.html (accessed 31 December 2016).
215. *See* Case C-62/14 *Peter Gauweiler and others*, para. 80.
216. *See* Chapter 8 section §8.05[A] for the consideration of the ESM as the fiscal backstop in the EBU.

To conclude, this section has demonstrated that also the last resort/rescue measures play an important role for supranational financial stability in EU law and policy. This is because these measures guarantee that certain *ultima ratio* instruments are capable of avoiding risks or shocks that can jeopardise or even compromise supranational financial stability. In Europe the LOLR assumes a peculiar role in this sense. However, in the absence of a clear determination of the LOLR in Europe at present, supranational financial stability still remains incomplete.

§3.04 SUPRANATIONAL FINANCIAL STABILITY AS THE MAIN DRIVER OF REFORM TO THE EU LEGAL FRAMEWORK

Having completed the analysis of the normative instruments for supranational financial stability as a foundational objective in EU law and policy, the final part of this chapter looks at the two main areas where the objective of financial stability has been a major driver for reform and on which this study concentrates. These are the EMU reform (section [A]) and the creation of the EBU (section [B]).

[A] Financial Stability and the Reinforced EMU

The EMU reform is a reaction to the consequences of the financial crisis. The financial crisis required a redefinition of the role of economic governance, monetary policy and financial assistance mechanisms in the EMU project. The major constitutional and institutional reforms to reinforce the EMU have been triggered by the increasingly problematic fiscal sustainability of some Member States as well as by the turbulences of sovereign financial markets as of 2010. These have been motivated by the relevant risks caused by the absence of a normative framework for financial stability. As put by Chiti and Teixeira, the new EMU has undergone an essential development as:

> the original EMU as a community of benefits gradually turns into a more complex community with some forms of risk-sharing mechanisms, with a gradual removal of the fiscal sovereignty of Member States, and oriented to the values of solidarity and loyalty among Member States.[217]

Europe, and in particular the euro area, have been driven by the need to change the existing rules on economic governance and to provide financial assistance to Member States in financial distress. Public finances of euro area Member States have suffered from the increasingly worrisome vicious circle between banks and sovereigns. Meanwhile certain Member States required financial assistance. This has necessitated major changes in the EMU framework and has brought a redefinition of targets, institutions and powers at the supranational level. While the lack of strong supranational powers to control fiscal policies and to sustain public finances has been a major issue, the EU institutions have provided at various times a forum of discussion for reforms to the pre-crisis EMU legal framework. The need for immediate assistance to

217. Chiti, Teixeira *supra* n. 2, 699.

Member States in financial difficulties has prompted the establishment of transitional, and then permanent, financial assistance mechanisms. At the same time, the ECB has exercised its price stability mandate with unprecedented monetary policy measures in order to strengthen the monetary policy transmission system in the euro area.

At the same time, the Heads of State and Government and the European Council published reform proposals at various meetings aiming at reforming the existing EMU legal framework. As the following chapters will show, these have then taken the form of new intergovernmental instruments for the reinforcement of the EMU as well as new secondary EU legislation measures. In 2012, the Van Rompuy Report included proposals to the effective refinement of the EMU.[218] The Commission has backed the Van Rompuy Report with a Blueprint providing institutional reflections on the need to deepen EMU reforms.[219] More recently, the adoption of the Five Presidents' report in 2015 is a more recent – yet timid – attempt to provide further political momentum for the strengthening of the EMU.[220]

Against this background, this study contends that the main driver of the EMU reform is the need to attain supranational financial stability in Europe in order to strengthen the system of supranational economic surveillance, provide financial assistance to sovereigns if needed and generate adequate incentives to financial markets and the real economy. Within this picture, financial stability is at the centre of the reform process to establish the EMU. While the reinforcement of the EMU shows limitations and inconsistencies, the need to achieve supranational financial stability as a new foundational objective of the EMU has played a major role in the EMU reform processes.

[B] Financial Stability and the EBU

The EBU is the second area where supranational financial stability has driven reform. The EBU has been triggered by the deepening of the financial crisis in 2012 when systemic problems arose both in the banking system and in fiscal and economic sustainability of sovereigns.[221] In particular, the euro area revealed that the costs of public bank rescues and the vicious circle between the banking system and sovereigns

218. Hermann Van Rompuy, *Towards a Genuine Economic and Monetary Union*, Report by the President of the European Council in close collaboration with the President of the European Commission, the President of the Eurogroup, and the President of the ECB, 5 December 2012 at www.consilium.europa.eu/uedocs/cms_data/docs/pressdata/en/ec/134069.pdf (accessed 31 December 2016).
219. European Commission, *A blueprint for a deep and genuine Economic and Monetary Union: Launching the European Debate*, COM(2012)777 final.
220. Five Presidents' Report, 22 June 2015 at http://ec.europa.eu/priorities/economic-monetary-union/docs/5-presidents-report_en.pdf (accessed 31 December 2016).
221. Rishi Goyal et al., *A Banking Union for the Euro Area*, IMF SDN/13/01 7 (2013). *See also* generally Danny Busch & Guido Ferrarini, *European Banking Union* (Oxford University Press 2015).

brought to the euro-area a new phase of the sovereign debt crisis.[222] While the ECB announced the OMT programme in July 2012 and financial assistance programme for the financial sector was agreed for Spain in June 2012, the European Council and the Eurogroup formation agreed in June 2012 to establish a centralised system of banking supervision and resolution which would break the vicious circle between failing banks and sovereigns and the euro area in general.[223] Subsequently, the Commission published a 'roadmap' in September 2012 on the reform agenda to establish the EBU as a new institutional and substantive framework with the SSM, a common system of deposit guarantees and an integrated crisis management framework.[224] In between 2013 and 2016, the SSM and the SRM were established as the two main pillars of the EBU.[225] Most recently in November 2015, the Commission has adopted a Communication on the completion of the EBU.[226] Furthermore, it has unveiled a plan for the completion of the EBU in particular with the proposal to create the EDIS as a supranational DGS arrangement, and urging the establishment of bridge-financing measures for resolution and a common fiscal backstop as last resort.[227]

As put by Moloney, the EBU framework is a legal matrix:

> which is composed of multiple interlinked components which have different Treaty bases and which operate in the internal market and the euro area to differing extents.[228]

These legal acts are of diverse nature and content. It is clear that the building block of the EBU are the SSM, the SRM, and their founding legal instruments and now recently the proposed EDIS. At the same time, the single rulebook on banking regulation complements the EBU. All these aspects of the EBU reforms express to various degrees a revolutionary reform to the pre-crisis system of banking regulation and supervision. As it will be argued throughout this study, the main driver of the EBU reform is the need to attain financial stability in Europe through:

> the degree of mutualisation of losses achieved under the SRM, the cession of supervisory sovereignty under the SSM, and the development of legal technology to grapple with the complex euro area/internal market asymmetry.[229]

In sum, supranational financial stability is at centre of the reform process to establish the EBU. While there are still some risks inherent in the project to create and complete the EBU, it is contended that financial stability has primarily driven the institutional and substantive framework to shape the EBU as a new foundational objective in EU law and policy.

222. Niamh Moloney, *European Banking Union: Assessing Its Risks and Resilience*, 51 Common Market Law Review 1622 (2014).
223. Hermann Van Rompuy, *Euro Area Summit and European Council Statement*, 29 June 2012.
224. European Commission, *Communication on a roadmap towards Banking Union* COM(2012)510.
225. *See* Chapter 7 for the SSM and Chapter 8 for the SRM.
226. European Commission, *Towards the completion of the Banking Union*, COM(2015) 587.
227. European Commission, *Proposal amending Regulation (EU) 806/2014 in order to establish a European Deposit Insurance Scheme*, COM/2015/0586 final.
228. Moloney *supra* n. 222, 1625.
229. *Ibid.*, 1629.

§3.05 CONCLUSION

This chapter has discussed the critical question of the role of supranational financial stability in EU law and policy. Since the outbreak of the financial crisis, EU law and policy have developed crisis-related reforms that are largely driven by the foundational objective of financial stability.

In this chapter, the concept of financial stability, its nature, scope and normative instruments were assessed. The financial crisis has exacerbated the 'public good' dimension of financial stability in Europe and shown that EU law and policy shall be driven by financial stability as a supranational foundational objective. The crisis-related reforms suggest that, although being at the intersection of economics, law and politics, financial stability is a new supranational and foundational – yet evolving – objective in EU law and policy.

As outlined in this chapter, before the financial crisis, financial stability in EU law and policy remained a neglected concept subject to limited legal analysis. This was exemplified by the widespread consideration of Union membership as a 'community of benefits' and not of 'risks'.[230] With the outbreak of the financial crisis, this chapter has demonstrated that the attainment of financial stability as a supranational public good objective has acquired a central focus in Europe through the focus on preventing and managing shocks and risks as well as in the development of its normative instruments analysed in this chapter. It has been argued that the recent regulatory responses in Europe indicate that the EU has taken a firm stance to develop an unprecedented financial stability normative framework. However, it was also shown that some aspects of supranational financial stability still need to be improved.

With this said, the role of financial stability requires an examination of the existing and desirable legal frameworks to achieve financial stability in Europe. The next chapters will assess in practice whether and to what extent financial stability plays a foundational role in EU law and policy.

230. Chiti, Teixeira *supra* n. 2, 687.

CHAPTER 4
European Economic Governance

§4.01 INTRODUCTION

The financial crisis has prompted important reforms in the context of the European economic governance, the weak EMU pillar.[1] These crisis-related reforms have taken various forms in the direction of attaining a higher degree of financial stability for Member States' public finances. These take the form of *ex ante* crisis prevention measures that aim to attain some degree of supranational regulation and a reinforced use of macro-economic surveillance instruments. These reforms show that the Member States, and in particular the euro area Member States, have promoted the achievement of a higher degree of surveillance integration motivated by the need to maintain a sufficient level of financial stability in Europe.

As examined in the third chapter of this book, financial stability has acquired a foundational role in EU law and policy that, as is argued in this chapter, can be partially seen in the reinforcement of the European economic governance rules. This chapter will look at the new framework for economic governance that the financial crisis has generated both in the form of EU law measures and in the intergovernmental TSCG. At the same time, it discusses to what extent the foundational objective of financial stability appears to frame the new normative framework for economic governance. In effect, the role of financial stability can be seen in the development of stricter instruments for preventive and corrective measures and in tighter surveillance rules in the context of the European economic policy. Nonetheless, as pointed out in this chapter, financial stability efforts remain limited in nature in the European economic governance as Member States are reluctant to give away sovereign powers in their budgetary, fiscal and social fields.

1. *See* Francis Snyder, *EMU-Integration and Differentiation: Metaphor for European Union* in Paul Craig & Grainne de Búrca (eds.), *The Evolution of EU Law*, 687 (Oxford University Press 2011).

This chapter focuses on the financial stability dimension of the new economic governance. The main question that this chapter addresses is whether the renewed European economic governance has developed an economic surveillance model for supranational financial stability. The reinforcement of the European economic governance framework from a purely EU constitutional law perspective lies beyond the scope of this chapter.[2]

After looking at the legal framework of the European economic governance before the outbreak of the financial crisis (§ 4.02), this chapter looks into the mutation of the surveillance model in the European economic governance. The chapter is divided into two subsections that will show how the European and the intergovernmental paths have been followed to reinforce supranational financial stability of Member States' finances (§4.03). Then, the chapter aims to evaluate the current development of economic governance regime in light of the objective of financial stability (§4.04). It will demonstrate that the current economic governance reinforces the degree of financial stability only to a limited extent. Then the chapter looks at possible measures to improve economic governance in Europe (§4.05). This could take place in particular through a reinforcement of the current framework by providing an enhanced level of integration to public finances surveillance and by structuring a pan-European system of supranational bonds to finance government debt. Indeed, the assessment takes into account the political difficulty to finding solutions towards supranational financial stability in the field of European economic governance. The last section concludes (§4.06).

§4.02 THE MAIN LIMITATIONS OF THE PRE-CRISIS EUROPEAN ECONOMIC GOVERNANCE FRAMEWORK: LOOSE COORDINATION AND INADEQUATE SURVEILLANCE OF MEMBER STATES' FINANCES

The European economic governance framework has been considered as one of the major flawed aspects exacerbated by the outbreak of the financial crisis.[3] The Maastricht Treaty did not introduce provisions for fiscal or economic supranational tasks and powers, differently from the ESCB monetary policy framework. Rather, the economic framework was based on the assumption that Member States would coordinate their economic policies.[4]

The Maastricht Treaty introduced a Chapter on the coordination of economic policies of the Member States. As argued by Craig, this policy was 'built on two related

2. For such analysis *see* Federico Fabbrini, *Economic Governance*, 181 (Oxford University Press 2016).
3. *See* Rosa Lastra, *International Financial and Monetary Law*, 291 (Oxford University Press 2015).
4. *See* generally Mads Andenas *et al.* (eds.), *European Economic and Monetary Union: The Institutional Framework* (Kluwer Law International 1997).

assumptions, preservation of national authority and preservation of national liability'.[5] This meant that the Member States agreed to exclude the conferral of fiscal powers to the EU and set clear prohibitions to restrict supranational powers to adopt economic and fiscal measures in the Member States.

The Maastricht Treaty established a loose system of economic policy coordination where Member States still decide on their fiscal and budgetary policies. Member States shall consider their economic policies as a matter of common concern and coordinate them in the Council.[6] Furthermore, 'sovereign liability brakes' were provided in the Maastricht Treaty. Member States or EU institutions cannot benefit from overdraft facilities or any other type of credit facility from the ECB or any NCB (Article 123 TFEU) and the EU or the Member States cannot be liable or assume the commitments of other Member States (Article 125 TFEU).[7]

After the Lisbon Treaty, the TFEU system remained unchanged and it is still limited to two loose economic policy procedures in primary EU law. The system of EU competences provides that 'Member States shall coordinate their economic policies within the Union' in Article 5 TFEU. This provision sits uneasily with the general structure of EU competences (exclusive, shared or supporting) and suggests that European economic governance is not strictly speaking an EU competence. At the same time, Article 2(3) TFEU includes coordination of economic policies in the system of competences. Some commentators have highlighted the strange nature of this provision.[8]

The TFEU contains a Chapter on economic governance where Article 119 TFEU repeats that Member States shall coordinate their economic policies. The same Chapter contains then further rules on economic governance. First, Article 121 TFEU establishes a system of broad guidelines of the economic policies of the Member States which form the basis for Council recommendations setting the broad guidelines. If the economic policies of the Member States are not consistent with the broad economic guidelines, or they risk jeopardising the proper functioning of the EMU, the Commission may address a warning to the relevant Member States. The Council can take the necessary recommendations or decisions to the concerned Member State. Second, Article 126 TFEU provides for the Excessive Deficit Procedure (EDP) which establishes a supranational surveillance system over excessive deficits in Member States. The procedure detailed in Article 126 TFEU may conclude a Council decision to impose corrective measures on the concerned Member State.

Two criteria drive budgetary discipline at the European level. First, Member States shall not exceed 3% of the planned or actual government deficit to GDP. Second, Member States shall not exceed the 60% of government debt to GDP. These are provided in Protocol 12 on the EDP to the EU Treaties.[9] The TFEU states that, in case

5. Paul Craig, *The Lisbon Treaty, Revised Edition: Law Politics and Treaty*, 460 (Oxford University Press 2013).
6. Art. 121 TFEU.
7. *See* Chapter 5 section §5.05[A][2] for a detailed analysis of Art. 125 TFEU.
8. *See* Alicia Hinarejos, *The Euro Area Crisis in Constitutional Perspective*, 74 (Oxford University Press 2015) and doctrine quoted therein.
9. Protocol 12 on the Excessive Deficit Procedure.

of failure to respect these criteria, non-interest-bearing deposit of an appropriate size and fines of an appropriate size may be imposed on Member States.[10]

Following the entry into force of the Maastricht Treaty, the Treaty framework on economic governance was further implemented with the adoption of secondary legislation to detail the provisions in the Treaty, the Stability and Growth Pact (SGP). This instrument was composed of two EU regulations setting out secondary law rules on the preventive and corrective arm implementing Articles 121 and 126 TFEU. Regulation 1466/1997[11] and Regulation 1467/1997[12] established specific rules for the economic policy primary law procedures. The SGP reinforced the commitment to budgetary balance over time.[13] Nonetheless, even with the SGP, the European economic policy framework was insufficient to coordinate properly Member State finances and their economic performances.[14] Practice showed that some euro area Member States departed from the EDP and the SGP rules. This led to the (in-)famous case *Commission v. Council*[15] where the ECJ held that the failure by the Council to adopt the decisions recommended by the Commission did 'not constitute an act challengeable by an action for annulment'. Further, in procedural terms the ECJ held that the conclusions of the Council to hold the EDP in abeyance for France and Germany were unlawful. Soon after, the Commission put forward a reform to the SGP in 2005.[16] However, the 2005 revision of the SGP made economic policy coordination even more flexible and discretionary.[17]

The financial crisis opened the debate on reforms both at primary and secondary EU law level to improve the established European economic governance framework. The following section explores the key reforms to strengthen fiscal surveillance and fiscal discipline in Europe and shows the differences between EU law and intergovernmental measures.

§4.03 REFORMING EUROPEAN ECONOMIC GOVERNANCE AS A RESPONSE TO THE FINANCIAL CRISIS IN EUROPE

As from 2010, an important set of reforms has resulted in newly strengthened surveillance and corrective rules in the European economic governance framework. The reforms are an expression of supranational regulation and tighter macro-economic supervision/surveillance as the main normative instruments to reach supranational financial stability. It is important to note that the crisis has urged new discussions on

10. Art. 126(11) TFEU.
11. Council Regulation 1466/1997 [1997] OJ L209/1.
12. Council Regulation 1467/1997 [1997] OJ L209/6.
13. *See* Fabian Amtenbrink & Jakob de Haan, *Economic Governance in the European Union – Fiscal Policy Discipline Versus Flexibility*, 40 Common Market Law Review 1075 (2003).
14. *See* Snyder *supra* n. 1, 691.
15. Case C-27/04 *Commission v. Council* ECLI:EU:C:2004:436.
16. Regulation 1055/2005 [2005] OJ L174/1 and Regulation 1056/2005 [2005] OJ L174/5.
17. *See* Jean-Victor Louis, *The Review of the Stability and Growth Pact*, 43 Common Market Law Review 85 (2006).

the degree of supranational regulatory integration of fiscal policies in the EMU. This is because the economic governance framework in the Maastricht Treaty did not establish an appropriate enforcement level of the rules to counteract three essential challenges to the EMU: fiscal discipline, structural imbalances and asymmetric shocks.[18] It has been argued that all these three challenges have been posed and – partially – addressed in the aftermath of the financial crisis.[19] As put by Bieber '[t]he common denominator of those acts is a *reduction* of Member States' competence in matters of general economic policy and a resulting transfer to the Union.'[20] However, at present these measures still leave considerable marge of manoeuvre to Member States in their economic, budgetary and fiscal policies.

This section analyses the main reforms to strengthen the European economic governance: the Six Pack, the Two Pack and the TSCG. These will be divided according to their legal nature.

[A] The EU Law Response

In the context of the Europe 2020 strategy,[21] the Commission presented a complex package of six legislative proposals aimed to reinforce economic governance in the EMU in September 2010. The Commission presented six regulatory proposals already in a Communication on 'enhancing economic policy coordination for stability, growth and jobs, tools for stronger economic governance'. This document contained the bulk of what would have been the Six Pack.[22] After fierce political negotiations, the Commission proposals have been adopted in October 2011 and have entered into force in December 2011.

The Six Pack is composed of six instruments (five Regulations and one Directive) which aim to strengthen European economic governance and the SGP. These instruments are based on Articles 121, 126 and 136 TFEU. Due to the tensions in financial markets and the problems of sovereign debt and deficit surveillance, the fiscal profligacy reached with the 2005 SGP revision needed a reform that could strengthen control over economic, budgetary and fiscal rules.[23] In general terms, the Six Pack aims to create a broad and enhanced surveillance framework for fiscal policies in Europe, and in particular for the euro area Members. Economic governance is framed in a European Semester cycle which ensures that Member States align their budgetary and economic policies with the objectives and rules agreed at the EU level. As argued by

18. Alicia Hinarejos, *Fiscal Federalism in the European Union: Evolution and Future Choices for EMU*, 50 Common Market Law Review 1621 (2013).
19. *Ibid.*, 1633.
20. Roland Bieber, *The Allocation of Economic Policy Competences in the European Union* in Loïc Azoulai (ed.), *The Question of Competence in the European Union*, 92 (Oxford University Press 2015) (emphasis in original).
21. See European Commission, Europe 2020 strategy at https://ec.europa.eu/info/strategy/european-semester/framework/europe-2020-strategy_en (accessed 31 December 2016).
22. *See* European Commission, *Communication Enhancing economic policy coordination for stability, growth and jobs – Tools for stronger EU economic governance* COM/2010/0367 final 2–3.
23. Dariusz Adamski, *National Power Games and Structural Failures in the European Macroeconomic Governance*, 49 Common Market Law Review 1336 (2012).

Adamski 'the legal response given in late 2011 is massive, complex and largely problematic'.[24] The Six Pack is composed of six legal instruments which can be divided in two groups.[25] The first group comprises three Regulations strengthening the existing European budgetary surveillance system and a Directive imposing minimum standards for Member State's national budgetary frameworks. The second group includes two Regulations introducing a new surveillance framework for macroeconomic imbalances, the Excessive Macroeconomic Imbalance.

[1] A Reinforced SGP

The first group of measures amends and strengthens the pre-existing SGP. It includes rules on a reinforcement of the SGP rules on the general government deficit and the public debt. The preventive arm involves a restructured multilateral surveillance of budgetary policies. The basic primary law framework requires that each Member State maintain the actual government deficit below 3% of GDP, unless either the ratio has declined substantially and continuously and reached a level that comes close to 3%. In the alternative, the excess over 3% is only exceptional and temporary and the ratio shall remain close to 3%.[26] Each Member State shall maintain its government debt below 60% of GDP, unless the ratio is sufficiently diminishing and approaching 60% at a satisfactory pace.[27] In case a Member State has a government debt above 60% of GDP, it must reduce it at a satisfactory pace, which assumes a reduction of the differential between the actual debt level and the 60% of the GDP threshold at an average rate of one-twentieth per year.[28] For euro area Member States, there is a penalty ground. This stage may lead to the imposition of financial sanctions.

The corrective arm of the SGP stems out of the Treaty provision under Article 126 TFEU where a special procedure for excessive deficit was introduced. Regulations 1177/2011 and 1173/2011 have substantially updated the corrective arm of the SGP. According to Regulation 1173/2011, the Commission shall, within twenty days of the adoption of the Council's decision, recommend that the Council, by further decision, requires the Member State in question to lodge with the Commission an interesting-bearing deposit amounting to 0.2% of its GDP in the preceding year.[29] The Council may reject the Commission's recommendation by qualified majority within ten days if it

24. *Ibid.*, 1337.
25. Regulation 1175/2011 amending Regulation 1466/97 on the strengthening of the surveillance of budgetary positions and the surveillance and coordination of economic policies [2011] OJ L306/12; Regulation 1177/2011 amending Regulation 1467/97 on speeding up and clarifying the implementation of the excessive deficit procedure [2011] OJ L306/33; Regulation 1173/2011 on the effective enforcement of budgetary surveillance in the euro area [2011] OJ L306/1; Directive 2011/85/EU on requirements for budgetary frameworks of the Member States [2011] OJ L306/41; Regulation 1176/2011 on the prevention and correction of macroeconomic imbalances [2011] OJ L306/25; Regulation 1174/2011 on enforcement measures to correct macroeconomic imbalances in the euro area [2011] OJ L306/8.
26. Art. 126 TFEU and Protocol 12 on excessive deficit procedure, Art. 1.
27. *Ibid.*
28. Regulation 1467/97 amended, Art. 2(1a).
29. Regulation 1173/2011, Art. 4.

disagrees with the Commission.[30] The main purpose of the 2011 reform has been to tackle the excessive reliance on national politics and the consequent soft enforcement by 'speeding up and clarifying the excessive deficit procedure'.[31] The main 2011 reforms tend to clarify what are the inter-institutional relationships and to provide new rules on enforcement. The Regulations set an economic dialogue between the EU institutions involved in the EDP. In particular, the European Parliament is involved to some extent on the process, and, most importantly, there is a reinforced Commission role as 'the Council, as a rule, is expected to follow the recommendations and proposals of the Commission or explain its position publicly'.[32]

The second ground of improvement relates to enforcement. The new SGP provides that a fine be applied as a rule only on a euro area Member State. However, there might be some leeway for Council arrangements or also in case of a severe economic downturn which affects the euro area or the Union as a whole to make more flexible the effective action that the Member State needs to take.[33] This means that there is a relaxation to the rules on deficit reduction recommendation and sanctions in some circumstances.[34]

The Six Pack comprises also Directive 2011/85/EU that aims to reinforce the decentralised dimension of budgetary frameworks of the Member States. It has been suggested that this Directive is part of a decentralised effort to implement European rules at the national level.[35] The Directive has been adopted pursuant to Article 126(14) TFEU as the Treaty provision indicating that the Council may 'lay down detailed rules and definitions for the application' of the Protocol on EDP. As indicated in the Preamble, the aim of the Directive is to facilitate the uniform compliance with budgetary discipline within the Union.[36] The Directive specifies what national authorities of the Member States must do to comply with the EU's EDP. They are required to maintain public accounting systems including bookkeeping, internal control, financial reporting and auditing.[37] The main purpose of a harmonised budgetary framework is the need for Member States to adopt the necessary budgetary measures to avoid EDPs.[38] The main aspects of the Directive are indicated in Articles 4-7. The Directive prescribes that Member States shall adopt reliable budgetary forecasts and numerical fiscal rules. The first one relates to an exercise of budgetary planning which shall lead to forecasts based on realistic scenarios. Member States should indicate the institutions responsible for the development of forecasts, and these should be subject to regular 'unbiased and comprehensive evaluation based on objective criteria'.[39] Finally, in order to achieve this objective, Member States shall establish a credible and effective

30. *Ibid.*, Art. 4(2).
31. Regulation 1467/1997, Art. 1(1).
32. *Ibid.*, amended Art. 2a(1).
33. *Ibid.*, Art. 3(5) and Art. 5(2).
34. Adamski *supra* n. 23, 1346.
35. Kenneth Armstrong, *The New Governance of EU Fiscal Discipline*, 38 European Law Review 613 (2013).
36. Directive 2011/85/EU, Recital 1.
37. *Ibid.*, Recital 2.
38. *Ibid.*, Art. 1.
39. *Ibid.*, Art. 4 paras 5 and 6.

medium-term budgetary framework which provides for a fiscal planning for at least three years in order to ensure that national fiscal planning follows a multiannual fiscal planning perspective.[40]

Most recently, the EU Commission has adopted a Communication providing for more flexibility to the existing rules in the SGP in 2015.[41] The document promotes a more flexible interpretation of the reformed SGP rules. In particular, it establishes a structural reform clause and an investment clause that favours national contributions to the European Fund for Strategic Investments (EFSI). This Communication is based on the rationale that SGP should be applied in a more flexible fashion to take into account the possible downturn in the economic conditions of the Member States.

[2] The New Macroeconomic Imbalances Procedure

The second group of measures included in the Six Pack establishes a new procedure of economic surveillance, the Excessive Macroeconomic Imbalance. This is established in Regulation 1176/2011 on prevention and correction of macroeconomic imbalances and Regulation 1174/2011 on enforcement measures to correct excessive macroeconomic imbalances in the euro area. While keeping a strong resemblance with the preventive arm of the new SGP, the Macroeconomic Imbalances Procedure (MIP) establishes a new mechanism for economic surveillance which introduces an alert mechanism to identify macroeconomic imbalances. The rationale behind the creation of this new framework lies in the need to broaden economic surveillance in the EMU in order to detect and address macroeconomic imbalances at an early stage.[42] The Commission is given a primary role in carrying out in-depth-reviews of the Member States imbalance while the Council decides on the recommendation of the Commission to make the sanction binding.

The first stage of the MIP comprises the Commission's analysis of national macro-economic positions. This is based on a set of economic and financial indicators – the macro-economic scoreboard.[43] This *ex ante* analysis serves to identify which Member State suffers from macroeconomic imbalances. These are defined:

> as any trend giving rise to macroeconomic developments which are adversely affecting, or have the potential adversely to affect, the proper functioning of the economy of a Member State or of the economic and monetary union, or of the Union as a whole.[44]

The Commission, if it realises that the Member State concerned experiences imbalances, recommends the Council to issue appropriate economic policy recommendations.[45] The Council does not have to follow the Commission's advice. However, the

40. *Ibid.*, Art. 9.
41. Commission Communication, *Making the best use of the flexibility within the existing rules of the stability and growth pact* COM/2015/012 final.
42. Regulation 1176/2011, Recital 9.
43. *Ibid.*, Arts 3 and 4.
44. *Ibid.*, Art. 2(1).
45. *Ibid.*, Art. 6(1).

Commission should recommend the Council to open the Excessive Imbalance Procedure (EIP) by adopting a 'recommendation establishing the existence of an excessive imbalance and recommending that the Member State take corrective action'.[46] Similar to the strengthened SGP rules, the macro-economic surveillance procedure provides for some additional 'reinforced' rules applicable to euro area Member States. In case of non-compliance with the first recommendation issued by the Council, Regulation 1174/2011 provides that the concerned Member State is subject to an interest-bearing deposit which amounts to 0.1% of the country's GDP.[47] In case of non-compliance with the second non-compliance decision or the second recommendation requiring new corrective measures, the Council shall decide to impose an annual fine of the same amount.[48]

The sanctioning part of the MIP shows that the economic union component in European economic governance remains rather weak. The role of the Commission as compared with that of the Council remains limited. Even if the Commission rules on the recommendations to advance in the MIP, the Council still governs the procedure as it is empowered and still not obliged to take formal steps.[49] Furthermore, what remains problematic is the degree of vagueness and discretion that characterise the EIP. The nature of financial sanctions does not appear credible, and these might be imposed when they would do more harm than good.[50] At the same time, the nature of the acts to be adopted in EIP is rather soft, and excessive flexibility in their use could be used. On a positive note, the EIP procedure appears to be a novel form of economic surveillance over national imbalances.

[3] The Two Pack: Strengthening Supranational Surveillance for Euro Area Member States?

The Two Pack is composed of two Regulations that apply to Member States which are part of the euro area. These two Regulations have been adopted at a later stage than the Six Pack for a number of reasons. First, these documents were subject to strong political negotiations at the Council as they intended to provide enhanced rules for euro area Member State economic governance. Second, the proposals were progressively watered down from the original Commission's proposals and had to be extensively negotiated. Third, these measures were supposed to take into account the progressive implementation of the new European governance regime and the macro-economic adjustment programmes in distressed Member States.

The two Regulations entered into force on 1 June 2013 and are based on Article 136(2) TFEU which allows Member State whose currency is the euro to strengthen the coordination and surveillance of budgetary policies with a view to allow budgetary (fiscal) discipline in the EMU. The main objective of the Two Pack is to ensure an

46. *Ibid.*, Art. 7(2).
47. Regulation 1174/2011, Art. 3(1) and (5).
48. *Ibid.*
49. Adamski *supra* n. 23, 1354.
50. *Ibid.*

enhanced budgetary coordination and surveillance in the euro area Member States. The Two Pack is to build on the Six Pack reforms to the SGP and establish an enhanced level of supervision to Member States in the euro area.[51]

Based on the rules established in Directive 2011/85/EU, Regulation 473/2013[52] sets out enhanced rules for monitoring budgetary policies in the euro area and for ensuring consistency in the economic policy framework built on the new SGP.[53] The Regulation introduces a new common budgetary timeline and common budgetary rules for the euro area Member States. These are structured in deadlines throughout the year requiring Member States to respect the surveillance rules intended to enhance fiscal discipline.[54] In particular, the euro area Member States are required to submit medium-term fiscal plans to the Commission and Stability Programmes, which outline the main medium-term fiscal plans.[55] The Regulation contains substantial deadlines for the submission of budgetary documents. By 15 October of each year, euro area Member States must publish their draft budget laws for the following year,[56] and by 31 December of each year, they must submit their budgets for the following year to the Commission.[57] One of the main novelties of Regulation 473/2013 is that the Commission will examine and give an opinion on the draft budget rules of each euro area Member State.[58] If the Commission believes that there is 'particularly serious non-compliance' with the budgetary obligations, it will ask for a revised plan to the concerned Member State for further evaluation.[59] For the purpose of compliance, the Regulation requires that the Commission makes a public opinion on a 'particularly serious non-compliance' which may exercise some influence on the concerned Member State.

Regulation 472/2013[60] contains new consolidated rules on the enhancement of fiscal discipline for Member States experiencing or threatened with serious difficulties as regards their financial stability. In other words, this Regulation sets the rules for the negotiation and the setting up of three specific instruments to allow an appropriate economic and budgetary surveillance for euro area Member States which are experiencing financial instability. First, the Regulation contains rules on the negotiation and the implementation of an enhanced surveillance status to allow the addressee Member State to be controlled in a more structured way.[61] Enhanced surveillance to a distressed

51. European Commission, *Two-Pack enters into force, completing budgetary surveillance cycle and further improving economic governance for the euro area* (2013) MEMO/13/457.
52. Regulation 473/2013 on common provisions for monitoring and assessing draft budgetary plans and ensuring correction of excessive deficits of the Member States in the euro area [2013] OJ L140/11.
53. *Ibid.*, Art. 1.
54. *See ibid.*, Recital 12.
55. *Ibid.*, Art. 4(1).
56. *Ibid.*, Art. 4(2).
57. *Ibid.*, Art. 4(3).
58. *Ibid.*, Art. 7.
59. *Ibid.*, Art. 7(2).
60. Regulation 472/2013 on the strengthening of economic and budgetary surveillance of Member States experiencing or threatened with serious difficulties with respect to their financial stability in the euro area [2013] OJ L140/1.
61. *Ibid.*, Art. 2.

Member State provides for a reinforced level of surveillance on the Member State that shall adopt the suggested measures. Second, the Regulation provides for rules on the negotiation and the implementation of a formal macro-economic adjustment programmes. These programmes are adopted when a euro area Member State receives financial assistance from one or several other Member States or third countries, the European Financial Stabilisation Mechanism (EFSM), the ESM, the European Financial Stability Facility (EFSF) or the IMF.[62] The Regulation consists of a systematisation of the formal procedure to negotiate and implement a macro-adjustment programme. Third, the Regulation contains rules on post-programme surveillance that allows for an extension on surveillance on euro area Member States under a macro-adjustment programme as long as a minimum of 75% of the financial assistance received has not been repaid.[63]

This concludes the analysis of the renewed EU law measures to reinforce the European economic policy. The following section will analyse the main provisions in the TSCG as the intergovernmental Treaty reinforcing economic surveillance.

[B] The Intergovernmental Measures for Reinforced Fiscal Discipline in the Economic Governance Framework: The TSCG

While the preceding policy and legal reforms were taken alongside the established rules under EU law, the Euro Plus Pact and the TSCG – erroneously known as the 'Fiscal Compact' as the latter is only one Chapter of the Treaty – have been adopted outside the EU legal framework.

Already in March 2011, some Member States acting on the side of the European Council, adopted the Euro Plus Pact, a non-binding intergovernmental declaration encouraging Member States to enhance the sustainability of public finances by translating EU fiscal rules into national legislation.[64]

Soon after, the Member States agreed on the TSCG. This is an intergovernmental agreement signed and adopted by twenty-five Member States in March 2012. This instrument intends to coordinate and supervise national fiscal policies beyond EU law. The need to create a closer fiscal union brought to the adoption of the intergovernmental agreement only as 'gesture politics' mainly because of the consequences of financial assistance interventions to distressed Member States and the need to foster further fiscal discipline in Europe.[65] The legal options on the table were three: the use of the special legal basis to replace Protocol 12 on the EDP as provided under Article 126(14) TFEU; the opening of an ordinary or simplified revision procedure provided in Article 48 TEU; or the conclusion of an intergovernmental agreement.[66] The third one

62. *Ibid.*, Art. 7(1).
63. *Ibid.*, Art. 14(1).
64. *See* European Council, *Conclusions* 24/25 March, 2011 EUCO 10/1/11, Annex 1, para. c.
65. Steve Peers, *The Stability Treaty: Permanent Austerity or Gesture Politics?*, 8 European Constitutional Law Review 441 (2012).
66. Van Rompuy Report, *Towards a Stronger Economic Union: Interim Report to the European Council*, 6 December 2011. *See* Editorial, *Some Thoughts Concerning the Draft Treaty on a Reinforced Economic Union*, 49 Common Market Law Review 1–2 (2012).

was the final – and unexpected – chosen option. From a political point of view, the final intergovernmental solution came out from the concerns on veto powers on specific Treaty amendments, lengthy and burdensome Treaty ratification processes and, most importantly, because of the political opposition of the UK to change the rules on fiscal coordination and governance established in the European Treaties. The UK veto in particular proved to be a deadlock for the natural attainment of new Treaty amendments.[67] Hence, the other Member States, with the exception of Czech Republic, agreed on having an intergovernmental treaty.

The negotiation stage of the TSCG was long and burdensome. As from the European Council conclusions in December 2011 the draft Treaty was subject to six revisions before reaching the final agreement. As emphatically put by Craig:

> the fact that 25 states agreed in principle to strengthened control over national economic policy did not mean that they would agree on the precise form or degree of that control.[68]

The purpose of the TSCG is indicated in Title I. Article 1 states that the aim of the TSCG is:

> to strengthen the economic pillar of the economic and monetary union by adopting a set of rules intended to foster budgetary discipline, to strengthen the coordination of their economic policies and to improve the governance of the euro area, thereby supporting the achievement of the European Union's objectives for sustainable growth, employment, competitiveness and social cohesion.[69]

While financial stability is not expressly mentioned in the objective of the TSCG, Article 1 provision indicates that – ideally – the TSCG is threefold as it aims to deal with budgetary discipline, coordination of economic policies and governance in the euro area. As demonstrated infra, only budgetary discipline in the 'Fiscal Compact' under Title III has binding legal value.

Article 2 refers to the relationship between the TSCG and the EU Treaties. In particular, the TSCG shall be interpreted in conformity with the Treaties in particular with Article 4(3) TEU on loyal cooperation as well as with EU law. Moreover, the same provision requires that the TSCG is compatible with the EU Treaties and does not encroach on competences of the Union in the field of the economic union. In other words, the TSCG applies in parallel with the established rules in the EU Treaties, but EU law has 'primacy' over the TSCG provisions. This means that in case of conflicts between rules, EU law rules shall prevail.

The essence of the Fiscal Compact is enshrined in Title III.[70] This part reinforces both the preventive and the corrective arms of the established SGP with new rules on budgetary discipline agreed outside EU law. The Fiscal Compact introduces the 'balanced budget rule' or 'golden rule' according to which the budgetary position of the

---

67. Paul Craig, *The Stability, Coordination and Governance Treaty: Principle, Politics and Pragmatics*, 37 European Law Review 232–233 (2012).
68. *Ibid.*, 233.
69. TSCG, Art. 1.
70. *See* further Fabbrini *supra* n. 2, 29.

government of the Member States 'shall be balanced or in surplus'.[71] This entails that the contracting parties shall implement rules of the revised SGP that do not overturn more than 0.5% GDP structural deficit extended to 1% for states having a debt under 60%. Under exceptional circumstances, the contracting parties may be allowed temporary deviations. The golden rule shall be implemented in national law 'through provisions of binding force and permanent character, preferably constitutional, or otherwise guaranteed to be fully respected and adhered to throughout the national budgetary processes'.[72]

Furthermore, the Fiscal Compact provides for an 'automatic correction mechanism' to be triggered in cases of significant deviations from the medium-term objective or the adjustment path towards it.[73] The correction mechanism shall be based on common principles that are proposed by the Commission on the nature, size and time, and the role and independence of the institution responsible for monitoring compliance at the national level.[74] The ECJ is given the mandate to decide on the TSCG as it is given full jurisdiction to adjudicate on infringements whenever a Member State fails to implement the TSCG fiscal rule.[75] This rule constitutes a special agreement between the Member States within the meaning of Article 273 TFEU.[76] The TSCG also indicates that, in case of an EDP, the euro area Member State shall 'commit to supporting the proposals or recommendations submitted by the European Commission',[77] unless a qualified majority of euro area Member State opposes to the decision.[78] This sets a reverse qualified majority (RQM) rule according to which the Council may oppose to the Commission's opinion or recommendation only if qualified majority is reached.

The TSCG includes a revision clause according to which, within five years of its entry into force, i.e., by 1 January 2018, the experience gained with its implementation shall be taken into account and necessary steps shall be taken with a view to incorporate the substance of the Fiscal Compact into EU law.[79] This provision suggests that the Fiscal Compact should become part of EU law after five years. This is also clear in the Fiscal Compact Preamble stating that 'the objective (...) is to incorporate the provisions of this Treaty as soon as possible into the Treaties on which the European Union is founded'.

This analysis shows that the European economic governance framework is now composed also of an intergovernmental body of binding law. This reveals that the Member States have agreed on strengthening the macro-economic governance in the EU and a closer coordination of domestic fiscal and economic policies by auto-imposing legal limitations to their budgetary rules. Two general remarks can be made

71. TSCG, Art. 3(1) letter (a).
72. *Ibid.*, Art. 3(2).
73. *Ibid.*, Art. 3(1) letter (e).
74. *Ibid.*, Art. 3(2).
75. *Ibid.*, Art. 8.
76. *Ibid.*, Art. 8(3).
77. *Ibid.*, Art. 7.
78. *Ibid.*
79. *Ibid.*, Art. 16.

at this stage. First, economic governance now includes an added layer of complexity shown by the adoption of an intergovernmental agreement outside the EU law framework. Second, the Member States have not yet made sufficient political efforts to transfer to the supranational level economic, budgetary and fiscal powers over national fiscal and economic policies. The next part of this chapter will assess the recent European economic governance reforms in light of the foundational objective of financial stability, in particular to show to what extent these reforms have been adopted to reinforce the supranational dimension of European economic governance and ultimately financial stability in EU law and policy.

§4.04 FINANCIAL STABILITY AND THE NEW EUROPEAN ECONOMIC GOVERNANCE FRAMEWORK: A TRUE PARADIGM CHANGE OR A 'TINY' SURVEILLANCE DEVELOPMENT?

After having analysed the new European framework for European economic governance, this section assesses the new economic governance framework and argues whether it offers a satisfactory paradigm change in light of the foundational objective of financial stability in EU law and policy as developed in this book. The new economic framework for the surveillance and control of public finances in Member States opens many complex issues that question whether the original European economic surveillance framework has been effectively modified after the financial crisis in Europe. This section shows that the recent legal developments in this field suggest that there are still considerable difficulties to move towards a stronger supranational regulatory and surveillance system in economic governance finances based on the normative instruments of supranational financial stability identified in the preceding chapter. This is because Member States are reluctant to give away sovereign powers over economic, budgetary and fiscal matters.

The first part of this section discusses whether the new European economic governance framework provides a satisfactory development to the pre-existing Maastricht Treaty surveillance model. Then, it assesses whether the new tools are sufficient to enforce fiscal discipline, avoid structural imbalances and react to asymmetric shocks. Finally, it elaborates on the role of EU institutions in the new economic governance framework.

[A] The Developing Model of European Economic Governance Surveillance

[1] The Supranational Surveillance Framework for Member States' Finances: Towards a Reinforced Model?

As from 2012, the regulatory reforms both under EU law and in the TSCG promoted a new economic surveillance model different from the original Maastricht Treaty framework. The assessment of this new model for economic surveillance shows that the responses to the financial crisis have reinforced the supranational economic governance rules setting budgetary discipline to the benefit of supranational financial stability.[80] This model has followed a multidimensional ground of reforms. This is noticeable in two ways. First, the new measures combine both soft law and hard law elements that, as demonstrated in Chapter 3, are part of the normative instrument of supranational regulation. In particular, this is clear in the procedural phases leading to the imposition of sanctions for the preventive and corrective arms of national budgetary surveillance. The renewed SGP provides for Commission's recommendations and opinions as well as Council decisions. Second, the new economic governance framework has been reinforced with secondary EU legislation and with the adoption of an intergovernmental Treaty signed by twenty-five Member States.

The new European surveillance model shows some degree of improvement as compared with the one existing before the financial crisis. When the SGP was reformed in 2005, literature expressed reservations as to the general level of budgetary rules and at the lack of enforcement powers.[81] Since the beginning of the financial crisis, the new measures have shaped a new supranational model of supranational economic governance. At the same time, the introduction of 'intergovernmentalism' in the European economic governance complicates the legal framework and is a problematic development in this context. The TSCG was adopted as a response to the need for strengthening the economic governance rules without amending the EU Treaties. The solution found by the Member States was motivated by the reluctance of some Member States to amend considerably EU primary law provisions and introduce stricter rules on budgetary surveillance in the Treaty. Although the TSCG contains a revision clause, its intergovernmental nature remains inconsistent with the need to develop further a supranational budgetary surveillance model in Europe. At the same time, the presence of a revision clause in the TSCG indicates that the intergovernmental solution is temporary in nature and will be integrated in the EU legal order in near future.

Notwithstanding the intergovernmental path followed to reinforce European economic surveillance, it is argued that two aspects make the new economic governance framework more oriented towards supranational financial stability in EU law and policy as compared with pre-financial crisis regime. There is now a wide framework for stricter budgetary surveillance on Member States, especially applicable to euro area Member States. This is noticeable in the adoption of both hard law and soft law measures that have extended the scope of supranational surveillance both at the level of strict budgetary policy and economic policy. First, surveillance measures have been extended to general national economic policies with the introduction of the MIP. Second, there has been a consolidation of the rules on budgetary scrutiny to Member States and fiscal surveillance in distressed Member States.

Furthermore, the new rules move towards a more detailed and enforceable regime for supranational budgetary and economic surveillance. This is visible in four normative trends. First, there are new procedural steps that, as the case may be, could lead to the application of sanctions for euro area Member States. This procedure involves both the Commission and the Council. Second, there has been a reinforcement

80. *See* for a similar perspective Fabbrini *supra* n. 2, 28.
81. Louis *supra* n. 17, 85.

of the sanctioning regime as the Council may apply interest-bearing deposits and fines. Third, there is the creation of the RQM as a new decision-making arrangement both in the EU law and in the TSCG. Fourth, supranational surveillance procedures have been strengthened, especially for distressed Member States under enhanced surveillance or macro-economic adjustment programme. Both the Commission and the Council may exert considerable influence on national economic, budgetary and fiscal provisions of Member States under financial distress.

In sum, the new European economic governance reforms have built a renewed model of supranational surveillance showing improvements to the pre-existing flexible and loose pre-financial crisis regime. However, at present European economic governance does not constitute a revolutionary paradigm change establishing a new supranational system for the supranational surveillance of economic, budgetary and fiscal decisions of Member States.[82] The current supranational framework is not sufficiently strong to shape a truly European model of budgetary and economic surveillance to achieve supranational financial stability in Europe as Member States still bear full sovereign powers and responsibility in economic, budgetary and fiscal matters. EU institutions do not have extensive economic, budgetary and fiscal powers over individual Member States. Moreover, recent institutional practice indicates that political compromises can still water down the power to adopt supranational instruments of the renewed European economic governance. For instance, in July 2016, the Commission decided not to impose sanctions for excessive deficits on Portugal and Spain, although a breach of the EDP was found.[83]

[2] A Stricter Surveillance Regime for Euro Area Member States?

While the European economic surveillance still shows considerable grounds of improvements, the new economic governance framework develops a special regime for euro area Member States. This comes from the higher level of integration that euro area Member States have developed. The EU legislation to reform economic governance provides for stricter rules to euro area Member States for the sake of economic, budgetary and fiscal discipline. This is already evident in EU primary law. While Articles 121 and 126 TFEU are applicable to all Member States, the Lisbon Treaty has included a new provision, Article 136 TFEU, applicable only to euro area Member States. This provision establishes that euro area Member States may adopt measures:

> a) to strengthen the coordination and surveillance of their budgetary discipline; b) to set out economic policy guidelines for them, while ensuring that they are compatible with those adopted for the whole of the Union and are kept under surveillance.

82. Hinarejos *supra* n. 18, 1633.
83. Council of the EU, *Excessive deficit procedure: Council agrees to zero fines and new deadlines for Portugal and Spain*, 8 August 2016 http://www.consilium.europa.eu/en/press/press-releases/2016/08/08-excessive-deficit-portugal-spain/?utm_source=dsms-auto&utm_medium=email&utm_campaign=Excessive+deficit+procedure%3a+Council+agrees+to+zero+fines+and+new+deadlines+for+Portugal+and+Spain (accessed 31 December 2016).

Some legal instruments in the Six Pack and the Two Pack have been adopted with the use of Article 136(1) TFEU as the legal basis. This has developed a stricter and more integrated system for euro area Member States economic surveillance as compared to non-euro area Member States. The use of this legal basis has been relied to modify the multilateral surveillance procedure as well as for the adoption of the two Pack Regulations. The literal interpretation of this legal basis would not give ground to adopt reinforced euro area surveillance measures as it strictly refers to multilateral surveillance procedures under Article 121 TFEU.[84] However, both the Regulation on effective enforcement of budgetary surveillance and the Two Pack legislation go beyond the letter of Article 126 TFEU. This innovative interpretation is justified by the legal limitations to adopt new measure to reinforce economic governance under Article 136(1) TFEU.[85]

In particular, Article 136(1) TFEU contains a specific phrasing that, from a literal interpretation, would not allow going beyond measures for the 'coordination and surveillance' and 'economic policy guidelines'. However, the adoption of the Six Pack for the euro area and the Two Pack shows that Article 136 TFEU has been interpreted in an extensive manner by including the power to impose deposits and fines and to monitor annual budgets as well as empowering the European institutions beyond the Treaty rules.[86]

The existence of a specific euro area Chapter in the EMU Treaty framework has empowered the European legislators to improve economic governance as regards the euro area. This suggests that Member States whose currency is the euro may develop further rules to improve supranational economic governance only among them. However, two main questions are open to debate. First, the extent of powers which euro area Member are granted might lead to further differentiation between the Member States sharing the same currency and those not. Second, the participation of some non-euro area Member State to part of the rules on the new economic governance contradicts the argument in favour of a stricter integration only for euro area Member States. This is in particular true for the TSCG that has been signed by twenty-five Member States and, as seen earlier, introduces a 'golden rule' of constitutional significance which has been implemented at the national level.

Overall, the use of Article 136 TFEU has been a useful instrument to reinforce the system of economic surveillance for euro area Member States. The euro area Member States have built a stronger surveillance system which could be used to reinforce further the existing euro area surveillance regime. However, at this stage, the current legal framework is not fully satisfactory as the normative instrument of supranational regulation has not yet established a fully-fledged euro area supranational economic governance system grounded on financial stability as a founding objective in EU law

84. Kaarlo Tuori & Klaus Tuori, *The Eurozone Crisis. A Constitutional Analysis*, 171 (Cambridge University Press 2014).
85. Specific measures for the euro area Member States may be adopted by referring to TFEU, Arts 121 and 126 'with the exception of the procedure set out in Article 126(14)'.
86. Tuori, Tuori, *supra* n. 84, 170.

and policy. There are still no binding and enforceable supranational powers to enforce fiscal discipline or to raise taxes in a generalised way or to absorb risks and asymmetric shocks within the euro area.

[B] Economic Governance and the Renewed Supranational Institutional Involvement

This section assesses the supranational institutional involvement in the renewed European economic governance under both the reinforced SGP and the TSCG. In particular, it reflects on the new institutional balance arising from this new structure.

Under the new European economic governance framework, there has been a partial reorganisation of the role of the EU institutions. The role of the European Council remains highly influential in the overall economic governance process as it guides the process at the general political level. The European Council's conclusions have had an important impact on the adoption of measures by other EU institutions and in particular in the process of adoption of the EU legislative packages. However, there remains a degree of ambiguity as to its institutional role.[87] It remains questionable whether the European Council is effectively supporting the development of a supranational surveillance model or rather promotes national interests in the conduct of economic policy.

The Council surely plays the most important role in the renewed European economic governance. This is clear both in the general role of the Council in European economic governance framework, in particular on economic and fiscal matters. As a general decision-maker, the Council, which acts both as a representative of the interests of the Member States and as a key decision-maker in the field, has established itself as the most important player in the renewed economic governance. The Council still adopts each economic governance recommendation or decision. This is the case of the non-compliance and sanction decisions in the multilateral surveillance procedure, in the MIP, in the EDP as well as in the decisions provided in the Two Pack and the TSCG. This clearly results from the EU Treaties rules themselves where the Council is given the final decision-making powers to take action in the multilateral surveillance procedure under Article 121 TFEU as well as to sanction Member States in the EDP under Article 126 TFEU. Notwithstanding such prominent role, the introduction of RQM voting is an interesting development to a supranational economic governance framework.[88] The RQM is a Council procedure according to which a Council act in the European economic governance shall be deemed to be adopted unless a qualified majority of the Council decides to reject the Commission's recommendation within ten days from the Commission's adoption. The RQM has been introduced in order to provide more automatism to decision-making bodies and to strengthen the role of the Commission in decision-making procedures. These justifications can be seen both in the TSCG and in the new secondary legislation (the Six Pack and the Two Pack).

87. Mark Dawson & Floris de Witte, *Constitutional Balance in the EU after the Euro-Crisis*, 76 Modern Law Review 830 (2013).
88. *See* Rainer Palmstorfer, *The Reverse Majority Voting under the 'Six Pack': A Bad Turn for the Union?*, 20 European Law Journal 186 (2014).

Nonetheless, the Council still enjoys a powerful position in the European economic governance, especially as regards the final decision on sanctions for non-compliance with the Council's positions. This limitation shows the reluctance of Member States to confer supranational powers to improve the European surveillance model.

The Eurogroup[89] as an informal gathering of finance ministers of the euro area has acquired an increasingly important role in the European economic governance framework. While the ministers of finance of the euro area Member States held meetings since 1997,[90] the Lisbon Treaty has explicitly recognised the Eurogrop as an informal gathering of the economics and finance ministers of the euro area.[91] This recognition has not gone in the direction of giving it the status of EU body or providing it formally binding powers.[92] However, this forum has acquired a specific status in the economic governance as well as in the discussions on financial stabilisation mechanisms and general financial issues. The Eurogroup has a semi-permanent president and the members hold political and technical discussions, but have no legislative functions.[93] Nevertheless, during the financial crisis it has effectively worked as a powerful informal forum complementing the Council in ECOFIN composition in promoting and assessing most of the economic policy initiatives adopted during the financial crisis.

The Commission has strengthened its role as the one EU institution dealing with the adoption of the new regulatory framework in European economic governance. The Commission's proposals as well as the Commission recommendations, opinions and advice in the field have played a considerable role during the financial crisis to strengthen the European economic governance framework. The Commission may suggest what policy-making should be taken at the national level in economic governance. In particular, the Commission publishes documents on a yearly basis which have a specific impact on Member States: country-specific recommendations giving an overview on the economic conditions of each Member State in May each year and opinions on draft budgetary plans of euro area Member States in November each year. Furthermore, the Commission exercises soft law decision-making powers with opinions and recommendations indicating what action the Council and Member States should take. For instance in 2016, the Commission recommended to the Council a review of the debt and the EDP for some Member States.[94] However, the Commission still does not exercise formal decision-making powers as the ultimate decision-making EU institution, especially on sanctions or adoption of budgetary laws. These are still exercised by the Council at the European level and the Member States at the national level. At the same time, the introduction of the RQM voting indicates that the Commission may still ensure that its proposals are taken as Council's final decisions. In sum, the Commission has an essential importance in making proposals and soft law

89. *See* Uwe Puetter, *The Eurogroup* (Manchester University Press 2006).
90. *See* European Council, *Conclusions*, 12–13 December 1997.
91. *See* Protocol No. 14 on the Eurogroup [2010] OJ C83/283.
92. See Case C-105/15 P *Mallis and Malli v. Commission and ECB* ECLI:EU:C:2016:702, para 61.
93. *Ibid.*
94. European Commission, *Spring 2016 European Semester package: Commission issues country-specific recommendations* http://europa.eu/rapid/press-release_IP-16-1724_en.htm?locale = en (accessed 31 December 2016).

surveillance of economic governance measures, but no powers to adopt final decisions in the field.

The European Parliament has no decision-making power in European economic governance, but only a consulting and advisory role. Analysing the role of the European Parliament in the field would go beyond the scope of this book.[95] It has been correctly argued that European democracy is the real loser in the context of the renewed economic governance reform.[96] This is especially true if one looks at the European Parliament role in the Six Pack or in the TSCG. The European Parliament has basically no decision-making power in the field and is only engaged in 'economic dialogues'. This is clear from both the EU legislation and the TSCG where there are only very limited references to the role of the European Parliament. This is a clear legitimacy deficit that should be solved in future reforms, perhaps by addressing the RQM and establishing a stronger involvement of the European Parliament in economic governance decision-making.[97]

The ECJ continues to have a limited jurisdiction in the renewed economic governance model. The only expressed reference on the role of the ECJ in the context of the new economic governance framework[98] relates to the new enforcement procedure to decide whether the golden rule in the Fiscal Compact is respected. Article 8 of the TSCG includes a sui generis enforcement procedure which empowers the ECJ to decide on whether the Member State has complied with the golden rule in the Fiscal Compact. This procedure is very similar to the enforcement proceeding provided for under Articles 259 and 260 TFEU, but it is still different as it is limited in its scope. Only the Contracting Parties may access the Court for failure to compliance by another Contracting Party. This means that the Member States signing the TSCG are the only ones deciding whether there should be a case on the infringement of the golden rule. Practice on the use of Member State to Member State infringement procedure under Article 259 TFEU remains statistically insignificant. Therefore, the procedure under TSCG Article 8 remains an 'unloaded pistol'[99] that would rarely be exercised in future.

Overall, the new European economic governance framework shows that institutional practice in the field has been improved as compared to the pre-crisis economic governance framework. However, the lack of hard law supranational decision-making powers by the Commission in national economic, budgetary and fiscal matters and the – undoubtedly – predominant role of the Council in coordinating European economic policy indicate that there is still not a clear framework to achieve supranational financial stability in EU law and policy in the context of European economic governance.

95. *See* Cristina Fasone, *European Economic Governance and Parliamentary Representation. What Place for the European Parliament?*, 20 European Law Journal 164 (2014).
96. See Tuori, Tuori *supra* n. 84, 213–215.
97. *See* Fabbrini *supra* n. 2, 190.
98. It remains clear that the ECJ can still be involved if legally binding EU acts in the context of the European economic governance are challenged.
99. Adamski *supra* n. 23, 1359.

[C] The New Surveillance Tools of the EU Economic Governance

After having assessed the developing institutional model of European economic governance, this subsection examines whether the new preventive and corrective tools of the current surveillance model are satisfactory.

The European governance framework contains new rules to exercise supranational surveillance on the budgetary policies of the Member States. As compared with the pre-crisis framework, some improvements can be found in the new preventive arm and in the TSCG. First, the Six Pack and the Two Pack reinforce the existing regulatory framework for budgetary surveillance by providing some new rules for budgetary discipline and grounds for sanctions if there is a divergence from the Medium-Term Budgetary Objective (MTO). Euro area Member States are subject to the application of more stringent rules than in the past. Second, there is a reinforced role for the Commission in conducting economic surveillance by adopting soft law measures to assess the economic and fiscal situation of Member States such as opinion on draft national budgets, and there is more ground for ECJ involvement. Third, the TSCG has introduced the 'golden rule' as a sovereign international law obligation to adopt a balanced budget which shall be incorporated in the domestic legal system of the Member States. Fourth, the introduction of the MIP monitoring and preventive tools is a welcome development as it broadens the scope of European economic governance by including surveillance assessments of major macro-economic trends in Member States.

However, on a more critical note, the preventive arm fails to achieve strict rules to achieve supranational financial stability in EU law and policy. First, the Council, which represents the Member States' interests, still has the final saying over the multilateral surveillance process, the decision to open infringement by the adoption of decisions. Second, the surveillance procedure still shows considerable leeway for Member States to change the content of the Commission recommendations and draft opinions as well as to 'escape' from the application of rules and sanctions. This is evidenced by the fact that the Council is not obliged to follow the recommendations of the Commission and still exercises full powers over final decision-making. Third, the Fiscal Compact creates only a partially enforceable mechanism as regards the golden rule. In fact, under strict constraints, the TSCG gives competence to the ECJ to adjudicate on the failure to implement the fiscal rule under the condition that a Member State activates the enforcement action.

Similarly to the preventive arm, as compared with the pre-crisis framework, some improvements can be found in the new corrective arm and in the TSCG. The corrective arms of the renewed economic governance framework address existing EDP, excessive government debts, macroeconomic imbalances as well as enhanced surveillance and macro-economic adjustment programmes. First, the new economic governance rules allow stricter sanctioning to Member States by addressing sanctions for non-compliance with the EDP as well as with excessive government debts. There is an important extension of the corrective arm also to excessive government debts. Second, the MIP broadens the scope of possible corrective interventions as there is now a specific procedure for the correction of macroeconomic imbalances which is not provided in EU primary law. This MIP allows the imposition of enforcement measures in the form of an interest-bearing deposit or even fines and sanctions. Third, the Fiscal Compact establishes an automatic correction procedure which can be launched to correct deviations from the MTO or the adjustment path towards it. This improves the corrective arm procedure by introducing specific rules to correct automatically national budgetary deviations. Fourth, Regulation 472/2013 introduces rules for the systematisation of rules regarding euro area Member States in financial difficulties. The introduction into the euro area legal order of enhanced surveillance as well as macro-economic adjustment programmes indicates a clear stance towards a consolidation of the macro-economic adjustment programmes in the EU legal order. This consolidation effort makes the system of financial assistance more transparent and legitimate under the rules of the EU Treaties.[100] Moreover, the progressive use of enhanced surveillance and macro-economic adjustment programme and post-programme surveillance show a supranational systematisation in the law.

However, the existing corrective tools in the new economic governance still show considerable problems as to their nature, scope and implementation. As argued earlier, the lack of compelling and binding supranational instruments, or truly supranational decision-making powers on national economic, budgetary and fiscal decisions are clear limitations to the existing corrective tools in European economic governance. As shown earlier, these problems were evident in the decision not to sanction some euro area Member States for excessive deficits in July 2016.

Overall, the European economic surveillance governance tools show some improvements as compared to the pre-financial crisis framework. However, there are still important limitations in order to achieve supranational financial stability in EU law and policy as developed in this book. Most evidently, the lack of hard law powers conferred to the Commission or EU agencies to control effectively Member States or to take over national decisions in economic, budgetary and fiscal decisions remain a problematic feature in the existing economic governance rules.

§4.05 A (RE-)RENEWED EUROPEAN ECONOMIC GOVERNANCE: THE POSSIBLE WAYS FORWARD

The picture delineated so far shows that there are still considerable supranational surveillance gaps in the reformed European economic governance framework. This final part proposes some solutions to the existing limitations in European economic governance to respond to the lack of a truly supranational system attaining the supranational objective of financial stability in EU law and policy. It proposes institutional and substantial developments to improve the existing supranational economic governance surveillance model in Europe.

100. For discussions on financial assistance in the Europe *see* Chapter 5 section §5.05.

[A] Institutional Developments

This section addresses the need to reinforce the institutional arrangements in European economic governance. The establishment of contractual arrangements to confer further institutional powers to EU institutions would be a first option to reinforce European economic governance. These agreements would provide for cross-border economic and fiscal governance reforms between Member States or between Member States and EU institutions. According to these arrangements, Member States would contractually enact some obligations vis-à-vis EU institutions to coordinate budgets, taxation, promote investments and implement structural reforms.[101] This would mean that Member States contractually ensure that EU institutions intervene in economic, budgetary and fiscal matters at the national level. Already in 2012, the President's Council conclusions on improving the EMU put forward the possibility to support structural reforms 'through limited, temporary, flexible and targeted financial incentives as Member States enter into arrangements of a contractual nature with EU institutions'.[102] In practice this would mean that the Member States would commit to certain reforms in exchange for support funds either from the EU Commission or from other Member States. However, these proposals do not appear satisfactory for the reinforcement of supranational economic surveillance of Member States' finances. Contractual arrangements would place the Member States at the centre of decision-making and would not improve the existing economic governance in a supranational way. This is because such arrangements would not strengthen supranational regulation and surveillance. Furthermore, Member States would be involved in the negotiations and in the enforcement of the arrangements while the EU institutions could end up having a limited role in the effective implementation of such arrangements. Finally, the 'contractual' nature of them does not make it a strongly enforceable solution for the purpose of further supranational integration.

As an alternative, the adoption of stronger and deeper enforceable supranational institutional measures looks more satisfactory in order to improve the current limitations of the existing European surveillance economic governance model. Improvements could be made through the strengthening of the already existing economic surveillance institutional arrangements by hardening the Commission approach to assess national fiscal, budgetary and economic decisions ('stick') while promoting instruments that provide incentives ('carrot') to Member States which successfully implement structural reforms and make use of investments.[103] The harmonisation of some areas of economic policy and stronger supranational powers to the Commission, to the European Parliament or to other EU agencies or bodies in preventing and

101. *See* the two Communications from the Commission to the European Parliament and the Council, *Towards a deep and genuine EMU: Ex ante coordination of plans for major economic policy reforms*, COM(2013)166 final; and *Towards a deep and genuine EMU: The introduction of a convergence and competitiveness instrument*, COM(2013)165 final.
102. *See* President of the European Council, *Final Report 'Towards a Genuine EMU'*, 5 December 2012, 9.
103. *See* in this sense European Commission, *Making the best use of the flexibility within the existing rules of the Stability and Growth Pact* COM/2015/012, 3.

correcting possible macroeconomic imbalances, structural shocks and asymmetric shocks should be put forward.[104] These proposals should establish a more intrusive control of the Commission or EU agencies or bodies, in full dialogue with the European Parliament, in order to scrutinise fiscal, budgetary and economic decisions of Member States, to provide additional quasi-binding recommendations in the country-specific reports and draft budgetary laws as well as to invite more firmly Member States to adopt specific structural reforms. In this sense, the proposal to create a European Fiscal Board is a discrete institutional development in this sense.[105] The establishment of an advisory body for the overall direction of fiscal policy in the euro area and in the Union may play an important role in evaluating independently how the EU's fiscal framework is implemented in the Member States. The main task of the European Fiscal Board is to provide evaluation of the implementation of the EU fiscal framework. Another proposal is the establishment of national group of national independent authorities subject to EU coordination – Competitiveness Councils – with the task to provide independent expertise notably on assessing competitiveness performance and competitiveness-related reforms.[106] While the role and function of the European Fiscal Board seem limited at the moment, the system of supranational surveillance may benefit from the conferral of more powers to such supranational bodies in future. In perspective, the conferral of a wider institutional role to the EU Commission or other EU agencies or bodies to reduce asymmetric shocks, to provide insurance mechanisms to unemployment, to raise some form of European taxes and to dismiss national budgetary decisions if necessary should be explored.

At the same time, new supranational institutional reforms should provide incentives to Member States implementing structural reforms and making good use of investments. These should allow Member States that successfully adopt structural reforms to benefit from flexible interpretations of supranational economic and fiscal rules. The creation of an investment fund managed by the EU Commission aimed at reforms in Member States (the European Fund for Strategic Investment) is a first, but insufficient, attempt to provide Union-wide investment resources through a pooling of financial resources in the form of EU guarantees and European Investment Bank (EIB) contributions.[107] While this investment fund is intended to provide financial incentives to investments aimed at economic growth and jobs in Member States, it does not look an institutional 'panacea' to the economic policy problems of the EU. Similarly, the establishment of a European Fiscal Board as well as national competitiveness boards look minor attempts to move institutional reform forward.

104. *See* Hinarejos, *supra* n. 18, 1634–1635.

105. Commission Decision (EU) 2015/1937 of 21 October 2015 establishing an independent advisory European Fiscal Board [2015] OJ L 282.

106. See European Commission, *Communication on steps towards Completing Economic and Monetary Union*, COM/2015/0600 final, section 3.3.

107. Regulation (EU) 2015/1017 of the European Parliament and of the Council of 25 June 2015 on the European Fund for Strategic Investments, the European Investment Advisory Hub and the European Investment Project Portal and amending Regulations (EU) No 1291/2013 and (EU) No 1316/2013 – the European Fund for Strategic Investments [2015] OJ L 169.

Finally, the European Parliament should be more involved in the assessment of European economic governance decisions. The European Parliament should become a true legislator and increase its decision-making powers in the field.[108] From an institutional point of view, the limited role of the European Parliament in the field, remains a contentious issue as demonstrated by the current democratic deficit of (re-)newed European economic governance.

[B] Substantive Developments: Building Fiscal Capacity with Supranational Powers and Issuing Supranational Bond in Europe

[1] Providing the EU with Fiscal Capacity and Taxing Powers at the Supranational Level

The ideas to address the EU with supranational fiscal capacity and taxing powers are fascinating – yet politically extremely difficult – alternatives to the current limits of the European economic governance.

In the 2012 Blueprint the Commission endorsed the idea of a fiscal capacity to reinforce structural reforms and provide a stabilisation tool at EMU level especially in support of adjustment in asymmetric shocks.[109] The Commission proposed the strengthening of economic governance with the introduction of a 'convergence and competitiveness instrument' (CCI) within the EU budget.[110] This would support the implementation of structured reforms with contractual arrangements of the Member States.[111] However, in the same document, the Commission held that:

> [m]oving further in terms of national budgetary policy control, for example by setting up a European right to require a revision of national budgets in line with European commitments, would require a Treaty change.[112]

Notwithstanding such limitation, the possibility to provide hard law powers to the Commission or an EU agency or body on draft budgetary laws of Member States should be developed within the existing Treaty rules. In particular, this development would allow discharging budgetary laws of Member States and requiring a EU-driven national budget. Furthermore, substantive powers could include the supranational dismissal of individual national budgetary law and a supranational set of European balanced budgetary rules. These could be based on an EU Regulation adopted on the basis of Article 136 TFEU in combination with Article 352 TFEU. However, from a literal interpretation of existing Treaty rules, it appears that such proposal would require changes in primary EU law which at the moment do not seem possible.[113]

108. *See* Hinarejos, *supra* n. 8, 159.
109. European Commission, *Communication A blueprint for a deep and genuine economic and monetary union Launching a European Debate* COM(2012) 0777 final.
110. *Ibid.*, 21.
111. *Ibid.*, section 3.
112. *Ibid.*, 26.
113. *Ibid.*, 26 and following. Equally, the Commission indicates a clear EU competence to harmonize national budgetary laws and to have recourse to the CJEU in case of non-compliance.

More recently, some policy suggestions have been in the direction of creating supranational central fiscal capacity and taxes.[114] The two main aspects of the proposed model are the resources of fiscal funding and the use of such fiscal resources. As for the former aspect, resources could be collected by making available resources from Member States, similarly to what happens to contributions to the EU budget, or direct tax collections from individuals or entities or borrowing resources by a separate institutional unit, for instance an ad hoc international fund, that would be repaid using taxes/contributions or revenues from its operations.[115] As for the latter aspect, the support may be either providing intergovernmental transfers or loans to Member States which would then use these funds to support demand or directly funding expenditures in Member States, such as infrastructure projects or transfers to individuals (in the form of unemployment benefits), or providing funding and incentives for the private sector to spend or invest them similar to what happens with the existing EFSI.[116]

The partial transfer of financial resources to increase the EU budget is an area that should be further explored. The power to raise a European tax could be used to allow EU institutions to raise taxes that would fund a European treasury.[117] These proposals are made in the context of the general debate on the creation of a supranational treasury or of supranational fiscal transfer mechanisms. In particular, the existing rules provide for the use of the own resources system of the Union to finance the European budget. It has been recently suggested that fiscal capacity of the EU could be enhanced with a combined use of the own resources legal basis under Articles 133 and 311 TFEU.[118] This combined use of legal bases would make it possible to provide some additional financial resources to the EU budget either from Member States' contributions or from new EU own resources with a view to establish a common budget for the expenses to be undertaken in a truly supranational governance framework. Alternatively, the integration of the ESM in the EU legal order[119] could give the opportunity to make the ESM a sovereign fund capable of supporting excessive government debts or address asymmetric shocks or provide fiscal transfers under certain conditions.

The use of these financing instruments would require that the Member States with the higher sovereign debt implement some structural reforms to lower the level of government debt to compensate the moral hazard problem. The increase of fiscal capacity through the EU budget would allow for the increase of financial resources at supranational level. However, in the absence of clear directions and actual political willing for such supranational reforms, European economic governance remains constrained. After having assessed some substantive options on strengthening the

114. *See* IMF, *Euro area policies. Selected issues*, 45 (2016) at https://www.imf.org/external/pubs/ft/scr/2016/cr16220.pdf (accessed 31 December 2016).
115. *Ibid.*
116. *Ibid.*
117. *See also* the Five Presidents' Report, 22 June 2015, 20 http://ec.europa.eu/priorities/economic-monetary-union/docs/5-presidents-report_en.pdf (accessed 31 December 2016).
118. Federico Fabbrini, *From Fiscal Constraints to Fiscal Capacity* in Maurice Adams, Federico Fabbrini, Pierre Larouche (eds), *The Constitutionalization of European Budgetary Constraints* 408 (Hart Publishing 2014).
119. *See* Chapter 5 section §5.06[B] for discussions on the integration of the ESM into the EU legal order.

existing European economic governance, the following section focuses on the creation of supranational debt instruments to finance sovereign public debts.

[2] Issuance of Supranational Debt Instruments

As demonstrated above, the increase of EU fiscal capacity is an option under the current Treaty constraints open to euro area Member States to refinance high government debts. It is clear that the perspective of proposing a supranational level for financial stability in Europe would require an appropriate backstop mechanism to counteract severe sovereign debt crises. At present, the solution is found in intergovernmental treaties where liability regimes are strictly separated between the EU and Member States.[120] An alternative to increasing the fiscal capacity of the Union could be the issuance of supranational bonds. These would strengthen the pursuit of supranational financial stability at the European level.

The issuance of supranational debt instruments or Eurobonds has generated some intense discussions in the first phase of the European financial crisis. Already in 2010, Juncker and Tremonti called for the creation of Eurobonds as the final solution of the crisis.[121] In literature, Eurobonds are seen as:

> the promised land to which the monetary union must direct its evolution; [while] they are regarded [...] as a treason to the principle that each Member State must remain liable for its budgetary decisions.[122]

A number of proposals on Eurobonds have been developed to date. Legal scholarship maintains that Eurobonds are legally conceivable under three different forms: 'proportionate liability'; 'joint and several liability'; or 'issuance under a guarantee'.[123] During the crisis, a number of academic contributions have been developed proposals for Eurobonds.[124] One of the most famous initiatives is the Blue Bond proposal.[125] This suggests providing the separation between blue and red national bonds. Sovereign debt below 60% would be pooled together and issued as a blue bond, while the debt beyond 60% would be red and have junior status. De Grauwe and Moesen suggested that the creation of Eurobonds could play a substantial improvement for financial stability. This would take place by establishing a system of

120. *See* Chapter 5 section §5.05[B] for similar discussions in the context of the ESM.
121. Jean-Claude Juncker & Giulio Tremonti, *E-bonds Would End the Crisis*, Financial Times, 5 December 2010.
122. Alberto de Gregorio Merino, *Legal Developments in the Economic and Monetary Union During the Debt Crisis: The Mechanisms of Financial Assistance*, 49 Common Market Law Review 1630 (2012).
123. Phoebus Athanassiou, *Of Past Measures and Future Plans for Europe's Exit from the Sovereign Debt Crisis: What Is Legally Possible (and What Is Not)*, 36 European Law Review 572 (2011).
124. *See* Stijn Claessens, Ashoka Mody & Shahin Vallée, *Paths to Eurobonds*, IMF WP 12/72 20 (2012).
125. Jacques Delpla & Jakob von Weizsäcker, *The Blue Bond Proposal*, Bruegel Policy Brief 2010/03 6 (2010).

differential interest rates between Member States related to their fiscal position.[126] In 2011, an alternative solution envisaged the creation of short-term common debt (i.e., Eurobills), intended to be about 10% of GDP.[127] These Eurobills would have a very short maturity and be backed up by several and joint liability. The short maturity would guarantee the respect of fiscal discipline. Furthermore, in 2011, the German Council of Economic Experts published a proposal aiming at establishing a European Debt Redemption Fund (EDRF) where the sovereign debt beyond 60% would be placed under a several and joint liability regime.[128] The beneficiary Member States would agree to repay the transferred amount to the EDRF over a number of years.

At institutional level, the Commission published a document outlining the feasibility of creating Stability Bonds, the Green Paper Stability Bonds in 2011.[129] The Commission acknowledges that Stability Bonds would provide extensive benefits in Europe: they would manage the crisis and prevent further sovereign crisis as well as reinforce financial stability in the euro area.[130] The Communication offers an official reconstruction on the creation of Eurobonds. This presents three possible models: the complete substitution of national debt by common bonds issued under a joint and several framework, the issuance of both common and national debts, and the issuance of stability bonds under several guarantees. The Commission states that the several and not joint liability instrument option would not require burdensome Treaty changes.[131] In this sense, the Commission blueprint favours the European Redemption Fund and the Eurobill proposals.[132]

Overall, the proposals of supranational bond issuance are interesting and have led to many debates. However, their feasibility in technical and political terms seems unlikely in the short- and medium-term.

[3] Assessment

Following one reading or the other, it appears that proposed substantive solutions to improve European economic governance would be beneficial to reach supranational financial stability and further integration in EU law and policy. Automatic fiscal transfers, asymmetric shock absorption mechanisms or supranational public bond issuance would increase the level playing field in economic governance and contribute to the completion of the EMU. However, it is expected that the Commission would

126. Paul de Grauwe & Wim Moesen, *Gains for All: A Proposal for a Common Euro Bond*, 33 Intereconomics 132 (2009).
127. Christian Hellwig & Thomas Philippon, *Eurobills, Not Eurobonds*, VoxEU 2 December 2011 http://www.voxeu.org/article/eurobills-not-euro-bonds (accessed 31 December 2016).
128. Peter Bofinger *et al.*, *A European Redemption Pact*, VoxEU 9 November 2011 at http://voxeu.org/index.php?q=node/7253 (accessed 31 December 2016).
129. European Commission, *Green Paper on the feasibility of introducing Stability Bonds*, COM(2011) 818 final, 2.
130. *Ibid.*, 4.
131. *Ibid.*, 20.
132. *See* European Commission, *A blueprint for a deep and genuine economic and monetary union Launching a European Debate*, 28, 30.

come with minor reform proposals in 2017 as part of the project to publish a White Paper on the future of the EMU.

The proposed initiatives show that a possible development of reinforced European economic governance would lead to the mutualisation of public debt and truly supranational surveillance in the medium to long-term. It has been suggested that a new EU fiscal sovereignty and new EU fiscal authorities would move Europe towards a fiscal Union.[133] Supranational fiscal transfer or debt issuance would create the conditions for stronger financial stability in Europe, would prevent future sovereign debt crisis and would eventually transform the Union into a true new quasi-federal entity. However, at present technical and non-technical concerns limit a supranational response to the reform of economic governance. As to the former, the limitation of moral hazard and the enforcement of market discipline on the part of the Member States would be the most significant challenges. Guaranteeing the fair balance between mutualisation and fiscal discipline is difficult to achieve in practice. As to the latter, existing Treaty prohibitions (Articles 123 and 125 TFEU) and the political unwillingness to embark on such projects seem insurmountable. After having provided some reform suggestions on the way forward in the European economic governance framework, it is appropriate to draw some conclusions.

§4.06 CONCLUSION

This chapter outlined the main aspects of the renewed economic governance framework in light of financial stability as a supranational foundational objective in EU law and policy. The impact of the financial crisis shows that the loose and flexible European economic governance framework needed to be reinforced in order to guarantee that the Member States – in particular the euro area ones – coordinate further their economic and fiscal policies. As part of the broader analysis made in this book on the role of financial stability in EU law and policy, this chapter has argued that the current reinforced economic governance framework is not itself sufficient to promote an effective supranational financial stability policy at the European level.

While there are still important aspects that have been improved to address economic governance, there remains a number of limitations. Loose EU primary law rules on multilateral surveillance and EDP still exist and the supranational level-playing field is not capable of addressing shocks or risks to financial stability for Member States. Political compromises led to adopt an intergovernmental Treaty imposing the 'golden rule' and show the difficulties of a common agreement on supranational measures to improve supranational economic governance over Member States. The Fiscal Compact is and will not be a 'panacea' to address supranational financial stability in Europe from the perspective of European economic governance. Similarly, the national imprinting of decision-making in the European governance framework, exemplified by the strong role of the Council in the renewed SGP, does not

133. Edoardo Chiti & Pedro Gustavo Teixeira, *The Constitutional Implications of the European Responses to the Financial and Public Debt Crisis*, 50 Common Market Law Review 700 (2013).

contribute to move the governance framework towards a new supranational dimension of economic surveillance. From this analysis, it emerges that the process of mutualisation of European economic and fiscal governance is achievable only through political consensus to amend EU primary law or through intergovernmental arrangements aiming at reinforcing the existing rules on supranational surveillance. At present, there are no Treaty provisions empowering the EU institutions to establish a system of supranational taxes or the mutual issuance of public debt or to empower EU institutions to set hard law rules on economic, budgetary or fiscal rules in Member States.

Overall, this chapter has shown that the (re-)newed European economic governance model shall still improve and evolve into a true system of economic, budgetary and fiscal federalism promoting supranational financial stability as one of its foundational objectives. Nonetheless, the absence of a political paradigm change towards the creation of a supranational European economic governance framework is partially counterbalanced by the establishment of supranational and intergovernmental financial stabilisation tools aiming at sustaining sovereigns in financial difficulties. Therefore, the book will now turn to examining the new – and unprecedented – creation of mechanisms to provide financial assistance to sovereigns in Europe.

CHAPTER 5
Stability Mechanisms in Europe

§5.01 INTRODUCTION

At the peak of the sovereign debt crisis in Europe, it was soon realised what the EU framework lacked: supranational backstops to address sovereigns or institutions in financial distress in Europe. The creation of stability mechanisms in Europe is a new expression of the current development of financial stability as a supranational foundational objective as developed in this book. While at international level the IMF is entitled to provide financial assistance to its members through a number of established lending instruments, the financial – and in particular the euro – crisis has developed a new set of stability mechanism instruments which apply in the Europe, and in particular to the euro area Member States. Public finances have been used to provide financial assistance to Member States in distress or to financial institutions established in a Member State.

Financial assistance mechanisms have the objective to grant stability support to Member States or financial institutions with a view to address financial distress. An essential part of a credible financial stability framework requires an adequate system of financial backstops in Europe that is capable of addressing shocks by providing financial resources to distressed Member States and financial institutions. The Member States and the EU have developed a number of financial assistance instruments that have taken different forms, made use of an unusual legal basis and questioned the existence of EU primary law provisions. In particular, the euro area Member States have concluded an international agreement to establish the ESM, a permanent intergovernmental institution based in Luxembourg that may provide financial assistance to euro area Member States or financial institutions in distress under certain conditions. The ESM is the most remarkable example of crisis-related stability mechanisms established to date in Europe. It is an international institution having a significant capital stock (up to EUR 700 billion) and offering financial instruments to assist euro area Member States or financial institutions in distress. In the context of the normative instruments for financial stability developed earlier in this book, the ESM implements normative instruments to attain financial stability, in particular the use of rescue measures for the management of risks and/or shocks to sovereigns with burden-sharing arrangements through the conditionality of intervention.

Reform efforts have agreed on two supranational public backstop-funding mechanisms in Europe: (i) EU instruments backed up by the EU budget to provide assistance facilities to Member States in distress; (ii) purely intergovernmental instruments to provide financial assistance. This chapter assesses to what extent the establishment of financial stability mechanisms in Europe is grounded on the foundational objective of financial stability in EU law and policy. It examines the way in which both the EU and the Member States have developed an extensive set of financial assistance instruments for financial stability purposes while having to cope with the lack of supranational financial resources to sustain public finances in Europe and to avert sovereign default risks for Member States. It argues that the path towards permanent stability mechanisms is now well established in Europe. Given the current political limitations to build up a truly supranational economic governance,[1] this chapter assesses the use of such intergovernmental means to provide financial assistance to Member States in distress. At the same time, this chapter explores the alternative path of grounding financial assistance mechanisms into the EU legal order.

The chapter is structured as follows. After a brief assessment on the role of the IMF in providing financial assistance arrangements to its membership (§5.02), the chapter refers to the Treaty provisions limiting the possibility of financial assistance and provides an overview of the early initiatives to create stability mechanisms in Europe (§5.03). Then, it assesses the ESM as the permanent financial assistance mechanisms for the euro area by also examining the ECJ *Pringle*[2] judgment on the compatibility of the ESM with EU law and assessing the use of intergovernmental financial instruments to provide financial stability in Europe (§5.04). Further, it discusses the main aspects of financial stability mechanisms under EU law both in substance and in form (§5.05). After that, the chapter investigates the possible ways forward to create reinforced crisis-related financial stability mechanisms in Europe (§5.06). The last section concludes (§5.07).

§5.02 FINANCIAL ASSISTANCE MECHANISMS AND THE IMF

The provision of financial assistance to sovereigns is a well-established feature in international economic law. This section attempts to provide a succinct overview on the instruments for financial assistance offered by the IMF, especially vis-à-vis Member States of the EU.

1. *See also* the discussions in Chapter 4 section §4.05.
2. Case C-370/12 *Thomas Pringle v. Governement of Ireland, Ireland and The Attorney General* ECLI:EU:C:2012:756.

[A] The IMF

The IMF is the international organisation that was conceived in 1944 at the Bretton Woods Conference and formally created in 1945.[3] The IMF's fundamental mission is to help ensure stability in the international system. The main objectives of the IMF are the promotion of international monetary cooperation and exchange stability, and the development of expansion and balanced growth of international trade. The IMF may make the general resources of the Fund temporarily available to its members to 'correct maladjustments in their balance of payments'.[4]

One of the key objectives of the IMF enshrined in the IMF Agreement is to provide lending facilities to countries with balance of payments (BoP) difficulties.[5] Over the years, the IMF has established a number of lending instruments to assist its Members. Under Article V of the IMF Agreement upon request by a member country, IMF resources are usually made available under a lending 'arrangement'. The IMF lending programmes are generally tailored with conditionality. In practice, the requesting member shall adopt and implement adjustment policies in order to receive financial assistance. Over the years, the IMF has developed various lending instruments which address the specific circumstances of its diverse membership. Facing the most recent challenges of the financial crisis, the IMF has undertaken a policy of revision of its arrangements in order to lend at concessional rates or to write down the debt of the highly indebted countries.[6]

[B] The IMF and Its Involvement in Assistance to EU Member States

While the IMF is an international economic institution, the impact of the financial crisis in Europe has witnessed an important IMF intervention in Europe.[7] In effect, the IMF has played a considerable role in assisting Member States in Europe and in guiding the negotiation and implementation of financial assistance programmes to some Member States. This is shown by two major policy developments. First, the IMF has provided considerable financial assistance to some euro area Member States as part of European macro-economic adjustment programmes (Ireland, Portugal, Greece, Cyprus) and non-euro area Member States (Hungary, Romania and Bulgaria). The agreed programmes have been established to the benefit of both euro area and non-euro area Member States. The euro area ones are larger and longer-lasting programmes than

3. *See* Matthias Herdegen, *Principles of International Economic Law*, Ch. XXXIX (Oxford University Press 2016).
4. *See* IMF Agreement, Art. I.
5. For the reinforced role of the IMF in surveillance *see* Chapter 2 section §2.05[D].
6. *See* IMF, *Lending by the IMF* http://www.imf.org/external/about/lending.htm#changing (accessed 31 December 2016).
7. Jean Pisani-Ferry *et al.*, *EU-IMF Assistance to Euro Area Countries: An Early Assessment*, Bruegel Report 27 (2013) http://www.bruegel.org/publications/publication-detail/publication/779-eu-imf-assistance-to-euro-area-countries-an-early-assessment/ (accessed 31 December 2016).

previous IMF programmes.[8] Second, the IMF has increasingly acquired an important role to shape and implement financial assistance mechanisms agreed in Europe. This is clear in the role it has acquired as a troika member. Together with the ECB and the EU Commission, the IMF has become a powerful institution and has profoundly contributed to shape conditionality requirements and structural reform needs for the benefiting Member States.

Overall, during the recent financial crisis, the IMF has played a substantial role in assuring financial stability in the international system.[9] First, the IMF has made use of its global mandate to lending operations to sovereigns. This spans from very high-income economies up to very low-income economies. Second, the IMF has developed a number of instruments throughout its seventy years of existence and has gained extensive experience in lending instruments. Third, the IMF has a wide mandate that comprises financial assistance, surveillance and technical assistance.

It can be concluded that the IMF acts as a global institution for financial assistance to its membership. However, the IMF stability assistance is different as compared with the new ESMs. The latter will be explored below in this chapter.

§5.03 THE DEVELOPMENT OF FINANCIAL ASSISTANCE MECHANISMS IN EUROPE: THE FIRST MEASURES

[A] Limitations to Establish Financial Stability Mechanisms Under the Maastricht Treaty 'Legacy'

The Maastricht Treaty did not provide for financial assistance mechanisms between Member States or from the Union to Member States as a rule. While the Maastricht Treaty established a system of economic policy coordination between Member States, it also introduced a number of prohibitions to preserve fiscal discipline and liability of the Member States and the Union. The most evident prohibition is the no-bailout clause under Article 125 TFEU. This states that the EU and the Member States shall not be liable for, or assume any commitments of another Member State. Similarly, Article 123 TFEU prohibits monetary financing of government debt.[10] The provision of Article 125 TFEU reads as follows:

> The Union shall not be liable for or assume the commitments of (...) any Member State, without prejudice to mutual financial guarantees for the joint execution of a specific project. A Member State shall not be liable for or assume the commitments of (...) another Member State, without prejudice to mutual financial guarantees for the joint execution of a specific project.

This article sets an outright prohibition of vertical and horizontal financial assistance measures under EU law. Article 125(2) TFEU provides that the Council, on

8. *Ibid.*, 30.
9. *See* Annamaria Viterbo, *International Economic Law and Monetary Measures*, 56 (Edward Elgar 2012).
10. *See* Chapter 3 section §3.02[A][4] for a brief analysis of Art. 123 TFEU.

a proposal from the Commission and after consulting the European Parliament, may, as required, specify definitions for the application of the prohibitions referred to in Articles 123 and 125 TFEU. This is an explicit legal basis which allows the Council to interpret the economic policy prohibitions. The Council adopted Regulation 3603/1993 specifying the scope of the no-bailout clause.[11]

Shortly after the entry into force of this provision, scholarship suggested that the no-bailout clause is an essential element of the 'budgetary code' of the Union. Thus, Member States are 'on their own' as to their budgetary commitments. It was argued that 'the rationale for the prohibition is (...) the application of full market rigour to the activities of Governments'.[12] At the same time, Article 122(2) TFEU allows the Council, on a proposal from the Commission, to grant financial assistance to a Member States in difficulty, or that is seriously threatened with severe difficulties caused by natural disasters or exceptional occurrences beyond its control.[13]

Furthermore, for Member States outside the euro area, Article 143 TFEU provides for a detailed system of BoP support to non-euro area Member States whenever the Member State encounters financial difficulties. According to Article 143 TFEU a Member State with a derogation from the use of the euro that is 'in difficulties or is seriously threatened with difficulties as regards its balance of payments (...)' may be granted financial assistance. This provision is specifically addressed to non-euro Member States and aims at providing non-euro area Member States medium to long-term financial assistance. The Council adopted Regulation 332/2002[14] under Article 352 TFEU establishing a BoP facility for non-euro area Member States.

[B] From Temporary to Permanent Stability Mechanisms in Europe

This section looks at the first instruments of financial assistance established in Europe at the end of 2010 during the most dramatic phases of the crisis. The imbalance in the EMU has been stigmatised by the outbreak of the financial crisis. The limited competences of the Union to control and supervise Member States' budgets have had a clear impact on the EMU framework. New solutions to avoid the default of some EU Member States were needed. As of 2010, special arrangements were established to assure rapid liquidity to weak Member States in the euro area. These measures have taken the form of bilateral loans to Greece followed by loan facilities to Member States in economic distress. Subsequently, the EFSM and the EFSF were established for the purpose of providing financial assistance to sovereigns.[15] These instruments will be briefly analysed.

---

11. OJ L 332, 31 December 1993.
12. René Smits, *The European Central Bank*, 76–77 (Kluwer Law International 1997).
13. *See infra* section §5.05[A] for the analysis of Arts 122 and 125 TFEU.
14. Council, Regulation (EC) No 332/2002 of 18 February 2002 establishing a facility providing medium-term financial assistance for Member States' balances of payments [2002] OJ L 53.
15. *See* Alberto de Gregorio Merino, *Legal Developments in the Economic and Monetary Union During the Debt Crisis: The Mechanisms of Financial Assistance*, 49 Common Market Law Review 1615–1621 (2012).

[1] *The Greek Loan Facility: The First Ad Hoc Financial Assistance Tool to Avoid a Sovereign Default*

During an informal meeting of the Heads of State and Government of the EU on 11 February 2010, the euro area Member States realised that the required level of Greek government debt could not be sustained and that spillover effects to other Euro zone economies could take place.[16] On 25 March 2010, euro area Member States decided to establish an ad hoc intervention tool as part of a joint euro area-IMF financing package via the conclusion of 'coordinate bilateral loans' that would complement the assistance provided by the IMF. These bilateral loans would be 'non-concessional loans i.e., not containing any subsidy element'.[17] The financial resources were pooled under strict conditionality of intervention.[18] The total amount of the pool of bilateral loans to Greece amounted to EUR 80 billion with the IMF contributing with a loan of EUR 30 billion.

[2] *The EFSM: The Limitation of an EU Funded Stability Mechanism*

The EFSM was created as an EU budget backed-up instrument to provide financial assistance possibly to all Member States. The Council agreed on the use of the legal basis under Article 122(2) TFEU to establish the EFSM on 9 May 2010. Council Regulation 407/2010[19] created the EFSM as a truly Union assistance facility. The EFSM funding has been used to provide financial assistance to Portugal and Ireland. The EFSM has been used for a total amount of up to EUR 48.5 billion (up to EUR 22.5 billion for Ireland and up to EUR 26 billion for Portugal), to be disbursed over three years (2011–2013). The EFSM is an emergency funding programme which relies on funds raised in the financial markets and backed by the EU budget. The ESFM is founded on the unusual legal basis of Article 122(2) TFEU and is backed by the EU budget as collateral. The concession of loans or credit lines of the EFSM are subject to conditionality.

[3] *The EFSF: A Temporary Euro Area Stability Mechanism*

While the Council agreed to create a specific EU budget instrument, the EFSM, the euro area Member States decided to establish a Special Purpose Vehicle, after renamed the

16. *See* Heads of State or Government of the European Union, *statement of 11 February 2010* at www.consilium.europa.eu/uedocs/cms_data/docs/pressdata/en/ec/112856.pdf (accessed 31 December 2016).
17. *See* Heads of State or Government of the euro area, *statement of 25 March 2010* at www.consilium.europa.eu/uedocs/cms_data/docs/pressdata/en/ec/113563.pdf (accessed 31 December 2016).
18. *Ibid.*
19. Council, Regulation (EU) No 407/2010 of 11 May 2010 establishing a European financial stabilisation mechanism [2010] OJ L 118.

EFSF.[20] The EFSF afforded financial assistance for up to EUR 440 billion. Soon after, the euro area Member States decided to raise the EFSF's guarantees to a total of EUR 780 billion at the conclusions of the Heads of State and Government of the euro area on 11 March 2011.[21] The shareholders of the EFSF were the euro area Member States. The Member States' contributions reflected the ECB's paid-up capital.

Overall, the EFSF was a temporary mechanism between euro area Member States based on guarantees. The beneficiary Member State had to respect appropriate conditionality by implementing appropriate rules and policies through a financial assistance programme. The EFSF expired on 30 June 2013, but it continues to service existing programme commitments. Its capacity has been absorbed by the ESM, which will be analysed infra in this chapter.

[4] Financial Mechanisms and Non-euro Area Member States

As held before, the Maastricht Treaty did not introduce specific provisions on financial stability mechanisms with the exception of the balance of payment assistance for non-euro area Member States under Article 143 TFEU. While the outbreak of the financial crisis has provided new financial stability mechanisms in the euro area, the non-euro balance-of-payment instrument has remained substantially unchanged. Non-euro area Member States may benefit from financial assistance from the EFSM and from the instrument provided under Regulation 332/2002.

More recently, non-euro area Member States have agreed with the euro area Member States that 'no financial (direct or indirect) liability will be incurred by the Member States which do not participate in the single currency' as regards the future involvement of the EFSM or other financial instruments for the assistance of euro area Member States.[22] In August 2015, the Council adopted a regulation guaranteeing that non-euro area Member States 'are immediately and fully compensated for any liability they may incur as a result of any failure by the beneficiary Member State to repay the financial assistance (...)'.[23] This recent development shows that non-euro area Member States remain unaffected by mutual systems for financial assistance, especially if such financial support means committing to instruments granted to euro area Member States.

20. EFSF Agreement at www.efsf.europa.eu/attachments/20111019_efsf_framework_agreement_en.pdf (accessed 31 December 2016).
21. Heads of State or Government of the euro area, *conclusions of 11 March 2011*, www.consilium.europa.eu/uedocs/cms_data/docs/pressdata/en/ec/119809.pdf (accessed 31 December 2016).
22. European Council, *Joint declaration by the Commission and the Council on the use of the EFSM*, 16 July 2015 at http://data.consilium.europa.eu/doc/document/ST-10994-2015-INIT/en/pdf (accessed 31 December 2016).
23. Council Regulation (EU) 2015/1360 of 4 August 2015 amending Regulation (EU) No 407/2010 establishing a European financial stabilisation mechanism, OJ L 210, 7.8.2015.

§5.04 THE ESM: CREATION, ROLE, POWERS AND JUDICIAL ENDORSEMENT IN *PRINGLE*[24]

After having analysed the first instruments for financial assistance to sovereigns, this section looks at the creation, role and power of the ESMT and assesses the ECJ *Pringle* judgment on the compatibility of the ESM under EU law.

[A] The Conclusion of the ESMT

In order to ensure balance and sustainable growth, at the meeting of 28 and 29 October 2010 the euro area Heads of State and of Government decided to create a *permanent* stability mechanism.[25] At the meeting of 16–17 December 2010, the European Council provided the features of the new stability mechanism and agreed to undertake the required consultations for an amendment of the Treaty to that effect.[26] The euro area Member States agreed on a first draft ESMT on 11 July 2011. However, soon after a second draft ESMT was agreed on 2 February 2012.[27] This second version contains a longer list of financial instruments for the euro area Member States such as precautionary assistance and assistance for the re-capitalisation of financial institutions. Following the adoption of the ESMT on 2 February 2012, all the euro area Member States have ratified the ESMT according to their national constitutional requirements and have paved the way for the entry into force of the agreement in September 2012.

[B] The Main Features of the ESM

The ESM is a Luxembourg-based international organisation under international public law which provides for financial assistance to euro area Member States in financial difficulties, subject to the requirement of strict conditionality. The ESM membership is exclusively open to euro area Member States that have signed the TSCG.[28] As provided in Article 2 of the ESMT, the purpose of the ESM is:

> to mobilise funding and provide stability support under strict conditionality (...) to the benefit of ESM Members which are experiencing or are threatened by, severe financing problems, if indispensable to safeguard the *financial stability* of the euro area as a whole and of its Member States (...).[29]

---

24. This section draws from Gianni Lo Schiavo *The Judicial 'Bail Out' of the European Stability Mechanism: Comment on the Pringle Judgment*, 5 Italian Journal of Public Law 188 (2013).
25. European Council, *conclusions of 30 November 2010* at http://www.consilium.europa.eu/uedocs/cms_data/docs/pressdata/en/ec/117496.pdf (emphasis added) (accessed 31 December 2016).
26. *Ibid.*
27. ESM, Treaty (hereinafter 'ESMT') at http://www.esm.europa.eu/pdf/esm_treaty_en.pdf (accessed 31 December 2016).
28. ESMT, Art. 44 and Recital 5.
29. emphasis added.

In other words, the purpose of the ESM is to provide stability support to euro area Member States, where needed and subject to conditionality to the benefit of financial stability.[30] According to the ESMT, stability support may be granted 'when severe risks to the financial stability of Member States whose currency is the euro may put at risk the financial stability of the euro area as a whole'.[31]

The ESM Board of Governors plays a central role in the ESM. It acts as the main body to take decisions to grant financial assistance to Member States in difficulty. The ESMT provides that only approximately EUR 80 billion are paid-in capital, while a remaining amount of EUR 620 billion are committed callable capital.[32] The maximum lending capacity of the ESM is EUR 500 billion. When activated, ESM loans have a preferred creditor status as compared with other credits.[33]

The ESMT provides for different instruments to assist the euro area Member States. It can provide precautionary financial assistance when the economic condition of a Member State is sound enough to retain access to the market, but financial aid is necessary in order to avoid a crisis.[34] Further, the ESM can grant loans to euro area Member States who have lost access to financial markets either due to excessive costs or due to lack of lenders. The Primary Market Support Facility (PMSF) allows the ESM to buy bonds in the primary bond market of the euro area Member State either to facilitate that it returns to the financial markets or to increase the efficiency of other ESM financial aid.[35] Intervention in the Secondary Market Support Facility (SMSF) is designed to reduce interest rates in the secondary market and to help euro area Members struggling with the refinancing of their banking systems.[36] Furthermore, financial assistance might be used to recapitalise indirectly the financial institutions of an euro area Member State.[37] In 2014, the ESM adopted a new instrument in the form of direct recapitalisation of a financial institution established in the euro area.[38]

In case a euro area Member State in distress needs financial assistance, the parties involved would prepare and sign a Memorandum of Understanding (MoU) which shall reflect the severity of the weaknesses to be addressed in order to receive financial assistance.[39] Following the decision to grant assistance and in liaison with the ECB, the Commission negotiates the MoU with the concerned Member State.[40] Thereafter, the

30. de Gregorio Merino *supra* n. 15, 1621.
31. ESMT, Recital 6.
32. *Ibid.*, Art. 8.
33. *Ibid.*, Recital 13.
34. *Ibid.*, Art. 14.
35. *Ibid.*, Art. 17.
36. *Ibid.*, Art. 18.
37. *Ibid.*, Art. 15.
38. ESM, *Guideline on Financial Assistance for the Direct Recapitalisation of Institutions* at http://www.esm.europa.eu/pdf/20141208%20Guideline%20on%20Financial%20Assistance%20for%20the%20Direct%20Recapitalisation%20of%20Institutions.pdf (accessed 31 December 2016).
39. *Ibid.*, Art. 13(3).
40. ESMT, Art. 13(3).

Commission signs the MoU on behalf of the ESM.[41] In the implementing phase, the ESM and the ECB monitor compliance with the conditionality laid down in the MoU.[42] The ESM entrusts the EU institutions with crucial tasks in granting and supervising financial assistance. The Commission and the ECB assess the needed financial needs[43] as well as the sustainability of the Member State's public debt and the corresponding risk of financial stability to the euro area as a whole.[44] Moreover, the ECJ is entrusted with the task of adjudicating disputes between the ESM and a Member State or among several Member States relating to the interpretation and application of the ESMT when a decision of the board on the matter is contested.[45]

Until now, the ESM financial instruments have been provided in three cases. First, the ESM provided financial assistance to Spain in the form of a bank recapitalisation programme. On 20 July 2012, the Eurogroup decided to grant financial assistance to Spain.[46] Financial needs of Spain were agreed for up to EUR 100 billion in order to safeguard the financial stability in the euro area as a whole.[47] Second, the ESM, after fierce negotiations, has provided financial assistance to Cyprus.[48] In 2015, Greece resorted to the ESM to provide for a maximum commitment of EUR 86 billion.[49]

[C] The ESM and *Pringle*: A 'Yes' from the European Judiciary

While the ESM has been adopted in 2012, some judicial challenges at the national level provided clarifications as to the possibility to create a pan-euro area intergovernmental stability mechanism.[50] The *Pringle* case reached the European judiciary. During the process of ratification of the ESMT, Mr Pringle brought an action before the High Court of Ireland. Following his claims, the Irish High Court dismissed his action in its entirety. Mr Pringle appealed before the Supreme Court of Ireland which decided to refer a number of questions to the ECJ for preliminary ruling.

Following the Advocate General (A.G.) Kokott's view on 26 October 2012,[51] the ECJ delivered the *Pringle* judgment on 27 November 2012. The Court's judgment

41. *Ibid.*, Art. 13(4).
42. *Ibid.*, Art. 13(7).
43. *Ibid.*, Art. 13.
44. *Ibid.*
45. *Ibid.*, Art. 37(3).
46. Eurogroup, *Statement*, 20 July 2012 http://www.consilium.europa.eu/uedocs/cms_data/docs/pressdata/en/ecofin/131914.pdf (accessed 31 December 2016).
47. ESM, *Spanish financial assistance programme* http://www.esm.europa.eu/about/assistance/spain/index.htm (accessed 31 December 2016).
48. ESM, *Cypriot financial assistance programme* http://www.esm.europa.eu/about/assistance/cyprus/index.htm (accessed 31 December 2016).
49. ESM, *Greek financial assistance programme* http://www.esm.europa.eu/assistance/Greece/index.htm (accessed 31 December 2016).
50. *See*, extensively, Federico Fabbrini, *Economic Governance*, 67 (Oxford University Press 2016).
51. Case C-370/12 *Thomas Pringle v. Governement of Ireland, Ireland and The Attorney General* ECLI:EU:C:2012:756, AG Kokott View delivered on 26 October 2012.

comprised three questions. The first question referred to the Court concerned the validity of the Treaty amendment of Article 136 TFEU and the use of the simplified revision procedure under Article 48(6) TEU. The Court scrutinised the impact of the amendment to the TFEU and ascertained whether the effects of such amendment concern solely provisions of Part Three of that Treaty and whether such amendment increased the competences attributed on the Union in the Treaties. The ECJ reached the conclusion that the ESM pursues the objective of maintaining the stability of the euro area as a whole whereas the Eurosystem pursues the objective of price stability. The Court observed that it is clear that the establishment of the ESM does not encroach on the monetary policy as the ESM's objective is:

> to safeguard the stability of the euro area as a whole, that is clearly *distinct* from the objective of maintaining price stability, which is the primary objective of the Union's monetary policy.[52]

With regard to the impact of the ESM on the EU monetary policy competence, the ECJ denied that the role and the tasks of the ESM would fall within the monetary policy under the TFEU under Article 127 TFEU. According to Articles 3 and 12(1) of the ESMT, the ESM is not entitled to set the key interest rates for the euro area or to issue euro currency, but it seeks to provide financial assistance entirely granted by the ESM from paid-in capital or by the issue of financial instruments.[53] Furthermore, the Court held that even if the activities of the ESM might have an influence on the rate of inflation, such influence would constitute 'only indirect consequence of the economic policy measures adopted'.[54]

Further, the Court conducted an extensive analysis on the interpretation of the ESM with the economic coordination provisions under Articles 2(3) TFEU, 119 TFEU to 121 TFEU and 126 TFEU. The judgment stated that 'the ESM is not concerned with the coordination of the economic policies of the Member States, but rather constitutes a financing mechanism'.[55] Even though the Court distinguished between the ESM's conditionality and economic policy coordination, it emphasised that the ESM comes within the economic policy element of the EMU as the conditionality attached to the ESM stability support shall be compatible with the TFEU-based coordination of economic policies.[56]

Then, the Court examined more in details the spirit of Article 125 TFEU. While not entering in the detailed assessment of A.G. view,[57] the Court stressed that:

> the ESM will not act as guarantor of the debts of the recipient Member State by referring to the spirit of the article inserted by the Treaty of Maastricht. In fact, the latter will remain responsible to its creditors for its financial commitments.[58]

---

52. *Pringle*, para. 56 (emphasis added).
53. *Ibid.*, para. 96.
54. *Ibid.*, para. 97.
55. *Ibid.*, para. 110.
56. *Ibid.*, paras 111–112.
57. A.G. Kokott View, paras 100–166.
58. *Pringle*, para. 138.

In referring to the foundations of the said provision in the Maastricht Treaty, the ECJ concluded that the no-bailout clause is not infringed by:

> the granting of financial assistance by one or more Member States to a Member State which remains responsible for its commitments to its creditors provided that the conditions attached to such assistance are such as to prompt that Member State to implement a sound budgetary policy.[59]

Finally, the judgment interpreted Article 13 TEU, which provides that each institution shall act within the limits of the powers conferred on it by the Treaty. First, the Court examined the role allocated to the Commission and to the ECB. It held that, in cases of non-exclusive competences of the Union, Member States can confer powers to the Union institutions, on condition that the Member States do not alter the essential character of the powers conferred on those institutions by the Treaties.[60] Second, as to the role allocated to the Court, the judgment confirmed that Article 273 TFEU[61] does not preclude the possibility to confer a judicial role to the Court in cases of international agreement outside the Union framework. On the contrary, the conditions laid out in the ESMT under Article 37 appear consistent with the provision under Article 273 TFEU.[62]

Therefore, the ECJ in the *Pringle* judgment provided an important interpretation of key Treaty provisions and concluded that the role, design and powers of the ESM are in line with EU law. This brings the chapter to assess the role of financial assistance mechanisms to benefit supranational financial stability in EU law and policy.

§5.05 FINANCIAL ASSISTANCE MECHANISMS TO THE BENEFIT OF SUPRANATIONAL FINANCIAL STABILITY IN EU LAW AND POLICY?

The ruling in the *Pringle* case is a seminal ECJ judgment.[63] The ESM and *Pringle* offer the essential argument to establish stability mechanisms in Europe in the context of the creation of supranational financial stability. At the same time, the nature of financial assistance is intergovernmental and is not grounded in EU law, mainly because of the lack of an adequate legal basis and of the existence of the no-bailout clause. As regards the legal basis, there is no explicit legal basis in the Treaties to establish a fund for the stability of the euro area as a whole. As regards the no-bailout clause, it is well known that the Maastricht Treaty did not provide for rules to establish adequate financial resources to finance Member States in distress neither through the EU budget nor through financial

59. *Ibid.*, para. 137.
60. *Ibid.*, paras 168–169.
61. *See* Art. 273 TFEU.
62. *Pringle*, paras 171–177.
63. *See* Vestert Borger, *The ESM and the European Court's Predicament in Pringle* 14 German Law Journal 113–140 (2013); Bruno de Witte & Thomas Beukers, *The Court of Justice Approves the Creation of the European Stability Mechanism Outside the EU Legal Order: Pringle*, 50 Common Market Law Review 805–848 (2013).

assistance between Member States.[64] On the contrary, the existence of the no-bailout clause has so far limited the possibility to make the Union or Member States liable for or committed to financial assistance to other Member States in the EU.[65] Nonetheless, it seems that the financial crisis has impacted the traditional reading of the no-bailout clause and has provided the conditions to establish stability mechanisms for the benefit of the EU legal order.

Pringle was a rather long awaited judgment, especially because of the incumbent entry into operation of the ESMT and the need to provide rapidly a safety net for euro area Member States in distress. The full Court discussed the essential conditions to create a stability mechanism of the ESM-kind to maintain financial stability in the euro area. By clarifying the nature of financial assistance as an economic or as a quasi-economic policy instrument,[66] the ECJ allowed the Member States to establish an intergovernmental mechanism which does not impinge on the exclusive EU competence for monetary policy in the euro area. At the same time, the *Pringle* judgment, for the first time since the adoption of the Maastricht Treaty, analysed core provisions in the economic and monetary policy title (in particular Articles 122–126 TFEU) and clarified the power to provide financial assistance in the euro area. The Court legitimised the possibility to use an international instrument between Member States to create stability support for the euro area. This section looks at the legitimate creation and use of stability mechanisms by assessing the creation of the ESM in substance and in form to the benefit of supranational financial stability as developed in this book.

[A] Financial Stability Mechanisms and Law in Substance

As held above, the ESM has been established outside the Union legal framework. This is because primary EU law rules do not provide for the establishment of *permanent* financial assistance mechanisms for euro area Member States. Articles 122 and 125 TFEU come into question. The Court interpreted them and concluded that the ESMT complies with these two provisions. This part reflects on the compatibility of stability mechanisms in light of the general debate on financial stability in EU law and policy.

[1] Stability Mechanisms and Article 122 TFEU

Article 122(2) TFEU includes a special legal basis to provide financial assistance to a Member State in difficulties or is seriously threatened with severe difficulties. The use of this provision is limited to natural disasters or similar occurrences. A strict reading of this provision would run counter to its use in other circumstances. However, the financial crisis has referred to this provision in a wide sense to provide ad hoc financial

64. *See* Paul Craig, *The Lisbon Treaty, Revised Edition: Law Politics and Treaty*, 460 (Oxford University Press 2013).
65. Rainer Palmstorfer, *To Bail or Not to Bail Out? The Current Framework if Financial Assistance for Euro Area Member States Measured Against the Requirements of EU Primary Law*, 38 European Law Review 773 (2012).
66. *Pringle*, paras 111–112.

assistance to Member States in financial distress.[67] Article 122 TFEU was used to establish the EFSM.[68] The *Pringle* judgment assessed this provision and offered a reading on its role. The special nature of Article 122(2) TFEU cannot act as a *carte blanche* to provide any kind of financial support, given the special conditions set out in that article. As such, Article 122(2) TFEU could not be stretched so much as to establish the ESM. This would clearly run counter the scope of the provision mainly because of the permanent nature of the ESM and the existence of the no-bailout provision under Article 125 TFEU.

Nonetheless, it is argued that the use of Article 122 TFEU should be stretched to provide reinforced use of EU assistance for Member States. This is for three reasons. First, the historical reading to Article 122 TFEU suggests that this article was introduced as a compromise solution between the Member States concerns on the creation of a transfer union and the Commission position to create a scheme for financial assistance for Member States under distress.[69] In this sense, the use of this legal basis dismisses to some extent the compromising solution found in Maastricht.[70] Second, from a contextual reading of the provision, Article 122 TFEU would be some sort of escape clause to the rigour of the no-bailout clause.[71] In this sense, the creation of mechanisms of financial assistance also beyond Union assistance would be possible within the reading of Article 122(2) TFEU. Even if the trigger to Article 122 TFEU is restrictive, it is argued that such provision should act as a counterbalance to the no-bailout clause under Article 125 TFEU. Third, the purposive interpretation of Article 122 TFEU would suggest that this provision comprises also the situation of serious difficulties for a Member States in gaining access to the financial markets to finance its public debt.[72] This reading 'reinvents' the substantive scope of Article 122 TFEU as it configures it as an emergency break to provide financial assistance to Member States.

Nonetheless, the ECJ position is cautious on this provision as it limits the use of Article 122 TFEU in future. *Pringle* examined whether Article 122(2) TFEU would run counter the establishment of the ESMT. The Court adopted a strict reading on the limits of Article 122 TFEU which referred to the strict views of the Heads of State and Government on the future use of Article 122 TFEU. The Court followed the strict line of the Heads of State and Government by excluding that:

> [A]rticle 122 (2) TFEU (...) constitute an appropriate legal basis for the establishment of a stability mechanism of the kind envisaged in [Decision 199/2011].[73]

In other words, the ECJ did not recognise that Article 122 TFEU might be used, generally, as the legal basis to provide *permanent* financial assistance to Member

67. *See* Jean-Victor Louis, *Guest Editorial: The No-Bailout Clause and Rescue Packages*, 47 Common Market Law Review 984 (2010); Palmstorfer *supra* n. 65, 779.
68. Council Regulation 407/2010.
69. Pipkorn, *Legal Arrangements in the Treaty of Maastricht for the Effectiveness of the Economic and Monetary Union*, 31 Common Market Law Review 263 (1994).
70. Louis *supra* n. 67, 983.
71. *Ibid.*, 971.
72. de Gregorio Merino *supra* n. 15, 1634.
73. *Pringle*, para. 65.

States in serious difficulty in the euro area. Rather, it can only be used to provide exceptional financial assistance within a limited timeframe. Similarly, scholars express concern on the use of Article 122(2) TFEU.[74] Scholars argue that Article 122 TFEU has a limited scope and cannot serve to establish permanent mechanisms of the kind.[75] Reference to Article 122(2) TFEU should be made only when support is provided to a Member State in temporary financial difficulties and not to create a permanent facility to assist Member States in distress.

Overall, *Pringle* confirms that Article 122(2) TFEU is a very special provision.[76] This is a regrettable step as the Court could have avoided such strong view on this Treaty article. On the contrary, Article 122(2) TFEU could have come into play as a legal basis to create other forms of financial assistance under EU law in future. The Court's approach on the use of Article 122(2) TFEU is severe and has had repercussion on the role of Article 122 TFEU for financial assistance. To conclude, Article 122 TFEU cannot be considered as a provision to attain supranational financial stability in EU law and policy, but only as an exceptional provision to provide ad hoc financial assistance interventions.

[2] Stability Mechanisms and Article 125 TFEU

As mentioned earlier, Article 125 TFEU contains the prohibition to financial liability or the assumption of financial commitments between Member States. *Pringle* offers the ground to reflect on the establishment of financial stability mechanisms and the no-bailout clause. Article 125 TFEU was inserted in the Treaty of Maastricht to ensure that the Member States follow a sound budgetary discipline.[77] So far, Article 125 TFEU has proven to be the real 'evil' for any possible mutualisation of public debt. Doctrinal positions have been divergent in this sense. In the context of the current financial crisis, doctrine appears divided between expansive and restrictive interpretations of Article 125 TFEU. Rüffert argued that the bilateral loans to Greece in 2010 and the establishment of the EFSF breached EU law as they would run counter Article 125 TFEU.[78] Similarly, Palmstorfer argues that the wording and the systematic reading of the provision 'covers and bans all forms of financial assistance given by the European Union or through a Member State to another'.[79] Thus, the Greek loan facility, the EFSF and the ESM would run counter Article 125 TFEU. Some others have tried to give a narrower interpretation of the no-bailout provision as it 'aims to force Member States to comply with their budgetary discipline following the logics of the markets when

74. Louis *supra* n. 67, 986.
75. de Gregorio Merino *supra* n. 15, 1632.
76. *See* Kaarlo Tuori & Klaus Tuori, *The Eurozone Crisis. A Constitutional Analysis*, 139 (Cambridge University Press 2014).
77. *Pringle*, para. 135 where the Court mentions the Bulletin of the European Communities, Supplement 2/91, 24 and 54.
78. Matthias Rüffert, *The European Debt Crisis and European Union Law*, 48 Common Market Law Review 1785 (2011).
79. Palmstorfer *supra* n. 65, 784.

incurring public debts'.[80] Louis sustained that in exceptional circumstances the no bailout can be potentially overturned 'if the situation (...) degenerates into an asymmetric shock or a shock common to a number of Member States'.[81] Smits suggested that the markets have yet not been reliable instruments to discipline financial assistance to Member States in difficulties and that, given the changed circumstances, a different view on the EMU rules is needed.[82] Similarly, Tuori and Tuori make clear that this prohibition has been restricted especially in crisis times.[83] Overall, the doctrinal position appears divergent as to the possible implications of Article 125 TFEU on financial assistance mechanisms. To that extent, it seems that practice has shown a rather restrictive interpretation of the no-bailout clause. This is also upheld in the ECJ's interpretation of Article 125 TFEU in *Pringle*.

Pringle offered the Court the opportunity to interpret for the first time on Article 125 TFEU and, in particular, the ESM in light of Article 125 TFEU. The Court considered that Article 125 TFEU does *not* preclude the adoption and ratification of the ESMT. This conclusion is made through a certain number of arguments to be assessed.

First, the Court conducted a literal interpretation of Article 125 TFEU and concluded that Member States are not prohibited from granting any form of financial assistance whatever to another Member State.[84] This result is achieved through a combined reading of Article 125 TFEU together with Article 122(2) and 123 TFEU. Correctly, the Court showed that financial assistance between Member States is allowed by some Treaty provisions even if Article 125 TFEU provides for the no-bailout clause. This is an important point as the Court considered that, notwithstanding the no-bailout clause, financial assistance between Member States is possible.

Second, the Court examined the objective of Article 125 TFEU. Paragraph 135 of the *Pringle* judgment affirms that Article 125 TFEU serves to ensure that Member States maintain budgetary discipline. This equals to say that Article 125 TFEU serves as a provision to guarantee the budgetary discipline of the Member States and *not*, strictly speaking, to prohibit financial assistance between Member States. However, this is not an invitation to create financial assistance instruments. In fact, the Court required that such intervention be indispensable for the safeguarding of the financial stability of the euro area as a whole and that it is subject to strict conditionality.[85] The Court based its interpretation on the different provisions contained in the ESMT according to which financial assistance is given only if special conditions are respected. This is not to say that Member States cannot provide assistance between each other. Indeed, one might take two different views on this issue. On the one hand, it can be argued that the Court clearly set the maximum limits on the possible exceptions to Article 125 TFEU. Member States cannot be liable for debts of other Member States, but they can only provide loans or similar means on condition that the beneficiary rests fully liable with its commitments. On the other hand, provided that assistance is given to the benefit of the

80. de Gregorio Merino *supra* n. 15, 1625.
81. Louis *supra* n. 67, 984.
82. René Smits, *Correspondence*, 49 Common Market Law Review 827 (2012).
83. Tuori, Tuori *supra* n. 76, 187.
84. *Pringle*, para. 130.
85. *Ibid.*, para. 136.

'financial stability of the euro as a whole' and that strict conditionality is respected, Member States can make use of financial assistance instruments without infringing Article 125 TFEU and, arguably, to the extent that they deem appropriate.

De Witte and Beukers argue that the interpretation of Article 125 TFEU in *Pringle* is based both on the requirement of indispensability and conditionality of intervention.[86] However, more emphasis should be put on the actual limits on Member States' commitments which flow from Article 125 TFEU. In fact, the Court legitimised Member States' money transfers through an international institution to bailout Member States in distress without infringing EU law.[87]

It is true that the recipient Member State remains fully responsible to its creditors for any financial commitments.[88] Financial assistance amounts to the creation of a new debt to the ESM and not to the establishment of debt liabilities assumed by the assisting Member States. The ESM does not establish a transfer Union with a mutualisation of public debts.[89] In particular, the ESM does not provide either for joint or several liability or for joint and several liability of the assisting Member States. In other words, the ESM is not an international organisation which provides for fiscal transfer to its membership. The ESM capital stock remains separated from the Member State finances and the assisted Member State remains fully responsible for its commitments.

Nonetheless, it can be argued that the Court legitimised Member States to bailout Member States in financial distressed through the creation of a separate international fund for these purposes. Such arrangement does not infringe the no-bailout clause. This is because the purpose of Article 125 TFEU is essentially to ensure that 'the incentive of the recipient Member State to conduct sound budgetary policy is [not] diminished'[90] and not to prohibit financial assistance between Member States as such.

If the Court's judgment is welcome as it held that the ESM is compatible with the no-bailout clause, regrettably, the ECJ interpretation does not appear as convincing as the reading of the A.G.'s view. First, the A.G. stated that Article 125 TFEU would not prohibit any form of financial support to a Member State.[91] In a more appealing way, the A.G. argued that the purpose of Article 125 TFEU is to assure that 'the disciplinary effect of interest rate spreads on the capital markets according to the individual financial positions of Member States'.[92] This would mean that the no-bailout provision is concerned with market discipline of Member States rather than with budgetary discipline.[93] Article 125 TFEU runs primarily counter Member State's arrangements subverting the credibility of individual financial positions of Member States and is not meant as a general prohibition to provide commitments or financial assistance measures from Member State to Member State.

86. De Witte, Beukers *supra* n. 63, 838–839.
87. *See Pringle*, para. 137.
88. *Ibid.*, paras 139 and 145.
89. *See* de Gregorio Merino *supra* n. 15, 1630–1632.
90. *Pringle*, para. 136.
91. A.G. View, para. 134.
92. *Ibid.*, paras 132 and 148.
93. *See* Borger *supra* n. 63, 135–137.

Second, the A.G.'s view contended that an extensive reading of the no-bailout prohibition would run counter the principles of sovereignty and solidarity of the Member States. Such argument equals to say that an extensive reading of the no-bailout clause would *infringe* two principles in the EU that, admittedly, 'rank as of at least equal importance to Article 125 TFEU'.[94] The *Pringle* judgment mentions neither of them to interpret Article 125 TFEU. This is regrettable, as the Court could have supported a more restrictive reading of Article 125 TFEU. If focus on Article 125 TFEU is on the ways in which Member States provide financial assistance, conditionality and even more indispensability of financial intervention have less importance than what one could see at first reading. As to the role of conditionality, the MoU is essential to granting financial and can also go further or can be different from what is required under the economic governance provisions contained in the Treaty. It is true that Article 13 ESMT requires strict conditionality of intervention. However, it is argued that conditionality is a flexible concept which depends on the nature of each intervention. As to the role of indispensability, this requirement does not seem essential for financial assistance. It is true that the ESM was created to guarantee the stability of the euro and Article 136(3) TFEU requires that intervention can be activated 'if indispensable to safeguard the stability of the euro area as a whole'. However, ESM funds could be used also to allow a Member State in difficulty not to exit the euro area[95] or to provide special safety nets to the sovereign economy of an euro area Member State. This suggests that the indispensability of intervention is not essential to trigger the ESM intervention.

Overall, the *Pringle* judgment and the ESM practice suggest that the Article 125 TFEU is not a strict prohibition on the use of financial assistance to Member States. What matters is that financial assistance to sovereigns is given agreeing on the commitments of the beneficiary Member State and with a MoU capable of addressing the financial difficulties of the Member State and moral hazard concerns. This moves the analysis to the form of financial stability intervention.

[B] Stability Mechanisms and the Law in Form

The assessment of the key Treaty provisions on financial assistance takes the analysis to the modalities through which financial assistance can be granted. This section looks at the use of intergovernmental agreements, the powers of EU institutions outside the EU legal order and the conditionality of intervention.

[1] Intergovernmental Mechanisms for Financial Stability Outside the EU Legal Framework

International agreements, such as the ESMT, provide for financial assistance mechanisms to the benefit of the EU legal order. *Pringle* supported the use of intergovernmental agreements outside the EU legal order. The ESMT was concluded as an *inter se*

94. *Pringle*, para. 136.
95. Borger *supra* n. 63, 138.

international agreement, thus between some Member States and outside the Union framework. While the Lisbon Treaty contains rules, codified from the ECJ case law, which give exclusive competences to the Union for the conclusion of international agreements with international organisations and third countries,[96] the Treaty does not contain rules allowing the creation of permanent financial assistance between Member States *inter se*. Furthermore, the introduction of paragraph 3 under Article 136 TFEU supports the use of intergovernmental agreements to safeguard the stability of the euro as a whole.[97] The ECJ was favourable to the use of intergovernmental agreements for financial assistance between Member States as a tool to safeguard financial stability in the euro area. The Court clearly stated that the ESMT shall be considered within economic policy, even if this area is not – strictly speaking – a common policy within the meaning of Article 3(2) TFEU. This argument served the Court to conclude that the ESM does not affect common rules because economic policy is not an area of *common* rules. The assumption, however, does not exclude any duty on the part of Member States. In fact, the Court reaffirms the *Gottardo* case law according to which, even when concluding international agreements outside EU competences, Member States need to comply with EU law when exercising their competence in their reserved competence area.[98]

In sum, *Pringle* held that financial assistance instruments in the form of intergovernmental agreements outside EU law between Member States are legitimate instruments to establish financial assistance mechanisms in EMU law. This suggests that intergovernmental agreements are a legitimate form to create financial stability mechanisms to the benefit of the EU legal order. In this way, intergovernmental agreements can reinforce supranational financial stability to sustain euro area Member State public finances in financial distress, although these arrangements have the nature of an intergovernmental agreement.

[2] The Use of EU Institutions for Stability Mechanisms Outside the EU Legal Order

The *Pringle* judgment gave some interesting clarifications on the use of Union institutions in international agreements.[99] *Pringle* gives ground to the Court to assess the use of the Commission, the ECB and the Court itself in situations where EU institutions are given competences outside the Union framework. Paragraph 158 of *Pringle* confirms that Member States can confer additional tasks to the Union institutions also when they use the intergovernmental means or they act outside the Union framework. However, one may argue whether the doctrine according to which

96. Art. 3(2) TFEU.
97. For the assessment of this new Treaty provision see Chapter 3 section §3.02[B].
98. Case C-55/00 *Elide Gottardo v. Istituto nazionale della previdenza sociale (INPS)* ECLI: EU:C:2002:16, para. 32.
99. *See* Steve Peers, *Towards a New Form of EU Law? The Use of EU Institutions Outside the Legal Framework*, 9 European Constitutional Law Review 37–72, 46–55, 61–65 (2013); Paul Craig, *Pringle and Use of EU Institutions Outside the EU Legal Framework*, 9 European Constitutional Law Review 263 (2013).

international agreements may confer additional functions to EU institutions has not been stretched too much. In other words, it should be determined up to what limits EU institutions may be 'borrowed' for international arrangements between Member States.

Reference to the previous ECJ case law allowed the Court to affirm in *Pringle* that additional tasks can be conferred to Union institutions so long as they 'do not alter the *essential character* of the powers conferred on those institutions by the EU and FEU Treaties'.[100] Some conditions need to be respected: the Union shall not have exclusive competence; the tasks conferred to EU institutions shall not entail any power to make decision of their own; and the additional tasks shall not alter the essential character of the powers conferred to them by the Treaties. Regrettably, the Court does not go into more details on each condition and bases its reasoning on previous case law rather than proposing some grounds to assess them in the *Pringle* case. In accordance with the ESMT, the Commission and the ECB should only play a role of assistance to the ESM. However, the ESMT indicates that both the Commission and the ECB exert quasi-decisional powers. A strict reading of the ESMT would suggest that these powers are against the second condition mentioned by the Court above. Nonetheless, the use of the Commission and the ECB in the negotiation and implementation of financial assistance has been confirmed in recent ECJ case law. In particular, the ECJ confirmed the lack of decision-making powers of EU institutions acting on behalf of the ESM, but highlighted the fact that they shall act always in consistency with EU law.[101]

Pringle scrutinised also the use of the ECJ jurisdiction as a special jurisdiction when Member States conclude a separate treaty to that effect. According to Article 273 TFEU the Court:

> shall have jurisdiction in any dispute between Member States which relates to the subject matter of the Treaties if the dispute is submitted to it under a special agreement between the parties.

This provision serves to avoid a divergent interpretation of EU law by other jurisdictions and to assure unity in the interpretation of EU law.[102] Accordingly, the ESMT states that if decisions of the ESM Board of Governors are contested, the dispute may be submitted to the Court of Justice. The Court's reasoning of Article 273 TFEU is quite open. First, the Court recognises that that article may be invoked also *ex ante causa*. It means that it is not necessary that the actual dispute has arisen.[103] Second, the subject matter of the dispute concerns the Treaties, and *a fortiori* EU law, as the ESMT requires that the stability support be fully consistent with EU law.[104] However, one may question the fact that the Court affirmed that the dispute will be *likely* to concern the

100. *Pringle*, para. 158 (emphasis added).
101. Case C-8/15 P *Ledra Advertising v. Commission and ECB* ECLI:EU:C:2016:701, paras 56-61.
102. Koen Lenaerts, Ignace Maselis & Kathleen Gutman, *EU Procedural Law*, 697 (Oxford University Press 2014).
103. *Pringle*, para. 172.
104. *Ibid.*, para. 174.

interpretation or application of EU law. Finally, the Court considered that disputes where international organisations are party may be submitted to it.[105]

Overall, the Court provided for an extensive interpretation of Article 273 TFEU which could serve to reinforce the role of EU institutions outside the EU legal order. The ECJ case law on the role of EU institutions outside the EU legal order supports the idea of the stability functions of the EU institutions also outside the EU legal order and their role in ensuring consistency with EU law. This role contributes to guarantee that intergovernmental arrangements on financial assistance are beneficial the EU legal order and ultimately to financial stability in EU law and policy.

[3] Financial Assistance Mechanisms and Conditionality of Intervention

The ESM financial arrangements are disbursed in accordance with the MoU agreed between the ESM and the concerned Member State. This enables the ESM, and the Commission and the ECB in their implementing roles, to verify whether the concerned Member State continuously honours the commitments in the MoU. The suspension on the granting of financial assistance is usually an effective incentive to allow the beneficiary Member State to implement the promised measures, even against potentially strong domestic decisions. The official programme reviews allow the ESM to monitor, through the Commission and the ECB, whether the agreed conditionality targets have been met in practice. The ESM's Board of Governors thus assesses the beneficiary's progress towards meeting the programme's objectives, with the possibility of reacting to changing circumstances. The positive review of the MoU usually means that the ESM would provide further disbursements of ESM funds to the beneficiary Member State.

Conditionality of intervention is therefore a guarantee to ensure that the disbursed financial means are given to improve the financial situation of the beneficiary Member States. This concludes the assessment of the financial assistance means in substance and in form. The analysis will move to the ways to increase the legitimacy and effectiveness of stability mechanisms in Europe.

§5.06 STABILITY MECHANISMS IN AND OUTSIDE THE EU LEGAL ORDER: INCREASING THEIR LEGITIMACY AND EFFECTIVENESS

This section analyses the possible evolutions of stability mechanisms outside or inside the EU legal order to reinforce supranational financial stability in Europe. The ESM appears as a permanent – still transitional - solution to legitimate financial assistance arrangements in Europe. The role of financial stability as a foundational objective in EU law and policy is at odds with intergovernmental measures as the latter are outside the EU legal order in providing a supranational response to the attainment of the objective of financial stability. At present, given the Treaty prohibitions in the Treaty (Article 125 TFEU in particular), Member States resorted to intergovernmental agreements. This

105. *Ibid.*, para. 175.

last section reflects on the creation of a more legitimate and effective framework for stability mechanisms in Europe.

[A] Solutions Outside the EU Legal Order

[1] The Current Limits of the ESM

Whilst the ESM is an essential institution for the stability of the euro area as a whole, this section provides an overview on the substantial limitations of the ESMT. These downsize the possibility to legitimately and effectively strengthen financial stability as a supranational foundational objective in EU law and policy by way of financial assistance mechanisms.

First, the ESMT is exclusively open to euro area Member States. The ESM does not foresee membership of non-euro area members. Non-euro area Member States may enjoy only the role of observers in the ESM. They can participate on an ad hoc basis alongside the ESM in a stability support role. This is acceptable as regards the rationale of creating a stability mechanism only for the euro area as a whole. However, at present the ESM falls short of any possible integration of the 'outs' inside the ESM decision-making system. Second, the ESM capital stock is divided into paid-up shares and callable shares. The total capital stock for the ESM activities is EUR 700 billion among which only EUR 80 billion is the paid-up capital. Such amount is considerable as compared with the EFSM capacity of EUR 50 billion. However, it does not appear sufficient to counteract a crisis which could let a big euro area economy in financial distress. Third, the liability regime of the ESM is limited to the capital contributions of the ESM Member States. As stated in Article 8, Member State's liability shall be limited to the authorised capital stock. This article provides for a distinction between the ESM and the Member State liability regimes. This limitation is also reinforced by Article 25 of ESMT on the coverage of losses. This provision states that the last source of ESM liability is the callable capital of the ESM stock. It is an essential guarantee to avoid the breach of the no-bailout clause under Article 125 TFEU. Fourth, as described earlier, the ESM instruments are those that are enlisted in Articles 14–18 of the ESMT. At present, the ESM's mandate is limited to provide financial support to *Member State* and to credit institutions through the direct recapitalisation instrument only in the form of stability support for financial crisis and not also by providing fiscal transfer or an equalisation function in the euro area. Furthermore, the ESM does neither comprise a specific instrument directed to private counterparties nor special funds that could be used to backup Member State liabilities. This is a limitation that is also evident in the EBU, and that will be discussed in subsequent chapter.[106] Overall, these five arguments show that the ESM has limited firepower and would require further improvement to increase its legitimacy and effectiveness.

106. *See* Chapter 8 section §8.05[A] for a discussion on the creation of a common fiscal backstop for the EBU.

[2] The Possible Improvements to the ESM

The ESM acts as a stability support international organisation for the euro area. Some changes to the ESMT or a new international agreements would improve supranational financial stability as argued in this book. First, the ESM could partially open itself to the non-euro area Member States. It would be possible to create a legal arrangement similar to the close cooperation agreements foreseen in the SSM.[107] These close cooperation agreements would create the conditions for non-euro area involvement in stability support to Member States in distress, thereby promoting the establishment of a truly European Monetary Fund not limited to the euro area Member States. Alternatively, another solution would be to allow some form of partial membership to non-euro area Member States. However, both these options would require substantial changes to the ESMT as well as increased financial solidarity of non-euro area Member States with euro-area Member States.

Second, the ESM could raise its capital stock to an amount higher than EUR 700 billion. This is already possible under the ESMT. Article 10 of the ESMT foresees a change in the capital stock via a decision of the ESM Board of Governors decision. Accordingly, a review of the capital stock shall take place at least once every five years. Thus, a mutual agreement of the Board of Governors could be sufficient to raise considerably the capital stock of the ESM. However, this would require unanimity in the ESM Board of Governors and also grounds to justify such increase.

Third, the liability regime is problematic as the ESMT provides for clear rules that separate the euro area sovereign Member States' and the ESM liability regimes. Amendments to the ESMT will need to be made in order to create a mutual liability regime between euro area Member States within the ESM. This would also be open to legal challenges on the no-bailout clause under Article 125 TFEU. However, such an amendment is not impossible. Arguably, raising the capital stock of the ESM or including a guarantee system on the euro area Member States would suffice to provide additional resources that may extend the ESM liability regime. At the same time, whilst the need of political consensus might be an obstacle, the creation of a new international agreement with a different liability regime could be an alternative solution.

Fourth, as stated earlier, the ESM contains specific financial instruments to make use of under the ESMT.[108] Some changes are possible. Article 19 ESMT provides that the Board of Governors can reform the ESM financial instruments. Similarly, Article 24 ESMT envisages the possibility to create 'where appropriate, other funds'. This means that the ESMT already contains provisions to create other instruments and other forms of funding. These provisions have been used to establish an instrument of the direct recapitalisation of credit institutions established in the ESM Members[109]. Therefore, Article 24 could be used to provide new funding to Member States at concessional rates

107. *See* Chapter 7 section §7.04[F] for an assessment of the close cooperation arrangements in the SSM.
108. ESMT, Arts 14–18.
109. ESM, *direct recapitalisation of credit institutions*, FAQ at http://www.esm.europa.eu/pdf/FAQ%20Direct%20Bank%20Recapitalisation%20280620131.pdf (accessed 31 December 2016).

or investment and funding opportunities open to Member States or to private entities.

Overall, the ESM could be improved to create a more effective system of stability mechanisms in Europe in order to strengthen financial stability in Europe. Alternatively, new international treaties could be concluded to reinforce the existing ESM and increase its legitimacy and effectiveness. These proposals are not easy to achieve at present and might be open to legal challenges both at national and at European level. However, they could extend the role and powers of the ESM as a truly European Monetary Fund in Europe.

[3] Beyond the ESM: Establishing a Common Management Mechanism for Sovereign Debt in Europe?

A parallel ground for future reform pertains to the introduction of a new sovereign debt management mechanism, inside or outside the ESM, to allow euro area Member States having an unsustainable government debt ratio to ease their sovereign debts. This mechanism would provide a solution in Europe to counterbalance the excessive government debts of some euro area Member States, allow debt sustainability and guarantee that a reinforced dimension of financial stability is achieved in the medium- to long-term by allowing sovereign debt sustainability. Arguably, this mechanism could be created with an intergovernmental agreement between euro area Member States or the introduction of sovereign debt management measures in the context of the ESM or even through an extensive reading of the legal bases under Article 126(14) TFEU in combination with Article 136(2) TFEU in EU law. In practice, some arrangements might be the following: introducing measures to back up sovereign debt maturities, guarantee Member States' debt instruments, support the repayment of sovereign bonds to creditors at regular intervals. In 2016, a first discussion on this topic was raised in the context of the ongoing macro-economic adjustment programme of Greece. The Eurogroup agreed in principle that some forms of debt relief measures would be implemented to address the Greek debt fiscal sustainability and to convince the IMF to participate in the third macro-adjustment programme.[110]

At present, the practical implementation of effective and structured government debt management seems premature, as there are many political constraints to the realisation of such mechanism. Nonetheless, it is submitted that the creation of a sovereign debt management mechanism in line with the principle of conditionality would be beneficial for the achievement of a truly supranational dimension of financial stability in EU law and policy.

---

110. Eurogroup, *statement on Greece*, 25 May 2016 available at http://www.consilium.europa.eu/en/press/press-releases/2016/05/24-eurogroup-statement-greece/?utm_source = dsms-auto&utm_medium = email&utm_campaign = Eurogroup + statement + on + Greece (accessed 31 December 2016).

[B] Solutions Inside the EU Legal Order: The Use of Enhanced Cooperation to Transfer the ESM into EU Law?

While the previous section reflected upon some solutions outside the EU legal order, this section looks at some normative solutions to integrate further the existing intergovernmental arrangements in the EU legal order. In order to legitimise the ESM in the EU legal order, two alternative constitutional tools could be used in the medium-term: the enhanced cooperation framework or the flexibility clause under Article 352 TFEU.

The use of enhanced cooperation procedure to transfer the ESM into EU law is an interesting proposal to increase legitimacy of the ESM. The Treaty of Amsterdam introduced enhanced cooperation.[111] After the entry into force of the Lisbon Treaty, Articles 20 TEU and Articles 326–334 TFEU regulate enhanced cooperation. Enhanced cooperation is conceived as a mechanism to allow a faster development in specific areas which involve a limited number of Member States while other non-participating Member States remain outside the enhanced framework. The Treaty framework provides that Member wishing to establish a legal regime of enhanced cooperation between themselves within the EU's non-exclusive competences may make use of the Union's institutions and exercise this supranational competence. Articles 326 and 327 TFEU hold that enhanced cooperation shall comply with the Treaties and secondary legislation and that the enhanced regime must respect the competences, rights and obligations of the non-participating Member States. Importantly, the enhanced cooperation shall further develop the objectives of the Union, protect the EU's interests and reinforce the integration process.[112] This brief assessment suggests the potential use of the reinforcement of stability mechanisms to create an ESM-kind instrument through enhanced cooperation in EU law and policy. In effect, the use of enhanced cooperation may provide sufficient to establish a European Monetary Fund for the purpose of financial assistance to euro area Member States for the benefit of supranational financial stability in EU law and policy.[113] However, the following arguments limit the use of enhanced cooperation: first, enhanced cooperation may be established within non-exclusive competences; second, it shall use the EU institutional framework.[114] In particular, the use of enhanced cooperation only where the Union does not have exclusive competence suggests that the Union needs to have some form of competence before the establishment of enhanced cooperation. At present, the ESM is an intergovernmental arrangement, hence outside the system of Union competences.

---

111. *See* Nico Groenendijk, *Enhanced Cooperation under the Lisbon Treaty*, Research Meeting on European & International Affairs 3 (2011) at http://doc.utwente.nl/80704/ (accessed 31 December 2016).
112. Art. 20 TEU.
113. *See* Michael Schwarz, *A Memorandum of Misunderstanding – The Doomed Road of the European Stability Mechanism and a Possible Way Out: Enhanced Cooperation*, 51 Common Market Law Review 389 (2014); Michele Messina, *Strengthening Economic Governance of the European Union Through Enhanced Cooperation: A Still Possible, but Already Missed, Opportunity*, 40 European Law Review 404 (2014).
114. Art. 329 TFEU.

Furthermore, the use of enhanced cooperation proves to be a difficult political solution as also its recent use in other fields shows.

At the same time, the nature of the ESM financial assistance is that of a measure in between the economic and monetary policies, thus between a sui generis competence and an exclusive competence in EU law. *Pringle* suggests that the nature of financial assistance to Member States is neither a monetary nor an economic policy competence. It appears therefore that the creation of a stability mechanism to sustain public finances in distressed Member States could be grounded on the foundational objection of financial stability as developed in this book.

In the alternative, the flexibility clause may be a useful tool to transfer the ESM into the EU legal order. Article 352 TFEU stipulates that the:

> If action by the Union should prove necessary, within the framework of the policies defined in the Treaties, to attain one of the objectives set out in the Treaties, and the Treaties have not provided the necessary powers, the Council, acting unanimously on a proposal from the Commission and after obtaining the consent of the European Parliament, shall adopt the appropriate measures.

This provision suggests that the Commission could put forward a proposal to integrate the ESM into the EU legal order by way of unanimity in the Council. The proposal would specify that ensuring the completion of the EMU and respect the limitations provided in Article 352 TFEU. Such proposal would require the unanimity of the Council, but could be a less problematic tool to constitutionalise the ESM into the EU legal order.

Recent attempts to strengthen the legitimacy of the ESM in the EU legal order have been put forward in the Five Presidents' Report of Summer 2015 which envisages three phases to strengthen and complete the EMU in future.[115] Enhanced cooperation could be used to integrate the ESM at a certain time in near future in the EU legal order. Interestingly, it is suggested that the ESM will be integrated into the EMU by use of the enhanced cooperation at a certain point in future. This will be analysed in the upcoming White Paper of the Commission in 2017. However, the Five Presidents' Report suggests that the ESM integration into the EU legal order is foreseen only at a later stage.[116]

§5.07 CONCLUSION

Financial stability is at the centre of concern for financial assistance instruments in the euro area. The ESM attempts to play the role of the euro area financial 'firewall' to avoid future sovereign debt crisis in Europe. The establishment of the ESM and the Court's approach on Article 125 TFEU in *Pringle* are welcome as they have given leeway to financial assistance between Member States beyond a strict reading of Article

115. Five President's Report, *Completing Europe's Economic and Monetary Union*, 22 June 2015, at https://ec.europa.eu/priorities/sites/beta-political/files/5-presidents-report_en.pdf (accessed 31 December 2016)
116. *Ibid.*

125 TFEU. The ECJ sustained that Member States can provide financial resources to other Member States without breaching the no-bailout prohibition. This is possible so long as such intervention is in line with sound budgetary discipline and with the indispensability to safeguard the stability of the euro as a whole. However, it has been demonstrated that these two requirements can become rather flexible in their application. At present, the liability regime of the financial instrument is the real limit of the no-bailout clause. Notwithstanding such limit, the creation of financial stability instruments for euro area Member States in distress is a novel phenomenon in Europe and is surely grounded on the objective of financial stability in Europe. The ESM is the first permanent step to provide stability support to Member States and possibly to their financial institutions. However, it remains clear that the intergovernmental nature of the ESM undermines a truly supranational dimension of financial stability in EU law and policy. At the same time, this chapter has shown that the ESM and *Pringle* clarify essential issues. The ESM and *Pringle* illustrate that financial stability mechanisms are not only compatible with the EU legal order, but that they are a new feature in Europe. The ESM provides a rudimentary euro area European Monetary Fund beyond the straightjacket of the no-bailout clause. Member States could establish financial arrangements which can be used beyond the prohibition of Article 125 TFEU.

The debate on the future of stability mechanisms shows that intergovernmental agreements are still essential components that indirectly reinforce supranational financial stability in EU law and policy. It remains true that Member States are not willing to lose sovereign powers on financial assistance and amend the Treaty accordingly. The intergovernmental path represents a politically easy path to reach an appropriate level of public backstop for crisis management. In perspective, the ESM structure and powers require new arrangements to improve the system of stability mechanisms in Europe in light of the objective of supranational financial stability. Considerable improvements could take place by relying further on intergovernmental instruments with appropriate and stronger links to the EU legal order or by fully integrating the ESM in the EU legal order via enhanced cooperation or the flexibility clause. At present, the solutions found do not seem to be fully in line with the foundational objective of financial stability in EU law and policy. However, they demonstrate that Europe has strengthened its financial stability dimension through the adoption of financial stability mechanisms.

Having concluded the assessment of financial stability mechanisms in Europe, the analysis moves to the reinforcement of the institutional and substantive dimensions of banking regulation in EU law and policy.

CHAPTER 6
EU Banking Regulation

§6.01 INTRODUCTION

The creation of a single regulatory market for banks[1] is a project that was conceived as part of the creation of the EU and that, as part of the regulatory effort to counteract the financial crisis, has been substantially reinforced in the last five years. In recent times, banking regulation is a field that has been subject to extensive regulatory reforms due to the topical role and functions of banks in society.[2] This is in particular due to the strong impact of the financial crisis on credit institutions' capital, activities and business models.

The institutional and substantive reforms in the field of banking regulation show to what extent the objective of financial stability is a key aspect in Europe. Two aspects are relevant to this examination: first, institutional reforms have established a system where European institutions and agencies through EU legislative, delegated, implementing and soft law measures are able to shape the prudential regulatory framework; second, there has been a reinforcement of the rules as regards the regulatory aspects of conducting banking activities in Europe. This dual dimension contributes to consider financial stability as a normative supranational objective for the prevention and management of risks or shocks in EU law and policy. As argued in this chapter, the European approach to banking regulation shows that the evolving normative instruments incorporated in objective of supranational financial stability in EU law and policy – notably reinforced hard and soft supranational regulation and a higher

1. Banks (or credit institutions) assessed in this chapter, and generally in this study, follow the definition of credit institution provided in the CRR under Art. 4(1) as 'undertaking the business of which is to take deposits or other repayable funds from the public and to grant credits for its own account'.
2. *See* Chapter 3 section §3.02[C][2] for the general discussion on the role of banks in the economy.

harmonisation paradigm – have produced a resilient and highly sophisticated supranational regulatory system for credit institutions in Europe. This is also through the development of a single 'rulebook' for banks in Europe.

The creation of a 'single rulebook' for banks in Europe was first coined in the Council conclusions in 2009 by affirming that a single rulebook should be established to provide:

> a core set of EU-wide rules and standards directly applicable to all financial institutions active in the Single Market, so that key differences in national legislations are identified and removed.[3]

So far, the creation and use of the single rulebook for banks has been a remarkable result for the reinforcement of banking regulation in Europe. While the reorganisation of domestic and international financial regimes, undertaken as part of the many reform projects launched during the financial crisis, have been analysed already in earlier parts of this book, this chapter focuses the attention on the main institutional and substantive aspects in banking regulation. Such analysis demonstrates that the strong regulatory efforts to establish prudential rules for banking activities have been put forward also in light of the foundational objective of financial stability developed in this book. Also, other areas such a supranational DGS and the EU rules on banking structures play an important role in the conduct of banking activities. However, they are still under development in Europe. After a brief account of the pre-crisis regulatory framework for credit institutions, the chapter looks at the evolving regulatory shape of banking regulation in Europe in order to analyse the role of financial stability in the context of banking regulation. Then, it critically examines the regulation of banks during the financial crisis both in its substantive and institutional dimensions and the possible ways forward in European banking regulation.

The chapter is structured as follows. The first part looks at banking regulation in Europe before the outbreak of the financial crisis and also in the first phase of the financial crisis (§6.02). Next, the chapter examines the current rules establishing a new regulatory framework for banking regulation both at substantive and institutional level (§6.03). In particular, it assesses the institutional structure of banking regulation and the different players in the process as well as at the substantive rules on banking regulation. The chapter proceeds then with an analysis of the evolving normative agenda for supranational banking regulation and examines the recent proposals to reform EU banking regulation (§6.04). The last part concludes (§6.05).

3. Council of the EU, *Conclusions on strengthening EU financial supervision*, 10 June 2009 http://register.consilium.europa.eu/doc/srv?l=EN&f=ST%2010862%202009%20INIT (accessed 31 December 2016). *See also* European Council, *Conclusions*, 18 and 19 June 2009, para. 20.

§6.02 SETTING THE PRE- AND IN-THE-FINANCIAL CRISIS BACKGROUND ON REGULATION OF CREDIT INSTITUTIONS IN EUROPE

Before looking and assessing the most recent substantive and institutional reforms in banking regulation in Europe, it is essential to examine the banking rules predating the financial crisis and adopted in the first phase of the financial crisis in Europe (2008–2011). This section will briefly look at the institutional (section [A]) and substantive (section [B]) dimensions for banking regulation in Europe.

[A] The Institutional Dimension: From the *Lamfalussy* Committee Structure to the ESAs

As regards the institutional regime for banking regulation in Europe, the Lamfalussy process, which lies in the Financial Services Action Plan (FSA Plan) of 1999,[4] is the first structured attempt to institutionalise banking regulation at European level. The FSA Plan indicated that regulatory divergences among Member States delimited substantial economic benefits arising from free cross-border provision of financial services.[5] The principles of mutual recognition, minimum harmonisation and home country control had failed to achieve full the purposes of integration, mainly because of shortcomings arising from distorted regulatory and enforcement processes.[6] The Lamfalussy Report proposed a new structured level for regulatory decision-making in financial services based on four levels to address the inadequacies of the existing procedures for financial law-making.[7] This structure was based on four levels. At Level 1, the European Parliament and Council of the European Union adopted a piece of legislation, establishing the core principles of a law and building guidelines on its implementation. Level 2 was a technical level with the Commission and sector-specific committees in charge of advising and adopting technical details. Level 3 was grounded on the committees for banking supervision, financial markets and insurance markets for the implementation and adoption of guidelines, recommendations and standards. Level 4 consisted in the implementation of the rules of the three preceding levels at the national level and then the control of the Commission. Although the Lamfalussy structure has been considered a success, shortcomings have been found over time.[8] For instance, the strong 'national imprinting' of the committees' functions or the absence of legally binding powers of the commitees have proved to be inadequate to coordinate efficiently national regulators and supervise financial markets.

4. European Commission, *Financial Services Action Plan* COM(1999)232.
5. *Ibid.*, 5, 8, 11.
6. *See* Rosa Lastra, *The Governance Structure for Financial Supervision and Regulation in Europe*, 10 Columbia Journal of European Law 49 (2003).
7. Alexandre Lamfalussy, *Final Report of the Committee of Wise Men* (2001) at http://ec.europa.eu/internal_market/securities/docs/lamfalussy/wisemen/final-report-wise-men_en.pdf (accessed 31 December 2016).
8. *See* Niamh Moloney, *EU Financial Market Regulation after the Global Financial Crisis: 'More Europe' or More Risks?*, 47 Common Market Law Review 1381 (2010).

During the financial crisis, the need for institutional reforms to European financial regulation was highlighted by important European reports that showed how the established committee system was inadequate to tackle the risks of cross-border financial crises and to avoid spillover effects. In particular, in February 2009, the Commission published the de Larosière Report. This document presented the inefficiencies of the Lamfalussy system of European financial supervisory model and called for a more institutionalised system of micro-prudential supervision and for the establishment of a macro-prudential system of supervision.[9] The Lamfalussy committee structure needed to be reformed in order to endure financial stability and to assure a more structured financial integration at European level.[10] Overall, the de Larosière report showed that the problems of the Level 3 Committees structure were the absence of legally binding powers, the insufficient level of accountability and transparency, and the lack of real independence from national and stakeholder interests.[11]

Soon after, the Council supported the de Larosière Report[12] and paved the way for the Commission proposing new regulatory measures on the institutional design of banking regulation. In September 2009, the Commission promptly proposed four regulations aimed at creating the ESFS. These consisted in establishing the ESRB in charge of monitoring macro-prudential risks in Europe and in upgrading the Lamfalussy Committee structure into three ESAs, EBA, ESMA and European Insurance and Occupational Pensions Authority (EIOPA). ESAs' functions include, among others, an intervention-based supervision over Member States and market participants, and preparatory law-making powers in EU financial legislation.[13] These entities were formally established in January 2011.

[B] The Substantive Dimension: Origins and Development of Banking Regulation in Europe

Substantive regulation of European banking law dates back to the first Banking Directive of 1977. The First Banking Directive was adopted in 1977,[14] and it set out the first founding block of the internal market for banks in Europe. At the same time, the ECJ shaped the liberalisation of the internal market through case law and negative harmonisation, in particular in the context of the free movement of goods, services and capitals. This took place in the well-known *Dassonville*[15] and *Cassis de*

9. Jacques de Larosière, *High Level Report of the Group on Financial Supervision in the EU* (2009) at http://ec.europa.eu/internal_market/finances/docs/de_larosiere_report_en.pdf (accessed 31 December 2016).
10. *Ibid.*, 46–48.
11. *Ibid.*, 54–55.
12. European Council, *Council conclusions on strengthening EU financial supervision*, para. 7.
13. *See* European Commission, *Communication on European Financial Supervision*, COM(2009)252.
14. Council Directive 77/780/EEC of 12 December 1977 on the coordination of the laws, regulations and administrative provisions relating to the taking up and pursuit of the business of credit institutions, [1977] OJ L 322. *See* Larisa Dragomir, *European Prudential Banking Regulation and Supervision: The Legal Dimension*, 68–71 (Routledge 2009).
15. Case 8/74 *Procureur du Roi v. Benoît and Gustave Dassonville* ECLI:EU:C:1974:82.

Dijon[16] rulings. These proved to be the cornerstone judgments for the progressive abolition of trade barriers in the internal market. After the adoption of the Maastricht Treaty, the late 1990s foresaw the need to consolidate the effects of the Treaty freedoms of establishment and the provisions of free movement of services and capitals. The Commission aimed to achieve an integrated market in financial services. The FSA Plan of 1999 contained forty-two substantial reform proposals to adopt at EU level. Three objectives guided the FSA Plan: the completion of the single wholesale market, the development of open and secure markets for retail services, the attainment of improved prudential rules and increased supervisory cooperation. In subsequent years, the adoption of the recast CRD and the Capital Adequacy Directive in June 2006 was an important legislative development in the White Paper 2005–2010 era.[17]

Soon after, the immediate reaction of the Commission to the financial crisis was to propose amendments to the CRD and the Capital Adequacy Directive. Directive 2009/111/EC ('CRD II') was adopted on 16 September 2009. Directive 2010/76 (the 'CRD III') made further amendments to the CRDII and the Capital Adequacy Directive. The CRD III dealt with three main issues. First, it strengthened the capital requirements for assets that credit institutions hold in the trading-book for short-term resale. Credit institutions were required to calculate potential losses on these assets in a 'worst-case scenario'. Second, it established higher capital requirements and strengthened disclosure requirements for re-securitisations (i.e., repackaging securitisations into new securities). Finally, credit institutions were required to have consistent remuneration policies and to promote sound and effective risk management.

Together with the progressive harmonisation of capital requirements rules for credit institutions, the EU legislated also in the field of deposit insurance. Already in 1994, the DGS Directive was adopted.[18] This Directive provided for the harmonisation of deposit insurance policies across the EU with the fourfold aims of boosting the freedom of establishment, provide services, ensuring the stability of the banking system, protect savers and depositors.[19] The DGS Directive followed a minimum harmonisation approach and set a minimum level of deposit protection as well as the maximum payout time.[20] These development show that the financial crisis has prompted supranational regulatory efforts to improve the existing rules in EU banking law.

16. Case 120/78 *Rewe-Zentrale AG v. Bundesmonopolverwaltungfür Branntwein* (Cassis de Dijon) ECLI:EU:C:1979:42.
17. Directive 2006/48/EC of the European Parliament and of the Council of 14 June 2006 relating to the taking up and pursuit of the business of credit institutions (recast) (2006) OJ L 177; Directive 2006/49/EC of the European Parliament and of the Council of 14 June 2006 on the capital adequacy of investment firms and credit institutions (recast) (2006) OJ L 177.
18. Directive 94/19/EC of the European Parliament and of the Council of 30 May 1994 on Deposit Guarantee Schemes [1994] OJ L 135.
19. *Ibid.*, Recital 1.
20. *Ibid.*, Arts 7 and 10.

§6.03 SUPRANATIONAL REGULATION OF CREDIT INSTITUTIONS IN EUROPE IN THE AFTERMATH OF THE EUROPEAN FINANCIAL CRISIS

The financial crisis has had an important impact on the regulation of banks in Europe. The waves of supranational regulation have continued also later during the financial crisis (2013–2016). These new reforms aimed to establish a resilient regulatory framework for credit institutions and promote supranational financial stability. The structure of the reinforced banking regulation reveals three main issues from an institutional perspective. First, there is a dynamic institutional balance on the exercise of EU banking regulation rules as evidenced by interrelations among EU institutions on the exercise of institutional powers on banking regulation both at the horizontal and vertical levels. Second, the increasing importance of the EU 'agencification' process has led to a reinforced framework of quasi-regulatory rule-making entities with EBA as the banking authority entrusted to shape the single rulebook for banks, but which still lacks full regulatory powers to adopt legally binding measures. Third, the conferral of supervisory powers to the ECB may impact the other EU institutions' tasks to adopt European regulations and decisions in their field of rule-making competence and EBA powers in rulemaking in the banking sector.

This part of the chapter examines the institutional dimension of regulation of credit institutions in Europe (section [A]), the role of EU agencies in banking regulation (section [B]) and provides a critical assessment of the new substantial rules in banking regulation as part of the CRR and CRDIV package (section [C]).

[A] The Institutional Dimension: The Role of EU Institutions in Banking Regulation

The new regulatory framework for credit institutions in Europe shows that a new balance between supranational institutions and agencies is being shaped in Europe. This is in particular the case for the relationship between the EU Commission, the Council and the European Parliament. It is argued that supranational financial stability has driven supranational regulation both because of the State failure to resolve regulatory issues and of the market failures arising from the inability of credit institutions to address the problems on their own.[21]

[1] The Role of the European Parliament, the Council and the Commission

As in the normal policy-making process in the EU, the European Parliament and the Council are the EU legislators for the adoption of supranational banking regulation. Ordinary legislative rulemaking is governed by the ordinary legislative procedure

21. *See* Chapter 3 section §3.02[C][2] for an assessment of the banking market failures.

which requires that the Council and the European Parliament agree on a common text following a formal proposal by the Commission.[22]

The adoption of the ordinary legislative procedure can become complex, cumbersome and intensive. This is why decision-making processes at the European Parliament and the Council may require time and may need to come to terms, also in light of national interests. The European Parliament conducts its legislating activities in committees before the vote takes place in the plenary. Committees discuss legislative proposals and propose amendments by drafting reports and resolutions that are submitted to the plenary session. Inside the committee, the work is given to the entrusted rapporteur who can play a major role for the inter-institutional negotiations and for a positive outcome of the discussed proposals.

The problems in the development of the decision-making process are quite evident in the Council. The Council represents the national interests and might be willing to discuss the matters so long as national interests are not fully protected. The organisation of the Council is supported by the role of Council committees which operate below it and are an essential component in coming up with a Council position and to deal with the decision-making phase. Through committees, the Council does not need to agree on the proposal, but simply consider the matter as an 'A' point at its meeting as the document has been agreed in advance of the Council's meeting. An important component of decision-making processes are the solution founds in 'trilogue' which are informal contacts between representatives of the Council, the European Parliament and the Commission that conduct bargaining to find decision-making solutions before the formal conclusion of the procedure. In practice, the beginning of the first reading, as part of the ordinary legislative procedure, starts only when the Council members have agreed their positions also vis-à-vis the European Parliament and the Commission. In sum, delegations, trilogues and institutional dialogues contribute to shape the decision-making process in the ordinary legislative procedure.

The Commission is the other essential institutional player in European banking regulation. It is important to clarify what the role of the Commission in developing the single rulebook for credit institutions in Europe is. The Commission is given the power to ensure the application of the EU Treaties, and of the measures adopted by the other EU institutions. Furthermore, it oversees the application of Union law and execute enforcement powers under the EU Treaties.[23] The main role of the EU Commission in banking regulation is thus to propose banking legislation, adopt delegated or implementing acts, participate in meeting and dialogues with experts, and verify the application of EU law in the Member States. Most importantly, the EU Commission has the task of proposing regulations, directives or decisions. Furthermore, it shall implement and execute legislation adopted by the EU co-legislators. In particular, it is important to clarify that the Commission is given the power to adopt delegated and implementing acts under Articles 290 and 291 TFEU. According to the new formal

22. Art. 289 TFEU.
23. Art. 17 TEU.

legislative and non-legislative distinction introduced in the Lisbon Treaty, the Commission can adopt delegated and implementing acts. The co-legislators (the European Parliament and the Council) adopt the general rules in banking regulation after the Commission has proposed them. Furthermore, the co-legislators are also empowered to delegate to the Commission the power to amend or supplement primary legislation with delegated or implementing acts.[24] In general terms, the Commission's delegated powers are subject to scrutiny provided in the legislative act and to control mechanisms for the delegated and implementing acts.[25] The power of delegation to the Commission is constrained by a number of conditions.[26] First, delegation of powers shall take place in a legislative act for delegated acts. Second, the delegating legislative act shall explicitly allow for the enactment of delegated acts. Third, the delegating act cannot delegate essential elements of the legislative act. Finally, there are also some constitutional safeguards to the power of delegation. Article 290(2) TFEU indicates that:

> (a) the European Parliament or the Council may decide to revoke the delegation;
> (b) the delegated act may enter into force only if no objection has been expressed by the European Parliament or the Council within a period set by the legislative act.

The category of implementing acts as provided in Article 291 TFEU empowers the Commission to adopt acts relating to the implementation policies adopted by the legislative authorities. The delegation of implementing acts does not allow the Commission to make policy choices or exert discretionary powers. The European legislators retain the power to control the use of implementing powers. As provided in Article 291 TFEU implementing acts remain a subsidiary form of regulation to the implementation in Member States. Thus, the Commission shall adopt implementing acts only as much as 'uniform conditions for implementing legally binding Union acts are needed'.[27]

On a critical note, these Treaty rules limit the power of the Commission to adopt any kind of delegated and/or implementing acts. On the one hand, the Commission is the promoter of supranational legislative acts, but is subject to the political positions of the Council and the European Parliament on the legislative act. The Commission has limited rule-making powers over the final content of the legislative proposals. This can be the case of the current CRR/CRDIV rules where the EU co-legislators have adopted rules of very detailed nature. On the other hand, the Commission has the power to endorse delegated or implementing technical standards as drafted by EBA and to adopt delegated or implementing acts as provided in legislative acts. This contrast suggests that the Commission is only one of the players in the context of banking regulation as it may be subject to decision-making positions promoted by the EU co-legislators and the rule-making of EBA. Notwithstanding these limits, the projects undertaken by the

24. Arts 290 and 291 TFEU.
25. Jürgen Bast, *New Categories of Acts After the Lisbon Reform: Dynamics of Parlamentarization in EU Law*, 49 Common Market Law Review 918 (2012).
26. *See* Robert Schütze, *From Rome to Lisbon: 'Executive Federalism' in the (New) European Union*, 47 Common Market Law Review 1399 (2010).
27. Art. 291(2) TFEU.

new Juncker Commission and the internal restructuring of the Commission directorates, in particular the introduction of DG FISMA, indicate that the normative goals of the Commission are certainly intended to promote market integration and supranational financial stability in the banking sector.

The core of supranational decision-making is based on the principle of institutional balance. The importance of institutional balance as a principle of law-making in Europe is well established in literature.[28] The interplay between the Commission and the co-legislators in adopting very detailed banking rules show that problems of balancing the institutional powers may arise. The adoption of rules of a legislative nature in banking regulation is given to the Council and to the European Parliament as they adopt European rules under the ordinary legislative procedure. However, the very detailed banking regulation rules show that the EU co-legislators keep their powers and supervision on the adoption of legislative rules on banking regulation. In this sense, the wide framework for supranational financial stability would require that the EU co-legislators limit themselves to principled-based regulations while leaving to the EU executives the technical rules on banking regulation.

For instance, the CRR and CRDIV as well as the DGS directive leave some space to the Commission and EBA to adopt delegated and implementing acts. The difficult balance of what constitute a legislative component and what does not may raise questions of institutional *in*-balance. For the sake of supranational financial stability, it would seem appropriate that the EU co-legislators adopt principle-based rules, while the Commission and EBA are empowered to adopt acts which, while being strictly confined as to their scope by the delegating institution, are technical in nature. In this way, institutional balance would be respected and problems of legitimacy and democracy would be overcome. Even if institutional balance is not under threat, the length and complexity of the CRR and the CRDIV questions whether the Council and the Parliament have really exercised their legislative powers or whether they have simply rubber-stamped the Commission's proposals. In this sense, the adoption of very detailed legislative rules does not provide sufficient clarity and transparency as to whether the co-legislators have fully respected the values of inter-institutional balance. This suggests that there should be an improved level of separation between what is necessarily of legislative nature as general principled-based regulation and what is not. This may take place through extensive use of delegation of non-essential aspects in legislative acts in future.

[2] The (Emerging) Regulatory Role of the ECB

The emerging regulatory powers of the ECB in the banking sector is an inter-institutional problem regarding the extent of institutional balance and the role of the EU institutions. The ECB has been progressively involved in the development of banking

28. *See* Jean-Paul Jacqué, *The Principle of Institutional Balance*, 41 Common Market Law Review 383 (2004).

regulation.[29] This questions the relationship between the EU Commission, EBA as the European administrative regulator and the ECB in the euro area, especially following the conferral of tasks in micro-prudential supervision.[30] The effective exercise of banking regulation tasks to the ECB is indicated in primary law both in the Treaty and in the ESCB Statute. The ECB as a non-basic task shall be consulted in the development of legislation of its competence under Article 127(4) TFEU and Article 4 ESCB Statute. The provisions in question confer a specific competence to the ECB to be consulted in all the fields of its competence also as regards the exercise of the issues related to prudential supervision and the stability of the financial system. The exercise of a consultative function for the ECB is wide and encompasses all draft EU acts. This consultative role is corroborated also under Article 25 ESCB Statute where it is stated that the ECB 'may offer advice and be consulted (...) on the scope and implementation of Union legislation (...)'.[31] The important consultative role of the ECB has been examined by the ECJ in the *OLAF* case. In that case, the ECJ held that the consultative function of the ECB is an essential aspect in the development of banking regulation.[32] Furthermore, the ECB is involved in the development of banking regulation by participating in the regulatory processes as an observer or membership status. This involvement contributes to the adoption of measures in Level 1 and 2. Finally, the ECB has been granted an autonomous - yet legitimate - regulatory power. According to Articles 132(1) TFEU and 34(1) ESCB Statute, the ECB may adopt legal acts, either regulations or decisions, necessary to the exercise of its functions. These can be regulations,[33] decisions, recommendations and opinions.

The Treaty empowers the ECB to adopt regulations, decisions and soft law measures that can be fully exercised in the banking sector. It is clear that the ECB has already exercised a consultative power as regards banking regulation and has acquired regulatory powers in the context of the SSM. The extent of the ECB's regulatory powers is considerable if one takes into account the exercise of supervisory powers in the SSM.[34] Pursuant to Article 4 of the SSM Regulation, the ECB should contribute to the adoption of EBA's rulemaking acts, and in particular technical standards. Article 4(3) of the SSM Regulation states that '[T]he ECB shall adopt guidelines and recommendations, and take decisions (...). The ECB may also adopt regulations only to the extent necessary to organise or specify the arrangements for the carrying out of the tasks conferred on it by [the SSM Regulation].' This provision suggests that the ECB within the scope of its supervisory tasks may adopt regulatory acts both of hard and soft law nature that may shape the exercise of supervisory tasks to credit institutions within the SSM. The SSM Regulation clearly states that the ECB does not act as a banking

29. Dragomir *supra* n. 14, 225.
30. *See* Chapter 7 section §7.04[D] for the relationship between the ECB and EU agencies in the SSM.
31. Dragomir *supra* n. 14, 228.
32. Case C-11/00 *Commission v. European Central Bank* ECLI:EU:C:2003:395, para. 110.
33. Art. 132(1) TFEU indicates that regulation shall be adopted only when 'necessary to implement the tasks defined in Art. 3.1, first indent, Arts 19.1, 22 and 25.2 of the Statute of the ESCB. However, it seems that ECB regulations are not restricted in their scope. *See contra* Dragomir *supra* n. 14, 233.
34. *See* Chapter 7 section §7.03[B][1].

regulator. However, it cannot be excluded that the ECB as a prudential supervisor may exercise its tasks not only by providing its views on delegated and implementing EU rulemaking as regards the other EU institutions and EBA within the euro area but also by adopting regulations in certain aspects of banking supervision. The exercise of such regulatory power is evident in banking supervision where the ECB has recently proposed regulations or decisions having a general nature such as the recent one on options and discretions in the CRR and therefore impacting on the content of EU banking regulation.[35]

Furthermore, from a regulatory perspective, the relationship between the ECB and EBA may be problematic. The participation as a non-voting member of the ECB to EBA's Board of Supervisors may impact the content of EBA draft standards to be submitted to the Commission or EBA soft law measures. In this sense, the introduction of the 'double majority' voting for EBA decisions is a rebalance towards a mitigation of an ECB-imposed view on regulatory matters at EBA level.

In sum, the role of the ECB as an emerging regulatory institution in banking regulation shows that an incorrect – or even aggressive – use of regulatory powers by the ECB could jeopardise the institutional balance between legislative and executive powers in Europe. At the same time, the conferral of supervisory powers to the ECB does not exclude an impact of the ECB regulatory powers in banking regulation. The chapter now moves to EBA, an important European player in banking regulations.

[B] The Role of EU Agencies in Banking Regulation: The Case of the EBA

This sections analyses the EBA role, legal basis and powers (subsection [1]) as well as EBA legitimacy and effectiveness (subsection [2]). A detailed examination of EBA shall be made as EBA has acquired a central role in developing supranational regulation in EU banking regulation.

[1] The Role, Legal Basis and Regulatory Tasks of EBA

The creation of EBA has been one of the remarkable institutional reforms during the financial crisis. This subsection assesses EBA's role in the construction of a supranational regulatory framework for credit institutions in Europe. The creation of ESAs in the EU has proved to be an 'evolution' in the current process of 'agencification', but still raises questions as to the effectiveness of ESAs in financial market regulation and supervision. Moloney argued that ESAs, and therefore EBA, could lead to a significant proliferation of delegated rule-making[36] and carry 'the real potential for

35. *See* Regulation (EU) 2016/445 of the ECB of 14 March 2016 on the exercise of options and discretions available in Union law (ECB/2016/4), OJ L78.
36. Moloney *supra* n. 8, 1345.

centralisation'.[37] Traditionally, the establishment of agencies in the EU legal order has been made through the use of Article 352 TFEU.[38] Depending on the sector, specific legal bases have been used to create new agencies. More recently, EU agencies have been established under the legal basis of Article 114 TFEU. The Preamble of EBA Regulation refers to Article 114 TFEU which has been used as the legal basis for the creation of ESAs because:

> [t]he purpose and the tasks of the [Authority] – assisting national supervisory authorities in the consistent interpretation and application of Union rules and contributing to financial stability necessary for financial integration – are closely linked to the objectives of the Union *acquis* concerning the internal market for financial services.[39]

The first aspect to assess is EBA's structure. It follows a structure similar to other agencies with a Board of Supervisors, a Management Board and an Executive Directorate. The Board of Supervisors acts as the main ESAs' decision-making body as its tasks include, *inter alia*, the guidance to the activities of the competent ESA, the preparatory decision-making activities, the adoption of the budget and the multiannual work programme and the annual report. The Management Board is composed of the Chairperson and six members of the Board of Supervisors who are elected by the voting members. The Executive Director is entrusted with the day-to-day management of ESAs, the preparation of the work of the Management Board and the implementation of ESAs' work programme. EBAs' organisational structure still follows the logics of an EU agency provided as a network structure which excludes that EBA acts as a fully supranational entity in Europe. The institutional structure has been clearly identified in the EBA Regulation as an 'integrated network of national and EU supervisory authorities'[40] with a formal institutional structure.

As regards EBA powers, the preparation of technical standards is one of the most important regulatory power ESAs possess. EBA can propose regulatory or implementing technical standards that, after the Commission's endorsement, will take the form of delegated or implementing Commission acts. EBA influence in the creation of technical standards is high as, in contrast with its predecessor, its input is direct and unmediated at the drafting stage.[41] The categories of regulatory and implementing technical standards, which EBA adopts, reflect the distinction between delegated acts and implementing acts under Articles 290 and 291 TFEU.[42] The former are based on Article 290 TFEU and shall consist of norms aimed at establishing 'a single rulebook [and] a

37. Niamh Moloney, *The European Securities and Markets Authority and Institutional Design for the EU Financial Market – A Tale of Two Competences: Part (1) Rule-Making*, 12 European Business Organisation Law Review 49 (2011).
38. Art. 352 TFEU (the 'flexibility' clause).
39. Regulation (EU) No 1093/2010 of the European Parliament and of the Council of 24 November 2010 establishing a European Supervisory Authority (European Banking Authority), amending Decision No 716/2009/EC and repealing Commission Decision 2009/78/EC [2010] OJ L331 ('EBA Regulation') Recital 17.
40. *Ibid.*, Recital 9.
41. *See* for ESMA Pierre Schammo, *The European Securities and Markets Authority: Lifting the Veil on the Allocation of Powers* 48 Common Market Law Review 1883 (2011).
42. *See supra* section §6.03[A][1].

level playing field and adequate protection to depositors, investors and consumers across the Union'.[43] The latter are based on implementing acts under Article 291 TFEU. The power to draft regulatory and implementing technical standards has clear limitations as these 'shall not imply strategic decisions or policy choices' and their 'content shall be delimited by the legislative acts on which they are based'.[44] The procedure for the adoption of the technical standards requires a qualified majority, an exception to the general rule of simple majority. EBA prepares the technical standards and submits them to the Commission which shall immediately send them to the European Parliament and the Council. Endorsement is the essential condition for the standards to become binding. In case the Commission does not intend to endorse the standard, to endorse it in part or to endorse it with amendments, it shall send it back to EBA together with an explanation of its objections. If EBA does not submit an amended standard or has submitted a standard which does not comply with the Commission amendment, the latter may adopt the standard with the amendments it considers relevant or reject it.[45]

The process of adoption of technical standards gives strong powers to EBA. It acts as the drafter of the technical standards while the Commission substantially follows them. In fact, the latter has limited powers to propose amendments only in 'very restricted and extraordinary circumstances'.[46] On the one hand, the Commission enjoys the final wording on the content of the standard through the 'endorsement'. On the other hand, EBA Regulation restrains the possibility of rejection or amendment by stating that amendments can be made only when:

> [the standards] were incompatible with Union law, did not respect the principle of proportionality or run counter to the fundamental principles of the internal market for financial services (...).[47]

In other words, while the Commission still participates in EBA's meetings, its possibility to review the proposed draft technical standards adopted by EBA is restricted only to specific infringements of EU law. Furthermore, the Commission cannot unilaterally revise the content of EBA's draft standard.[48]

This analysis has shown that the Commission is limited in the marge of manoeuvre to (re)-draft, amend or discard EBA's technical standards. At the same time, the power of the Commission to revise, amend or discard technical standards indicates that the Commission's approval is a necessary condition to ensure that the *Meroni* doctrine[49] is not infringed. This is a true guarantee in the decision-making process to avoid EBA exercising an uncontrolled and discretionary rule-making power. At the same time, the existence of strict conditions for the Commission to amend or

43. EBA Regulation, Recital 22.
44. *Ibid.*, Arts 10 and 15.
45. *Ibid.*
46. *Ibid.*, Recital 23.
47. *Ibid.*
48. *Ibid.*, Arts 10(1) and 15(1).
49. Cases 9/56 and 10/56 *Meroni and Co., Industrie Metallurgiche SpA v. High Authority* ECLI: EU:C:1958:7 para. 152.

discard the technical standards shows that EBA may play a powerful role in shaping the content of technical standards. Should the Commission agree on the draft technical standard, EBA has the 'first word' to make choices that can have the potentials of going beyond the rule-making process of the delegator.[50]

EBA can also adopt soft law acts in the forms of guidelines and/or recommendations addressed to competent national authorities and/or to market players. As stated in Article 16 of ESAs' Regulations, this prerogative serves as a way 'to ensure efficient and effective supervisory practices' and 'to ensure the common, uniform and consistent application of Union law'. These soft law acts are subject to some procedural requirements: open public consultations, proportionality in relation to the scope, nature and impact of guidelines and recommendations; and cost-benefit analysis. It appears that ESA's soft law powers are more stringent than generic soft law powers. First, EBA Regulation clearly specifies that the addressees shall 'make every effort to comply'[51] with these acts and in case of non-compliance they shall give reasons for non-compliance. Second, the National Competent Authorities (NCAs) can be required to report in a clear and detailed way whether they have complied with the guideline or the recommendation. Third, in case the national authorities do not comply or intend to comply, they are further obliged to state reasons (EBA's 'comply or explain' procedure). Further, ESAs shall publish the results of non-compliance and can decide to publish the reason provided by the competent authority for non-compliance ('naming and shaming'). Hence, EBA's recommendations and guidelines might act as de facto hard law measures as they may produce legal effects which can go beyond the general statement that they do not have binding force. In particular, it seems that the public 'naming and shaming' approach may ensure enforcement.[52] However, the indirect legal effects soft law powers might raise concerns of accountability and legal certainty.[53] Therefore, the analysis moves to the legitimacy and effectiveness of EBA.

[2] Legitimacy and Effectiveness of EBA as a Banking Regulation Law-Maker

This subsection assesses the legitimacy and effectiveness of EBA by critically evaluating its creation and the extent of its powers. A first subsection assesses the creation of EBA and in general EU agencies under Article 114 TFEU (subsections i). The second subsection looks at the extent of delegation powers to EBA, also in light of the ECJ case law (subsection ii).

50. Madalina Busuioc, *Rule Making by the European Financial Supervisory Authorities: Walking a Tight Rope*, 19 European Law Journal 117 (2012).
51. EBA Regulation, Art. 16(3).
52. Busuioc *supra* n. 50 118.
53. Takis Tridimas, *Financial Supervision and Agency Power: Reflections on ESMA* in Niamh Shuibhne, Laurence Gormley (eds), *From Single Market to Economic Union*, 72 (Oxford University Press 2012).

[a] EBA Legal Basis

Article 114 TFEU is an internal market provision that serves to adopt legal measures for the harmonisation or approximation of national rules in order to contribute to the establishment and functioning of the internal market. This is a general Treaty legal basis for the harmonisation of the internal market or approximation of law. Extensive case law before the ECJ has arisen in recent years.[54] To date the *Tobacco Advertising* case has been the most important legal challenge to the use of Article 114 TFEU. The case was seen as the seminal expression of the constitutional limits to the use of Article 114 TFEU. The ECJ affirmed that public health should be taken as a decisive factor in the choice of adopting the Directive at issue.[55] Subsequent case law blurred the boundaries of the Article 114 TFEU legal basis.[56]

Article 114 TFEU has been used extensively to create new EU agencies. Case law has arisen on such use. Two cases are of particular interest in the purposes of this analysis: *UK v. European Parliament and Council* (Smoke Flavourings) and *UK v. European Parliament and Council* (ENISA). In *Smoke Flavourings*, the Court held that the system adoption of authorisation for smoke flavourings for foods, which gave certain powers to the European Food Safety Authority (EFSA) and to the Commission, did not run counter Article 114 TFEU as legal basis.[57] The test used by the Court to uphold the decision was very low as it was ready to uphold mere differences between laws of Member States to use Article 114 TFEU. The *ENISA* case[58] concerned the establishment of the European Network and Information Security Agency (ENISA) under Article 114 TFEU. The Court applied a low threshold for the adoption of the contested Regulation and held that the legislator:

> may deem it necessary to provide for the establishment of a Community body responsible for contributing to the implementation of a process of harmonisation in situations where (...) the adoption of non-binding supporting and framework measures seems appropriate.[59]

The Court required that the objectives and the tasks of this body were closely linked to the subject matter which the legislation concerned intends to harmonise, and that its objectives and tasks supported and provided a framework for the implementation of that legislation.[60] This case shows that the Court did not restrict the use of

54. Case C-376/98 *Germany v. European Parliament and Council* (Tobacco I) ECLI:EU:C:2000:544, para. 84.
55. *Ibid.*, para. 88.
56. *See* Stephen Weatherhill, *The Limits of Legislative Harmonisation Ten Years After Tobacco Advertising: How the Court's Case Law Has Become a 'Drafting Guide'*, 12 German Law Journal 827 (2011).
57. Case C-66/04 *United Kingdom v. European Parliament and Council* (Smoke Flavourings) ECLI:EU:C:2005:743.
58. Case C-217/04 *United Kingdom v. Council and European Parliament* (ENISA case) ECLI: EU:C:2006:279.
59. *Ibid.*, para. 44.
60. *Ibid.*, paras 43–45.

Article 114 TFEU. On the contrary, it adopted an extensive approach on the establishment of ENISA which did not follow the strict ECJ interpretation in the *Tobacco Advertising* case.

Overall, in both cases the Court outlines the broad limits to the use of Article 114 TFEU. First, the necessity of the harmonising act shall be 'closely linked to the subject matter of the acts approximating the laws, regulations and administrative provisions of the Member States'.[61] Second, the harmonising act should constitute an appropriate means of preventing the emergence of disparities likely to create obstacles to the smooth functioning of the internal market in the area.[62] Third, in line with the principles applied by European courts, harmonisation shall be proportionate.

Despite presenting some limitations, these judgments have shed light on the use of Article 114 TFEU to create EU agencies. As recently stated, the use of Article 114 TFEU is 'attractive because it allows for flexible structures and far-reaching conferral of powers'.[63] This is precisely what happened with the creation and shaping of ESAs. It is uncontested that ESAs, and therefore EBA, have relied on Article 114 TFEU as legal basis. However, some commentators have argued that ESAs have been established on a rather precarious legal basis for radical institutional reform.[64] Nonetheless, it is submitted that in the context of financial supervision and regulation, Article 114 TFEU has acquired a role that was inconceivable before the outbreak of the financial crisis, although its legal boundaries are still uncertain and require more legal clarifications.

Moving to the extent of powers conferred to EBA and Article 114 TFEU the well-known *ESMA* case[65] sheds some light and takes a rather innovative approach on the use of Article 114 TFEU to confer powers to EU agencies. Shortly after the adoption of the Short Selling Regulation (SSR),[66] the UK filed an action for the annulment of Article 28 of the SSR. This provision empowers ESMA to either:

> (a) require natural or legal persons who have net short positions in relation to a specific financial instrument or class of financial instruments to notify a competent authority or to disclose to the public details of any such position; or (b) prohibit or impose conditions on, the entry by natural or legal persons into a short sale or a transaction which creates, or relates to, a financial instrument (...) where the effect or one of the effects of the transaction is to confer a financial advantage on such person in the event of a decrease in the price or value of another financial instrument.

---

61. *Ibid.*, paras 45, 47.
62. *Ibid.*, paras 62–63.
63. Herwig Hofmann & Alessandro Morini, *Constitutional Aspects of the Pluralisation of the EU Executive Through 'Agencification'*, 37 European Law Review 428 (2012).
64. *See* Eilis Ferran, *Understanding the New Institutional Architecture of EU Financial Market Supervision* in Guido Ferrarini, Klaus Hopt, Eddy Wymeersch (eds), *Financial Regulation and Supervision. A Post-crisis Analysis*, Chapter 5 (Oxford University Press 2012).
65. Case C-270/12 *United Kingdom of Great Britain and Northern Ireland v. European Parliament, Council of the European Union* (ESMA case) ECLI:EU:C:2014:18. *See* Gianni Lo Schiavo, *A Judicial Re-Thinking on the Delegation of Powers to European Agencies under EU Law? Comment on Case C-270/12 UK v. Council and Parliament*, 16 German Law Journal 315 (2015).
66. Regulation (EU) No 236/2012 of the European Parliament and of the Council of 14 March 2012 on short selling and certain aspects of credit default swaps, OJ L 86, 24.3.2012.

The UK framed its case on four grounds of annulment. First, it alleged that the provisions envisaged under Article 28 of the SSR exceed the limits set out by the Court in the *Meroni* judgment on the delegation of powers to EU agencies. Second, it argued that Article 28 empowers the ESMA to adopt non-legislative acts that are in breach of Articles 290 and 291 TFEU. Finally, the UK claimed that the power to adopt individual decisions that are legally binding on third parties is not correctly based on Article 114 TFEU, which is the legal basis for the harmonisation of the internal market and not for regulatory measures by an EU agency directed at individuals in Member States.

The attention of the ECJ went to whether the provision of Article 28 of the SSR can be adopted using Article 114 TFEU as the legitimate legal basis. This takes place with a discussion by the ECJ on the two main elements of the provision under Article 114 TFEU: the nature of the expression of 'measures for the approximation'; and the content of the measure that shall have as an object the establishment and functioning of the internal market.

The ECJ analysis of Article 114 TFEU was first on the expression 'measures for the approximation'. The ECJ took a rather open interpretation of the expression 'measures for the approximation'. The Court considered that the EU legislature may have a wide degree of discretion in adopting measures for the approximation. This means that it is also possible to confer EU agencies the power to adopt measures of approximation for special professional and technical expertise. The Court is conscious that the measures for the approximation shall be loose enough to allow also EU agencies to adopt acts having a general application. However, the ECJ did not indicate what the more general limitations for 'the measures for the approximation' are. Rather, it preferred to describe the provision of Article 28 SSR without setting a more general framework for the interpretation of 'measures for the approximation'. The ECJ's approach shows that the Court is rather deferential on the action of the EU legislature, and that it prefers to exercise limited judicial review in the matter.

The expression 'measures which have as their object the establishment and functioning of the internal market' under Article 114 TFEU is the second element that the Court addresses in the case. The Court shows judicial deference to the EU legislator. It confirmed that the measures of approximation may also be addressed to reduce obstacles of the internal market. The Court stated that the prohibition or the imposition of conditions on the entry by natural or legal persons into a short sale or a transaction at ESMA level prevents 'the creation of obstacles to the proper functioning of the internal market and the continuing application of divergent measures by Member States'.[67] On the one hand, this judicial deference is positive as it allowed the Court to endorse the EU legislator. On the other hand, it is argued that this is not sufficient to confer more legal certainty to the EU legislator in adopting measures whose object is the establishment and functioning of the internal market. In such way, the ECJ leaves

67. Case 270/12 *United Kingdom of Great Britain and Northern Ireland v. European Parliament, Council of the European Union* (ESMA case), para. 114.

the EU legislator free to adopt measures, albeit without an effective assessment of the measures that would go beyond the legal sphere of Article 114 TFEU. In sum, the ECJ makes use of a deferential approach to the EU legislator to adopt measures which confer powers to EU agencies. This brings the analysis to the extent of delegation powers to EBA, also in light of the *ESMA* judgment.

[b] Delegation of Powers to EBA

As regards the exercise of delegation powers to EU agencies, it is undisputed that legal constraints have obstructed EU agencies' powers. This comes after what the ECJ stated in the *Meroni* judgment.[68] In *Meroni*, the Court reasoned under what circumstances delegation to agencies or bodies could be lawful by saying that:

> delegation of powers [to agencies] can only relate to clearly defined executive powers, the use of which must be entirely subject to the supervision of the [Commission].[69]

It put forward a number of arguments to prohibit a *carte blanche* delegation to EU agencies. In brief, the *Meroni* doctrine contends that institutions cannot delegate their essential powers to other entities. This is the essential argument that runs counter the possibility to delegate power without an effective system of supervision and control by the delegating entity.

The consequences of the *Meroni* ruling have been immense in the following decades. The *Meroni* principle enshrined in the judgment 'has stood for (...) 50 years as a constitutional limit to delegation'[70] as a constitutional doctrine on limitations of agency delegation. As Ellen Vos puts it, the risk of a distortion to institutional balance is the true limit set out in the *Meroni* judgment. A delegation of discretionary powers to agencies would upset this balance.[71] The delegation of substantial powers to agencies has been discussed extensively in literature.[72] If the post-*Meroni* case law appears rather restrictive in considering delegation of power, many counterarguments in doctrine have been put forward to reduce or even annul its *diktat*. In particular, Chiti argued that the institutional balance referred in *Meroni* is a fluid concept that should be reinterpreted over time by the Court.[73] Accordingly, he held that it would be time to give also discretionary powers to agencies and go beyond a strictly legal reading of *Meroni*.[74]

---

68. Cases 9/56 and 10/56 *Meroni and Co., Industrie Metallurgiche SpA v. High Authority* ECLI :EU:C:1958:7.
69. Case C-270/12 *United Kingdom of Great Britain and Northern Ireland v. European Parliament, Council of the European Union* (ESMA case), para. 152.
70. Paul Craig, *EU Administrative Law*, 155 (Oxford University Press 2012).
71. Ellen Vos, *Agencies and the European Union* in Luc Verhey, Tom Zwart (eds), *Agencies in European and Comparative Perspective*, 131 (Intersentia 2003).
72. *See* recently Merijn Chamon, *EU Agencies: Legal and Political Limits to the Transformation of the EU*, 135 (Oxford University Press 2016).
73. Edoardo Chiti, *An Important part of the EU's Institutional Machinery. Features, Problems and Perspectives of European Agencies*, 46 Common Market Law Review 1423 (2009).
74. *Ibid.*, 1424.

Limitations to delegation are well reflected in EBA rule-making powers as EBA cannot adopt legally binding measures without the Commission's endorsement. In this context, the *ESMA* case has made an important clarification on the scope of application of the *Meroni* doctrine with a relaxation of the strict line followed in the ECJ case law. The ECJ adopts an evolutionary approach to *Meroni*. The *ESMA* doctrine renews the *Meroni* doctrine and leaves behind the structural difficulties of delegation of powers to agencies.

According to the ECJ, the delegation of powers is allowed under EU law so long as control mechanisms are in place to avoid the exercise of a pure discretionary power by the delegated agency.[75] This means that the main concern shall be to introduce limitations to delegated powers and control mechanisms that allow that delegated agencies respect their attributed powers. In that sense, the ECJ pointed to two arguments to exclude that the powers conferred under Article 28 breach the *Meroni* doctrine. First, the Court held that ESMA is not conferred any autonomous power that 'goes beyond the bounds of the regulatory framework established by the ESMA Regulation'.[76] Second, conditions and criteria to the exercise of this power limit ESMA's discretion effectively to exercise its delegated powers. These suggest that there are clear limits and control mechanisms provided by the legislators to the exercise of the specific ESMA's powers. The ECJ argumentations make clear that the *Meroni* doctrine cannot be considered as an absolute limitation to the conferral of powers to a delegated agency or body.

On the contrary, delegation of powers to agencies is *Meroni*-compatible so long as there are non-fully discretionary powers delegated and that control mechanisms to assess delegation are put in place. First, the *ESMA* ruling recognises the private law nature of the agencies in *Meroni* and distances the findings of *Meroni* with the case at issue. This allows taking some distances from the *Meroni diktat*. Second and more important, the ECJ holds that limitations to discretionary powers and control mechanisms are sufficient elements to make delegation of powers to EU agencies compliant with the *Meroni* doctrine. Hence, the ECJ makes a 're-styling' of the *Meroni* doctrine and moves beyond its straitjacket so long as pure discretionary powers are not given to an EU agency and some institutional safeguards are guaranteed. In other words, so long as the EU legislators give powers to agencies and include clearly delineated control mechanisms, there is no breach of the *Meroni* doctrine.

Therefore, the *Meroni* doctrine still exists although with flexible contours especially in regulating European financial (and in this case banking) markets. This means that the *Meroni* doctrine is more flexible than in the past. As applied to EBA, the *ESMA* case is a step further in the judicial endorsement of regulatory EU agency in banking regulation. Yet, the *ESMA* case does not overrule the basic limitation of the *Meroni* judgment by elaborating a new constitutional doctrine allowing fully fledged decision-making powers to EU agencies. It is submitted that such change should take place in a

75. Case C-270/12 *United Kingdom of Great Britain and Northern Ireland v. European Parliament, Council of the European Union* (ESMA case), para. 53.
76. *Ibid.*, para. 44.

changing European constitutional and institutional post-crisis environment. Nonetheless, the ECJ has succeeded in relaxing the constitutional boundaries of EU agency delegation.

The new supranational financial stability environment as set out in this book calls for further relaxation of the *Meroni* doctrine. Such development would suggest a reconsideration of the *Meroni* limitations, which do not seem to be valid anymore.[77] So long as certain constitutional safeguards such as conferral of powers and judicial review are warranted, the attribution of fully fledged decision-making powers to EU agencies would solve legal constraints on the conferral of full discretionary powers to EBA.[78] In perspective, such development would allow EU agencies exercising full powers in Europe.

[C] The Substantive Dimension: The Reinforcement of Supranational Regulation in the Banking Field

Having completed the assessment of the institutional dimension of banking regulation, this section looks at the substantive dimension of banking regulation. The regulatory developments regarding the adoption of the 'CRDIV'[79] and the creation of a 'single rulebook' for credit institutions in Europe show that EU banking regulation has undergone considerable improvements in light of the normative instruments of supranational regulation as developed in this book. Without being a detailed assessment of each provision on banking regulation, which would go beyond the scope of this book, this section looks at the new substantive reforms and discusses them in light of the emergence of financial stability as a foundational objective in EU law and policy. In particular, it examines to what extent the existing rules are an expression of a 'harmonised' effort where European rules replace national rules. Hence given the extensive banking rules in the banking field, this section will concentrate on the most important prudential provisions to ensure the supranational dimension of financial stability of credit institutions in Europe. The first subsection looks at the harmonisation efforts in the CRR and the CRDIV (subsection [1]). The second subsection looks at the DGS renewed directive (subsection [2]).

[1] The New Capital Requirements Rules Under EU Law: Shaping the Single Rulebook in the CRR and the CRDIV

On 26 February 2010, the Commission launched public consultations on possible further amendments of the CRD, CRD II and CRD III. These consultations were focused on the question of how the financial soundness of banks and investment firms could be

77. *See* Edoardo Chiti, *In The Aftermath Of The Crisis: The EU Administrative System Between Impediments and Momentum*, EUI WP Law 2015/13, 5 (2015).
78. *See* for a similar discussion on the SRB Chapter 8 section §8.04[C].
79. Directive 2013/36/EU of the European Parliament and of the Council of 26 June 2013 on access to the activity of credit institutions and the prudential supervision of credit institutions and investment firms, amending Directive 2002/87/EC and repealing Directives 2006/48/EC and 2006/49/EC [2013] OJ L 176.

assured and thus on how the minimum capital requirements for credit institutions in the EU should be revised. The amendments were substantially aligned with the amendments to the Basel III Framework.[80] The regulatory package consists of Regulation 575/2013[81] and Directive 2013/36/EU and Member States needed to apply the new rules from 1 January 2014, with full implementation by 1 January 2019. This regulatory effort is in line with the reinforcement of supranational regulation as normative instruments to the attainment of financial stability in EU law and policy.[82] At the same time, the prudential regulatory reforms for credit institutions in Europe reflect a *sui generis* European implementation into binding rules of the international prudential standards developed in Basel III.[83]

[a] The Maximum Harmonisation Paradigm in the CRR

The CRR is the first EU Regulation that introduces directly applicable capital requirements in the internal market for credit institutions. It aims to realise a 'single rulebook' for credit institutions and investment firms in Europe. The CRR is a very long Regulation comprising more than 500 articles. This section does not aim to cover all the aspects included in the CRR, but to show what the most important aspects are and whether these are intended to shape banking regulation in light of supranational financial stability.

The CRR is intended to provide uniform rules on the general prudential requirements that supervised institutions need to respect. In this sense, Recital 7 indicates that the main purpose of the Regulation is to include prudential requirements for credit institutions that are meant to ensure financial stability of the operators on financial markets as well as a high level of protection of investors and depositors. This applies in particular to own funds, requirement to limit large exposures, liquidity risks, reporting requirements and public disclosure requirements.[84] These are analysed below.

Capital Adequacy

The first and foremost important element in banking regulation is having sound capital adequacy. The authorisation of a business activity of credit institutions presupposes that an initial capital is present and that the institution respects the capital adequacy requirements. These are essential elements in order to incentivise banks to take less risk and to create buffers to absorb losses in cases of unexpected economic shocks. The

80. For a brief account of the Basel framework *see* Chapter 2 section §2.05[C].
81. Regulation (EU) No 575/2013 of the European Parliament and of the Council of 26 June 2013 on prudential requirements for credit institutions and investment firms and amending Regulation (EU) No 648/2012 [2013] OJ L 176 ('CRR').
82. *See* Directive 2013/36/EU, Recitals 5 and 50; Regulation 575/2013, Recital 7.
83. On Basel III *see* Chapter 2 section §2.05[C].
84. CRR, Art. 1.

CRR addresses capital uncertainties and improves the capital adequacy in the pre-existing European legal framework. It sets own funds requirements as the required holding of capital and expressed as a percentage of Risk Weighted Assets (RWAs).

The CRR identifies the way how to weigh the institution assets according to their risks. In this sense, the RWA amount is reflected in the types of capital. Traditionally, the Basel Committee divided capital between Tier 1 and Tier 2. The former consists mainly in shareholder's equity and disclosed reserves, while the latter corresponds to hybrid capital and subordinated debt. The CRR reproduces the well-established 8% ratio of minimum own fund requirements as developed in the Basel standards, but it requires that credit institutions have 4.5% of Common Equity Tier 1 (CET1) ratio.[85] CET1 is the purest form of capital which need to respect the capital ratio rule of 4.5% as provided in the CRR. Furthermore, in the 8% rule, the capital comprises Additional Tier 1 (AT1) as additional capital instruments whose capital ratio would qualify as Tier 1 for the purpose of capital requirements. Tier 2 capital is the other component of the own funds. Tier 2 comprises capital instruments that are not sufficiently reliable to constitute Tier 1 capital instrument. Tier 2 capital instruments have less qualitative criteria to be Tier 1, but are still an important part for loss absorption for a credit institution. The CRR requires that Tier 2 amounts to 2%.

Limits to Large Exposures

An important set of regulatory requirement imposed on credit institutions is the limit on certain large exposures that credit institutions may incur. The harmonised rules require that credit institutions avoid being excessively exposed to a single client. Therefore, the CRR provides a general prohibition for credit institutions to incur an exposure to one client or a group of connected clients the value of which amounts to more than 25% of its own funds.[86] The CRR introduces a definition of large exposure as where 'its value is equal to or exceeds 10%' of the own funds of the credit institution.[87] There are a number of exemptions to such rules that are notably calculated on the basis of RWAs. For instance 'Exposures to central governments, central banks or public sector entities which, unsecured, would be assigned a 0% risk-weight' are exempted from the calculation of large exposures.[88]

The Liquidity Ratios

An important aspect of the financial crisis has been to reinforce liquidity requirements so as to allow a number of liquid financial resources to withstand financial crises. Following the Basel III, the CRR introduces two liquidity instruments: the liquidity coverage ratio (LCR) and the Net Stable Funding Ratio (NSFR).

The LCR consists in a requirement to hold liquid assets in order to ensure that institutions maintain a certain level of liquidity in case of liquidity shortage. The LCR

85. CRR, Art. 92(1).
86. CRR, Art. 395.
87. CRR. Art. 392.
88. CRR, Art. 400.

is meant to withstand the crisis over a period of thirty days by holding some liquid assets covering the liquidity outflows less the liquidity inflows in stressed conditions.[89] The LCR has been object of fierce negotiations as a high level of liquidity buffer might have an adverse impact on the real economy.[90] In theory, an excessively high LCR would promote the shift from lending to liquid assets. In 2015, the Commission adopted a delegated Commission Regulation setting a binding LCR.[91] This instrument introduces a high quality liquid assets ratio to cover the difference between the expected cash outflows and the expected capped cash inflows over a thirty-day stressed period. The LCR is set at 100% of high quality liquid assets. The CRR sets an implementation schedule of the LCR along the phased-in percentage: '(a) 60% of the liquidity coverage requirement in 2015; (b) 70% as from 1 January 2016; (c) 80% as from 1 January 2017; (d) 100% as from 1 January 2018.'[92]

Furthermore, following Basel III, the CRR introduces the NSFR as the second liquidity ratio requiring an acceptable amount of stable funding to support the institutions assets and activities over the medium-term. This is a complementary liquidity instrument that envisages to hold funding instrument over a longer period. NSFR is calculated by assessing the amount of available stable funding minus the amount of required stable funding. However, the CRR does not expressly introduce yet binding rules on NSFR. This may be explained by the fact that the Commission did not intend to adopt a binding liquidity requirement before an observation period had taken place. The CRR indicates that credit institutions shall respect long-term obligations are met with some stable funding requirements under both normal and stressed conditions.

The Definition and Role of Leverage Ratios

The CRR foresees the leverage ratio as a new instrument for the safeguarding of risks associated with risk models. The leverage ratio is calculated as Tier 1 capital divided by a measure of non-risk weighted on- and off-balance sheet items.[93] The leverage ratio is a new regulatory tool introduced in the CRR which is not binding for institutions as from the entry into force of the CRR. Initially it will be considered as an optional measure to be introduced by credit institutions. This entails that credit institutions need to respect a disclosure obligation as of 1 January 2015 with the purpose to introduce more transparency in the financial sector.[94]

---

89. CRR, Art. 412.
90. The issue was also discussed at Basel Committee Level which decided to adopt a standard on liquidity ratio in January 2013 *see* Basel Committee on Banking Supervision, Liquidity Coverage Ratio and Liquidity Risk Monitoring Tools, January 2013 at www.bis.org/publ/bcbs238.pdf (accessed 31 December 2016).
91. Commission Delegated Regulation (EU) 2015/61 of 10 October 2014 to supplement Regulation (EU) No 575/2013 of the European Parliament and the Council with regard to liquidity coverage requirement for Credit Institutions, OJ L 11, 17.1.2015
92. CRR, Art. 460(2).
93. CRR, Art. 429.
94. *See* CRR, Art. 430.

[b] *The Partial Harmonisation Paradigm in the CRD*

While the CRR intends to achieve full harmonisation on capital requirements, relevant prudential sectors are subject to national implementation as part of the CRDIV, the second component of the EU legislative reform adopted in 2013. Differently from the CRR, the CRDIV needs to be implemented by the Member States into national law and in general gives certain discretionary powers to the Member States to regulate the implementing national law.

The CRDIV includes rules for access to taking up/pursuit of banking business, exercise of freedom of establishment and free movement of services, prudential supervision, capital buffers, corporate governance and sanctions. While the CRDIV can have a maximum harmonisation approach in some areas, the CRDIV provisions as such are not directly prescriptive and enforceable, but shall be implemented in national law.

Rules on the Taking Up the Business of Credit Institutions

The criteria for taking up the business of credit institutions is the first essential condition to the exercise of banking activities. Article 5 of the CRDIV provides for the authorisation conditions and requires that national authorities decide in their own procedure whether to authorise an institution so to allow the fulfilment of some minimum requirements. Member States are also required to notify the authorisation requirements to the EBA. Most importantly, the initial requirement for the pursuit of the banking business is that the credit institution shall have separate own funds and have an initial capital of EUR 5 million. Furthermore, other conditions need to be complied with to be granted authorisation. First, the Directive stipulates that competent authorities require an application of authorisation to the institution with a programme of operations indicating among other aspects the type of business envisaged and the structural organisation of the credit institution. Second, competent authorities are not allowed to authorise entities in light of economic needs.[95] Third, the competent authorities shall grant authorisation only to credit institution which are effectively directed by at least two persons of sufficiently good repute and with sufficient expertise to perform such duties. The Directive now includes specific criteria to assess whether the two persons fulfil this mandate. Fourth, the competent authorities shall consider the characteristics of the important shareholders of the credit institution. The authorities need to be informed on the identities of the shareholders or members that have qualifying holdings in the credit institutions as well as the amounts of these holdings.

As for the credit institution, the authorisation may be withdrawn in case the said institution does not fulfil some requirements. Article 18 lists the cases in which withdrawal of authorisation may take place. Among other situations, two are the most relevant ones. Letter (c) prescribes withdrawal of authorisation in case the institution does not respect the conditions for authorisation as granted under the conditions

95. CRDIV, Art. 11.

examined earlier.[96] This means that the requirements for the initial authorisation are not fulfilled any longer. This applies for the initial capital condition of EUR 5 million, for the requirement that at least two persons direct the institution, for the required robust governance arrangements, risk management processes or internal control mechanisms and the remuneration policies. Letter (d) lists a series of situations that would lead to the withdrawal of authorisation. First, withdrawal would apply when the credit institution does no longer meet the prudential requirements provided in the CRR.[97] Second, withdrawal would apply when the specific capital requirements on additional own funds or on specific liquidity imposed by competent authorities are not fulfilled with. Finally, withdrawal would apply if the institution can no longer be relied on to fulfil its obligations towards its creditors with particular attention to the fact that it 'no longer provides security for the assets entrusted to it by depositors'.[98]

Rules on the Exercise of the Business of Credit Institutions

The new CRDIV harmonises also to a certain extent the requirement on credit institutions for the pursuit of their business activities. This has a dual dimension, as both the Member State and the authorised institutions need to fulfil some requirements.

As for the Member States, once the conditions for authorisation have been complied with, the CRDIV allows the authorised institution to benefit from the 'single passport'. This means that each Member State needs to comply with the home country principle which provides that credit institutions may establish branches or provide services without any other authorisation.[99] The new harmonisation paradigm means that Member States cannot derogate from the rules on authorisation and from the home country principle.

The conduct of business requires also that competent authorities monitor the changes in qualifying holdings in the credit institution. It requires that the changes in such holdings need to be notified in writing to the competent authorities in case the holding increases by reaching or exceeding 20%, 30% or 50% or so that the credit institution would become a subsidiary.[100] The CRDIV contains rules on the acquisition of qualifying holdings, setting out the requirement and the procedure to be followed for such acquisitions.[101] Qualifying holding is defined in the CRR as a 'direct or indirect holding in an undertaking which represents 10% or more of the capital or of the voting rights or which makes possible to exercise a significant influence over the management of that undertaking'.[102]

Furthermore, the CRDIV contains rules on Pillar 2 measures as additional capital requirements imposed by the competent supervisor on credit institutions. While Pillar

96. CRDIV, Art. 18(1) letter (c).
97. This applies in particular to Part Three (Capital Requirements), Four (Large Exposures) and Six (Liquidity) of the CRR.
98. CRDIV, Art. 18 letter (d).
99. *See* CRDIV Art. 33.
100. CRDIV, Art. 22(1).
101. CRDIV, Arts 22 and following.
102. CRR Art. 4(1) point (36).

1 measures are those imposed in the CRR as minimum own funds requirements, Pillar 2 requirements are additional institution-specific measures that could be used to address risks to which an institution is exposed. The competent supervisory authorities perform the Supervisory Review and Evaluation Process (SREP) as an assessment and review of risks of supervised entities. This includes an assessment of: '(a) risks to which the institutions are or might be exposed; (b) risks that an institution poses to the financial system (...); and (c) risks revealed by stress testing (...)'.[103]

Corporate Governance

The CRDIV contains also rules on the harmonisation of corporate governance of credit institutions.

The CRDIV requires that the credit institutions have robust corporate arrangements in place, adequate internal control mechanisms, and remuneration policy and practice consistent with and promote sound and effective risk management.[104]

As regards corporate governance rules, the CRDIV contains rules that concern the composition of boards, their functioning and their role in risk oversight and strategy. The CRDIV provides that Member States introduce principles and standards to ensure effective oversight in order to monitor the adequacy of internal governance arrangements.[105] The new regulatory framework introduces rules on diversity in the management board composition in order to avoid the process of 'groupthink' according to which board decisions are taken by a group and not by each because of the lack in diversity.[106] Furthermore, the CRDIV introduces rules on transparency and reporting as regards the disclosure of important information on turnover, profits, taxes and public subsidies as well as the return on assets.[107]

These are in particular rules on organisational structures, personal requirements for board members, and board members duties and responsibilities. The first group consists of rules imposing requirements on banks' corporate structures. The CRDIV contains rules that concern the composition of boards, their functioning and their role in risk supervision and strategy. The CRDIV provides that Member States introduce principles and standards to ensure effective supervision in order to monitor the adequacy of internal governance arrangements such as maximum numbers of directorships by managers.[108] First, the chairman of the management body in its supervisory function shall not hold simultaneously the function of chief executive officer within the same institutions, unless justified by the institution and authorised by the competent

103. CRDIV, Art. 97(1).
104. CRDIV, Art. 74(1).
105. CRDIV, Recital 54.
106. *See* CRDIV, Recital 60.
107. CRDIV, Arts 89 and 90.
108. CRDIV, Recital 54.

supervisory authority.[109] Second, the CRDIV contains rules on the establishment of special committees. These are the risk committee, the remuneration committee, the nomination committee as well as the audit committee. The second group establishes fit and proper rules both for executive and non-executive members of the board and its committees.[110] The CRDIV includes provisions on individual and collective qualities of executive and non-executive board members, limitations on directorships as well as rules on board diversity. In particular, the fit and proper requirements establish rules on sufficient knowledge, skills and experience for the performance of duties as board members. The third group includes rules on how the management body defines, oversees and is accountable for the implementation of governance arrangements that ensure effective and prudent management of the institution.[111] The board is responsible in particular for the implementation of sound remuneration policies and efficient risk governance. As regards risk governance, the CRDIV devotes some provisions on the role of the management body to approve and review the strategies and policies for taking up, managing, monitoring and mitigating risks.[112] The focus of these provisions is to ensure that risks are controlled and managed, and that an appropriate institutional structure for risk control is in place.

As regards remuneration, the CRDIV lists a series of standards on remuneration policies. These deal with the governance, but most importantly, the design of remuneration. They provide for the form, structure and level of performance-based pay systems. The CRDIV reproduces the existing rules on remuneration already provided in the CRDIII. It contains technical criteria on the total remuneration policies of staff of credit institutions whose professional activities have an impact on the institution risk profile. This means that these rules apply only to a specific category of staff, those whose professional activities have a material impact on the risk profile activities of the credit institutions. Adding to the pre-existing CRDIII remuneration policy, the CRDIV introduces two new main remuneration rules. First, it increases transparency and disclosure requirements by requiring disclosure on remuneration policies for the number of natural persons in each institution that are remunerated EUR 1 million or more each year.[113] Second, it strengthens the essential conditions for the relationship between the variable component (the bonus) and the fixed component of remuneration (the salary).[114] In particular, the CRDIV sets a cap on bonuses whereby the variable component shall not exceed 100% of the fixed component of the total remuneration for each individual.[115] Therefore, credit institutions shall balance the fixed and variable component of the executive pay.

109. CRDIV, Art. 88(1)(e).
110. CRDIV, Art. 91.
111. CRDIV, Arts 88, 92 and 94.
112. CRDIV, Art. 76.
113. CRDIV, Art. 75(3).
114. CRDIV, Art. 94(1)(g), 94(2).
115. It should be noted that the new provisions on transparency and bonus cap have been contested by the United Kingdom and brought to the ECJ. The A.G. delivered the opinion in case C-507/13 *United Kingdom of Great Britain and Northern Ireland v. European Parliament, Council of the European Union* ECLI:EU:C:2014:2394. In November 2014, the UK withdrew its challenge.

Capital Buffers

The CRDIV introduces provisions on the introduction of capital buffers that may complement the existing basic capital requirements as contained in the CRR. The CRDIV introduces the capital conservation buffer, the counter-cyclical capital buffer, the global systemic institution buffer, the other systemically important institutions buffer and the systemic risk institution buffer.

The capital conservation buffer is a new prudential tool that consists of total exposures of a bank that needs to be met in CET 1 capital equal to 2.5% of the institution total exposure. The CRDIV stipulates that Member State may require credit institutions to adopt this buffer. The objective of this instrument is to conserve a bank's capital and to allow for automatic safeguard to apply in order to limit the amount of dividend and bonus payment the credit institution can make.

The second instrument is the counter cyclical buffer whose purpose is to counteract the effects of the economy cycle. By accumulating capital resources during economic growth, the capital buffer is used in case of a countercyclical situation and provides additional capital resources.

Furthermore, the CRDIV introduces a mandatory systemic risk buffer, the Global Systemic Institution Buffer, for credit institutions considered as being systemically important. The identification of globally important institutions is based on the size, cross-border activity and interconnectedness. The Global Systemically Important Institutions (G-SIIs) need to apply a mandatory surcharge which will be between 1% and 3.5% of CET1 of RWAs. As clearly indicated in the CRDIV, the main reason for the introduction of the G-SII buffer is 'to compensate for the higher risk that G-SIIs represent for the financial system and the potential impact of their failure on taxpayers'.[116]

The CRDIV introduces also the faculty for Member States to require other systemically important institutions to maintain other systemically important institution buffers. This would apply to domestically important as well as other institutions that are considered as such according to their size, cross-border activities and interconnectedness. The inclusion of this instrument requires that the competent authorities notify the justification, the likely positive and/or negative impact and the buffer rate to establish.[117] These safeguards are introduced in order to avoid disproportionate adverse effects for the integrity of the internal market.[118]

Finally, the systemic risk buffer is the last category of buffer introduced in the CRDIV. Each Member State may introduce this buffer as corresponding to CET1 for the financial sector or one specific sub-sector. This instrument serves to 'prevent and mitigate long-term non-cyclical systemic or macroprudential risks'.[119] In other words, the systemic risk buffer is an additional tool that Member States could introduce to avoid potential disruptions to the financial system. In case the proposed systemic risk buffer rate is between 3% and 5%, its introduction is subject to a procedure whereby

116. CRDIV, Recital 90.
117. CRDIV, Art. 128(7).
118. CRDIV, Art. 128(6).
119. CRDIV, Recital 85.

the Member State notifies the proposed measure to the Commission, the EBA and the ESRB.[120] The Commission provides an opinion and, if this is negative, then the Member State will need to follow a 'comply or explain' procedure. In case the proposed systemic risk buffer rate is above 5%, the Commission needs to adopt it with an implementing act.[121]

[c] Assessment

This subsection intends to summarise and assess the main regulatory trends on prudential requirements for banks as stemming from the CRR/CRIV regulatory package. Reflections are made in light of the normative instrument of supranational regulation developed in Chapter 3 of this book. These concentrate on the degree of harmonisation reached with the CRR/CRDIV, the level of options and discretion contained in the existing CRR/CRDIV package and the level of complexity of Level 1 regulation.

The increased level of harmonisation in capital requirements is a positive development as compared to the previous EU legislation. The first and most evident improvement is the fact that the most important capital requirements are now contained in an EU regulation rather than an EU directive. The de Larosière Report already held that Europe suffers from 'the lack of a consistent set of rules'[122] and invited EU institutions to use regulations rather than directives.[123] As emphasised by the Report, the lack of harmonised rules creates market distortions, and, by creating regulatory inconsistencies, threatens financial stability.[124] This point suggests that directly applicable EU rules shall be adopted whenever possible as they constitute directly applicable obligations while Member States are not allowed to impose any stricter requirements than those laid down in the instrument itself, and not even further options ('maximum harmonisation'). The outcome of the reform efforts was to introduce the CRR while retaining less harmonised rules in the CRDIV.

Second, the overall general harmonised approach followed in the reform package is a welcome development that is intended to set a European regulatory on capital requirements and the limitations to large exposure. For instance, there are now fully harmonised rules on the calculation of capital and recognition/qualification of capital instruments. Similarly, there is a general legal limit to large exposures of credit institutions to 25% of their capital. These two regulatory developments are the most important changes as compared with the previous framework where the EU attempt has been to reduce the number of national options and, thus, uncertainties.

Third, the European approach to prudential regulation is very comprehensive, as the EU has followed the approach of the 'one-size-fits-all'. The CRR and the CRDIV substantive rules apply to all credit institutions. This is an important requirement to

120. CRDIV, Art. 133(14).
121. CRDIV, Art. 133(13) last indent.
122. de Larosière report *supra* n. 9, 27.
123. *Ibid.*, 29.
124. *Ibid.*

ensure that business models in Europe follow certain rules and ensure an adequate level-playing field in the banking sector. Conversely, it may still be argued whether the application of the same rules for big and small credit institutions or different business models is justifiable from the perspective of the impact on banking business. This is in particular evident if one considers the difference between the standardised and internal risk based (IRB) bank model for risk assessment. While big banks may well develop their own internal models, small banks may not have enough resources to 'personalise' their models and need to make use of the standardised model.

If the CRR intends to achieve maximum harmonisation on capital requirements, many prudential elements are still subject to national implementation in the CRDIV, an EU directive, or in options and discretions to Member States or to competent authorities. Differently from the CRR, the CRDIV includes provisions that require Member States' implementation in national law and which may differ considerably from jurisdiction to jurisdiction. As in general for directives in EU law, articles in a directive are not directly prescriptive, but need to be implemented in national provisions leaving Member States wide marge of manoeuvre to adopt different rules. There may be exceptions where the directive sets maximum harmonisation rules and Member States are not allowed to deviate from these rules. Nonetheless, Member States may still retain some discretion on how to implement procedural aspects. There is still considerable margin of manoeuvre for Member States to adopt divergent prudential measures. There may be also the risk of 'gold-plating' measures.

Furthermore, the CRR/CRDIV contains a large number of options and discretions in the regulatory framework that limit the adoption of a complete harmonised approach in Europe and do not contribute to achieve a truly supranational level of financial stability. At the same time, the increasing complexity of the European rules transposing the Basel III standards and being part of Level 1 regulation shows that finding an appropriate balance between what needs to be regulated at Level 1 and what can be delegated or implemented at Level 2 or Level 3 remains an open question. The general capital requirement package appears extremely complex and may be considered itself a source of concern as there are intricate rules that may raise difficult interpretations. A number of examples show the above-mentioned problematic aspects in the CRR/CRDIV package. First, the definitions of capital and capital instruments might lead to divergences as Member States may choose to introduce additional buffers going beyond the capital requirements, leverage and liquidity ratios. The latter are not still fully harmonised and give broad spaces for divergent approaches. Second, Member States can adopt exemptions to a list of exposures fully or partially exempted from the large exposure rule.[125] These may be problematic as divergences can lead to fragmented approaches between regulators. Third, the introduction of capital buffers in the CRDIV is not yet harmonised as Member States may adjust the level of buffers over time, and there is not yet a supranational level playing field for capital buffers. Fourth, the CRDIV includes rules for access to taking up/pursuit of banking business, exercise of freedom of establishment and free movement of services, prudential supervision and

125. CRR, Art. 395(1) and (5).

supervisory powers, capital buffers, corporate governance and sanctions which may vary considerably in national laws. For instance, Article 5 and following of the CRDIV provides for the authorisation procedure, requires that national authorities decide as part of national law whether to authorise an institution so to allow the fulfilment of some minimum requirements and sets out general rules on the withdrawal of authorisation. The criteria for taking up the business of credit institutions are the first essential condition to the exercise of banking activities. However, banking authorisations are not fully harmonised at European level and the type, models and criteria for banking licensing still differ among Member States. Similarly, the rules on supervisory powers provided in Europe are still not supranational as their national implementation can lead to different provisions. This is the case of Article 104 of the CRDIV which lists only certain supervisory powers, but does not set an exhaustive list of supervisory powers and Member States can still introduce further national powers. Fifth, it remains also open the problem that CRR/CRDIV do not contain certain explicit provisions or minimum requirements on important banking operations or activities. This is the case of mergers, acquisitions - apart from qualifying holding in credit institutions-, asset transfer and divestments, covered bond issuance, corporate structures of credit institutions, activities of credit institutions in third countries. The lack of EU harmonised law on such topics remains an open problem.

The above analysis reveals that there are still supranational regulatory limits leading to supranational divergences – or even fragmentations – in Member States as regards banking rules. These are mainly national laws implementing EU law, the absence of EU rules in certain banking fields, as well as options and discretions contained in EU secondary law. As supranational regulation still requires that directly applicable EU rules supersede national laws in many areas, supranational banking regulation only partially contributes to attain supranational financial stability in EU law and policy as developed in this book.

[2] The 2014 Directive on DGS as a New (Limited) Effort to Harmonise DGSs in Europe

A second strand of banking law reforms concerns the creation of a harmonised framework for deposit insurance schemes. In banking theory, deposit insurances serve as an instrument for the protection of depositor's assets held by credit institutions.[126] Without going into the details of deposit insurance theory, many authors have assessed the importance of deposit insurance as a source of stability for the financial system and as a system for the protection for medium and small depositors, predominantly the retail ones.[127] The main objectives of deposit insurance schemes are to avoid deposits runs from an ailing bank and to allow a third-party guarantee on bank deposits.

126. *See* Christine Blair, Frederick Carns & Rose Kushmeider, *Instituting a Deposit Insurance System: Why? How?*', in Andrew Campbell, John La Brosse, David Mayes, Dalvinder Singh (eds), *Deposit Insurance*, 73 (Palgrave MacMillan 2007).
127. *See* Nikoletta Kleftouri, *Deposit Protection and Bank Resolution*, 3 (Oxford University Press 2015) and Jennifer Payne, *The Reform of Deposit Guarantee Schemes in Europe*, 12 European Company Financial Law Review 540 (2015).

Following the financial crisis, a new wave of reforms for the harmonisation of DGSs in Europe has taken place. The new Recast DGS Directive was adopted in April 2014.[128] It does not create a single pan-European DGS. Rather it aims to strengthen the network of national DGS regimes, and to deal with some of the pitfalls of national DGS systems in an internal market.

In particular, the Directive provides for some improvements as regards the applicability of rules for DGSs. First, it reproduces the covered deposit agreed in the 2009 Directive[129] for an amount up to EUR 100,000.[130] Second, it strengthens the level of protection by progressively reducing the repayment days from twenty working days up to seven working days in 2024.[131] Third, it improves the overall level of protection of covered depositors in the context of resolution or insolvency proceedings. The directive provides a rule on creditor preference for all deposits below EUR 100,000 as well as for deposits held by natural persons and Small and Medium Enterprises (SMEs) above the coverage of EUR 100,000. Finally, funding depositor guarantee schemes is, to some extent, harmonised as the credit institutions will have to pay *ex ante* as well as *ex post* contributions. The Directive introduces an obligation to reach a target level of 0.8% of the amount of the covered deposits to be reached by 3 July 2024, so ten years after the entry into force of the Directive. However, Member States retain discretion as to the possible target funding levels for DGS by allowing Member States to raise the available financial means above the target level set in the Directive.[132]

The European approach towards DGS has been improved as compared with the 2009 rules. Two developments are particularly welcome: first, the introduction of priority rules in DGS resolution or insolvency proceedings is a welcome development also in light of the risks that depositors face during the financial crisis; second, the requirement to establish DGS in national law with *ex ante* contributions to reach certain funded levels over time. Although these two main developments are surely an improvement to protect further depositors and assist them in case a credit institution needs to be resolved or fails, European attempts to create a reinforced system for depositor protection falls short both from a substantive and institutional point of view. The existing supranational law on DGS is still not a sufficient safeguard against Member State divergences in the application of DGS rules that may lead to regulatory divergences and fragmentation which are not in the line with the supranational dimension of the financial stability objective in EU law and policy. There is still scope for national choices in the context of deposit guarantees as Member States might set higher targets for guaranteeing the DGS system. Furthermore, while the 2014 Directive proposes a new role for deposit insurers in the context of cross-border issues, i.e. to provide a single point of contact for depositors and banks, and the coordination of

128. Directive 2014/49/EU of the European Parliament and of the Council of 16 April 2014 on deposit guarantee schemes [2014] OJ L 173.
129. Directive 2009/14/EC of the European Parliament and of the Council of 11 March 2009 amending Directive 94/19/EC on deposit-guarantee schemes as regards the coverage level and the payout delay [2009] OJ L 68.
130. Directive 2014/49/EU, Art. 6(1).
131. *Ibid.*, Art. 8.
132. *Ibid.*, Art. 10(4).

reimbursement procedures, it falls short of sufficient clarity as to the way to deal with home/host issues, especially in a crisis situation. Moreover, at present, a common supranational institutional framework for deposit insurance does not exist. Its creation would allow having a harmonised deposit insurance system where the same level of protection of depositors is guaranteed at European level.

Overall, the current European regulatory environment on DGSs still lacks a system of fully harmonised and institutional rules affording the same degree of depositor protection throughout Europe. This is a major limitation in an effort to attain supranational financial stability in EU law and policy.

§6.04 THE EVOLVING NORMATIVE AGENDA ON SUPRANATIONAL BANKING REGULATION

The analysis undertaken as part of this chapter has revealed that supranational financial stability is clearly emerging in European banking regulation. As discussed in Chapter 3 of this book, it was argued that financial stability is a dynamic objective rather than a static one. Hence, the assessment of the main reforms, which have been politically agreed upon and implemented as part of the renewed EMU and the EBU, show that a truly supranational dimension of financial stability has been developed in Europe. However, the above analysis has also shown that certain improvements are needed in banking regulation at European level. This last section has the purpose to assess the most recent and ongoing regulatory attempts to reinforce the supranational financial stability objective in EU banking law and other related fields. This allows examining some recent regulatory reforms in Europe to reinforce financial stability as a supranational objective. Such analysis reveals that financial stability has a broad scope and 'guides' the recent regulatory initiatives undertaken at the supranational level.

Against this background, this section covers four main reform projects. First, it looks at some possible improvements to the CRR/CRDIV also in light of the June 2016 Council conclusions on the EBU[133] and the recent November 2016 Commission's proposals to amend specific provisions of the CRR/CRDIV.[134] Second, it looks at the

133. Council of the EU, *Council Conclusions on a roadmap to complete the Banking Union*, Press Release, 17 June 2016 at http://www.consilium.europa.eu/press-releases-pdf/2016/6/472446 42837_en.pdf (accessed 31 December 2016).

134. The European Commission published two proposals for CRR/CRDIV review in November 2016: Proposal for a Regulation of the European Parliament and of the Council amending Regulation (EU) No 575/2013 as regards the leverage ratio, the net stable funding ratio, requirements for own funds and eligible liabilities, counterparty credit risk, market risk, exposures to central counterparties, exposures to collective investment undertakings, large exposures, reporting and disclosure requirements and amending Regulation (EU) No 648/2012, COM(2016) 850 final; and Proposal for a Directive of the European Parliament and of the Council amending Directive 2013/36/EU as regards exempted entities, financial holding companies, mixed financial holding companies, remuneration, supervisory measures and powers and capital conservation measures, COM(2016) 854 final.

EDIS[135] as the essential, though missing, third pillar of the EBU. Third, it looks at the development of the European Capital Markets Union (CMU) as a recent policy initiative related to banking regulation to strengthen capital markets from a European perspective.[136] Fourth, it evaluates the Commission's proposal on banking structural reform in banking regulation.[137] These four inter-related projects are considered as missing pieces to move forward towards a stronger attainment of supranational financial stability in EU banking and financial law. They combine normative instruments of supranational regulation, supervision and rescue measures as developed in Chapter 3 of this book. The main objective of this section is therefore to assess the current strengths and weaknesses of these four reforms. At the same time, it remains clear that these prospected reforms are under negotiations and at the moment it is difficult to determine whether these proposals will be eventually adopted at the European level.

[A] Reviewing the CRR/CRD IV

Revisions of the CRR/CRDIV are the first, and most important, area that would improve banking regulation in Europe. As examined above, the European regulatory framework established in banking regulation still suffers from considerable divergences and national implementations that do not contribute to a truly supranational regulatory framework. Even if prudential supervision and resolution have to a certain extent be transferred to the supranational level, EU banking regulation still suffers from relevant banking rules being national and divergent in Member States. In June 2016, the Council has made clear that some changes to the regulatory framework of banks are needed, and that the Commission should put forward a proposal to amend the CRR/CRDIV. In this context, some proposal can be made on what rules are to be improved in the current regulatory framework.

Preliminary, as the structure of the CRR/CRDIV is made of a regulation and a directive, amendments should strive to transfer CRDIV provisions into the EU regulation in order to reinforce the supranational nature of banking regulation. As a second best solution, the level of harmonisation of the CRDIV could be improved by making more sections subject to the principle of maximum harmonisation. This would allow national legislators not provide for differential measures in their jurisdictions.

---

135. Proposal for a Regulation of the European Parliament and of the Council amending Regulation (EU) 806/2014 in order to establish a European Deposit Insurance Scheme COM/2015/0586 final - 2015/0270.
136. *See* EU Commission, *Communication, Action Plan on Building a Capital Markets Union*, COM(2015) 468 final and, most recently, EU Commission, *Capital Markets Union: First Status Report*, SWD(2016) 147 final.
137. Commission, Proposal for a Regulation on structural measures improving the resilience of EU credit institutions COM(2014) 043 final (hereinafter 'Commission proposal on structural measures').

The Council has identified some areas for improvements on the CRR/CRDIV. In November 2016, the Commission published the proposal to amend the CRR/CRDIV.[138] There are three main aspects.

First, the Commission proposal includes new prudential requirement ratios: the Leverage Ratio and the NSFR. As mentioned earlier, the Leverage Ratio was formally introduced in the CRR, but its binding nature was postponed to legislative proposal of the Commission. It would bind credit institution having a certain percentage of capital measures divided by the credit institution's total exposures. The Commission suggests introducing a binding leverage ratio of at least 3% for systemic banks. The leverage ratio would enhance financial stability by determining capital requirements on the basis of non-RWAs, would avoid building excessive leverage and would ensure having a backstop to internal model based capital requirements. As for the NSFR, this is considered as a liquidity-based ratio stable calculating the funding profile of a credit institution in relation to its on- and off-balance sheet activities. The NSFR would allow credit institutions finance their long-term activities (assets and off-balance sheet items) with stable sources of funding (liabilities). The NSFR is calculated by multiplying an institution's assets and off-balance sheet exposures by certain factors that reflect their liquidity characteristics. The NSFR would be expressed as a percentage and set at a minimum level of 100%.

Second, the Commission introduces a regulatory distinction in calculating capital requirements between additional Pillar 2 requirements and Pillar 2 guidance. The former are the mandatory requirements imposed by supervisors. The latter refers instead to the possibility for competent authorities to communicate expectations to supervised entities to hold capital in excess of Pillar 1 capital requirement, Pillar 2 capital requirements and combined buffers requirements in order to cope with certain situations.

Third, the Commission proposes additional authorisation requirements for financial holdings, mixed financial holdings for credit institutions established in Europe. Similarly, the proposal requires for third-country banks to have an intermediate EU parent undertaking where two or more institutions established in the EU have the same ultimate parent undertaking in a third country.

Other changes in the proposed package relate to a reform of trading books for calculations of capital requirements for market risk, exemptions from the prudential rules to certain categories of very small or special credit institutions, reinforcements to the prudential rules on large exposures, expansion of waivers from capital and liquidity.

However, the proposal falls short on some aspects that could have been included in the amendments. First, options and discretions provided to Member States should reduce considerably in the context of CRR/CRDIV amendments. These are provisions in the CRDIV that mainly grant discretions or options directly to a Member State. The use of such discretions or options may generate an uneven playing field with

---

138. *See* European Commission, *Frequently Asked Questions: Capital requirements (CRR/CRD IV) and resolution framework (BRRD/SRM) amendments*, Fact Sheet (2016) at http://europa.eu/rapid/press-release_MEMO-16-3840_en.htm?locale=en (accessed 31 December 2016).

differential rules in Member States. Most of these measures are macro-prudential measures that Member States may impose to banks at the national level. These have the highest impact on prudential requirements for credit institutions across the EU. There is no change on that in the Commission's proposal.

Furthermore, an important aspect that is left open in the Commission proposal is the treatment of sovereign exposures of credit institutions. At present, the Basel Committee is still developing its stance on the prudential treatment of such exposures on banks.[139] It is submitted that CRR/CRDIV amendments should include changes to the zero-risk rule. Sovereign risks have to be taken into account and should be given some risk-weight or at least assign sovereign exposures a concentration limit. Such changes would reduce the vicious circle between banks and sovereigns.

Moreover, the CRR/CRD would benefit from other regulatory amendments. These in particular concern the content of the CRD as it has provisions that have led to considerable divergences at the national level. For instance, fit and proper requirements as well as governance arrangements stemming from the CRDIV are still subject to a divergent degree of national implementation. Furthermore, other regulatory provisions should be included at the EU level. This is the case of merger by or concerning credit institutions, activities of credit institutions in third countries having an impact on prudential requirements, specific banking authorisations such as covered bonds issuance.[140]

Indeed, the CRR/CRDIV regulatory amendment package is a welcome development to reinforce supranational regulation as a normative instrument for financial stability in EU law and policy. However, the still existing different rules at the national level and single supervisory and resolution authorities for significant credit institutions – the ECB and the SRB – require further harmonisation efforts to avoid a differential application of rules.[141]

[B] The EDIS: Towards Supranational Deposit Insurance?

The creation of a supranational system of deposit insurance is a second important reform to strengthen supranational financial stability in EU law and policy. This section intends to analyse the EDIS Commission's proposal as a new supranational attempt to enhance risk sharing with the creation of a single deposit insurance scheme in Europe. The EDIS is conceived as a supranational system of deposit insurance where a single authority is in charge of protecting covered depositors of credit institutions in case of an ailing credit institution. This would allow deposit insurance to be exercised at

139. See Basel Committee on Banking Supervision, *The Basel Committee's work programme for 2015 and 2016*, 2016 http://www.bis.org/bcbs/about/work_programme.htm (accessed 31 December 2016).

140. The EBA has recently published a report on further harmonisation of the covered bond rules in Europe at https://www.eba.europa.eu/documents/10180/1699643/EBA+Report+on+Covered+Bonds+%28EBA-Op-2016-23%29.pdf (accessed 31 December 2016).

141. *See also* Ignazio Angeloni, *Challenges Facing the Single Supervisory Mechanism*, Speech 6 October 2016 https://www.bankingsupervision.europa.eu/press/speeches/date/2016/html/se161006.en.html (accessed 31 December 2016).

supranational level through a mutualised fund for deposit insurance purposes. The EDIS goes beyond the established system of European harmonisation of DGS, which was recently improved with the 2014 Directive. In November 2015, the Commission put forward a proposal for a Regulation setting up of such system. This would be the 'third' pillar of the EBU and would consist in a new supranational framework for deposit insurance that would apply to deposits below EUR 100,000 of credit institutions in the euro area.[142] The Commission Communication of 2015 on completing the EBU states that a common deposit insurance scheme would be an essential measure to reduce risks and shocks and to improve financial stability.[143] This would be the case as large local shocks may justify the use of a supranational deposit insurance system in case the national DGS is insufficient.

Without going into too many details, the EDIS is analysed.[144] The EDIS would include DGSs established in euro area Member States and in those Member States willing to enter into a close cooperation. The cover scope provided by the EDIS would be limited to the mandatory part of participating DGSs under the DGS directive.[145] The EDIS would be based on the pooling together of financial resources levied by the banking sector in a form of an EDIS Fund. The Commission's proposal envisages three consecutive phases: re-insurance, co-insurance and full insurance to be developed over a certain number of years.

The reinsurance phase would allow that the EDIS Fund resources are used only when the resources of the participating DGSs have already been exhausted.[146] When a bank faces liquidity crisis or is placed in resolution and it is necessary to pay out deposits or to finance their transfer to another bank, the national DGSs and EDIS will intervene.[147] In this phase, the EDIS Fund would only contribute a certain amount of payouts and provide assistance to the national DGS up to a specified percentage of the DGS shortfall and subject to a specified overall cap. The liquidity shortfall would trigger EDIS funding if the amount of covered deposits is more than those of the participating DGS and the amount of *ex post* extraordinary contribution that the participating DGS can provide in three working days.[148] In case of a resolution, the liquidity shortfall is calculated on the amount of the participating DGS contribution minus the amount of the participating DGS should have. Moreover, the EDIS would cover also 20% of the national DGS's excess loss.[149]

Subsequently, in the co-insurance phase, the participating DGS contributions would be combined with the Fund. The contribution from the Fund to depositor

142. *See* European Commission, *Communication Towards the completion of the Banking Union* COM/2015/0587 final.
143. *Ibid.*
144. For an analysis of the EDIS *see* Michael Huertas, *EDIS - the third-pillar of the EU's banking union: big, bold but can it be beautiful?*, 31 Journal of International Banking Law and Regulation 587-604 (2016).
145. Commission, proposal for a Regulation, Art. 1(2).
146. *Ibid.*, Art. 9(2).
147. *Ibid.*, Art. 41a.
148. *Ibid.*, Art. 41b.
149. *Ibid.*, Art. 41c.

payouts would progressively increase to 100%. This phase would allow that participating DGSs may request both funding and loss cover directly to the EDIS Fund.[150] The main difference with the re-insurance phase is that the EDIS Fund would be able to provide funding or cover losses as from the first contribution, while the share borne by the EDIS would increase gradually over some years. The EDIS share would reach 80% in the last year of co-insurance.

Finally, a third phase of full insurance would provide that only the European Fund insures participating DGSs. The Fund contribution to depositor payouts would not be considered State aid unless this contribution would be used for restructuring credit institutions. Full insurance would ensure full funding of the liquidity needs and would cover all losses arising from a payout event or a request to contribute to resolution. The mechanism would work as in the co-insurance phase, but the EDIS would cover a share of 100%. To mitigate 'moral hazard' situations, the incorrect or unwarranted use of the EDIS by the national DGS would be excluded if this fails to comply with the obligations set out in EU and national law or if the Member State has failed to implement correctly the proposed EDIS rules.[151] In this final stage of the EDIS set-up, which is envisaged in a transitional phase until 2024, the protection of covered deposits will be fully financed by EDIS and supported in a close cooperation between EDIS and national DGSs.

In the EDIS, the SRB would be entrusted with the administration of this Fund.[152] In case circumstances resulting in a payout event or a request to contribute for resolution purposes arise, the participating DGSs would inform the SRB immediately of these situations and the need to make use of the EDIS Fund.[153] Once detailed information is received,[154] the SRB would determine within twenty-four hours whether the conditions for an EDIS intervention are met and, in a positive case, would specify the amount of funding to be provided to the participating DGS. EDIS funding would then be given immediately after in cash to the participating DGSs. After the provision of funding, the SRB would then determine the excess loss or loss of the participating DGS, monitor the use of the funding for payouts of depositors or for contributing for resolution, and monitor the participating DGS collecting deposit claims back.[155]

The EDIS Fund would be financed by *ex ante* contributions owed and paid directly by the banking sector to the SRB. As of the co-insurance phase, the SRB may also claim extraordinary *ex post* contributions from the banks when the available means are insufficient for funding and loss cover. As regards decision-making, the EDIS would be administered by the SRB in its executive and plenary sessions. Decisions involving both SRM and EDIS matters would be taken by a joint plenary session.

150. *Ibid.*, Art. 41d.
151. *Ibid.*, Art. 41i.
152. The SRB is discussed extensively in the context of bank resolution as part of Chapter 8 section §8.04[C].
153. Commission, proposal for a Regulation, Art. 41i.
154. *Ibid.*, Art. 41k.
155. *Ibid.*, Art. 41o.

The establishment of the EDIS would be an extremely welcome reform for the attainment of supranational financial stability in EU law and policy. The establishment of the EDIS would strengthen supranational regulation and rescue measures as the main normative instruments to attain supranational financial stability in EU law and policy. The creation of a truly European system of deposit insurance would ensure that local shocks and risks related to deposits in credit institutions are solved at the European level. This would both avoid that depositors generate bank runs to withdraw their deposits as a crisis prevention measure, and that DGS would face risks of insufficient resources to repay covered depositors as a crisis management measure. National DGSs still remain vulnerable to large local shocks. EDIS would ensure equal deposit protection within the EBU regardless of the Member State where the deposit is located. Furthermore, it would guarantee that the decision to pay out depositors is taken at the European level, with less risks of national political or local influence. Moreover, it would deal adequately with cross-border issues of banking groups and limit problems related to the home/host regime.

Nevertheless, at the time of writing, the proposed EDIS Regulation is still under political discussions by the EU legislators, and it is far from clear whether it will be eventually adopted. Political negotiations on the EDIS design seem to have reached a deadlock.

[C] The CMU: Building a Stronger Capital Economy Legal Framework in Europe?

This section examines the CMU as a recent plan to strengthen the integration of capital markets in the EU and to ensure that capital markets are a viable and resilient source of financing to the economy. The CMU is not strictly legally speaking a banking regulation reform, but it is seen as a side EU reform having an impact on the banking sector, and more in general, on the attainment of supranational financial stability. The CMU can be seen as a 'flanking' supranational policy reform to reinforce supranational financial stability in Europe. This justifies a brief examination of the main aspects of the CMU.

In 2015, the EU Commission has launched a plan to establish a CMU that sets out an ambitious regulatory agenda to strengthen rules in capital markets and create a truly single capital market in Europe.[156] The CMU agenda is designed to 'build a true single market for capital' and to 'strengthen investment for the long term'.[157] The CMU reforms are organised in some main areas: the 'path to growth' (early stage funding for start-ups and for SMEs – this form of funding is often termed the 'funding escalator'); facilitating company access to the public markets; investing for the long term and for infrastructure and sustainable investment; fostering retail and institutional investment; leveraging banking capacity to support the economy; and facilitating cross-border

156. European Commission, Green Paper, *Building a Capital Markets Union* COM(2015) 63 final; European Commission, *Action Plan on Building a Capital Markets Union* COM(2015) 468 final.
157. European Commission, Green Paper (2015) 2.

investing.[158] The CMU agenda has three main objectives: to unlock more investment from the EU and the rest of the world; to better connect financing to investment projects across the EU; to make the financial system more stable.[159] The main pillars of the CMU agenda thus far are three. First, there are proposed reforms to the harmonised EU prospectus regime governing access to the capital markets by companies. The Commission proposal was presented in November 2015.[160] The prospectus reform intends to restructure the current Prospectus Directive[161] into a Regulation and proposes a series of largely deregulatory reforms designed to facilitate capital-raising, particularly by smaller companies.

Second, the Commission proposed a harmonised EU regime for securitisations,[162] which includes a specific regime for 'simple, transparent, and standardised' securitisations. This securitisation reform intends to streamline the current patchwork of rules that apply to securitisations (notably with respect to due diligence, risk retention and transparency requirements). It aims to make the capital treatment of securitisations more risk-sensitive. Moreover, it introduces a new harmonised regime for the identification and regulation/supervision of 'simple, transparent, and standardised' securitisations (including a more risk-sensitive capital treatment) that is designed to promote such securitisations and thereby to increase bank-lending capacity. At present, the EU institutions reached a political agreement on the securitisation regime at the ECOFIN Council in December 2015.

Third, a number of other specific reforms are also under development: the harmonisation of covered bonds rules across Europe,[163] the establishment of harmonised European Venture Capital Fund (EuVECA) and European Social Entrepreneurship Fund (EUSEF) regimes.[164]

The Commission in the CMU aims to bring forward long-term reforms such as facilitating SMEs' access to finance; supporting corporate bond markets; enhancing alternative means of financing, including crowdfunding; developing and diversifying the supply of funding, including through reforms to the EU's harmonised fund management regulation regimes, notably the 2015 European Long Term Investment Fund (the ELTIF) structure;[165] promoting stronger household/retail investment in the financial markets, such as what is envisaged in the Green Paper on Retail Financial

158. *Ibid.*, 3.
159. *Ibid.*, 2.
160. European Commission, Proposal for a Regulation of the European Parliament and of the Council on the prospectus to be published when securities are offered to the public or admitted to trading COM(2015) 583 final.
161. Directive 2003/71 [2003] OJ L345/64.
162. European Commission, *Proposal for a Regulation laying down common rules on securitisation and creating a European framework for simple, transparent and standardised securitization* COM(2015) 472 final.
163. European Commission, Consultation Document, 'Covered Bonds in the European Union' (2015).
164. Regulation 345/2013 [2013] OJ L115/1 and Regulation 346/2013 [2013] OJ L115/18. The Commission has consulted on the reforms needed to strengthen the capacity of these funds to support fund-raising: Commission, Consultation Document, *Review of the European Venture Capital Funds and European Social Entrepreneurship Funds Regulations* (2015).
165. Regulation 2015/760 [2015] OJ L123/98.

Services;[166] reforming company law, corporate governance requirements, insolvency law and taxation. In Autumn 2016, the Commission has issued a new Communication seeking to accelerate the CMU reforms and providing additional grounds for regulatory improvements of capital markets in Europe.[167]

The main aspects of the CMU require detailed analysis that cannot be made in this book.[168] Nonetheless, some conclusions on this new ambitious reform project can be made. The CMU is a regulatory reform based on supranational regulation as a normative instrument for the attainment of financial stability in EU law and policy. The main objective of the CMU is to enlarge capital market choices by providing for resilient and reliable capital sources alternative to banking funding. The Commission has designed the CMU project in order to address risks and shocks that can derive from excessive banking funding. Hence, the CMU reveals itself as a good policy initiative to attain supranational financial stability in Europe. The CMU intends to broaden the sources of funding sources, protect the EU economy against reduction in bank funding, and strengthen the shock-absorbing capacity of the EU economy.[169] It purports to reduce obstructive regulatory or supervisory divergences and strengthen the capacity of EU funding markets to deliver diversification to capital suppliers and to reduce thereby the costs of capital.[170] The CMU agenda 'pays tribute' to the continued importance of bank funding to the EU economy.[171]

At the same time, differently from the EBU, the CMU has two main limitations. First, it does not centralise the regulatory framework at the European level. It aims to reinforce existing rules, but it does not establish a top-down system of positive full harmonisation in all fields of non-banking finance. Second, the institutional dimension of the CMU remains weak. There is no attempt to create a supranational system of supervision of capital markets with the conferral of new tasks to EU institutions or agencies. This justifies its limited attention in this book.

[D] Banking Structural Separation: An 'Outdated' Structural Reform?

Before concluding, this final section looks at the Commission's proposal on structural measures as an interesting regulatory attempt to separate banking structures in Europe.

Structural separation of credit institutions is generally considered as being a regulatory power to protect core banking activities and depositors from riskier trading activities. Structural separation is based on the rationale that investment banking activities, generally of a risky nature, shall be separate from activities essential for

166. European Commission, *Green Paper on retail financial services Better products, more choice, and greater opportunities for consumers and businesses* COM/2015/0630 final.
167. European Commission, Communication, *Capital Markets Union – Accelerating Reform* COM(2016) 601 final.
168. *See* further Niamh Moloney, *Capital markets union: 'ever closer union' for the EU financial system?*, 41 European Law Review 307 (2016); Lucia Quaglia, David Howarth, Moritz Liebe, *The political economy of European capital markets union*, 54 Journal of Common Market Studies 185 (2016).
169. Commission, *Green Paper* (2015) 4.
170. *Ibid.*, 5.
171. *Ibid.*, 4.

small customers, consumers and the general economy. Separation is needed to prevent risky activities being undertaken by credit institutions that then have financial repercussions not only for the credit institutions itself, but also for the economy. The purpose of such separation is to reduce the risk of contagion that may spread from trading or other investment activities to traditional retail banking and deposits. Moreover, bank structural measures are intended to reduce banking complexity and to improve the resolvability of banking groups. As EU banking regulation currently stands, there are no harmonised or supranational rules for the separation of banking activities.

In 2012, the Commission established an expert group to examine the possible structural reform to be undertaken in Europe. The mandate of the Liikanen group was to explore structural reforms to strengthen financial stability as well as to improve market efficiency and consumer protection. In particular, the Group's task was to assess:

> whether additional reforms directly targeted at the structure of individual banks would further reduce the probability and impact of failure, ensure the continuation of vital economic functions upon failure and better protect vulnerable retail clients.[172]

The Liikanen Report followed a number of reforms taken in the US, the UK, France and Germany. It suggested that some improvements were needed in Europe in order to separate investment from commercial/retail services.[173] In particular, the report indicated that proprietary trading of all assets or derivative positions incurred in specific investment activities would need to be carried out by a separate trading entity.

Following the Liikanen Report, the Commission tabled a Regulation proposal in January 2014 on the structural reform on bank. This was intended to address risks and intra-group exposures linked with certain trading activities as well as to enhance resolvability. The Commission's proposal, inspired by the US Volcker Rule and the 2012 Liikanen Report, combines two general aspects: the ban on specific trading activities defined as proprietary and the requirement that certain trading activities are carried out by separate entities.

The scope of application of the proposed Regulation is limited to some specific G-SIIs that are considered as being globally systemic as well as for entities that have total assets amounting to at least EUR 30 billion and trading activities amounting to at least EUR 70 billion over a period of three consecutive years.[174] This scope of application would mean that around thirty banking groups would fall under the draft Regulation. The draft Regulation has also a broad territorial scope as it would apply to banks' overseas operations and EU-based subsidiaries and branches of non-EU banks, unless an 'equivalence' regime applies.

172. Erkki Liikanen, *High-level Expert Group on reforming the structure of the EU banking sector*, 4 (2012).

173. *Ibid.*

174. European Commission, *Proposal for a Regulation on structural measures improving the resilience of EU credit institutions* COM(2014) 043 final (hereinafter 'Commission proposal on structural measures'), Art. 3.

The proprietary trading prohibition is contained in Article 6. This indicates that entities covered under the Regulation shall not engage in proprietary trading in financial instruments, trading financial commodities, trading physical commodities and investing in hedge funds. Furthermore, the Regulation contains potential separation from certain trading activities. The first approach shows that the ban on proprietary trading is subject to a narrow scope, but the ban includes also investment activities that do not qualify per se as proprietary trading. The proposal specifies that the competent authority shall decide on restricting the activities both for the deposit-taking and trading entities. To ensure enforcement, Article 7 provides that the banned and restricted activities may not be encouraged or rewarded by the entity's remuneration policies. At the same time, the narrow wording of the proposed Regulation does not include underwriting activities, market making-related activities, or transactions to hedge risks result from client activities. Moreover, specific commodities trading are exempted from the ban as well as certain sovereign bonds. The prohibition of activities on the trading implies that the trading entities shall not take deposits eligible for protection under the DGS nor provide associated retail payment services.

As regards the second aspect, the Commission's proposal links the separation requirements to trading activities in general. These are defined in the negative as any activities that do not consist in deposit-taking, lending or other enumerated services.[175] The competent supervisory authority would regularly review specific metrics linked to the trading activities of EU banks taking eligible deposits, EU parents having deposit-taking banks in their group and EU branches from non-EU banks.[176] Should the separation be initiated, a group of entity that is legally, economically and operationally separate from the deposit-taking bank may only carry out the trading activities.[177] These activities would be prohibited from taking deposit-guarantee-eligible deposits or provide retail payment services.[178] On the contrary, the deposit-taking bank may then only carry out trading activities for the purpose of prudentially manage the capital, liquidity and funding.[179]

Having analysed the main aspect of the bank structural reform proposal, some critical remarks are made. Although the Commission's proposal is a welcome document to improve supranational financial stability in Europe, it is still a controversial document. This is for two main reasons. First, this proposal falls short of a harmonising approach to impose structural separation between investment and proprietary activities. Rather, it gives Member States quite much manoeuvre for divergent application of bank separation. Similarly, the Regulation proposal does not break up the universal banking model. Rather, it would still allow universal banks to conduct their services.

Second and most important, the examination of the Commission's proposal for banking structural changes questions whether the regulatory ambitions for the creation of a truly European regulatory structural measure exist at present. The Commission's

175. *Ibid.*, Art. 8.
176. *Ibid.*, Art. 9.
177. *Ibid.*, Art. 13.
178. *Ibid.*, Art. 20.
179. *Ibid.*, Art. 11.

proposal came too late in the regulatory responses to the financial crisis in Europe and only once national measures on structural separation for credit institutions had been adopted in key Member States – Germany and France. Furthermore, at present, the problem of systemically relevant trading activities, which may have powerful repercussions for financial stability in Europe, are subject to important political discussions that make the Commission's proposal unlikely to be adopted any soon. In other words, the proposal falls short on timing as the legislative process would not find agreement on the text now that the EBU has been put into place and other initiatives are under discussion. Moreover, some Member States have already enacted stricter structural requirements for credit institutions within their jurisdictions.

The Regulation proposal does not appear as a strong attempt to integrate further financial markets in light of a supranational objective of financial stability. Arguably, the alternative solution is currently to supervise thoroughly big banking groups' activities at the ECB level while ensuring that the level of capital, liquidity and solvency respects certain ratios. Proprietary trading and investment activities are a source of systemic instability that should be addressed at European level with a view to create a more integrated financial market. However, requiring a structural separation of banking activities is not currently an envisaged option at European level. This is mainly because resolution authorities have been vested with powers to change the organisational structure or business activities of a credit institution[180] while banks are required to implement Minimum Requirements for Eligible Liabilities (MREL) to ensure that bail-in can work effectively. These suggest that structural measures can already be taken by the competent authority in other ways. Similarly, it could be argued that the competent supervisory authority is empowered to make structural changes under the existing EU banking regulation.[181]

In sum, the Commission's proposal is a regulatory attempt to prohibit the exercise of proprietary trading and impose structural separation of activities for systemically relevant credit institutions. However, at present it appears that its value is substantially reduced by the reformed EU banking rules.

§6.05 CONCLUSION

The financial crisis has triggered important regulatory reforms for credit institutions at the European level. This chapter has analysed the development aiming to strengthen the supranational regulatory framework for credit institutions in Europe along the lines of the supranational objective of financial stability in EU law and policy. Both the institutional and substantial dimensions of banking regulation have undergone considerable improvements that are justifies by the need to promote supranational financial stability in Europe. The various initiatives undergone in order to strengthen the European regulatory framework suggest that the normative preventive instruments

180. BRRD, Art. 17(5).
181. *See*, in particular, Art. 16(2)(e) of the SSM Regulation and Art. 104(1)(e) of the CRDIV.

for financial stability in EU law and policy are pursued as a leading feature in EU banking law and policy.

However, the objective of attaining supranational financial stability with common regulatory responses in Europe faces two main challenges that were addressed in this chapter. First, EU banking regulation shows a complex constitutional and institutional compromise between the co-legislators and the administrative executives. The role of EBA and the *Meroni* doctrine in this context as well as in that of the ECB as a supervisor[182] might be controversial. A reconsideration of the *Meroni* doctrine has been proposed. Second, this chapter has argued that the promotion of strengthened banking regulation is only partially pursued as options and discretions at the national level and even the absence of supranational rules in certain areas of banking regulation still limit the attainment of financial stability as a supranational objective in EU law and policy.

The above analysis suggests that only a truly European level of harmonisation and rule-making might achieve further supranational financial stability in banking markets. The chapter has criticised some aspects on the new single rulebook that are in conflict with the development of maximum harmonisation and supranational regulation. The structural challenges of a truly European harmonised regulatory environment are not over yet. It is still unclear whether the new CRR/CRD review proposals would be successful in improving the existing rules and whether they would be sufficient to strengthen the supranational dimension of financial stability in Europe. Moreover, the limited scope of the DGS directive, the controversial EDIS proposal, the ongoing discussions on the impact of the CMU on banking regulation and the criticisable Commission's proposal on structural requirements for credit institutions reveal that the supranational regulation of banking and related fields is still subject to fierce negotiations and political discussions. At the same time, future regulatory improvements in the context of EU banking laws are needed in order to attain an even stronger regulatory benchmark in pursuing supranational financial stability in EU law and policy. This concludes the analysis of banking regulation. The next part will examine the SSM as the new institutional reform to centralise banking supervision to the ECB at supranational level.

182. *See* Chapter 7 section §7.04[D] for an assessment of the relationship between the ECB and EU agencies.

CHAPTER 7

EU Banking Supervisory Law[1]

§7.01 INTRODUCTION

The economic and financial crisis has had a great impact on prudential supervision of credit institutions and the overall financial stability of credit institutions in Europe. The creation of a single currency and the conferral of extensive monetary powers to the ECB did not correspond to the creation of a centralised level of prudential supervision over credit institutions in the euro area. Prior to the outbreak of the financial crisis, the financial architecture on banking supervision in Europe remained substantially national. Apart from the regulatory efforts to harmonise prudential requirements in the internal market, the architecture of financial stability was based largely on national supervision, national resolution and national safety nets.[2] In 2011, ESAs were established with EBA as the new EU agency[3] dealing with the general regulation and supervision of banking actors and markets but without the conferral of day-to-day supervisory powers at the supranational level neither to this new EU agency nor to an EU institution.

The recent financial and sovereign debt crisis has shown that the European banking system is vulnerable. The liquidity and solvability of credit institutions are still at risk and contagion effects can spread to other banks and to the real economy in Europe. This has generated many difficulties for supranational financial stability and

1. This chapter is an updated and revised version of Gianni Lo Schiavo, *From National Banking Supervision to a Centralized Model of Prudential Supervision in Europe: The Stability Function of the Single Supervisory Mechanism*, 21 Maastricht Journal of European and Comparative Law 110 (2014).
2. Rishi Goyal *et al.*, *A Banking Union for the Euro Area*, IMF Staff Discussion Note 7 (2013).
3. *See* Chapter 6 section §6.03[B][1] on the establishment of EBA. In literature *see* Edoardo Chiti, *An important part of the EU's Institutional Machinery. Features, Problems and Perspectives of European Agencies*, 46 Common Market Law Review 1395 (2009); Madalina Busuioc, *Rule-Making by the European Financial Supervisory Authorities: Walking a Tight Rope*, 19 European Law Journal 111 (2013).

for the single currency, especially because of the banking supervision at the national level.

In 2014, the European institutions succeeded in adopting a new institutional set-up for banking supervision in the euro area: the SSM.[4] This chapter assesses the seminal reform to establish the SSM and argues that the conferral of new supranational supervisory tasks to the ECB is a reform pursuing supranational financial stability in EU law and policy as argued in this book. It discusses to what extent the SSM reform aims to institutionalise the level of supervision at European level, to allocate responsibility at a central level, to integrate the single market for banks and to centralise supervision in a top-down fashion. To a large extent, these goals follow the normative instruments of supervision in its micro- and macro-dimension as outlined in chapter 3 of this book. The analysis concludes that the SSM is a seminal example of the attainment of financial stability as a supranational objective in EU law and policy.

The chapter proceeds as follows. After a brief examination of the pre-crisis and in-the-crisis attempts to centralise banking supervision in Europe (§7.02), the main aspects of the SSM are assessed (§7.03). This part outlines the main critical elements of European banking supervision inside and outside the SSM both from the institutional and substantive perspectives. Then, the most controversial elements of the SSM will be analysed to support the argument that the SSM acts as a founding pillar for financial stability as a supranational objective in EU law and policy (§7.04). The last section concludes (§7.05).

§7.02 SUPERVISION OF CREDIT INSTITUTIONS IN EUROPE PRIOR TO THE SSM

This section looks at the pre-crisis and in-the-crisis attempts to a European centralised banking supervision. The main findings are that before the SSM reform, the main actors for banking supervision remained NCAs. Before the outbreak of the crisis, it was well established that central banks or other supervisory entities at the national level exercised an extensive mandate for supervisory policies.[5] Even after the creation of the ESCB and the conferral of exclusive monetary policy to the ECB, prudential supervision remained at a national level.[6] Member States conducted banking supervision based on the principle of home country control and mutual recognition in the EU internal market.[7] Home country control has become an essential aspect in the internal market

4. Council Regulation (EU) No 1024/2013 of 15 October 2013 conferring specific tasks on the European Central Bank concerning policies relating to the prudential supervision of credit institutions [2013] OJ L 287 (hereinafter 'SSM Regulation').
5. Larisa Dragomir, *European Prudential Banking Regulation and Supervision: The Legal Dimension*, 238 (Routledge 2009).
6. *See* Jean Pisani-Ferry *et al.*, *What Kind of European Banking Union?*, Bruegel 2012/12 6 (2012).
7. *See* George Walker, *European Financial Programme: Content, Structure and Completion*, 15 European Business Law Review 305 (2004).

for credit institutions and has contributed to foster cross-border mobility and ultimately market integration. However, the home country principle is not absolute, but some powers or areas of action generally remain in the hands of the host state supervisors, especially when the public good derogation is invoked to restrict market integration.[8] At the same time, the conduct of day-to-day supervision with powers of imposing prudential requirements, inspections and authorisations in prudential matters remained a prerogative of NCAs.

The establishment of a supranational system of banking supervision at ECB level was not conceived as the leading model of prudential supervision in Europe.[9] The use of the 'enabling clause' under Article 127(6) TFEU remained unexplored.[10] Rather, scholarship promoted the creation of a new system of financial supervision through reinforced coordination and cooperation between national authorities in network-based structures or committees. In 2001, the Lamfalussy Report addressed the issue of who should provide the law-making competence for financial regulation by proposing the establishment of a Committee structure.[11] The Committee on European Banking Supervisors (CEBS) was established as an advice body aimed at providing adequate supervisory convergence in law-making and implementation of supervisory functions.

The impact of the crisis for the EU led the EU institutions to respond quickly to market pressure to reform and reinforce the system of prudential supervision. When in February 2009 the de Larosière Report was published, the need to put forward a reform of the system of financial – and thus banking – supervision was envisaged.[12] The findings of this report were an important step that prompted a change in the approach to be taken at supervisory level by creating the ESFS.[13] First, the Commission promoted the creation of the ESRB as a new European macro-prudential supervisory body.[14] Second, the Commission proposed the creation of ESAs.[15] In particular, EBA is defined as the authority that would be part of 'an integrated network of national and Union supervisory authorities, leaving day-to-day supervision to the national level'[16] at

8. *See* Dragomir, *supra* n. 5, 165.
9. *See* Rosa Lastra, *The Governance Structure for Financial Regulation and Supervision in Europe*, 10 Columbia Journal of European Law 55 (2003).
10. Rosa Lastra, *International Financial and Monetary Law*, 357 (Oxford University Press 2015). On Art. 127(6) TFEU see further section §7.04[A] of this chapter.
11. Alexandre Lamfalussy, *Final Report of the Committee of Wise Men*, (2001) 6 at http://ec.europa.eu/internal_market/securities/docs/lamfalussy/wisemen/final-report-wise-men_en.pdf (accessed 31 December 2016).
12. Jacques de Larosière, *Report of the High-Level Group on Financial Supervision in the EU*, 38 (2009).
13. *See* Eilis Ferran, *Understanding the New Institutional Architecture of EU Financial Market Supervision* in Eddy Wymeersch, Klaus Hopt, Guido Ferrarini (eds), *Financial Regulation and Supervision. A Post-Crisis Analysis*, 132 (Oxford University Press 2012).
14. Regulation (EU) No 1092/2010 of the European Parliament and of the Council of 24 November 2010 on European Union macro-prudential oversight of the financial system and establishing a European Systemic Risk Board [2010] OJ L 331, Art. 2.
15. *See* Chapter 6 section §6.03[B][2] for EBA's regulatory role.
16. EBA Regulation, Recital 9.

banking level. However, the de la Larosière Report rejected the use of the enabling clause to confer direct prudential supervisory powers to the ECB.[17]

Over time, the ESFS, conceived in the de Larosière Report and put into place in 2011, remained constrained for a number of reasons. Its structure was not as evolutionary as expected: the ESRB has very limited macro-prudential soft law powers[18], while EBA excludes exercise of day-to-day supervisory powers at the supranational level. In particular, EBA had a limited impact on prudential supervision in Europe.

This is for a number of reasons. First, the efforts to centralise supervision with the establishment of ESAs have not been sufficient to overcome the limits to delegation of powers to entities other than EU institutions. The *Meroni*[19] doctrine and ESAs' national-oriented governance had constrained evolutionary moves towards a supranational dimension of prudential functions attributed to EU institutions. EBA lacks real-teeth powers to supervise market players and to enforce decisions, as the *Meroni* doctrine does not allow an EU agency to enjoy full discretionary powers. Second, the absence of a European-wide supervisory regime and the excessive limits on the exercise of effective powers to control financial markets acted as limitations to a reliable level of centralisation of prudential functions at European level. EBA's operational functioning is nationally centred as EBA's structure acts as an integrated network of national supervisors and not as an independent and strong decision-making European authority. Third, the level of supervision remained substantially nationally orientated. EBA is based on cooperation and consultation between NCAs and does not establish a central authority for the conduct of micro-prudential supervision. This led to different approaches in Europe on the micro-level of supervision of credit institutions. The principles of home country control at national level and mutual recognition regulated the supervision of credit institutions. These principles have generated, to a large extent, fragmentation and differentiation in the internal market that have not created the appropriate conditions for further legal integration. Fourth, the system was characterised by a lack of a European level of supranational supervision with the exercise of supranational decision-making powers over credit institutions in Europe. National supervisors kept full powers to control banking structures at the cross-border level. Supervision remained at a national level, split among the national supervisors.

§7.03 BANK SUPERVISION IN EUROPE: THE POST-FINANCIAL CRISIS SCENARIO

The creation of the SSM in the context of the EBU has completely changed banking supervision in Europe by centralising it for SSM participating Member States (participating Member States) at ECB level and has upgraded the level-playing field in

17. de Larosière, *supra* n. 12, 43.
18. Eilis Ferran & Kern Alexander, *Can Soft Law Bodies Be Effective? The Special Case of the European Systemic Risk Board*, 35 European Law Review 751 (2010).
19. Cases C-9/56 and 10/56 *Meroni v. High Authority* ECLI:EU:C:1958:7.

prudential supervision. In this section, the new level of prudential supervision in Europe is explored both in the institutional and the substantive dimensions.

[A] The Institutional Framework for Banking Supervision

The SSM constitutes a tremendous development that requires the examination of the institutional dimension as regards the Member States jurisdictions participating and those not participating to the SSM.

[1] Micro-Prudential Supervision Inside the SSM

The financial turmoil of the first half of 2012 has been the turning point in the establishment of the SSM. The process of adoption of the SSM officially began in September 2012. Together with the 'Roadmap towards the Banking Union',[20] the Commission tabled two proposals for Regulations on 12 September 2012. These aimed at establishing the SSM by conferring new direct supervisory tasks to the ECB and by revising EBA's decision-making procedures.

In the words of Barroso, the SSM would create a:

> new system, with the European Central Bank at the core and involving national supervisors (…) [to] restore confidence in the supervision of all banks in the Euro area (…).[21]

Most importantly, the European Council conclusions of 14 December 2012 changed the content of the Commission proposal, especially with regard to the scope of application of the ECB direct supervision. Nevertheless, the process of adoption of the SSM founding Regulations was completed in October 2013 when the Council agreed on the adoption of the two SSM founding Regulations, the SSM Regulation and the EBA amending Regulation.[22] With this said, it is essential to analyse the SSM Regulation in some detail.

[a] Scope, Tasks and Cooperation

The SSM Regulation refers to the impact of the financial crisis and the need to adopt an integrated system of banking supervision. It is important to quote Recital 2 of the SSM Regulation as it clearly shows the rationale that has driven the Regulation:

> 'The present financial and economic crisis has shown that the integrity of the single currency and the internal market may be threatened by the fragmentation of the financial sector. It is therefore essential to *intensify the integration of banking*

20. European Commission, *A Roadmap towards a Banking Union*, COM(2012)510.
21. José Barroso, *Commission Proposes New ECB Powers for Banking Supervision as Part of a Banking Union* Press Release IP/12/953, 12 September 2012.
22. *See* Eddy Wymeersch, *The Single Supervisory Mechanism or 'SSM', Part One of the Banking Union*, ECGI WP 1 (2014); Niamh Moloney, *European Banking Union: Assessing Its Risks and Resilience*, 51 Common Market Law Review 1630 (2014).

supervision in order to bolster the Union, restore financial stability and lay the basis for economic recovery.' (emphasis added)[23]

This Recital is noteworthy in affirming that there is a need to intensify the integration of banking supervision with a view to restoring *financial stability* as well as to proceeding with economic recovery. This reinforces the argument that the normative instrument of supervision with the SSM aims to attain supranational financial stability in Europe as developed in this book.

The SSM Regulation is divided into five chapters: Subject matter and definitions (Chapter I), Cooperation and tasks (Chapter II), Powers of the ECB (Chapter III), Organisational Principles (Chapter IV), General and Final Provisions (Chapter V). Chapter I sets out the scope of the SSM Regulation and includes some key definitions that are useful to analyse. Article 1 deals with the main subject matter and scope of the regulation. The first indent refers to the objective of conferring specific tasks to the ECB as the supervision of the credit institutions will contribute to the safety and soundness of credit institutions and the stability of the financial system. This article is very careful in setting the boundaries of the supervisory power conferred to the ECB.

The same article of the SSM Regulation includes additional paragraphs and subparagraphs which provide some limitations as to the scope of the ECB supervision.[24] In particular, the fourth indent specifies that 'no action, proposal or policy of the ECB shall, directly or indirectly, discriminate against any Member State or group of Member States'.[25] This indent shows that financial integration is at the centre of the SSM. However, it may be questioned whether the differentiated scope between euro area and non-euro area membership might result in discrimination of treatment especially in cases of cross-border credit institutions. At the same time, it seems that the ECB has the essential task to guarantee a sound and consistent level of supervision especially for cross-border banks having subsidiaries or branches in participating and non-participating Member States.

Chapter I provides also the definitions of 'NCAs' and 'credit institution'. These definitions make reference to the CRDIV.[26] Both references contribute to foster the single rulebook of the internal market for banking services and to guarantee consistency in legislation as they set the appropriate links with financial market regulation applicable in all Member States.

The ECB cooperation and tasks Chapter contains the most important aspects to establish the institutional and substantive system of ECB supervision. The terms 'cooperation' and 'tasks' are very much interlinked as they both explain the degree of power of the ECB to conduct its supervisory powers. The required level of cooperation in good faith spans to every institution, agency and organisation both at European and at national level. However, the SSM Regulation makes clear that the ECB is responsible

23. Regulation 1024/2013, Recital 2.
24. *See also* SSM Regulation, Recital 28. *See* Eilis Ferran & Valia Babis, *The European Single Supervisory Mechanism*, 13 Journal of Corporate Legal Studies 255 (2013).
25. *See* SSM Regulation, Recital 30.
26. The SSM Regulation states that 'credit institution' means a credit institution as defined in point 1 of Art. 4(1) of Regulation (EU) No 575/2013.

primarily to conduct direct supervision especially in cross-border situations at the European level. The most stringent level of cooperation is envisaged with ESAs and the ESRB. This is obvious as the ESFS had been already established for supranational micro- and macro-prudential supervision at the European level. Cooperation in good faith shall also be exercised with NCAs, public financial assistance facility as well as authorities of the non-participating Member States.[27] Cooperation with NCAs is the most important one. Given the division of supervisory competences between the ECB and the NCAs, an appropriate 'supervisory balance' is essential. Therefore, the SSM Regulation attempts primarily at providing an extensive degree of cooperation between the supranational and the national level of supervision.

Article 4 is the key provision setting out the supervisory tasks of the ECB in the SSM. It provides as follows:

> The ECB shall be exclusively competent to carry out some tasks in relation to credit institutions established in the participating Member States: (a) to authorise credit institutions and to withdraw authorisations of credit institutions; (b) for credit institutions established in a participating Member State, which wish to establish a branch or provide cross-border services in a non participating Member State, to carry out the tasks which the competent authority of the home Member State shall have under the relevant Union law; (c) to assess notifications of the acquisition and disposal of qualifying holdings in credit institutions; (d) to ensure compliance with the acts which impose prudential requirements on credit institutions in the areas of own funds requirements, securitisation, large exposure limits, liquidity, leverage, and reporting and public disclosure of information on those matters; (e) to ensure compliance with the acts which impose requirements on credit institutions to have in place robust governance arrangements; (f) to carry out supervisory reviews, including where appropriate in coordination with EBA, stress tests and their possible publication; (g) to carry out supervision on a consolidated basis over credit institutions' parents established in one of the participating Member States; (h) to participate in supplementary supervision of a financial conglomerate in relation to the credit institutions included in it and to assume the tasks of a coordinator where the ECB is appointed as the coordinator for a financial conglomerate in accordance with the criteria set out in relevant Union law; (i) to carry out supervisory tasks in relation to recovery plans, and early intervention.[28]

This provision proves to be very wide and confers the ECB sufficient tasks to carry out comprehensive micro-prudential supervision. Among others, the ECB is competent to authorise the exercise of banking activities, qualifying holding in SSM established banks and supervise prudential requirements and corporate governance of credit institutions.

Article 6 on cooperation within the SSM contains the most important paragraph on the scope of application of the ECB direct supervision. In fact, under paragraph 4 of Article 6 the term 'significance' provides the yardsticks for the exercise of ECB or NCAs supervision. The institution is not 'less significant' when:

> (i) the total value of its assets exceeds EUR 30 billion; (ii) the ratio of its total assets over the GDP of the participating Member State of establishment exceeds 20%, unless the total value of its assets is below EUR 5 billion; (iii) following a

27. SSM Regulation, Art. 3.
28. *See* SSM Regulation, Art. 4.

> notification by its NCA that it considers such an institution of significant relevance with regard to the domestic economy, the ECB takes a decision confirming such significance following a comprehensive assessment by the ECB, including a balance-sheet assessment, of that credit institution.[29]

These combined criteria of 'significance' are not exhaustive. Other circumstances may justify exclusive ECB supervision. First, the ECB can also consider an institution of 'significant relevance' if: 'it has established banking subsidiaries in more than one participating Member States and its cross-border assets or liabilities represent a significant part of its total assets or liabilities'.[30] Second, the ECB exclusive supervision also includes the banks that have received direct financial assistance directly from the EFSF or the ESM.[31] Third, the last provision subparagraph[32] states that the ECB is competent to exercise its tasks also for the three most significant credit institutions in each of the participating Member States, unless justified by particular circumstances. Finally, the ECB may also decide to exercise directly itself all the relevant powers for one or more credit institutions regardless of their significance but based on high supervisory standards.[33] 'Less Significant' institutions continue being supervised by NCAs. Therefore, Article 6 sets out the main difference in scope between supranational and national prudential supervision.

[b] SSM Decision-Making

The SSM involves the exercise of considerable decision-making powers in the hands of the ECB. The SSM Regulation makes clear that the ECB has extensive decision-making powers. Pursuant to Article 4(3), the ECB can adopt guidelines, recommendations and decisions to exercise the tasks conferred by the regulation, as well as adopting regulations to the extent necessary to organise or specify the arrangements for the carrying out of the tasks conferred on it by the SSM Regulation. Furthermore, Recital 34 of the SSM Regulation makes clear that the ECB 'will apply the material rules relating to the prudential supervision of credit institutions'. This means that the ECB can apply national legislation based on EU regulation giving national options or national legislation transposing EU directives.[34]

Chapter IV of the SSM Regulation deals with the organisational principles in carrying out the supervisory functions conferred to the ECB. The SSM provides for a new organisational structure inside the ECB. This is essential as the SSM Regulation envisages a separation between supervisory and monetary policy functions of the ECB. In particular, Article 25 provides that the ECB separates between the monetary and the supervision functions. The degree of separation between the two functions is a crucial principle that shall be respected in order to conduct a sound monetary policy and an

29. *Ibid.*, Art. 6(4).
30. *Ibid.*
31. *Ibid.*
32. *Ibid.*
33. *Ibid.*, Art. 6(5).
34. *Ibid.*, Recital 34 and Art. 4(3).

effectively independent supervision.[35] This obligation derives directly from the overall ECB tasks as framed in the TFEU. While pursuant to Article 127(1) TFEU monetary policy functions are aimed at maintaining price stability as the overarching objective of the ECB, the exercise of supervision has a different objective that is to 'protect the safety and the soundness of credit institutions and the stability of the financial system'.[36] Correctly, Goodhart and Schoenmaker argued that this is mainly to avoid conflicts of interest in conducting different functions.[37] Therefore, this important aspect needs to be taken into account in the exercise of monetary policy powers.[38] The SSM Regulation thus requires that separation exists in exercising each function.

Article 26 of the SSM Regulation provides for an evolutionary change in the structure of the ECB as it establishes an independent and autonomous internal body that undertakes the ECB supervisory functions, the Supervisory Board. This body is a new internal organ of the ECB that carries out the required supervisory functions established in the regulation. This is an internal body composed of a Chair, a Vice Chair, four representatives of the ECB and one representative of the NCA of each participating Member State.[39] It shall undertake the planning and the execution of the supervisory tasks conferred on the ECB.

Among other provisions, Article 26(6) and 26(7) of the SSM Regulation indicate that the Supervisory Board approves draft supervisory decisions by simple majority (paragraph 6). Article 26(8) of the SSM Regulation further provides that the Supervisory Board carries out all preparatory work for the Governing Council. In particular, it provides that:

> the Supervisory Board shall carry out preparatory works regarding the supervisory tasks conferred on the ECB and propose to the Governing Council of the ECB complete draft decisions to be adopted by the latter.

Instead, the Governing Council of the ECB adopts the draft supervisory decisions approved by the Supervisory Board with a non-objection procedure. This procedure does not apply to ECB regulations in prudential matters that the ECB might adopt pursuant to Article 4(3). This means that the Governing Council still has the final say on prudential decision by following a procedure of non-opposition to the draft decision prepared by the Supervisory Board within a normal period of ten working days.

From an efficiency-oriented perspective, it remains problematic that the Supervisory Board submits to the Governing Council all acts having binding force in carrying out supervisory functions as the ultimate decision-maker of ECB legal acts. However, appropriate independence safeguards have been included, especially to ensure separation of the monetary policy and supervisory tasks.[40]

---

35. *See* Charles Goodhart & Dirk Schoenmaker, *Should the Functions of Monetary Policy and Banking Supervision Be Separated?*, 47 Oxford Economic Papers 539 (1995).
36. SSM Regulation, Recital 65.
37. *Ibid.*
38. *See* Chapter 3 section §3.02[A][3][b] for ECB unconventional monetary policy powers.
39. SSM Regulation, Art. 26.
40. *See* Ibid., Art. 19.

[2] Outside the SSM

While the SSM has conferred supervisory tasks to the ECB, EBA remains the EU agency on banking regulation and supervision in EU law and policy. EBA still acts as the authority in charge of regulation and supervision of all credit institutions established in the Member States, also those not participating to the SSM. As discussed in the previous chapter,[41] EBA is the quasi-regulatory agency in the banking sector having general regulatory and supervisory powers. EBA possesses some limited supervisory powers consisting of EBA's tasks to promote convergence of supervisory practices to a high standard in order to ensure that regulatory and supervisory rules are implemented equally across all Member States. However, EBA does not conduct day-to-day supervision.[42]

Following the establishment of the SSM, EBA has changed its organisational status in order not to compromise the voting powers of non-participating Member States in EBA Board of Supervisors. Regulation 1022/2013 complements the SSM Regulation. It amends EBA founding Regulation in order to reflect the specific tasks of the ECB concerning policies relating to the prudential supervision of credit institutions.[43] The need to have a complementary Regulation lies in the objective to ensure the proper functioning of EBA as well as the representation of supervisory authorities not participating to the SSM. As stated in the preamble, Regulation 1022/2013 states that:

> the interests of all Member States are adequately taken into account and to allow for the proper functioning of EBA (...) the voting arrangements within its Board of Supervisors should be adapted.[44]

In substance, this accompanying Regulation modifies the voting modalities of EBA. Overall, the NCAs of non-participating Member States to the SSM exercise the supervisory tasks and powers for the credit institutions established there. The NCAs outside the SSM still conduct day-to-day micro-prudential supervision. In cross-border situations, NCAs exercise supervisory tasks and powers in a college of supervisors whenever a credit institution has cross-border activities and needs to be evaluated by NCAs completely or partially outside the SSM, but within the EU. Outside the SSM, colleges of supervisors still play an important role as the main structures to allow cross-border cooperation between supervisory authorities in the EU and to ensure the supervision of cross-border banking groups. Colleges of supervisors are supervisory structures composed of NCAs, and possibly the ECB, assessing and examining

41. *See* Chapter 6 section §6.03[B].
42. EBA Regulation, Arts 20 and 30.
43. Regulation (EU) No 1022/2013 of the European Parliament and of the Council of 22 October 2013 amending Regulation (EU) No 1093/2010 establishing a European Supervisory Authority (European Banking Authority) as regards the conferral of specific tasks on the European Central Bank pursuant to Council Regulation (EU) No 1024/2013 [2013] OJ l 287/5.
44. *Ibid.*, Recital 14.

cross-border groups. EBA shall promote the activities carried out by the colleges of supervisors.[45]

[3] Macro-Prudential Supervision: The ESRB and the ECB

The supranational dimension of macro-prudential banking supervision is centred at the ESRB and now also at the ECB level in the SSM jurisdiction. The ESRB is the soft law macro-prudential supervisor in Europe. It is responsible for the macro-prudential oversight of the EU financial system in order to contribute to the prevention or mitigation of systemic risks to financial stability.[46] The ESRB has no legal personality, cannot adopt legally binding powers and its instruments are limited to warnings of systemic risks and recommendations for remedial action that should be taken to address the risk identified.[47] These limitations have questioned the real effectiveness of the ESRB to conduct macro-prudential supervision.[48]

Importantly, Article 5 of the SSM Regulation introduces for the first time binding supranational macro-prudential powers that the ECB may exercise under particular conditions. If deemed necessary, the ECB can in fact 'apply higher requirements for capital buffers' instead of national authorities or national designated authorities of the participating Member State and 'apply more stringent measures aimed at addressing systemic or macroprudential risks at the level of credit institutions'.[49] These requirements would be higher than the ones applied by the national authorities of the participating Member States where the credit institutions are established. If any of the NCAs or national designated authorities objects, the ECB can exercise such macro-prudential tasks and tools by providing its statement of reasons within the very short timeframe of five working days.

[B] Substantive Rules on Supervision

The creation of the SSM has also considerable repercussions on the extent of substantive powers for prudential supervision as compared with the past. This section deals with substantive rules applicable to participating Member States and those applicable to non-participating Member States.

[1] Micro-Prudential Supervision Inside the SSM

Under the SSM, the ECB is both the home and host supervisor for significant supervised entities. This is a very important development as compared with the previous practice where the NCAs were responsible as home and host supervisors. The ECB is now fully

45. EBA Regulation, Art. 21(1).
46. ESRB Regulation, Art. 3(1).
47. *Ibid.*, Art. 16.
48. Alexander, Ferran *supra* n. 18, 760.
49. SSM Regulation, Art. 5(2).

competent to exercise supervisory powers vis-à-vis credit institutions, financial holding companies and mixed financial holding companies. Furthermore, the ECB is the host supervisor whenever a non-participating Member State credit institution establishes a significant branch in a participating Member State.[50]

The use of a wide array of ECB supervisory powers is one of the most remarkable aspects of the SSM. Articles 9 and following of the SSM Regulation introduce ECB supervisory and investigatory powers. Article 9 sets out the general notion of supervisory and investigatory powers in affirming that the ECB exercises the powers that it has been conferred on the basis of the ECB tasks under Article 4 of the SSM Regulation. Furthermore, Recital 35 of the SSM Regulation states that the ECB can require national authorities to make use of their own powers where the SSM Regulation does not confer such powers to the ECB.

[a] Specific ECB Supervisory Powers

Chapter III section 2 of the SSM Regulation deals with ECB specific supervisory powers. In general terms, the SSM Regulation is more stringent on the role of the ECB as compared with the initial Commission's proposal of the SSM Regulation. Articles 14 and 15 of the SSM Regulation deal with licences and qualifying holdings. Article 16 of the SSM Regulation sets out specific supervisory powers that the ECB enjoys in controlling credit institution, financial holding company or mixed financial holding company in participating Member States. Among others, Article 16 of the SSM Regulation allows the ECB:

> (a) to require institutions to hold own funds in excess of the capital requirements; (b) to require the reinforcement of the arrangements, processes, mechanisms and strategies; (c) to require institutions to present a plan to restore compliance with supervisory requirements; (d) to require institutions to apply a specific provisioning policy or treatment of assets in terms of own funds requirements; (e) to restrict or limit the business, operations or network of institutions or to request the divestment of activities that pose excessive risks to the soundness of an institution; (f) to require the reduction of the risk inherent in the activities, products and systems of institutions; (g) to require institutions to limit variable remuneration; (h) to require institutions to use net profits to strengthen own funds; (i) to restrict or prohibit distributions by the institution to shareholders, members or holders of Additional Tier 1 instruments where the prohibition does not constitute an event of default of the institution; (j) to impose additional or more frequent reporting requirements; (k) to impose specific liquidity requirements; (m) to remove at any time members from the management body of credit institutions.

These supervisory powers are clearly in line with the wide ECB supervisory mandate and are essential to exercise an intrusive and fair supervision over significant supervised entities. The fact that these are only some and not all supervisory powers suggests that the ECB may exercise also other supervisory powers beyond the non-exhaustive list provided in Article 16.

50. SSM Regulation, Art. 4(2).

Three main ECB supervisory powers, reflecting ECB tasks, are analysed below: licence and withdrawal of licence; acquisition of qualifying holdings; and SREP.

As to the licensing power, the ECB has the exclusive task and power to confer and withdraw all banking licenses in the SSM.[51] Article 14 of the SSM Regulation establishes for a bottom-up administrative procedure where the NCAs analyse the application for an authorisation on the part of the credit institution.[52] The NCA will issue a draft decision for the ECB to assess. This will be followed by an assessment by the ECB. Only when the draft decision does not comply with the conditions for authorisation, the ECB will object to the authorisation.[53] The role of the national authority is quite important, as the authorisation will be first assessed at national level and, only once the draft decision is submitted to the ECB, the ECB will conduct its assessment. The licence application is assessed on the basis of the criteria contained in the CRDIV[54] and national law. In case the ECB does not object the draft decision, this is deemed to be adopted as a positive silence.[55] The procedure appears to foster expediency and efficiency in authorisation. However, the ten working days for the ECB assessment of banking licensing seems too short. Withdrawal of licences are subject to a similar procedure, with the notable difference that the ECB shall adopt an explicit decision withdrawing the licence without the possibility of having a silent decision. The ECB assesses the withdrawal of licence in light of the criteria established in the CRDIV and in national law.[56]

As to the qualifying holding power, the ECB has the exclusive task and power of authorising qualifying holdings in all credit institutions established in the SSM.[57] Article 15 of the SSM Regulation provides for the supervisory power for such authorisation. The procedure is based on the assessment criteria contained in the CRDIV[58] and follows a bottom-up administrative procedure where the NCA issues the draft decision to the ECB that ultimately adopts a decision within the timeframe provided in the CRDIV.[59]

As to the SREP, the ECB has the task and power to adopt supervisory decisions imposing significant institutions to hold own funds beyond the CRR/CRDIV regulatory requirements. SREP is the most important power based on Article 16 of the SSM Regulation. This power allows the ECB to impose capital requirements and other additional quantitative and qualitative measures to supervised entities.[60]

51. SSM Regulation, Art. 4(1)(a) in conjunction with Art. 6(4).
52. SSM Regulation, Art. 14.
53. *Ibid.*, Art. 14(2).
54. CRDIV, Arts 8–16.
55. SSM Regulation, Art. 14(5) and (6).
56. CRDIV, Art. 18.
57. SSM Regulation, Art. 4(1)(c) in conjunction with Art. 6(4).
58. CRDIV, Art. 23.
59. CRDIV, Art. 22.
60. SSM Regulation, Art. 16(2) in conjunction with CRDIV, Art. 97.

[b] ECB Investigatory Powers

The ECB is able to request information and conduct on-site inspections. The scope of intervention of the power to request for information is quite wide as the requests span from credit institutions established in the participating Member States up to third parties to whom activities have outsourced functions or activities.[61]

The ECB has a wide spectrum of powers. According to Article 11 of the SSM Regulation, the ECB can: (a) require the submission of documents; (b) examine the books and records of the persons indicated in Article 10 and take copies or extracts from such books and records; (c) obtain written or oral explanations from any person referred to in Article 10(1) or their representatives or staff; (d) interview any other person who consents to be interviewed for the purpose of collecting information relating to the subject matter of an investigation; interview any other person who consents to be interviewed.

Furthermore, pursuant to Article 12 of the SSM Regulation, the ECB can conduct on-site inspections at the business premises to both the legal persons indicated under Article 10 and to any other undertaking included in supervision. The power of on-site inspection might also extend to the sealing of any business premises and books and records. The investigatory powers in the SSM Regulation draw extensively from the Commission's enforcement in antitrust.

[c] ECB Sanctioning Powers

Article 18 of the SSM Regulation provides for the 'administrative penalties' that the ECB can impose in cases of breaches of supervised entities. The SSM Regulation states that the ECB can impose administrative pecuniary sanctions of up to twice the amount of the profits gained or losses avoided, or up to 10% of the total annual turnover.[62] The scope of direct ECB sanctioning powers is limited to the credit institutions, financial holding companies, or mixed financial holding companies within the SSM scope having breached direct applicable EU law. In cases where breaches have occurred in accordance with national law implementing EU directives or any relevant national legislation which confers specific powers which are currently not required by Union law, the ECB may require NCAs to open the proceedings.[63] Accordingly, Recital 53 stresses that the ECB cannot impose penalties on natural or legal persons other than credit institutions, financial holding companies or mixed financial holding companies. The ECB sanctioning powers mark a new stage in sanctioning credit institutions in the euro area when breaches of prudential requirements have occurred.

61. *Ibid.*, Art. 10(1).
62. *Ibid.*, Art. 18.
63. *Ibid.*, Art. 18(4).

[2] Micro-Prudential Supervision Outside the SSM

As regard the jurisdiction of SSM non-participating Member States, the supranational supervisory tasks and powers remain limited to those of EBA with wide space for powers on authorisation, monitoring, inspection and sanctioning credit institutions at NCA's level.

EBA keeps its formal power of enforcement to ensure compliance of supervisory authorities to clear and unconditional obligations in EU financial markets law[64] and the general power to facilitate and coordinate supervisory responses in emergency situations.[65] Finally, EBA has the important role of mediator by settling and mediating disputes between national supervisors.[66] These EBA powers are applicable to all NCAs in the EU.

§7.04 FINANCIAL STABILITY AND SUPRANATIONAL BANKING SUPERVISION: REFRAMING THE LEVEL-PLAYING FIELD?

Many reflections arise from the creation and the entry into force of the SSM. For the present purposes, this section argues that the institutional and substantive rules of the SSM and the role of the ECB therein foster financial stability as a supranational objective in EU law and policy. This is shown by the exercise of the normative instruments of micro- (and to a certain extent macro-) prudential supervision to achieve financial stability in EU law and policy as developed earlier in this book. As shown below, a number of reflections justify that the SSM is a true paradigm shift towards supranational financial stability.

[A] Article 127(6) TFEU (the 'Enabling Clause'): The Special Legal Basis to Centralise the Supervision of Credit Institutions at ECB Level

Both the TFEU and the ESCB Statute refer to the possibility of enabling the ECB to have supervisory functions in prudential supervision. Article 127(6) TFEU is the explicit legal basis which envisages the possibility to centralise supervisory functions within the ECB.

Article 127(6) TFEU reads as follows:

> The Council, acting by means of regulations in accordance with a special legislative procedure, may unanimously, and after consulting the European Parliament and the European Central Bank, confer specific tasks upon the European Central Bank concerning policies relating to the prudential supervision of credit institutions and other financial institutions with the exception of insurance undertakings.[67]

64. EBA Regulation, Art. 17.
65. *Ibid.*, Art. 18.
66. *Ibid.*, Art. 19.
67. *See* René Smits, *The European Central Bank*, 356 (Kluwer Law International 1997).

The European Council mandate to explore fully Article 127(6) TFEU led the Commission to make the appropriate use of this article with a view to creating the SSM. Scholarship argued that the limits of this legal basis are not circumvented to confer an extensive mandate to the ECB.[68] This is the correct reading as Article 127(6) TFEU provides for extensive ground to centralise supervisory functions even beyond the current SSM Regulation.[69] Other legal bases such as Article 352 TFEU, the flexibility clause,[70] or Article 114 TFEU would not be sufficiently founded. Similarly, the centralisation of prudential supervision by the implied powers doctrine[71] through an extensive reading of Article 127(5) TFEU, cannot be upheld.

The use of this enabling clause is in line with the objective of supranational financial stability. This is because Article 127(6) TFEU is an explicit legal basis to confer prudential tasks to the ECB and is a strong basis to achieve supranational financial stability in the specific case of banking supervision.

The existence of Article 127(6) TFEU is important for a number of reasons. First, the addressee of the 'tasks' is the ECB, an EU institution which is not limited in its decision-making powers by the restrictive interpretation held by the CJEU in *Meroni*.[72] EBA's rules show that the Commission put some limits on the decision-making and the EBA enforcement powers.[73] On the contrary, the ECB is an EU institution that can exercise full decision-making powers. No limitations on the scope of supervisory powers are contained in Article 127(6) TFEU, with the notable exception of supervision on insurance undertakings. Correctly, Wymeersch submits that the expression in the article 'conferring tasks (...) concerning policies relating to prudential supervision (...)' does not create limits for the legislator.[74] The rather open expression in the Treaty article suggests that extensive supervisory tasks and powers can be conferred to the ECB. In particular, the term 'policies' is sufficiently broad to confer day-to-day supervision of credit institutions and regulatory powers to the extent that they serve the tasks of the ECB. This is also confirmed in the recent case General Court case *UK v. ECB* (location policy).[75] As regards the powers granted to the EU institutions, the General Court held:

> [W]hen an article of the Treaty confers a specific task on an institution, it must be accepted, if that provision is not to be rendered wholly ineffective, that it confers on that institution necessarily and per se the powers which are indispensable in order to carry out that task.[76]

68. Wymeersch, *supra* n. 22, 18–19.
69. Another open legal problem is whether the use of 127(6) TFEU could be extended to non-euro area Member States. Article 139(3)(c) TFEU extends Art. 127 TFEU also to Member States with a derogation. However, Art. 139(2)(e) TFEU excludes acts of the ECB from applying to non-euro area Member States.
70. Smits, *supra* n. 67, 356.
71. Lazaros Panourgias, *Banking Regulation and World Trade Law: GATS, EU and Prudential Institution Building*, 173 (Hart Publishing 2005).
72. Cases C-9/56 and 10/56 *Meroni v. High Authority*.
73. *See* Chapter 6 section §6.03[B] for a discussion on the *Meroni* doctrine.
74. Wymeersch, *supra* n. 22, 19.
75. Case T-496/11 *United Kingdom v. ECB* (ECB location policy) ECLI:EU:T:2015:133.
76. *Ibid.*, para. 104.

This paragraph clearly indicates that EU institutions may be granted powers that are necessary to ensure the practical effect of a Treaty provision, while being respectful of the principle of conferral of powers and institutional balance.[77]

Second, Article 127(6) TFEU places the ECB as the best EU institution to exercise banking supervision without concerns about the problem of delegation of powers or legitimacy.[78] Three arguments support this. First, according to Article 25(1) ESCB Statute, the ECB enjoys wide advisory competence also in banking matters.[79] Second, the ECB plays an important role in contributing to the regulatory activities of establishing the financial market and the stability of the financial system. This takes place through the consultative task that the ECB can exercise when EU or national banking regulation is adopted.[80] It has been suggested that this is already well established in ECB practice.[81] Third, the ECB has explicit regulatory powers as stated in Article 132(1) TFEU which do not explicitly include prudential functions of supervision, but which do not exclude them either. These arguments indicate that the ECB has already been given regulatory powers in the Treaty and the ESCB Statute. The ECB can thus enjoy full prudential powers on the basis of Article 127(6) TFEU.

Third, the (re-)use of such legal basis for the supervision of non-bank financial institutions will exclude the need to Treaty changes to insert new legal bases.[82] It is a fast and efficient solution that avoids the opening of lengthy and burdensome revisions procedures to the Treaty. Article 127(6) TFEU is already very wide and could be used to further reinforce the ECB tasks and powers. Yet, this legal basis could be used to provide further centralisation of tasks and powers to the ECB. However, the limits of using this legal basis by way of unanimity in the Council still poses challenges to the future use of this legal basis.

In sum, a number of arguments support the use of Article 127(6) TFEU as the appropriate legal basis to confer prudential tasks and powers to the ECB. This legal basis creates the required legal certainty on the conferral of prudential functions to the ECB and establishes an adequate level of legitimacy for the SSM. Its use remedies the established institutional difficulties in conferring full discretionary prudential tasks to EU agencies and authorities. Article 127(6) TFEU is in line with the attainment of financial stability at supranational level. The possibility that this legal basis will be used again in future to reinforce prudential supervision is not excluded.

[B] The SSM Institutional Governance: A 'Stable' Structure?

The SSM provides for a new organisational structure inside the ECB. This attempts to solve the problem of a 'national imprinting' in the decision-making processes for bank supervision that had not been overcome in ESAs as well as the limits of having another

77. *Ibid.*, para. 105.
78. *See* Pisani-Ferry *et al.*, *supra* n. 6, 11.
79. *See* Dragomir, *supra* n. 5, 226–230.
80. *See* ESCB Statute, Art. 25.
81. Dragomir, *supra* n. 5, 232–234.
82. *See* Moloney *supra* n. 22, 1659.

ECB body that can adopt legally binding acts. However, the current structural arrangements with the Supervisory Board as the decision-maker may be open to criticism. The Supervisory Board is fully independent in conducting supervisory functions within the decision-making structure of the ECB.[83] However, the decision-making procedure and the strong links with the Governing Council might overtime undermine the required level of independence to carry out supervisory functions. Nonetheless, the Governing Council does not seem to obstruct decision-making effectiveness.[84] An alternative solution would have been to create an independent Supervisory Board capable of adopting legally binding decisions or a separation of tasks in the Governing Council structure as established in the ESCB Statute. However, these proposals would not have been simple and fast to implement. The former option would have left the Supervisory Board in a 'non-Treaty limbo' with possible challenges on its institutional legitimacy. The latter would have required an amendment of the ESCB Statute pursuant to Article 48 TEU.[85]

Without going into the details of independence and accountability of the ECB supervisory functions, another critical aspect is the degree of separation between supervisory and monetary policy functions in order to conduct a sound monetary policy and to achieve an effectively independent prudential supervision. The submission of the Supervisory Board preparatory work to the Governing Council may question the real effectiveness of the regulatory arrangements to separate monetary and supervisory functions. While, pursuant to Article 127(1) TFEU, ECB monetary policy functions are aimed at maintaining price stability as the primary objective of the ECB, the exercise of prudential supervision has a different objective, which is to 'protect the safety and the soundness of credit institutions and the stability of the financial system'.[86] The conferral of prudential tasks and powers to the ECB supports the foundational nature of supranational financial stability in EU law and policy, but still may challenge the conflict of tasks within the same institution.

Overall, the SSM governance structure is in line with the need for an institutional mandate on the exercise of prudential supervision at the supranational level. It establishes a Supervisory Board to carry out supervisory tasks, while it preserves the ECB Governing Council as the final decision-maker. Thus far, the subordinate place of the Supervisory Board in the ECB institutional structure and the dual functions of the Governing Council have reached an appropriate level of decision-making efficiency, as shown by the lack of objections to ECB supervisory acts by the Governing Council members.[87]

83. *See* Ferran, Babis, *supra* n. 24, 258.
84. Moloney, *supra* n. 22, 1652.
85. The ESCB Statute provides also for simplified amendments. These are limited only to a number of procedural provisions and not to separation of monetary and supervisory functions.
86. SSM Regulation, Recital 65.
87. ECB, *Annual Report on supervisory activities*, March 2016, 19.

[C] Allocation of Responsibilities Between the ECB and National Authorities: A Truly Single Supervision?

[1] The Allocation of Supervisory Tasks and Powers Between the ECB and the NCAs

The allocation of supervisory responsibilities in the form of tasks and powers between the ECB and the NCAs requires some reflections. Although the SSM establishes a centralised level of prudential supervision, there is still considerable scope for supervisory intervention of NCAs as provided in the SSM Regulation and under national laws. The Commission proposal gave full supervisory tasks of the ECB over all participating Member States' banks.[88] After the December 2012 Council conclusions, the scope of ECB supervision has been considerably reduced, mainly for political reasons. Full centralisation of supervisory functions at the ECB level was not desirable either. If the Commission text was adopted as such, the ECB would anyway not have been able to exercise supervisory tasks and powers for all credit institutions in SSM participating Member States, but only for the largest and more relevant credit institutions in the participating Member States regardless of the type of task or power to exercise. This is because the ECB's supervisory knowledge and resources are limited and by definition centralised.[89]

The SSM Regulation establishes that only banks that are considered as 'significant' are directly supervised by the ECB. 'Less significant' banks are supervised by NCAs with the exception of adopting licenses, withdrawal of licenses and qualifying holdings. As put by Ferran and Babis, the question that remains open is 'whether the allocation of supervision of less significant banks to national authorities may not afford the ECB with sufficient visibility'.[90] The result is that the ECB may lose track on supervision or not impinge on NCAs' competences if an adequate level of supervision at national level is not assured. Nonetheless, the ECB is fully committed to aim for uniformity in the application of the SSM rules also as regards less significant banks.[91] Thus far, the ECB has carefully supervised 'significant' credit institutions and those that may have repercussions on (systemic) risk, even if these are less significant.[92] This is in line with the main argument that financial stability needs to be achieved at the supranational level in order to avoid risks or shocks in the European financial system.

In this context, the allocation of supervisory powers between the ECB and the NCAs is an issue of great importance. The question is whether, in the application of national law as provided in the SSM Regulation, the ECB can exercise all possible

88. European Commission, *Proposal for a Council Regulation conferring specific tasks on the European Central Bank concerning policies relating to the prudential supervision of credit institutions*, COM/2012/0511, Art. 4.
89. *See* Goyal *et al.*, *supra* n. 2, 15.
90. Ferran, Babis, *supra* n. 24, 270.
91. Danièle Nouy & Sabine Lautenschläger, *We aim to improve the resilience of banks and reduce system-wide risks,* 16 November 2016 at http://www.ecb.europa.eu/pub/pdf/other/prudentialsupcbrole_en.pdf (last accessed 31 December 2016).
92. *See* Moloney, *supra* n. 22, 1645.

supervisory powers on 'significant' credit institutions that NCAs had so far. For the first time in European integration, the ECB as an EU institution can also directly apply national law. Article 4(3) of the SSM Regulation provides that the ECB shall apply:

> where (...) Union law is composed of Directives, the national legislation transposing those Directives. Where the relevant Union law is composed of Regulations and where currently those Regulations explicitly grant options for Member States, the ECB shall apply also the national legislation exercising those options.

In the absence of a truly harmonised single rulebook, i. e. only EU law rules in banking matters, this provision is extremely important as it allows the ECB to apply directly national law, without having to instruct the NCAs. However, the determination of what constitute transposition of EU directives, the different degree of implementing measures under national law and the existence of specific supervisory powers under national law may be highly problematic.[93]

In certain areas, the national transposition of the CRDIV shows different legal regimes in participating Member States. For instance, the national transposition of fit and proper requirement shows that national laws have in place different administrative procedures or substantive rules to consider a candidate in a management body suitable.[94] Furthermore, explicit supranational banking law provisions in EU regulations and directives, which give scope to ECB powers under Article 4(3) SSM Regulation, are not sufficiently detailed and comprehensive to include all supervisory powers provided in national law. This is for instance the case of authorisation powers regarding mergers, acquisitions by credit institutions in non-credit institutions or other strategic operations in banks. These supervisory powers do not have any clear and explicit provisions in EU law. However, they are still relevant operations in the conduct of prudential supervision and that come within the scope of the ECB tasks. At the same time, Article 9(1) third sentence of the SSM Regulation states that 'the ECB may require, by way of instructions, those national authorities to make use of their powers (...) where this Regulation does not confer such powers on the ECB'. This provision does not make it clear to what extent the ECB has the supervisory tasks but not the direct supervisory power. It seems that Article 9(1) third sentence of the SSM Regulation should be interpreted as giving the ECB the opportunity to instruct NCAs whenever some national provisions outside the supervisory tasks may have an impact on the ECB supervisory tasks.

Overall, allocation of responsibility between the ECB and NCAs remains a key aspect in the SSM. ECB supervision without a distinction between 'significant' and 'less-significant' credit institution or with a large scope of application of national supervisory powers would have been more in line with the attainment of supranational financial stability as developed in this book. This moves the reflections to the day-to-day cooperation and execution between the ECB and the NCAs.

93. ECB, *Annual Report on supervisory activities*, March 2016, 67.
94. *Ibid.*, 41.

[2] Cooperation and Execution of Supervisory Tasks Between the ECB and the NCAs

The ECB/NCAs' allocation of responsibilities is an essential aspect of the SSM. The SSM creates a cooperative and integrated supervisory framework with the exercise of prudential tasks and powers both by the ECB and the NCAs. In particular, the SSM Regulation establishes that NCAs supervise less significant credit institutions, and prepare and implement guidance on the ECB's supervision. As argued by Ferrarini and Chiarella:

> resource constraints and political expediency, but also (...) the existence in the eurozone of different legal, accounting and taxation frameworks, as well as of many languages and business contexts[95] excluded the conferral of direct ECB supervision for all credit institutions. The distinction between ECB and NCA supervision opens for some critical remarks.

First, the SSM Regulation is designed to create an integrated framework of activities between the ECB and NCAs. Shortly after the entry into force of the SSM Regulation, the ECB adopted a regulation specifying the cooperation between the ECB and the NCA, the SSM Framework Regulation.[96] This indicates that a duty to cooperate in good faith and exchanges of information between the ECB and NCAs are essential. The SSM Framework Regulation establishes the main modalities to achieve cooperation in supervising 'significant' banks: the 'Joint Supervisory Teams' (JST) composed of ECB and national officials with an ECB JST coordinator.

Second, the SSM Regulation contains important clauses that provide that the ECB is responsible of prudential supervision beyond the notion of 'significant' credit institutions under specific circumstances. These may be helpful to avoid risks of national fragmentation in the conduct of supervision in participating Member States. In fact the ECB might develop standards, policy stances and methodologies for supervised entities regardless of their 'significance'.[97] The NCAs are required to provide all the information necessary as well as assist the preparation and implementation of ECB direct supervision. Furthermore, the ECB may even take upon itself direct supervision of banks established in participating Member States, even if they are not 'significant' under the SSM Regulation.

Third, the ECB exercises some key prudential tasks in the banking sector, such as having the final say on authorisation, licensing, withdrawal of authorisation, qualifying holding and the supervision on significant banks. At the same time, NCAs conduct extensive tasks especially as regards 'less-significant' banks. The NCAs' exercise of supervisory tasks and powers for medium or small credit institutions might still be not

95. Guido Ferrarini & Luigi Chiarella, *Common Banking Supervision in the Eurozone: Strengths and Weaknesses*, ECGI Law Working Paper 54 (2013).
96. SSM Framework Regulation (EU) No 468/2014 of the European Central Bank of 16 April 2014 establishing the framework for cooperation within the Single Supervisory Mechanism between the European Central Bank and national competent authorities and with national designated authorities (SSM Framework Regulation) (ECB/2014/17) [2014] OJ L 141, Arts 20 and 21.
97. *See* ECB, *Annual Report on supervisory activities*, March 2016, 41–46.

fully in line with the ECB supervisory policy.[98] A good cooperation depends on the ability of the ECB to exercise its SSM functions in a proactive and structured way.

Overall, it appears that the SSM works in a 'supranational cooperative fashion'.[99] The SSM is not only a *Single* Supervisory Mechanism, but also a *Cooperative* Supervisory Mechanism where both the ECB and NCAs conduct supervision over credit institutions in participating Member States. The ECB prudential tasks and powers mark a new stage in the supervision of banks in the euro area as banking supervision has become an 'exclusive' EU competence as regards significant institutions and a 'shared' EU competence as regards less significant institutions. In this sense, a proactive ECB in the exercise of supervisory tasks and powers is certainly an important aspect to attain supranational financial stability in Europe.

[3] The SSM Supervisory Procedures

The SSM reforms the system of authorisation, withdrawal of authorisation, acquisition of qualifying holdings as well as the establishment of branches and subsidiaries for credit institutions in Europe. The rules for the authorisation, the withdrawal of authorisation and the assessment of the acquisition of qualifying holding are important elements showing that the SSM follows a model of cooperative supervisory centralisation with the ECB at the centre of the system. The ECB is in fact responsible for authorisation, withdrawal of authorisation and qualifying holding on all credit institutions regardless of their significance.[100]

The SSM Regulation involves the national authorities in the exercise of ECB powers the authorisation and the withdrawal of authorisation for banking activities within the SSM. The procedure appears to provide expediency and efficiency in the authorisation, but it does not completely overcome the home/host country principle as the NCAs remain the entry point in the procedure. This might result in the ECB not being sufficiently capable of assessing authorisations, the withdrawal of authorisations or acquisitions of qualifying holdings, especially because of the limited amount of time to assess these authorisations.

The SSM innovates also the application of the rights to provide services and the right of establishment of the credit institutions as the ECB is 'at the centre of gravity' in the new system.[101] Therefore, the ECB oversees cross-border exercises to open branches and/or provide cross-border services in participating Member States. This centralised degree of supervision reduces the differences in home and host country control in participating Member States. However, it does not mean that the principle of home/host country is superseded. Differently, the proposal for SSM Regulation innovated on the home/host country control principle as it indicated that the:

98. Moloney, *supra* n. 22, 1647.
99. *See* Robert Schütze, *From Rome to Lisbon: 'Executive Federalism' in the (New) European Union*, 47 Common Market Law Review 1421 (2010).
100. *See supra* section §7.03[A][1].
101. SSM Regulation, Arts 4(1)(b) and 17(1).

> ECB [would] assume the role of both home and host supervisor for credit institutions exercising the right of establishment and the free provision of services in other participating Member States.[102]

This provision could have simplified the exercise of the right of establishment and the free provision of services within the SSM. Similarly, the proposal for the SSM Regulation did not establish a bottom-up system for qualifying holdings, but only for licences and withdrawal of licences.

Furthermore, NCAs are the entry points for notifications for some authorisation decisions under the SSM Regulation and the SSM Framework Regulation, and notifications from banks to NCAs will continue to apply. Notably – and controversially –, this is the case for fit and proper assessment of significant institutions.[103] Such bottom-up procedures might suggest that conflicts or non-cooperation between the ECB and NCAs on the application of supervisory assessment criteria might take place in practice. Given the exercise of exclusive ECB tasks and powers for significant institutions, a system based on an NCA phase in the procedure followed by the ECB assessment is not in line with the attainment of supranational financial stability.

In all other cases, the SSM supervisory procedures follows the distinction between 'significant' and 'less significant' institutions. The ECB applies Article 95 of the SSM Framework Regulation, which sets out the procedural rules for direct notifications, requests and applications to the ECB.

Overall, while the SSM Regulation does not provide for a full operational centralisation[104] of banking activities, authorisations and processes, it makes clear that the ECB exercises a central prudential role as the final decision-maker.

[D] The SSM and EU Agencies: Rebalancing Prudential Supervision within a New Institutional Framework?

The relationship between the ECB and EU agencies is an important element in the context of the SSM. The ECB relationship with EU agencies, in particular the EBA and the SRB[105], poses a number of issues in relation to the level of coordination between supranational regulation, standard-setting, supervision and resolution of credit institutions. These two EU agencies have different tasks. EBA does not supervise credit institutions on a day-to-day basis, but has the mandate to develop guidelines and recommendations as well as to draft technical standards to be adopted by the Commission in EU banking regulation.[106] The SRB has the tasks to prepare and manage resolutions as well as prepare documents ensuring orderly resolutions. These two agencies question the balancing of horizontal competences between the ECB and the EU agencies.

102. COM/2012/0511, *Explanatory memorandum*, 4.3.2.
103. *See* SSM Framework Regulation, Art. 93.
104. See Pisani-Ferry *et al.*, *supra* n. 6, 11 (emphasis added).
105. For the SRB see further Chapter 8 section §8.04[C].
106. SSM Regulation, Recital 32.

The ECB relationship with EBA and the SRB shows that the conferral of supervisory powers to the ECB has necessarily changed the established set of rules as regards regulation and supervision in the euro area. As regards EBA, the need to adopt Regulation 1022/2013 proved to be essential for a correct rebalancing of powers between EBA and the ECB, especially to ensure participation and involvement of non-SSM competent authorities in banking regulation and standard-setting.

The SSM Regulation provides for a degree of close cooperation between the ECB and ESAs as well as the SRB. Recital 32 addresses the issue of the relationship between the ECB and ESAs and affirms that the ECB should carry out its tasks in compliance with relevant Union law. This means that the ECB should not exercise its powers in a way that compromises ESA's role in:

> developing draft technical standards and guidelines and recommendations ensuring supervisory convergence and consistency of supervisory outcomes within the Union.[107]

Furthermore, the relationship between the ECB and the SRB as the resolution authority require close cooperation and close participation.

However, the degree of cooperation may be problematic as the ECB disposes the power to adopt regulations and decisions under Article 132 TFEU[108] as well as the power to adopt regulations in supervisory tasks under Article 4(3) of the SSM Regulation. The ECB may adopt regulations in supervisory matters, which not only cover its supervisory task, but which could also encroach on EBA's or SRB's tasks. However, so long as ECB regulatory powers are exercised in respect of the two EU agencies' tasks these do not give rise to conflicts between the three.

The level of regulatory functions that EBA, SRB and the ECB exercise may be a source of concern.[109] Apart from Recital 31 in the SSM Regulation, there is no clear prohibition on the part of the ECB to adopt an act having some indirect impact on the EBA or SRB sphere. Furthermore, it is not excluded that EBA or SRB would be constrained by their nature as agencies to carry out restrained regulatory functions that need the Commission's endorsement. At the same time, to counterbalance this potential problem of legitimacy of EBA, Regulation 1022/2013 provides that a double simple majority (qualified majority) of Member States participating in the SSM and non-participating Member States is needed for deliberations of EBA board of supervisors, both in its regulatory and enforcement/conflict resolution tasks.[110] However, the intention to modify the voting modalities is tempered by the provision stating that the board of supervisors of EBA shall 'strive for consensus' when taking decisions.[111] The new voting modalities provided in the SSM EBA Regulation aim to safeguard the consistency of EBA's rulemaking. Similarly, the explicit exclusion of resolution tasks to the ECB under Article 4 of the SSM Regulation as well as the guarantees in ensuring the

107. *Ibid.*
108. *See* Chapter 6 section §6.03[A][2] for discussion on the regulatory role of the ECB in banking regulation.
109. Moloney, *supra* n. 22, 1667–1668.
110. *See* Regulation 1022/2013, Art. 1.
111. *Ibid.*

participation of the SRB in ECB tasks suggest that the ECB does not encroach with the tasks and powers of the SRB.

While a clear dividing line between banking regulation, supervision and resolution does and shall not exist, the EBA-SRB-ECB arrangements in the SSM provide for sufficient clarity on the competences held by them. Scholarship held that the ECB-EU agencies arrangements may be problematic from a practical perspective as it is not clear to what extent the ECB and the EU agencies will follow similar policies or contrast with each other.[112] The ECB may provide binding indications to the regulator in the exercise of supervision of credit institutions established in the SSM. Nevertheless, EBA remains responsible to adopt such documents if so provided in Level 1 regulation and the SRB is in charge of resolution planning and management. The ECB could probably encroach on EU agencies' tasks and powers within the jurisdiction of the participating Member States. At the same time, EBA has been mainly created to draft regulation in the banking field, both in the form of hard law and soft law, and the SRB to prepare and manage resolution. Therefore, these EU agencies do not seem undermined under the SSM structure,[113] also because there are safeguards in ensuring their good relationship such as cooperation arrangements, MoUs and informal high-level contacts.

Overall, it can be concluded that the ECB-EU agencies relationship shows a positive degree of coordination for the pursuit of the supranational objective of financial stability in EU law and policy. The ECB, EBA and the SRB are strongly linked with each other while keeping their own competences.

[E] Where Does Macro-Prudential Supervision Lie in Europe?

The exercise of macro-prudential supervision remains a controversial aspect in banking supervision. The de Larosière Report stressed that there should be a European macro-prudential policy.[114] As a result, the ESRB was established in 2011. However, the regulatory reforms on banking law implemented so far show that the focus of supranational banking supervision is mainly at micro-prudential level. Europe still lacks a European institution or agency exclusively and strongly dealing with macro-prudential regulation from both the institutional as well as the substantial dimension. The ESRB does not seem so successful in dealing with macro-prudential measures as it currently stands. As it was envisaged since its creation, the ESRB has been a 'supervisory platform with vague lines of responsibility involving in an equivocal way a plurality of other EU bodies'.[115] At the same time, the ECB has been conferred some macro-prudential tasks and tools within the SSM under Article 5(2) of the SSM Regulation.

112. Moloney, *supra* n. 22, 1668–1669. *See also* Karl-Philipp Wojcik, *Bail in the Banking Union*, 53 Common Market Law Review 115 (2016)
113. *See* Ferran, Babis, *supra* n. 24, 277.
114. de Larosière Report, *supra* n. 12, 44.
115. Dragomir *supra* n. 5, 293.

Two main issues are still open to debate and - certainly - future will provide some answers. First, it is important to see to what extent the ECB supervisory tasks in relation to the ESRB. Along the financial crisis, the ESRB has achieved its macro-prudential mandate only to a limited extent. This is due to the lack of legal personality and legally binding powers. Moreover, the large composition and the limited powers of intervention are seen as problematic aspects for the ESRB functioning. These views have been also expressed in the recent report on the mission and organisation of the ESRB published in August 2014 by the Commission.[116]

Second, the SSM may change macro-prudential policy as the ECB is now vested with a new macro-prudential competence under Article 5. The SSM Regulation states that strong cooperation should take place between the ECB and the ESRB. While the SSM Regulation stresses that the supervisory tasks conferred on the ECB shall not interfere with its tasks in relation to the ESRB,[117] the ECB is also vested with macro-prudential tasks and tools pursuant to Article 5 SSM Regulation.[118] Nonetheless, the provision leaves open the question of the relationship between the ECB and the ESRB mandate on macro-prudential supervision. The establishment of the SSM has certainly increased the ECB's role while the role of the ESRB as a stand-alone body to exercise macro-prudential supervision remains limited. It is expected that macro-prudential supervision is progressively exercised under the sphere of the ECB tasks under Article 5 of the SSM Regulation in participating Member States. This would be a positive development for supranational financial stability as an EU institution, which supervises directly credit institutions with legally binding powers, may well exercise macro-prudential functions. This follows the argument that macro-prudential tools in the euro area should predominantly be exercised by the ECB with a view to contribute to supranational financial stability.

In sum, while the ESRB has developed a 'soft' European dimension for macro-prudential policy, there is not yet a truly supranational exercise of macro-prudential policy at present. National regulators and supervisors remain substantially competent as regards macro-prudential decisions. The ESRB is not sufficiently resilient to perform the function of supranational macro-prudential supervisor in Europe. Some reforms are needed to strengthen the European macro-prudential policy either by establishing a stronger agency regulator for macro-prudential purposes or by letting the ECB exercise further macro-prudential tools. In August 2016, the Commission has launched a consultation to reform the macro-prudential supervisory framework.[119] Some regulatory developments may take place in the coming months.

116. European Commission, *Report on the mission and organisation of the European Systemic Risk Board (ESRB)*, COM(2014) 508 final.
117. SSM Regulation, Art. 25(2).
118. *See supra* §7.03[A][3].
119. *See* EU Commission, *Consultation Document. Review of the EU macro-prudential policy Framework* at http://ec.europa.eu/finance/consultations/2016/macroprudential-framework/docs/consultation-document_en.pdf (last accessed 31 December 2016).

[F] The SSM and Non-euro Area Membership: Dis-integration at Stake?

Another concern that comes from the SSM is whether the ECB supervision may create divergences between euro area and non-euro area Member States. It is questioned whether the SSM has put market integration in Europe at risk by creating further differentiation in Europe or even dis-*integration* between euro area and non-euro area membership. However, at a closer look on the SSM Regulation, dis-*integration* concerns are not founded as there are sufficient safeguards in the SSM that avoid such concern. Rather, it is argued that the SSM is a benchmark reform for further market convergence, for non-euro area Member States too, and it will enhance stability and generate positive spillover effects in the EU financial market.[120]

Two main arguments can be made to that effect. First, the SSM Regulation provides that the non-participating Member States shall conclude MoUs with the ECB and exercise their supervisory activities in colleges of supervisors together with the ECB.[121] While these instruments establish the background for cooperation between non-SSM supervisory authorities and the ECB,[122] the SSM Regulation recognises that the responsibility of non-participating Member States shall be fully respected.[123] The content of the MoU shall be in line with the established practice of providing detailed provisions on information sharing and supervision coordination. The degree of consistency in MoUs would reinforce the argument that non-euro area membership does not (dis-)integrate the established legal order.

Second, to support further the argument of further integration, the SSM Regulation provides that non-euro area Member States might join the SSM through 'close cooperation' agreements.[124] Even if scholarship has questioned its legal and policy strength,[125] it is argued that the inclusion of this level of cooperation is beneficial for consistent supranational supervision in Europe.[126] The SSM Regulation is favourable to the position of non-euro area members as the non-euro area Member States are in a position comparable, but not equal, to the euro area members as regards the exercise of supervisory tasks.

However, within a close cooperation under the SSM, problems of differential conditions are not entirely solved in the SSM Regulation. Most importantly, non-euro area members cannot be represented in the Governing Council. While the participating non-euro area Member States would be represented in the Supervisory Board, their position cannot be the same in the Governing Council. This is because the Treaties and the ESCB Statute do not allow the non-euro area members to participate in the Governing Council.[127] The SSM Regulation attempts to solve this legacy of the ESCB Statute by giving the participating Member State the possibility to express

120. *See* Goyal et al. *supra* n. 2, 28.
121. *See* ECB, *Annual Report on supervisory activities*, March 2016, 55–56.
122. SSM Regulation, Recital 14.
123. *Ibid.*, Recital 44.
124. *Ibid.*, Art. 7.
125. Ferran, Babis, *supra* n. 24, 280.
126. Moloney *supra* n. 22, 1663.
127. *See* ESCB Statute, Art. 10.

disagreement on the Supervisory Board's draft decision,[128] and to terminate the close cooperation. Equally, the SSM Regulation states that the participating non-euro area Member States are invited to express their disagreement with the draft decision of the Supervisory Board to the Governing Council.[129] However, it remains clear that the impossibility for the non-euro area NCAs to participate in the Governing Council is an open problem that can be solved only with an amendment of the Treaty and the ESCB Statute.

From this analysis, it is evident that the close cooperation arrangement is a problematic solution from the point of view of ECB governance. Nevertheless, it is submitted that the limitations on close cooperation arrangements are not as serious as they seem. First, close cooperation should not be seen as a negative status as compared with euro area membership. On the contrary, it is an inviting position, especially for small non-euro area Member States or those whose currency is pegged to the euro. The ECB would provide the adequate level of supervision also to non-euro area banks and would create the conditions for further integration in financial markets. Second, close cooperation agreements would give ground to an equal membership and voting in the Supervisory Board that is the actual body where the essential supervisory decision-making processes take place. Non-euro area Member States would be equally represented in the Supervisory Board. Third, close cooperation would boost confidence in market integration, especially for those non-euro area Member States that have banks exercising many cross-border activities.[130]

Overall, it is submitted that the SSM framework for close cooperation does not generate a 'disintegrating instability' in the internal market. On the contrary, it is argued that the SSM Regulation attempts to reach centralisation and integration also in relation to non-euro area Member States in light of the overarching objection of supranational financial stability. However, at present close cooperation has not been established with any non-euro area Member State.[131]

[G] The Stability Function of the ECB as a Supervisor: Its Legitimacy and Effectiveness

Before concluding, this subsection offers the opportunity to summarise and look into the main reasons as to why the ECB can exert supranational financial stability acting as prudential supervisor. This last section argues that the ECB expresses a normative instrument for supranational financial stability as the supranational supervisor in SSM participating Member States. The conferral of specific functions of prudential supervision on the ECB shows that the SSM puts the ECB at the centre of gravity of the system. The ECB as an EU institution is the most appropriate entity to exercise day-to-day

128. SSM Regulation, Art. 7(8). *See* Moloney, *supra* n. 22, 1663.
129. *Ibid.*, Recital 72.
130. Jörg Asmussen, *The Single Resolution Mechanism and the Limits of Bank-Regulation*, 8 November 2013 at https://www.ecb.europa.eu/press/key/date/2013/html/sp131108_1.en.html (accessed 31 December 2016).
131. ECB, *Annual Report on supervisory activities*, March 2016, 57.

supervision of banks in accordance with the normative components to achieve supranational financial stability in EU law and policy as developed in this book.

First, the decision to confer prudential tasks to the ECB as regards the supervision of credit institutions is undeniably more efficient than the conferral of such prerogatives to an ad hoc EU authority or agency created for such a purpose,[132] in the absence of a reconsideration of the *Meroni* doctrine. The role of EBA in banking supervision shows that its activities together with its limits in decision-making powers and budget have not developed an efficient system of supervision of credit institutions. EBA mandate was itself insufficient to achieve the required level of supervision in the euro area. In this sense, EBA would not have been the most appropriate agency to conduct prudential supervision on a vast scale. Both the limited EBA powers of intervention as well as the national structuring of EBA are not in line with the idea of establishing a centralised level of banking supervision to enhance financial stability.[133]

Second, it is submitted that the ECB may well be considered the best-placed EU institution to conduct supervisory tasks in the euro area. These raise the issue of whether the Treaties contain such prerogatives. According to the principle of conferral of powers under Article 5(2) TEU, the EU shall 'act within the limits of the powers conferred upon it by the Treaty and the objectives assigned therein'. The ECB can legitimately exercise such tasks in light of the principle of the conferral of powers of the EU as provided in Article 127 TFEU. Both the Treaty and the ESCB Statute confer the possibility for the ECB to perform specific tasks relating to the prudential supervision of credit institutions (Article 127(6) TFEU and Article 25 ESCB Statute). Furthermore, the ECB is vested with advisory functions on prudential supervision of credit institutions and a contributing role for the stability of the financial system.[134] As correctly argued by Padoa-Schioppa financial stability concerns are situated at the crossroads between monetary policy and supervision and there the ECB can play a role.[135] The ECB is thus the appropriate supervisor for banks established in the euro area.[136]

Third, the ECB is the best institution in place for its role and supervisory tasks as it has already adequate resources, instruments, governance, budget, structure and, most importantly, institutional capabilities and expertise to perform the role of supervisor for credit institutions. The high number of data, information-sharing and synergies within this institution are very useful for the proper conduct of prudential supervision at ECB level.

Finally, it is submitted that the role of central banking in supervising credit institutions is common in Europe.[137] Many NCBs have already been conferred extensive competence to exercise prudential supervision of credit institutions. This reinforces the argument that the ECB is the best institution to conduct prudential supervision at European level rather than ad hoc institutions or agencies that do not

132. *See* Wymeersch, *supra* n. 22, 25–28.
133. *See* Busuioc *supra* n. 3, 111.
134. Art. 127(5) TFEU.
135. Tommaso Padoa-Schioppa, *Regulating Finance*, 128 (Oxford University Press 2004).
136. Lastra, *supra* n. 10, 302.
137. *See* ECB, *The Role of Central Banks in Prudential Supervision* (2001) at http://www.ecb.europa.eu/pub/pdf/other/prudentialsupcbrole_en.pdf (last accessed 31 December 2016).

have the same expertise as the ECB in conducting monetary policy. However, it is be essential that the ECB exercises its prudential tasks while respecting the principles of accountability and independence.[138]

Overall, the above arguments suggest that the conferral of prudential tasks to the ECB is a clear expression of the normative instrument of supervision to attain supranational financial stability in EU law and policy.

§7.05 CONCLUSION

This chapter has demonstrated that the SSM and the role of the ECB therein are an essential evolution in attaining financial stability at the supranational level. The powers conferred to the ECB in the SSM for the supervision of credit institutions established in participating Member States are unprecedented, and contribute to attain supranational financial stability in EU law and policy.

Even with some limits and uncertainties as to its current functioning, the SSM is an essential reform for the development of supranational financial stability in EU law and policy. The tasks and powers conferred to the ECB in the SSM for the supervision of credit institutions established in participating Member States are unprecedented and – hopefully – contribute to establish a better model framework for top-down supervisory governance, supervisory convergence, regulatory harmonisation and lead to a strengthened model of bank supervision in participating Member States. At the same time, other areas of financial regulation and supervision in Europe remain nationally centred without supranational governance frameworks. For instance, this is the case of the competences in the matters of consumer protection and money laundering as well as the supervision of financial institutions other than credit institutions such as central counterparties. The SSM experience could promote institutional integration also in other areas of financial regulation.

Back in 1999 Padoa-Schioppa argued that:

> in the future the needs will change and the multilateral mode will have to deepen substantially. Over time such a mode will have to be structured to the point of providing the banking industry with a true and effective collective euro area supervisor. It will have to be enhanced to the full extent required for banking supervision in the euro area to be as prompt and effective as it is within a single nation.[139]

It seems that the SSM is eventually putting into place this proposal. In the words of Draghi, the 'SSM offers a tremendous opportunity to move from different national approaches to the treatment of banks to a genuinely European perspective'.[140] In this sense, it is important that the ECB exercises strong powers in supervising

138. SSM Regulation, Arts 19 and 20.
139. Tommaso Padoa-Schioppa, *EMU and Banking Supervision*, Lecture in the London School of Economics, 24 February 1999.
140. Mario Draghi, *Opening Speech at the European Banking Congress The Future of Europe*, 22 November 2013 at https://www.ecb.europa.eu/press/key/date/2013/html/sp131122.en.html (last accessed 31 December 2016).

significant credit institutions, and that it is not reliant on NCAs and/or on national political interplays. At the same time, the ECB should be ready to address critical issues and to supervise fairly 'significant' banks in the euro area. It is not an easy path and many challenges exist. However, it is argued that, to date, the SSM is a critical evolutionary reform, and is correctly described as 'the most ambitious and encompassing reform of the EU architecture since the institution of the single currency'.[141] In this sense, the ECB in the SSM has played a central role in attaining supranational financial stability in EU law and policy. With that being said, the establishment of the SSM calls for the assessment of the new banking recovery and resolution legal framework in Europe, which is the object of the next chapter.

141. Peter Praet, *Fixing Finance* Panel intervention 18 February 2014 at http://www.ecb.europa.eu/press/key/date/2014/html/sp140218.en.html (last accessed 31 December 2016).

CHAPTER 8

EU Banking Recovery and Resolution

§8.01 INTRODUCTION

The purpose of this chapter is to examine the role of EU banking recovery and resolution in the debate on supranational financial stability in EU law and policy. The chapter demonstrates to what extent supranational regulation has established burden-sharing measures and rescue measures that follow the objective of supranational financial stability as developed in this book.

The special treatment of credit institutions requires particular attention especially as a consequence of the financial crisis in Europe. This is because 'the distress of Systemically Important Financial Institutions (SIFIs) and its subsequent disorderly liquidation can create risks to overall financial stability'.[1] Until the outbreak of the financial crisis, the European legal system did not provide for harmonised and cross-border rules on resolution or winding down of credit institutions. At the international level, soft law measures have been adopted to frame the debate on orderly procedures for cross-border insolvencies for non-banking companies and for banks.[2]

A part of the regulatory response to the global financial crisis, a resilient regime for dealing with ailing banks and financial institutions became a priority for the international standard-setters.[3] This process led also to the adoption of

1. Jianping Zhou *et al.*, *From Bail-out to Bail-in: Mandatory Debt Restructuring of Systemic Financial Institutions Paper on Bail in*, IMF SDN/12/03, 4 (2012).
2. *See* among others Matthias Haentjens, *Bank Recovery and Resolution: An Overview of International Initiatives*, 3 International Insolvency Law Review 255 (2014).
3. G-20, Leaders' Statement The Pittsburgh Summit, 24–25 September 2009, 9; International Monetary Fund and World Bank, *An Overview of the Legal, Institutional, and Regulatory Framework for Bank Insolvency* (April 2009); Basel Committee on Banking Supervision, *Report and Recommendations of the Cross-Border Bank Resolution Group* (Bank for International Settlement, March 2010); IMF, *Resolution of Cross-Border Banks – A Proposed Framework for Enhanced Coordination* (June 2010).

the FSB Key Attributes of Effective Resolution Regimes for Financial Institutions,[4] which have been considered as an essential document for the adoption of resolution regimes for financial institutions at regional and national level.

Consequently, as of 2009 Europe has developed a new statutory framework for banking recovery and resolution throughout the financial crisis in order to allow administrative authorities to deal effectively with ailing financial institutions.[5] This supranational response, which led to the adoption of the BRRD and the Single Resolution Mechanism (SRM), was prompted by the massive recourse to State aid measures to financial institutions by the Member States in Europe and the lack of cross-border cooperation in dealing with ailing financial institutions. The new regulatory framework at European level aims to provide early intervention, prevention of resolutions and resolution measures for financial institutions in Europe.[6] The main objective of this new regulatory regime for the post-crisis scenario is to maintain financial stability, minimise losses for society, and specifically for taxpayers, and integrate further the single market for credit institutions. Hence, the recent European initiatives to create a cross-border and supranational system of crisis management for financial institutions have created a regulatory framework for the prevention of bank crises and for the orderly resolution of credit institutions. This is because an orderly liquidation of financial institutions may jeopardise financial stability in the system.

The chapter explores the recent regulatory developments in the recovery and resolution framework and assesses whether the established supranational resolution regime of the BRRD and the SRM is sufficiently resilient to resolve the 'too-big-to-fail' problem, and whether it effectively reinforces supranational financial stability in EU law and policy.

The chapter proceeds as follows. The first part shows that before the outbreak of the financial crisis, EU law and policy did not provide for a common framework for orderly banking resolution (§8.02). The section assesses in particular the de facto Commission's powers to recover or resolve credit institutions by approving State aid measures as compatible aid under Article 107(3) TFEU. The second part examines the current rules establishing a new regulatory framework for bank recovery and resolution both at substantive and institutional level (§8.03). In particular, it assesses the substantive recovery and resolution tools provided in the BRRD and the institutional framework established as the SRM. The third part assesses the current reforms in light of the debate of supranational financial stability and the role of the statutory recovery and resolution framework for banks to achieve this objective in Europe (§8.04). The fourth part looks at the possible reforms to improve further the European system of

---

4. FSB, *Key Attributes of Effective Resolution Regimes for Financial Institutions* (October 2011; revised October 2014); FSB, *Recovery and Resolution Planning for Systemically Important Financial Institutions: Guidance on Developing Effective Resolution Strategies* (July 2013).
5. European Commission, Communication on *An EU framework for crisis management in the financial sector*, COM(2010) 579 final.
6. *See* Eva Hüpkes & Diego Devos, *Cross-Border Bank Resolution: A Reform Agenda* in Mario Giovanoli, Diego Devos (eds), *International Monetary and Financial Law*, 359 (Oxford University Press 2010).

banking resolution and proposes a number of measures to be introduced in future (§8.05). The last part concludes (§8.06).

§8.02 THE RESOLUTION OF CREDIT INSTITUTIONS IN EUROPE BEFORE THE BRRD AND THE SRM: ACTING BY DEFAULT?

The intention to adopt new legislation for the recovery and the resolution of credit institutions lies at the core of the debate on supranational financial stability in EU law and policy. Before the outbreak of the financial crisis in Europe, a common regime for the recovery and resolution of credit institutions did not exist. On the contrary, Member States were exclusively competent to adopt national measures to recover and resolve financial institutions if these measures existed under national and to support ailing institution with state support measures.

[A] The Lack of a European Framework on Banking Resolution and Insolvency Before the Financial Crisis

While in 1999 the FSA Plan[7] intended to set up a European regime for the orderly winding-down of credit institutions in Europe, it did not establish a European regime to resolve credit institutions in Europe. The result of this process was the adoption of Directive 2001/24/EC on the reorganisation and winding-up of credit institutions.[8] This Directive, which had an extremely long negotiation process for adoption, included principles applicable to the single market for credit institutions and in particular the home country control.[9] It establishes rules based on a 'universalist' approach. This means that ailing financial institutions are subject to the measures concerning the reorganisation or winding-up taken by the administrative or judicial authorities of the home Member States of that institution. However, the mutual recognition approach adopted in the Directive does not provide adequate rules for an orderly winding-down of credit institutions and in particular for those entities running cross-border activities. Two main limitations are noticeable in the Directive. First, it does not extend to cross-border subsidiaries. Second, it does not harmonise insolvency proceedings, but it only provides some general rules on the mutual recognition of insolvency proceedings.[10]

The need to develop a new regulatory framework was envisaged in the de Larosière Report where a chapter was dedicated to crisis management and resolution. The report stressed that:

7. European Commission, *Financial Services Action Plan* COM(1999)232.
8. Directive 2001/24/EC of the European Parliament and of the Council of 4 April 2001 on the reorganisation and winding up of credit institutions [2001] L125/15.
9. *See* Georgina Peters, *Developments in the EU*, in Rosa Lastra (ed.), *Cross-Border Bank Insolvency*, 128 (Oxford University Press 2011).
10. *See also* Case C-526/14 *Kotnik and Others*, ECLI:EU:C:2016:570, paras 104 and 105.

> [t]he lack of consistent crisis management and resolution tools across the Single Market places Europe at a disadvantage vis-à-vis the US and these issues should be addressed by the adoption at EU level of adequate measures.[11]

However, the de Larosière Report did not go as far as to provide specific regulatory proposals for the creation of a new European resolution or insolvency regime for credit institutions. The problem of the too-big-to-fail dogma remained unresolved and required a solution in the short-term. In the meantime, the Commission exercised an increasingly important role as to determine the compatibility of State aid measures to financial institutions in the context of State aid control.

[B] Granting Compatible State Aids to Credit Institutions as a Recovery and Resolution Measure: From De Facto EU Rule to Exception[12]

During the first phases of the financial crisis and in the absence of a European regulatory framework for bank resolution or liquidation, the de facto statutory European reaction came from the Commission's role in enforcing State aid in the internal market. As of 2008, Member States provided extensive public support measures to the banking sector. Rescuing financial institutions was required in order to avoid the collapse of the financial system in many Member States. The single market had to rely on some other means to control the structure and functioning of the cross-border banking markets. The Commission's mandate to preserve the integrity of the single market and to avoid distortion of competition under State aid control as provided for in Article 107 TFEU served as a strong and swift supranational response to control distressed credit institutions. As held by Almunia, 'State aid was the only available means at EU level that could be quickly deployed to control the massive public bailout of banks in distress'.[13]

State aids are in principle prohibited under Article 107(1) TFEU. State aid is incompatible under Article 107(1) TFEU, 'save as otherwise provided in this Treaty'. Article 107(2) and (3) TFEU are considered exemption clauses from the first paragraph as markets may not always work properly left alone mainly. One derogation is important: letter (b) of Article 107(3) TFEU refers to aid to 'remedy a serious disturbance in the economy of a Member State'. Therefore, Article 107(3)(b) TFEU acted as the default European regulatory mechanism for bank restructuring and resolution before the adoption of the BRRD.

The adoption of a special framework for the assessment of State aids by the Commission shows that supranational financial stability has been pursued in the Commission control of State aids to banks in Europe. This was essential to avoid the collapse the European banking market. State aid control and the creation of a de facto

11. Jacques de Larosière, *Report of the High-Level Group on Financial Supervision in the EU* 32 (2009).
12. This is a condensed and updated version of Gianni Lo Schiavo, *State Aids and Credit Institutions in Europe: What Way Forward?*, 25 European Business Law Review 427 (2014).
13. Joaquín Almunia, *The Economic and Monetary Union, the euro and the financial crisis*, Speech 22 October 2012.

recovery and resolution regime for banks in distress were taken along the Treaty provisions. The Commission's decisions on compatible State aid under Article 107(3) TFEU included conditions and obligations imposing structural or behavioural measures to aided credit institutions in Europe.[14]

Following a first phase on State aid control[15] and without going into the details of such phase, the Commission adopted a second Banking Communication (the Banking Communication II) in July 2013.[16] This document, which already reflects the plan to establish a statutory regime for banking resolution and the EBU,[17] provides for stricter rules to the recovery and restructuring processes for banks receiving State aids than it did in the first phase of the financial crisis. Furthermore, it reinforces the burden-sharing requirements in light of the objective of undistorted competition and, more importantly, financial stability. In particular, the Commission has adopted a clear stance to the need to consider supranational financial stability as the overarching objective for crisis-related State aids. The Communication shows the need to:

> prevent major negative spill-over effects for the rest of the banking system which could flow from the failure of a credit institution as well as the need to ensure that the banking system as a whole continues to provide adequate lending to the real economy lies at the heart of the Commission's policy.[18]

In particular, it sets burden-sharing requirements in the form of own contribution by the beneficiary bank. In this sense, point 15 of the Communication clearly states that:

> aid should be limited to the minimum necessary and an appropriate own contribution to restructuring costs should be provided by the aid beneficiary. The bank and its capital holders should contribute to the restructuring as much as possible with their own resources. State support should be granted on terms which represent an adequate burden-sharing by those who invested in the bank.

In practice, this would mean, as provided in point 41, that:

> [a]dequate burden-sharing will normally entail, after losses are first absorbed by equity, contributions by hybrid capital holders and subordinated debt holders. Hybrid capital and subordinated debt holders must contribute to reducing the capital shortfall to the maximum extent.

At the time of writing, the Banking Communication is still applied by the Commission in assessing State aid measures. The ECJ has also had the chance to

14. See extensively European Commission, *The effects of temporary State aid rules adopted in the context of the financial and economic crisis* (2011) at http://ec.europa.eu/competition/publications/reports/working_paper_en.pdf (accessed 31 December 2016)
15. *See* Lo Schiavo, *supra* n. 12, 431.
16. European Commission, *Communication on the application from 1 August 2013, of State aid rules to support measures in favour of banks in the context of the financial crisis* (hereinafter 'Banking Communication II') [2013] OJ C/216.
17. *Ibid.*, para. 12.
18. *Ibid.*, para. 7.

pronounce itself on the nature of such Communication in the recent *Kotnik* judgment.[19] The preliminary reference in *Kotnik* was submitted to the ECJ in the context of State aid measures granted to Slovenian banks. National law had established burden-sharing measures 'transposing' the Banking Communication burden-sharing rules. Without entering into the details of the dispute, the ECJ has confirmed the strict stance of the Commission on State aids in the financial sector and the burden-sharing requirement provided in the Banking Communication. In particular, the burden-sharing measures are regarded as being measures that could lead the Commission to declare aid incompatible if the Member State decides not to apply such measures before granting the aid and takes the risk of granting incompatible State aid.[20] At the same time, the ECJ accepts the exception to the application of burden-sharing measures if implementing such measures to all subordinate debt would endanger financial stability.[21] Hence, it appears that the Commission shall carefully examine the degree of burden-sharing measures as provided in the Banking Communication.

The *Kotnik* judgment shows the essential role of the Commission in assessing the compatibility of State aids in the internal market as well as its strict(er) role in such assessment. Some general remarks can be made on the importance of State aid control for the rescuing and restructuring of banks in Europe, especially after *Kotnik*. First, the outbreak of the financial crisis has forced the Commission to adopt a special de facto legal framework to declare compatible state support measures to credit institutions. This development was founded on a more flexible interpretation to Article 107(3)(b) TFEU. The first phase of the financial crisis revealed extensive reliance on state support measures, while the more recent trends go in the direction of limiting State aids under a strict(er) Commission's control. Second, the Commission's policy on State aid has been guided by essential objectives or principles to declare the compatibility of State aid measures to banks. Over time, financial stability and burden-sharing have acquired an increasingly essential role in the assessment of State aid to banks. Third, the Banking Communication II aims to reduce reliance on State aid in the financial sector. This is shown by the reinforced degree of burden-sharing that is required and the imposition of *ex ante* stricter conditions before the granting of compatible State aids.

In sum, the policy adopted so far by the Commission goes in the direction of enforcing burden-sharing measures as a key normative instrument for the attainment of supranational financial stability in EU law and policy. This shows that the normative instrument of burden-sharing is somehow pre-ordinated to the normative instrument of rescue measures as developed in this book. While some remarks on State aids and the banking sector are provided *infra* whenever relevant to the banking recovery and resolution framework, the next part will move to the development of the regulatory reforms for bank resolution in Europe.

19. Case C-526/14 *Kotnik and Others*, ECLI:EU:C:2016:570.
20. *Ibid.*, para. 100.
21. *Ibid.*, 101.

§8.03 THE RECOVERY AND RESOLUTION OF CREDIT INSTITUTIONS: THE POST-FINANCIAL CRISIS REGULATORY SCENARIO[22]

This part looks at the key substantive features and recent reforms to create a supranational recovery and resolution framework (section [A]) prior to assessing the major institutional reform with the establishment of the SRM in participating Member States (section [B]).

[A] The Substantive Framework of EU Banking Recovery and Resolution: The BRRD

[1] The Path Towards the Adoption of a European Framework of Bank Recovery and Resolution

As argued earlier, it is well established that before the outbreak of the financial crisis no common European regulatory framework existed for the recovery and resolution for credit institutions and more generally for financial institutions. EU law did not regulate on resolution and winding-down of financial institutions.[23] After the outbreak of the financial crisis in Europe, the Commission issued a number of Communications proposing the creation of a new European architecture for the resolution of individual financial institutions and EU-based financial groups.[24] At the same time, the Commission launched a consultation on a new framework for recovery and resolution of financial institutions and published a Communication on EU Framework for Cross-border Crisis Management in the banking sector.[25] It emphasised the gaps and limits of the resolution regime for early intervention, bank resolution and insolvency framework and, accordingly, it proposed a wide-ranging reform.[26] Shortly after, the European Parliament published a resolution with recommendations to the Commission on cross-border crisis management in the banking sector in 2010. This document invited the Commission to propose a new regulatory regime for the resolution of banks to set 'a common minimum set of rules and ultimately a common resolution and insolvency law, applicable to all banking institutions operating in the Union'.[27] Subsequently, the Commission presented some proposals to introduce new European rules for the recovery and resolution of financial institutions. In 2010, a Commission Communication stressed that the ambitious EU regulatory reform is to ensure that:

---

22. Part of this section is a revised and updated version of Gianni Lo Schiavo, *The Development of a New Bank Resolution Regime in Europe: Fit for Purpose?*, 29 Journal of International Banking Law and Regulation 68 (2014).
23. *See* Hüpkes, Devos *supra* n. 6, 374.
24. *See* Emilios Avgouleas, *Governance of Global Financial Markets* 394 (Cambridge University Press 2012).
25. *See* European Commission, Communication, *An EU Framework for Cross-Border Crisis Management in the Banking Sector* COM(2009) 561 final.
26. *Ibid.*, 2–3.
27. European Parliament, *Resolution of 7 July 2010 with recommendations to the Commission on Cross-Border Crisis Management in the Banking Sector* (2010/2006(INI)).

> distressed institutions of any type and size, and in particular systematically important institutions, can be allowed to fail without risk to financial stability whilst avoiding costs for taxpayers.[28]

Subsequently, the Commission published a discussion paper on the bail-in instrument as a major tool in the context of resolution.[29] After a public consultation on resolution regimes, the Commission published the BRRD proposal in June 2012, which was eventually adopted in 2014.

[2] The BRRD: Definition, Scope and Resolution Authorities

The BRRD has been adopted in April 2014[30] after a legislative process of almost two years. The BRRD contains many technical provisions setting out the substantive powers of resolution that Member States should implement into national law as a minimum harmonisation approach. These will be analysed in a holistic manner.

The definition and scope of the resolution regime are the first important element to analyse. The expression 'resolution' is different from insolvency or bankruptcy procedure. 'Resolution' is a special regulatory proceeding for credit institutions in distress. It takes into account the special role of credit institutions by providing the means to deal with banking failure outside the ordinary bankruptcy legislation.[31] This excludes the situation whereby normal bankruptcy procedures are triggered leading to the immediate cessation of banking activities. However, the BRRD does not provide for a clear definition of what resolution is, but it specifies that resolution is different from normal insolvency proceedings.[32] The BRRD could have contained a general definition of what 'resolution' is.

The BRRD has a minimum harmonisation approach. Emphatically, it indicates that:

> Member States may adopt or maintain stricter or additional rules to those laid down in the Directive and in the delegated and implementing acts adopted on the basis of the Directive.[33]

---

28. European Commission, *An EU framework for crisis management in the financial sector*, COM(2010) 579.
29. European Commission, *Discussion paper on the debt write-down tool – bail-in* http://ec.europa.eu/internal_market/bank/docs/crisis-management/discussion_paper_bail_in_en.pdf (accessed 31 December 2016).
30. Directive 2014/59/EU of the European Parliament and of the Council of 15 May 2014 establishing a framework for the recovery and resolution of credit institutions and investment firms and amending Council Directive 82/891/EEC, and Directives 2001/24/EC, 2002/47/EC, 2004/25/EC, 2005/56/EC, 2007/36/EC, 2011/35/EU, 2012/30/EU and 2013/36/EU, and Regulations (EU) No 1093/2010 and (EU) No 648/2012, of the European Parliament and of the Council [2014] OJ L 173 (hereinafter 'BRRD').
31. *See* Seraina Grünewald, *The Resolution of Cross-Border Banking Crises in the European Union*, 13–15 (Kluwer 2014).
32. BRRD, Art. 2(1) number 49: normal insolvency proceedings are defined as 'proceedings which entail the partial or total divestment of a debtor and the appointment of a liquidator or an administrator normally applicable to institutions under national law and either specific to those institutions or generally applicable to any natural or legal person'.
33. *Ibid.*, Art. 1(2).

This paragraph was absent in the Commission proposal, and it strengthens the role of Member States in regulating resolution procedures. The minimum harmonisation approach is a welcome development as compared with the absence of a resolution regime in Member States. However, it may generate regulatory divergences among Member States, especially between those that participate in the SRM and those that do not.

Article 1(1) affirms that the BRRD lays down rules and procedures relating to the recovery and resolution of a number of entities. These rules apply not only to credit institutions, but also to financial institutions, financial holding companies, parent financial holding companies, branches of institutions established outside the Union according to the specific conditions of the BRRD.[34] Its scope is wide as it is not limited to SIFIs. This is because there is no certainty on which entities could create a systemic crisis, and a widespread failure of a number of smaller firms may cause devastating effects to the economy of a Member State.[35] In sum, the resolution regime applies to all covered institutions regardless of their size.

As regards the statutory institutions in charge of resolution, the BRRD provides that the Member States 'design' the resolution authorities.[36] So long as the resolution authorities are public administrative authorities, the Member States are free to designate the resolution authority in that Member States.[37] The BRRD envisages that the supervisory authorities or the central banks may also be entrusted with resolution tools, provided that a structural separation between the functions is in place.[38] In practice, in most Member States the competent supervisory authority has been entrusted also with resolution powers. However, as shown below, at the European level the entrustment to the competent resolution authority has been given to the SRB and not to the ECB as the competent supervisory authority.

[3] Prevention, Recovery and Early Intervention

Crisis prevention is one of the main aspects that the BRRD intends to address by avoiding the recourse to resolution. Substantive rules in the BRRD are intended to recover financial institutions and to prepare the earliest phase of resolution at the preventive stage. Furthermore, before resolution is triggered, early intervention measures may apply. In view of avoiding the trigger of resolution, BRRD Title II requires Member States to ensure that each institution draws up and maintain recovery and

34. *Ibid.*, Art. 1(2) and Art. 2(1).
35. Proposal for a Directive of the European Parliament and of the Council establishing a framework for the recovery and resolution of credit institutions and investment firms and amending Council Directives 77/91/EEC and 82/891/EC, Directives 2001/24/EC, 2002/47/EC, 2004/25/EC, 2005/56/EC, 2007/36/EC and 2011/35/EC and Regulation (EU) No 1093/2010 COM/2012/028, Explanatory Memorandum 4.3.
36. BRRD, Art. 3(1).
37. BRRD, Art. 3(2).
38. BRRD, Art. 3(3).

resolution plans. These are two essential documents ensuring that institutions within the scope of the BRRD have in place a robust recovery and resolution planning. Competent authorities are entrusted to assess recovery and resolution plans.

Recovery and resolution planning are expected to significantly improve supervision, especially with regard to systemically important institutions and groups.[39] The recovery plans are prepared by the financial institutions to set out how to restore their financial position in case of a significant deterioration of the latter. These plans are then submitted to the financial institution's relevant supervisor. First, competent authorities are required to evaluate whether the implementation of the arrangements is reasonably likely to maintain or restore the viability of the institution and the financial position of the institution.[40] Second, competent authority need to assess whether the plan and the specific options envisaged in the said plan are likely to be implemented quickly and effectively in case of financial stress while avoiding any significant adverse effect in the financial system.[41] In case the recovery plan is not submitted or it does not adequately respect the established requirements, already at this stage, the competent authority may require the institution to reduce its risk profile, enable recapitalisation measures, change institution's strategy and structure, review the funding strategy and make changes to the governance structure.[42]

Resolution authorities shall prepare also resolution plans for each institution with a view to provide the resolution actions that the resolution authority may take, in particular the resolution tools and powers.[43] Article 9 indicates the elements of the resolution plans. This article makes clear that the resolution plan shall demonstrate, among others, how critical functions and core business activities could be separated from other functions.

As part of their tasks, resolution authorities shall assess the extent to which the institutions are 'resolvable'. This is made by an assessment determining how it is feasible and credible that the resolution authority can either liquidate the institution under normal insolvency proceedings or resolve it by applying the resolution tools and powers.[44] It could be that the assessment of 'resolvability' shows that there are potential impediments for the institutions. In case the measures proposed by the institution do not reduce[45] or remove its resolvability, the competent authority will have, among others, certain powers such as limit exposures, request additional information, divest specific assets, limit or cease specific activities.[46]

Furthermore, the BRRD introduces early intervention measures under Title III. The objective of early intervention is to remedy the situation before triggering the

39. Avgouleas, *supra* n. 24, 425.
40. BRRD, Art. 6.
41. *Ibid.*
42. *Ibid.*
43. *Ibid.*, Art. 9.
44. *Ibid.*, Art. 13.
45. These are not mandatory as indicated under BRRD, Recital 10.
46. BRRD, Art. 14(4).

resolution of the institution.[47] Early intervention powers should be taken when the institution does not meet or is likely to breach the prudential requirements provided in the CRR/CRD.[48] The competent supervisory authorities shall be empowered to exercise the prerogatives indicated under Article 104 CRR and those set out in Article 23(1) BRRD.

Among other early intervention powers, the management body can be required to implement the measures indicated in the recovery plan; examine the problem situation, identify the measures to overcome the problem and draw up an action plan to resolve the problem; convene shareholders' meetings; remove and replace board members and managing directors; draw up debt restructuring plans. If these early intervention measures are insufficient, the BRRD allows the competent authorities to appoint a temporary administrator. This appointment is possible if the removal of the senior management and management body is insufficient to remedy the situation.[49] The special manager has all the powers of the management of the institution and shall take all necessary measures to promote solutions to address the financial situation. However, the special manager has some limitations on his/her power and temporal limits. Furthermore, he/she cannot override the shareholder rights under EU and national law[50] and the appointment cannot last more than one year.[51]

[4] Objectives, Conditions and Principles Governing Resolution

While planning and early intervention measures aim to prevent resolution from taking place, the case may be that the institution(s) may be resolved. The BRRD sets out a new European framework for the resolution of financial institutions with resolution tools conferred on resolution authorities. It is essential to outline the conditions, principles and conditions of resolution.

It is first essential to determine what resolution means. Resolution can be defined as the restructuring of one or more financial institutions with the resolution tools implemented under the BRRD with the aim to ensure the continuity of critical functions, to avoid adverse impact on financial stability, to minimise reliance on public funds, to protect depositors and to protect client funds and client assets.[52] It appears that what identifies resolution is the use of statutory measures to ensure the continuity of function of the institution. Resolution has the main objectives:

(a) to ensure the continuity of critical functions;

---

47. *Ibid.*, Recital 23.
48. *Ibid.*, Art. 27. EBA has adopted guidelines determining further the conditions for early intervention measures: EBA, *Guidelines on triggers for use of early intervention measures pursuant to Article 27(4) of Directive 2014/59/EU* EBA/GL/2015/03 (2015) http://www.eba.europa.eu/documents/10180/1151520/EBA-GL-2015-03_EN + Guidelines + on + early + intervention + measures.pdf/9d796302-bbea-4869-bd2c-642d3d817966 (accessed 31 December 2016).
49. BRRD, Art. 29.
50. *Ibid.*, Art. 29(7).
51. *Ibid.*, Art. 29(8).
52. *See* BRRD, Art. 31.

(b) to avoid a significant adverse effect on the financial system, in particular by preventing contagion, including to market infrastructures, and by maintaining market discipline;
(c) to protect public funds by minimising reliance on extraordinary public financial support;
(d) to protect depositors covered by Directive 2014/49/EU and investors covered by Directive 97/9/EC;
(e) to protect client funds and client assets.[53]

The BRRD indicates that the objectives of resolution are of equal importance and resolution authorities 'need to balance them as appropriate to the nature and circumstances of each case'.[54] Arguably, it does not appear possible that all these objectives may be treated at the same level, but a certain level of prioritisation will take place in practice.

Article 32 of the BRRD contains the fundamental provision to determine whether an institution needs to be resolved. As already provided in the Commission proposal, there are three cumulative conditions to put an institution under resolution: (a) that the institution is failing or likely to fail; (b) that there are no other possible alternatives, which would prevent the failure of the institution within a reasonable timeframe; (c) that a resolution action is necessary under the public interest. Condition (a) is the key prudential condition as it is necessary to identify the situation of failure (or likeliness to failure) in order to apply resolution. Thus, the failing or the likeliness to fail is defined under Article 32(4) of the BRRD as when one or more of the circumstances indicated below are fulfilled. These are: (a) that the institution breaches or is likely to breach the requirements for the authorisation and licensing of its activity; (b) that the assets are or will be less than the liabilities; (c) that the institution is or will be unable to pay its debts or other liabilities; (d) that extraordinary public financial support is required.[55] Public interest under condition (c) is defined as a situation where a resolution action achieves and is proportionate to one or more of the resolution objectives, while the winding up of the institution pursuant to normal insolvency proceedings would not meet the same resolution objectives.[56]

The BRRD conditions to initiate resolution show that the competent authority has much discretion in assessing whether an institution shall be resolved or be subject to other measures. This in particular is the case of the second and third criteria for resolution. At the same time, the formulation of the resolution conditions may generate regulatory competition between competent authorities and increase legal

53. BRRD, Art. 31(2).
54. *Ibid.*, Art. 31(3).
55. *See* further EBA, *Guidelines on the interpretation of the different circumstances when an institution shall be considered as failing or likely to fail under Article 32(6) of Directive 2014/59/EU* EBA/GL/2015/07 (2015) http://www.eba.europa.eu/documents/10180/1156219/EBA-GL-2015-07_EN_GL + on + failing + or + likely + to + fail.pdf/9c8ac238-4882-4a08-a940-7bc6d76397b6 (last accessed 31 December 2016).
56. *Ibid.*, Art. 32(3).

uncertainties among market operators as to whether resolution will apply in the specific case.[57] Finally, Member States may still give extraordinary public support under Article 32(4)(d) BRRD.

Article 34 of the BRRD contains general principles governing resolution. These are that:

(a) the shareholders of the institution under resolution bear first losses;
(b) creditors of the institution under resolution bear losses after the shareholders in accordance with the order of priority of their claims under normal insolvency proceedings, save as expressly provided otherwise in [the BRRD];
(c) management body and senior management of the institution under resolution are replaced, except in those cases when the retention of the management body and senior management, in whole or in part, as appropriate to the circumstances, is considered to be necessary for the achievement of the resolution objectives;
(d) management body and senior management of the institution under resolution shall provide all necessary assistance for the achievement of the resolution objectives;
(e) natural and legal persons are made liable, subject to Member State law, under civil or criminal law for their responsibility for the failure of the institution;
(f) except where otherwise provided in [the BRRD], creditors of the same class are treated in an equitable manner;
(g) no creditor shall incur greater losses than would have been incurred if the institution or entity (...) had been wound up under normal insolvency proceedings (...);
(h) covered deposits are fully protected; and
(i) resolution action is taken in accordance with the safeguards in [the BRRD].

Letters (a) and (b) are intended to indicate rules regarding the order of losses that resolution tools will entail. This clarifies that shareholders and creditors will be involved when resolution powers are exercised. Letter (c) involves a change in the management bodies of the institution under resolution. This means that those involved in the management activity of the institution under resolution will be excluded from the activities of management of the institution under resolution. Letter (g) refers to the 'no creditor worse off principle' which indicates that if a proper evaluation of bank assets and liabilities establishes a difference between the treatment that shareholders and creditors are actually afforded and the treatment they would have received under normal insolvency proceedings, they are entitled to compensation.[58] Letter (h)

57. Grünewald, *supra* n. 31, 89.
58. *See* BRRD, Recital 50. On this principle, *see further* Karl-Philipp Wojcik, *Bail in the Banking Union*, 53 Common Market Law Review 120 (2016).

establishes that covered deposits shall be fully protected. This is to guarantee that covered deposits are always protected whenever resolution takes place. DGS ensure that covered deposits are protected.[59]

[5] Resolution Tools

Resolution tools are provided in Articles 37–58 of the BRRD. These are analysed from the softer to the harder tool. The sale of business is aimed to achieve an efficient and easy transfer of the shares, the assets, the rights or the liabilities to a purchaser.[60] This means that resolution authorities have the power to sell the business without requesting the consent of the shareholders, the institution or other third parties. The transfer needs to be made on commercial terms with due attention to the circumstances of the case.[61] Resolution authorities shall find ways to comply with commercial conditions for the sale. Procedural requirements establish that the sale of business shall be transparent, fair and effective, and it shall aim to maximise the sale price for the instruments involved.[62] In case the sale of business to a private party is not possible, resolution authorities may make use of the bridge institution tool.

The bridge institution tool consists in the set-up of a legal entity to which shares, instrument of ownership, assets, rights or liabilities are transferred.[63] The bridge institution is wholly or partially owned by public authorities and is created for the purpose of receiving and holding the shares or the instruments, or the assets, rights and liabilities.[64] The resolution authority exercises considerable powers on the bridge institution. In particular, it appoints the bridge institution's board of director. The main objective of the bridge institution is to sell its business to a private sector buyer when market conditions are appropriate.[65]

The asset separation tool aims to transfer assets, rights and liabilities to an asset management vehicle, which is a legal entity wholly owned by public authorities.[66] This is a special resolution tool which aims at transferring assets, rights or liabilities only when normal insolvency procedures would have adverse effects on the market. It can be used only in conjunction with other resolution tools.[67]

59. For discussions on deposit guarantee schemes and deposit insurance, *see* Chapter 6 section §6.03[C][2] and §6.04[B].
60. BRRD, Art. 38(1).
61. *Ibid.*, Art. 38(3).
62. *Ibid.*, Art. 39.
63. *Ibid.*, Art. 40(1).
64. *Ibid.*, Art. 40(2).
65. *Ibid.*, Art. 40(5).
66. *Ibid.*, Art. 42(1) and (2) according to which that shareholders and creditors of the failing institution shall suffer appropriate losses and bear an appropriate part of those costs arising from the failure of the institution.
67. *Ibid.*, Art. 42(4).

The bail-in instrument is the most intrusive and important tool under the new European resolution regime.[68] The BRRD puts a great emphasis on the role of the bail-in tool for an appropriate resolution of credit institutions. Article 2 defines bail-in as:

> the mechanism for effecting the exercise by a resolution authority of the write-down and conversion powers in relation to liabilities of an institution under resolution.

The bail-in is an enforcement mechanism for shareholders and private sector creditors of the costs of a bank rescue/recapitalisation. Its objective is to ensure that 'shareholders and creditors of the failing institution suffer appropriate losses and bear an appropriate part of those costs arising from the failure of the institution'.[69] According to the Commission, bail-in shall serve as an instrument to resolve large and complex financial institutions when other resolution tools are not sufficient.[70] In other words, the bail-in instrument 'punishes' shareholders, creditors, bondholders and uncovered depositors for the losses that the institution suffers by their conversion into equity or their reduction and avoids bailouts funded by taxpayers. Article 44 of the BRRD specifies the scope of application of the bail-in tool. It provides that the bail-in applies to all liabilities of an institution save as the general exclusions contained under Article 44(2). Furthermore, the Directive contains other exceptions that apply in exceptional circumstances by the resolution authority.[71]

The BRRD requires some minimum conditions to trigger the bail-in tool. The resolution authority may decide whether to apply the bail-in tool or not. The BRRD provides a minimum requirement condition for the exercise of the bail-in tool. This is set by the resolution authorities and shall provide that the institutions maintain a sufficient aggregate amount of own funds and eligible liabilities.[72] The implementation of the bail-in tool requires that the resolution authorities establish the aggregate amount by which eligible liabilities must be written down.[73] This assessment will allow for the establishment of the amount of eligible liabilities that need to be written down or converted.[74] Most importantly, Article 48 contains the hierarchy in the exercise of the bail-in tool. CET1[75] instruments are reduced first, then, if, and only if, the CET1 is not sufficient, AT1 instruments are reduced. Further, the other aggregates that should

---

68. On the bail-in instrument, *see further* Wojcik, *supra* n. 58, 120; Emilios Avgouleas, Charles Goodhart, *Critical Reflections on Bank Bail-ins*, 2 Journal of Financial Regulation 3 (2015); and Clifford Chance, *Legal Aspects of Bank Bail-ins* (2011) at http://www.cliffordchance.com/publicationviews/publications/2011/05/legal_aspects_ofbankbail-ins.htm (accessed 31 December 2016).
69. BRRD, Recital 44.
70. European Commission, Communication on *An EU framework for crisis management in the financial sector*, 5.
71. BRRD, Art. 44(3).
72. BRRD, Art. 45.
73. BRRD, Art. 46(1).
74. BRRD, Art. 48(2).
75. *See* Chapter 6 section §6.03[C][1] for an explanation of CET1, Additional Tier 1 and Tier 2.

be reduced are in turn and one following the other AT1,Tier 2, and senior eligible debt.[76]

Article 44(2) BRRD provides for a list of liabilities that are mandatorily excluded from the bail-in tool. This list includes covered deposits, secured liabilities, any liability arising from the holding by the bank of client assets or by virtue of a fiduciary relationship, liabilities to other banks, liabilities with a remaining maturity of less than seven days towards securities settlement and clearing systems and liabilities towards employees (except variable remuneration components of material risk takers), towards commercial or trade creditors for critical operations of the bank, towards tax and security authorities and towards DGSs. Resolution authorities have discretion as to fully or partially exclude other liabilities. The exercise of such discretionary exclusion of liabilities from the scope of the bail-in tool is limited to exceptional circumstances and is subject to specific conditions.[77]

To ensure that sufficient resources are present to allow a workable bail-in, the BRRD establishes that institutions shall meet the minimum requirement for own funds and eligible liabilities. This allows that 'losses could be absorbed and the Common Equity Tier 1 ratio of the bank could be restored at a level necessary to enable it to continue to comply with the conditions for authorization ...'.[78] Determining an appropriate level of MREL and the interactions between resolution objectives and prudential requirements established in the CRR/CRD are essential aspects for a workable and effective bail-in instrument.[79] At present, the Commission has adopted a delegated Regulation specifying the criteria related to the methodology to set the MREL and consultations are ongoing between the resolution and the supervisory authority.[80]

Finally, the BRRD provides also that, in critical systemic crises, the ministry or the government may make use of government stabilisation tools i.e. state aids including the use of public money to support the resolution of the institution.[81] The tools are subject to strict conditions[82] and shall be seen as 'a last resort after having assessed and exploited the other resolution tools to the maximum extent practicable whilst maintaining financial stability'.[83]

76. BRRD, Art. 48(1).
77. BRRD, Art. 44(3).
78. BRRD, Art. 45(6).
79. Wojcik, *supra* n. 58, 114–115.
80. Commission, Delegated Regulation C(2016)2976 2016 http://ec.europa.eu/finance/bank/docs/crisis-management/160523-delegated-regulation_en.pdf (accessed 31 December 2016).
81. *See* BRRD, Art. 56.
82. *See* BRRD, Art. 37(10). The conditions are that (a) 8% of total liabilities including own funds of the institution under resolution, has been made by the shareholders and the holders of other instruments of ownership, the holders of relevant capital instruments and other eligible liabilities through write down, conversion or otherwise; (b) the Commission has approved their use under the State aid framework.
83. BRRD, Art. 56(3).

[6] Financing Arrangements

The BRRD sets out also national financing arrangements that together form a European System of Financing Arrangements.[84] The objective of such financing arrangements is to ensure the effective application of the resolution tools and powers by the resolution authorities. The creation of financing arrangements aims to let the banking sector pay the costs of resolving ailing banks. Article 101 of the BRRD contains an exhaustive list of authorised uses of financing arrangements, avoiding thus the risks of an inappropriate use of the funds. Even if the financing arrangements are publicly managed, the financial means originate exclusively from contributions paid by the banks.[85] Each national financing arrangement needs to attain a target level of at least 1 % of covered deposits of all banks authorised in the relevant territory by 2024.[86] Should national financing arrangements be insufficient in a Member State, the BRRD allows borrowing between national financial arrangements.[87]

Having completed the assessment of the main substantive elements of the BRRD, the following section looks at the key institutional aspects regarding the institutional framework on banking regulation, namely the SRM.

[B] The Institutional Framework of EU Banking Resolution: The SRM as a New Supranational Recovery and Resolution Framework

This part examines the SRM Regulation and the intergovernmental agreement regarding resolution. The SRM constitutes the second pillar of the EBU and establishes a supranational framework for the resolution of banks by means of an EU regulation, which is directly applicable EU law. It shall be made clear that the SRM Regulation needs to be read in close relationship with the BRRD, as the latter is the backbone of the SRM Regulation. This is important as the BRRD and the SRM are interlinked with each other. The BRRD provides for the substantive rules on resolution, while the SRM mirrors such rules, but establishes also the institutional framework for banking resolution in participating Member States, empowers the SRB to exercise its resolution tasks and creates a Single Resolution Fund (SRF). The most important difference between the BRRD and the SRM Regulation is that while the BRRD applies to all the twenty-eight Member States, the SRM Regulation applies only to participating Member States to the SSM that – at present – correspond to the euro area Member States.

84. BRRD, Arts 99–100.
85. *See* Commission Delegated Regulation (EU) 2015/63 of 21 October 2014 supplementing Directive 2014/59/EU of the European Parliament and of the Council with regard to *ex ante* contributions to resolution financing arrangements, O.J. 2014, L 11/44.
86. BRRD, Art. 102(1).
87. *Ibid.*, Art. 106.

[1] The Adoption of the SRM Regulation and of the Intergovernmental Agreement on the Resolution Fund

The European Council Conclusions of June 2012 promoted the creation of a single mechanism for the resolution of credit institutions. The Communication backed the European Council in the Communication on 'a Roadmap towards a Banking Union'.[88] The Commission stated that an SRM 'would govern the resolution of banks and coordinate in particular the application of resolution tools to banks within the banking union'.[89] In December 2012, the Four President Report stressed that an integrated financial framework will require the establishment of the SRM for the euro area. This would complement the set-up of the SSM as the SRM would be based on 'robust governance arrangements, including adequate provisions on independence and accountability, as well as an effective common backstop'.[90]

EU Regulation 806/2014,[91] the SRM Regulation, is the main legal instrument for the establishment and functioning of the SRM. This Regulation was adopted in April 2014 by the European legislators under the legal basis of Article 114 TFEU. In parallel to the adoption of the SRM Regulation, Member States in the Council resorted to the adoption of an Intergovernmental Agreement outside the EU legal framework.[92] This Agreement, concluded on 21 May 2014 between the EU Member States with the exception of the UK and Sweden, sets out, among others, the transfer of contributions raised at national level in accordance with the BRRD and the SRM Regulation to national compartments related to the progressive development of the SRF.

[2] Scope and Division of Tasks in the SRM

The first articles of the SRM Regulation provide for the scope of application of the SRM. The SRM Regulation identifies as a subject matter of the mechanism 'uniform rules and a uniform procedure for the resolution of credit institutions'. Article 1 of the SRM Regulation stresses that uniform rules will be applied by the Council, the SRB and the national resolution authorities (NRAs) of the participating Member States.[93] The resolution mechanism will be supported by the SRF that will be created upon the entry into force of the Intergovernmental Agreement among the participating Member States

88. Commission, *A Roadmap towards a Banking Union* COM(2012)510, section 3.2.
89. *Ibid.*
90. Four Presidents' Report, 5 December 2012, 7 at http://www.consilium.europa.eu/uedocs/cms_Data/docs/pressdata/en/ec/134069.pdf (last accessed 31 December 2016).
91. Regulation (EU) No 806/2014 of the European Parliament and of the Council of 15 July 2014 establishing uniform rules and a uniform procedure for the resolution of credit institutions and certain investment firms in the framework of a Single Resolution Mechanism and a Single Resolution Fund and amending Regulation (EU) No 1093/2010 [2014] OJ L 225.
92. Agreement on the Transfer and Mutualisation of Contributions to the Single Resolution Fund, available at http://register.consilium.europa.eu/content/out?lang=EN&typ=ENTRY&i=SMPL&DOC_ID=ST%208457%202014%20COR%201 (accessed 31 December 2016).
93. *Ibid.*, Art. 1.

to transfer the funds raised at national level.[94] The SRM applies to (a) credit institutions established in participating Member States; (b) parent undertakings established in one of the participating Member States, including financial holding companies and mixed financial holding companies; (c) investment firms and financial institutions established in participating Member States when they are covered by the consolidated supervision of the parent undertaking. Hence, the SRM applies to participating Member States of the SSM.[95] Similarly to the SSM, there may also be the conclusion of a close cooperation agreement with non-euro area Member States that will give the status of participating Member State to the one joining close cooperation.[96]

The SRM division of tasks reflects the differentiation between significant and less significant entities under the SSM.[97] Article 7 of the SRM Regulation provides for an explicit division of tasks between the SRB as the new EU agency responsible for banking resolution and the NRAs. The former is responsible to draw up the resolution plans and to adopt all schemes related to the possible resolution of significant credit institutions in compliance with the SSM Regulation, of those in relation to which the ECB is the competent supervisor as well as of other cross-border groups.[98] Conversely, Article 7(3) of the SRM Regulation attributes the resolution planning and functions of the other institutions to the NRAs. These are responsible for executing bank resolution schemes under the SRB's instructions.[99] Nonetheless, if resolution action requires the use of the SRF, then the SRB is responsible to conduct the resolution regardless of the significance of the credit institutions.[100] This is an important exception that confers resolution powers to the SRB also for 'less significant' or non-cross border entities under the SRM.

[3] The Single Resolution Board

As mentioned above, the SRM Regulation establishes a new agency: the SRB. The SRB is an EU agency with legal personality[101] with its seat in Brussels.[102] The SRB is composed of an Executive Director (the chair), four full-time members and a member appointed by each Member State representing the NRAs.[103] The Commission and the ECB are permanent observers in plenary and executive sessions. The SRB convenes in plenary and executive sessions.[104] Among other functions, the plenary sessions comprise the power to adopt the annual work programme, the annual budget and

94. *Ibid.*
95. *Ibid.*, Art. 4.
96. *See* SSM Regulation, Arts 2 and 7.
97. Art. 4 of the SRM Regulation refers to the distinction between 'significant' and 'less significant' credit institutions in Regulation 1024/2013.
98. It shall be noted that in the SSM not all cross-border supervised groups are directly supervised by the ECB as they may not meet the 'significance' criteria.
99. SRM Regulation, Art. 28.
100. SRM Regulation, Art. 7(3) second sentence.
101. *Ibid.*, Art. 42.
102. *Ibid.*, Art. 48.
103. *Ibid.*, Art. 43.
104. *Ibid.*, Art. 49.

resolution schemes.[105] Importantly, the plenary session is convened when the action to be taken requires more than EUR 5 billion in capital or twice that amount in terms of liquidity from the SRF. The plenary session shall also evaluate the application of resolution tools, including the use of the SRF, in case EUR 5 billion or more have been used throughout the calendar year. Moreover, the plenary session is convened to decide the necessity to raise extraordinary *ex post* contributions, borrowing of the SRF and financing arrangements in case the resolution of a group with entities in participating and non-participating Member States is above the EUR 5 billion threshold. Conversely, the executive session takes all decisions to implement the SRM Regulation.[106] Importantly, the executive session is represented only by the responsible NRAs. The executive session takes specific decisions relating to a single credit institutions or a banking group. This is a key difference with the supervisory board of the ECB in the SSM.

Article 51 of the SRM Regulation regulates the decision-making of the SRB. Both in cases of a deliberation on an individual entity or on a cross-border group, the SRB in executive session requires consensus among the SRB's members. If this is not possible, then the SRM Regulation provides that the SRB members shall take decision by a simple majority. Similarly, decisions in the executive session are to be taken by consensus, but if this is not possible, the Chair and the executive members take decision by simple majority. No member has a veto power.

[4] The Supranational Resolution Procedure in the SRM

The resolution procedure under the SRM Regulation is set out in Article 18 of the SRM Regulation. This is the most important provision on the decision-making process in the SRM. First, the ECB or the national supervisory authority signals when a credit institution or group in a participating Member States is failing or likely to fail. This first appraisal can also come by the SRB that, under particular conditions, can trigger the process on its own initiative. Second, the SRB determines that there is no reasonable prospect of a timely private sector rescue and that a resolution action is in the public interest. Third, the SRB, with the support of the relevant NRAs, prepares and adopts the resolution scheme. The adoption of a resolution scheme somehow involves a margin of discretion. The arrangement finally adopted in Article 18 is that the assessment of discretion is attributed to the Commission's responsibility. However, the Commission simply endorses the resolution scheme or may object to its discretionary aspects. In addition, the Council has a right to object, but only on a proposal from the Commission and on a limited number of matters (the existence of a public interest or a material modification of the amount of SRF to be used in a specific resolution action). The Commission and the Council have only twenty-four hours from adoption of the resolution scheme by the SRB in which they can object. The procedure should take place within twenty-four hours or, at most, thirty-two hours (eight hours being the

105. *Ibid.*, Art. 50.
106. *See ibid.*, Art. 53.

period for the SRB to modify the scheme in response to Commission or Council objections). The Commission is empowered to adopt delegated acts to further specify the criteria or conditions to be taken by the SRB in the exercise of its tasks.[107] The SRM Regulation expressly limits the power of intervention of the Council and the SRB on the impact over Member States' budgetary sovereignty. It states that neither the SRB nor the Council can require participating Member States to provide extraordinary financial support or impinge on budgetary or fiscal responsibilities.[108]

[5] Financial Arrangements Within the SRM

In the context of the SRM, there are certain financial arrangements to fund resolution. The SRF is the essential, but not the exclusive financial arrangement. The creation of the SRF is mandated by the need to:

> ensure a uniform administrative practice in the financing of resolution and to avoid the creation of obstacles for the exercise of fundamental freedoms or the distortion of competition in the internal market due to divergent national practices.[109]

This means that the SRF is a European fund to assist the competent resolution authority in exercising resolution tools. This will ensure the availability of medium-term funding support while a credit institution is being restructured. The SRF will take over national resolution financing arrangements and will constitute the main financing arrangement to deal with resolution expenses within the SRM once it is fully mutualised. The target level for the SRF is indicated as at least 1% of the amount of deposits of all credit institutions authorised in the participating Member States.[110] The resources are taken directly by covered entities. The individual contribution to create the SRF shall not exceed 12.5% of the target level each year.[111] The calculation of the contribution of each individual institutions consists of a flat contribution based on the institution's pro rata share of the liabilities of all institutions in the participating Member States and a risk-adjusted contribution based on the institution's own risk profile.[112] The target level will be achieved in a period no longer than eight years since the entry into force of the provision on the constitution of the SRF, hence by 2024.[113] Upon completion of the *ex ante* contributions, the SRF will reach EUR 55 billion once full mutualisation takes place. Similarly to the financing arrangements provided in the BRRD, the SRF can be used for a range of purposes, including providing guarantees, making loans, purchasing assets and providing compensation to shareholders or creditors. It can be used to provide capital to a bridge bank or asset management

107. SRM Regulation, Art. 93.
108. *Ibid.*, Art. 6(6).
109. *Ibid.*, Recital 19.
110. *Ibid.*, Art. 69.
111. *Ibid.*, Art. 70.
112. *Ibid.*
113. *Ibid.*, Art. 77.

vehicle, but it must not be used directly to absorb the losses of a failing institution or for direct recapitalisation.[114]

At the same time, extraordinary *ex post* contributions can be raised to cover shortfalls and the SRB may borrow or arrange other means of support to increase the funding available to the SRF.[115] Finally, alternative funding means may be borrowings or other forms of support from institutions, financial institutions or other third parties in case the amount raised with *ex ante, ex post* contributions and voluntary arrangements are not sufficient.[116] To increase the financing arrangements in the SRM, in December 2015, the SRM Member States agreed on a Loan Facility Agreement with the SRB, providing national credit lines to the SRB to support the national compartments of the Fund in case of possible funding shortfalls in that compartment following resolution cases of banks during the transition period.[117]

The SRF is aimed to provide the resolution financing within the SRM. As indicated above, the Council involved in the adoption of the SRM framed a separate intergovernmental agreement. The main objective of the intergovernmental agreement is to regulate the way in which the establishment of national compartments will be progressively mutualised over a transitional period of eight years to give full financial capacity to the SRF. The use of the compartments is subject to a progressive mutualisation with a view to make it possible for the SRF to conduct effective operations and functioning after eight years. The SRF will be funded by national compartments to be merged over time during the transitional period. These are national financing structures that collect *ex ante* contributions from covered entities each year.[118] The functioning of the compartments is to provide the collection of national resources for financing arrangements before the SRF is fully capitalised.

This concludes the assessment of the main provisions of the BRRD and the SRM. The next section evaluates the recovery and resolution framework established in Europe.

§8.04 THE NEW EUROPEAN RECOVERY AND RESOLUTION FRAMEWORK: DEVELOPMENTS AND CHALLENGES TO ACHIEVE SUPRANATIONAL FINANCIAL STABILITY IN EU LAW AND POLICY

This third part looks at some critical issues in the creation of a new recovery and resolution framework in Europe in light of the attainment of supranational financial stability in EU law and policy as developed in this book. The new EU framework opens up a number of remarks, which cannot fully be addressed in this section. Hence, the purpose is to provide reflections on the most contentious aspects related to the use of the normative instruments of supranational regulation, burden-sharing and rescue

114. *Ibid.*, Art. 76.
115. *Ibid.*, Art. 71.
116. *Ibid.*, Art. 73.
117. SRB Press Release, December 2015 https://srb.europa.eu/sites/srbsite/files/20151208-press-release_en.pdf (accessed 31 December 2016).
118. SRM Regulation, Art. 5.

measures to attain supranational financial stability. First, this part looks at the use of Article 114 TFEU to establish the SRM and to adopt the BRRD (section [A]). Second, it analyses the establishment of a supranational framework for the conduct of resolution of significant credit institutions (section [B]). Then, it assesses the extent of resolution powers provided in the BRRD and the SRM Regulation and the financing arrangements in the SRM. (section [C]).

[A] Use of the Legal Basis to Establish Recovery and Resolution Frameworks in Europe: Is Article 114 TFEU the Correct Legal Basis?

The BRRD and the SRM establish tasks and powers on the recovery and resolution of credit institutions and financial firms in Europe. Both the SRM institutional framework and the BRRD substantive framework are legitimate measures for the internal market in order to pursue supranational financial stability as a foundational objective in EU law and policy. However, the development of a common system of resolution procedures in Europe faces a basic problem: the choice of the appropriate legal basis in EU law and policy.

The conferral of resolution tasks and powers required a sound and effective legal basis for such purposes. Differently from the SSM,[119] the legal basis used to adopt the BRRD and to create the SRM was Article 114 TFEU. This Treaty provision allows for the adoption of measures for the approximation of the provisions laid down by law, regulation or administrative action in Member States that have as their object the establishment and functioning of the internal market. However, it may be questioned whether the legal basis of Article 114 TFEU is sufficiently broad to establish a fully fledged substantial and institutional resolution regime.[120]

Banking crisis management has been indicated as the main reason for further harmonisation of the internal market and, thus, for the use of Article 114 TFEU. The use of Article 114 TFEU could be questioned as its use may be seen as overcoming the legal limitations contained in Article 114 TFEU. While the use of Article 114 TFEU is accepted when a measure has the objective of the establishment and functioning of the internal market, it could be questioned whether this Treaty provision has sufficient grounds to establish a pan-European or pan-euro area system for banking crisis management.[121] The ECJ has favoured a wide interpretation on the use of Article 114 TFEU. Recently, the ECJ held in the *ESMA* case that Article 114 TFEU gives grounds to attribute wide powers to EU agencies – in the specific case to ESMA to prohibit short selling under specific conditions. The expression 'measure for the approximation' is broad enough to include also measures adopted by EU agencies in the context of

119. *See* Chapter 7 section §7.04[A] on the use of Article 127(6) TFEU to establish the SSM.
120. *See* George Zavvos & Stella Kaltsouni, *The Single Resolution Mechanism in the European Banking Union: Legal Foundation, Governance Structure and Financing*, in Matthias Haentjens & Bob Wessels (eds), *Research Handbook on Crisis Management in the Banking Sector*, 123 (Edward Elgar 2015).
121. The debate on the use of Art. 114 TFEU was already framed in previous Chapters: *see* Chapter 6 section §6.03[B].

banking regulation and supervision. Furthermore, the ECJ held that the measure assessed in the *ESMA* case reduces the obstacles to the proper functioning of the internal market.[122] Therefore, the ECJ concluded that the European legislator enjoys a certain level of discretion in adopting measures to reduce obstacles to the internal market, such as the one scrutinised in the ESMA case. This raises the questions of whether the BRRD and the SRM respect this interpretation.

As regards the BRRD, the choice of Article 114 TFEU for the resolution of credit institutions is compliant with the scope of Article 114 TFEU as it generally improves the functioning of the internal market by creating common resolution powers in all Member States as regards resolution procedures. This is an important point as the BRRD provides a minimum harmonisation framework for the creation of a European-wide system of resolution to be implemented into national law. This is in line with the purpose of harmonising the internal market in the banking field. The scope of Article 114 TFEU is respected, and its use reveals that the attempt to harmonise resolution substantive rules aims to crisis prevention and crisis management under the normative framework of supranational financial stability in Europe.[123] In this sense, the use of supranational regulation is a normative instrument for supranational financial stability as developed in this book. Therefore, the use of Article 114 TFEU fills the gap in dealing with banking resolution from a regulatory point of view. Its use shows that a resolution regime can be well established to harmonise the internal market. This is justified also by the need to move from the unconventional use of the de facto recovery and resolution with an assessment on the compatibility of State aid under Article 107(3) TFEU to a new harmonised regulatory regime to deal with banking recovery and resolution. In the context of the normative instrument of supranational regulation by way of positive harmonisation it is argued that the use of Article 114 TFEU for the adoption of the BRRD attains supranational financial stability in EU law and policy.

As regards the SRM, there are a number of arguments in favour of the use of Article 114 TFEU to establish a supranational institutional framework for banking resolution. First, the proper functioning of the single market is highly dependent on the level of integration of Member States that share the single currency. This justifies the use of Article 114 TFEU for the establishment of a system that applies to euro area Member States, and is ideally open to all the Member States. Second, the use of Article 114 TFEU is the most practical legal basis to the integration of financial markets. The effectiveness of the EBU is subject to the appropriate use of the legal tools to establish an integrated financial market. This justifies the creation of a euro area system for resolution that aims to reduce the obstacles that can arise in the context of market integration where certain Member States have opted for further integration. Third, it is essential that resolution authorities do not create obstacles to the cross-border resolution arrangements and be able to act swiftly and effectively for crisis management. A fragmented and lengthy national decision-making framework has shown evident problems in the recent past, especially with regard to cross-border recovery and

122. Case C-270/12 *United Kingdom of Great Britain and Northern Ireland v. European Parliament, Council of the European Union* (ESMA case) ECLI:EU:C:2014:18.
123. *See* Chapter 3 section §3.03[A][1] for the general discussion on harmonisation in the EU.

resolution measures.[124] This suggests that Article 114 TFEU reduces obstacles and promotes harmonisation to 'ensure a coherent and uniform approach' for resolutions in the internal market, also in the case of the SRM.

In terms of institutional framework, it may be questioned whether Article 114 TFEU embraces the possibility to adopt the SRM agency structure for supranational European resolution regime. However, Article 114 TFEU has been used extensively, especially during the financial crisis to establish new EU agencies.[125] The ECJ has upheld almost all EU legislation that relies on Article 114 TFEU as a legal basis to establish EU agencies when the agencies' responsibilities derive from its founding regulation and show how the agency improves the conditions for the establishment and functioning of the internal market. The ECJ also held that the legislator enjoys a wide margin of discretion in adopting legal acts under Article 114 TFEU. The Council Legal Service in this sense approved the content of the SRM proposal Regulation as it contained sufficient grounds to comply with the scope of Article 114 TFEU.[126] As the centralised decision-making procedure is considered an element contributing to the harmonisation of the internal market, the Council Legal Service concluded that the creation of such institutionalised framework is compatible with EU law.[127] In this respect, Article 114 TFEU is fully respected in reinforcing the institutional framework for banking recovery and resolution. In particular, the conferral of resolution powers to the SRB as well as the introduction of a supranational procedure for the resolution of credit institutions subject to SRM resolution is compliant with the purpose of reducing obstacles to the functioning of the internal market as well as distortions of competition. Furthermore, it has also been argued that the need to avoid divergent solutions followed for the ad hoc resolution or the bailout of credit institutions are sufficient grounds to make use of Article 114 TFEU to establish a new institutional framework.[128]

Overall, these reasons suggest that the use of Article 114 TFEU is the appropriate legal basis for the creation of a European or euro area substantial and institutional system of bank recovery and resolution.

[B] Extent of Recovery and Resolution Tools: Effective for Purpose?

The creation of resolution tools as provided in the BRRD and in SRM is an extremely important development for the attainment of supranational financial stability in EU law and policy. The de facto solution for temporary bank restructuring in dealing with state support measures was neither practicable nor legitimate in the medium- and long-term. The exception to the State aid regime under Article 107 TFEU and the proactive role of the Commission in dealing with bank restructuring are not satisfactory solutions for

124. *See* Niamh Moloney, *European Banking Union: Assessing Its Risks and Resilience*, 51 Common Market Law Revivew 1617 (2014).
125. *See* Chapter 6 section §6.03[B][1] on EU agencies.
126. Council of the EU Legal Service, *Examination of the proposed legal basis*, 13524/13, 11 September 2013.
127. *See* Moloney *supra* n. 124, 1657.
128. *See* Eilis Ferran, *European Banking Union: Imperfect but It Can Still Work* in Danny Busch, Guido Ferrarini (eds), *European Banking Union*, 79–80 (Oxford University Press 2015).

banking crisis management. The idea to establish a European resolution regime reveals that recovery and resolution tools are of critical importance for the functioning of the European financial system, in particular in case of cross-border activities.[129]

The recovery phase is an essential phase in the context of the new resolution regime as it intends to prevent and anticipate to the extent possible the trigger of resolution. The preparation of recovery plans, the possible use of early intervention measures by the competent supervisor and the approval of resolution plans make clear that financial institutions shall be prepared to take preventive measures to avoid deterioration of their financial situation and bear the burden to avoid resolution in any possible way. The interaction between the financial institutions, the competent supervisors and the resolution authorities remains an important paradigm in this sense.[130] At the same time, awareness of the solvency problems of financial institutions together with an appropriate planning on the actions to take in case of the deterioration of the situation are key elements to avoid the trigger of resolution. This is also important from the perspective of banks and their investors. Furthermore, recovery planning allows the appropriate consideration of measures to recover to the extent possible ailing institutions and may enhance transparency and awareness of banking problems. Hence, this bulk of recovery and pre-resolution tools is in line with the normative instrument of supranational regulation to prevent risks and shocks as developed in this book. At the same time, the role of early intervention measures under the existing recovery and resolution regime remains doubtful. These measures are intended to prevent the use of resolution, but they may still generate problems on the institution. This is because the public impact of using early intervention measures may go against the purpose of avoiding the resolution of the institution and could deteriorate the situation of the institution further. Furthermore, it is not clear whether early intervention measures have a purely supervisory nature or they are intended to have other purposes.

The new recovery and resolution framework is an important development in EU law and policy especially because of the introduction of specific statutory resolution instruments available to resolution authorities. The bridge bank, sale of assets and asset separation tools are useful to strengthen the instruments available to competent authorities. Further, the introduction of the bail-in tool stands out as a true 'regulatory revolution'. The bail-in is the strictest resolution tool to avoid recourse to public resources, break the vicious circle between financial institutions and the sovereign as well as to avoid initiating burdensome insolvency proceedings. The underlying idea of the bail-in instrument reveals that supranational financial stability is at the centre of gravity to safeguard the stability of the system as a whole and to justify that those who have invested in an ailing bank pay the costs of their choice. Instead of liquidating the entity, the bail-in instrument imposes losses on shareholders and creditors to allow the entity continue its activities. It has been correctly argued that creditors will reassess

129. *See* Avgouleas, Goodhart, *supra* n. 68, 15.

130. *See* Jens-Hinrich Binder, *Resolution Planning and Structural Bank Reform Within the Banking Union*, in Juan Castañeda, David Mayes, Geoffrey Wood (eds), *European Banking Union*, 145 (Routledge 2015).

their investment in a bank's debt instruments if the risk of bail-in may be present.[131] At the same time, the bail-in is considered as a positive development to allow the management of a credit institution to be more vigilant in conducting its business activities[132] and to avoid contagion risks in case of liquidation.[133] Hence, the bail-in is an important instrument to achieve the restructuring of the banking activities rather than making use of public money or terminating banking businesses with considerable contagion effects. The use of the bail-in ensures that the stakeholder primarily bear the cost of a bank failure, but also that the affected institution does not threaten financial stability in the Member State and in the EU. Turning to the critical aspects of the SRM, the following section offers the opportunity to look at some aspects of the new supranational resolution regime.

[C] The SRM: A Problematic Supranational Resolution Framework

This section looks at some key aspects of the SRM: the rationale of the SRM, the agency problem of supranational resolution, the procedural conundrum in the exercise of supranational resolution powers, as well as into the resolution financing for credit institutions in distress. While some critical remarks are made to the SRM design, the overall assessment shows that the establishment of the SRM is a welcome development in order to achieve supranational financial stability.

[1] Rationale of the SRM

The rationale to create the SRM lies in the need to have an appropriate European system of common resolution powers with tools and instruments framed at supranational level. This means that there is an institutional framework for the recovery and resolution of credit institutions. While the BRRD empowers national authorities with resolution tasks and establishes financing arrangements with the conferral of substantive powers to resolve credit and financial institutions, the SRM creates a supranational institutional framework at European level to resolve credit institutions. The SRM is essential to reach effective decisions to resolve credit institutions within participating Member States. Four main reasons are in favour of a single system for resolution in Europe: – the presence of a single authority can facilitate timely and cross-border resolutions; – it provides a mechanism to internalise home-host concerns and reach agreement on resolution and burden-sharing; – it is necessary to align incentives for least cost resolution; – it may achieve economies of scale, avoid incoherence and duplication, and accumulate expertise that would prepare and implement recovery and resolution plans.[134] Time, effectiveness and resource savings could be considered as the main benefits arising for the creation of the SRM.

131. Wojcik *supra* n. 58, 127.
132. *Ibid.*, 128–129.
133. *Ibid.*, 130.
134. *See* Rishi Goyal *et al.*, *A Banking Union for the Euro Area*, IMF Staff Discussion Note 16 (2013).

In this context, the SRM is as an institutional development to enhance enforcement of cross-border crisis management situations in Europe. However, its institutional complexity, the SRB discretionary use of powers and the role of the NRAs in implementing resolutions may over time have a significant impact on property rights and broader economic rights.[135] This may question the SRM effectiveness and legality under EU law and policy. Furthermore, the BRRD provides for a minimum harmonisation framework where Member States and NRAs still retain considerable powers on the ways in which they can configure the national resolution framework. This is especially true for the non-participating Member States, which implemented the BRRD, but could still adopt divergent rules than euro area Member States. An aspect to be explored in future is the reinforcement of existing substantive framework providing for EU rules going beyond a minimum harmonisation approach and look at centralised substantive instruments to deal with bank recovery and resolution.

[2] The 'Agency Problem' in Supranational Resolution

The role of the SRB is central for the correct functioning of the SRM. The SRB is a new EU agency. As argued above, the use of Article 114 TFEU allows for the establishment of EU agencies also for cross-border resolution purposes. The detailed technical area of banking resolution led to the establishment of an ad hoc EU agency for such purposes rather than conferring resolution powers to an already established EU agency or to an EU institution such as the Commission or the ECB. The establishment of a new agency in banking resolution is an important development that nonetheless needs to be framed in the context of the existing constitutional constraints to the establishment of EU agency in EU law.[136] As held in previous chapters, the power to establish an EU agency through Article 114 TFEU is legally possible. However, it is open to question whether and to what extent an EU agency might be empowered to deal effectively with resolution. The EU legislator possesses discretion on the 'harmonisation technique most appropriate for achieving the desired result',[137] and it can achieve so by establishing a new agency for such purposes. The establishment of a new EU agency for the exercise of resolution powers to ensure a coherent and uniform approach to bank resolution within the SRM is feasible, although open to competence and powers challenges.[138]

A major issue is the extent of powers that have been conferred to the SRB. This was a source of contention for the adoption of the SRM Regulation. The ECJ provided for the limitation to the delegation of powers with the (in-)famous *Meroni* doctrine. The debate on the *Meroni* doctrine was discussed earlier when dealing with EBA's role in

135. Alexander Kern, *European Banking Union: A Legal and Institutional Analysis of the Single Supervisory Mechanism and the Single Resolution Mechanism*, 40 European Law Review 184 (2015).
136. *See* Chapter 6 section §6.03[B] for the assessment of the *Meroni* doctrine and the creation of EU agencies.
137. Case C-217/04 *United Kingdom v. Council and European Parliament* (ENISA case) ECLI: EU:C:2006:279, para. 43.
138. *See* Moloney, *supra* n. 124 1657.

banking regulation.[139] With the *ESMA* ruling, it appears that the *Meroni* doctrine has been downgraded to some extent.[140] EU agencies can be empowered so long as a pure discretionary power is not conferred to EU agencies and that appropriate safeguards are established to that effect. The ECJ *ESMA* judgment plays an important role to support the legitimate use of agency-making and to improve the decision-making powers conferred to the SRB for future revisions. While the *Meroni* doctrine is inadequate to the current constitutional challenges arising from the financial crisis especially with a view to integrate financial markets further, it still prevents the SRB to possess full decision-making discretionary powers to deal with resolutions. In looking at the provision of the SRM Regulation, the extent of the SRB powers has been restrained as compared with the initial Commission's Regulation proposal. The SRB possesses much discretion in the realm of resolution planning but limited powers in resolution taking. For instance, the SRB may require banks or banking groups to change their organisational structure if the SRB determines that the bank or banking group's organisational structure is a substantial impediment to a feasible and credible resolution of the bank or group.[141] Furthermore, if the SRB determines that there are substantial impediments to the implementation of the resolution plan, it may order the institution to remove the impediments, including changing its organisational structure or business activities.[142] Moreover, the SRM Regulation provides that if the firm's or group's proposals are considered inadequate, the resolution authority will have the power to take specific actions that address or remove the impediments to resolvability.[143] This selection of provisions shows that the SRB can exercise wide discretion to choose a measure based on the nature of the impediment. This goes beyond the simple technical analysis. It can imply substantial degree of discretionary decision-making based on criteria that belong to an assessment made by the SRB.

However, the *Meroni* doctrine is strictly reflected in the resolution decision-making. The SRB's resolution scheme shall be endorsed by the Commission and – in certain circumstances – also by the Council. This was justified by the need to have a *Meroni*-compliant agency and perhaps the exigence not to dissociate the SRB too much from other EU political institutions such as the Commission and the Council. In particular, resolution powers will be subject at least to the Commission's scrutiny. Furthermore, the NRAs are responsible for the implementation of the resolution agreed at the supranational level in the SRM.

The final arrangements in the SRM Regulation question whether the SRB is such an effective entity in exercising its resolution mandate, as the limited degree of discretion remains an essential limitation in delegating powers to EU agencies.[144] In

139. *See* Chapter 6 section §6.03[B].
140. *See* Gianni Lo Schiavo, *A Judicial Re-Thinking on the Delegation of Powers to European Agencies under EU Law? Comment on Case C-270/12 UK v. Council and Parliament*, 16 German Law Journal 315 (2015).
141. BRRD, Art. 17(5).
142. BRRD and SRM Regulation, Arts 15 and 16.
143. BRRD, Art. 17(5) and SRM Regulation, Art. 10(11).
144. Moloney, *supra* n. 124, 1661.

practice, such limitations may considerably restrict the SRB's powers to play a primary and decisive role in the resolution procedure.

In sum, the creation of the SRB as an independent resolution EU authority in the SRM is a welcome development in the context of the creation of a supranational resolution regime for the attainment of financial stability. However, the lack of fully fledged discretionary powers to the SRB questions its real effectiveness in resolution-making and suggests that a reconsideration of the *Meroni* doctrine should take place in future.

[3] The Procedural Conundrum in the SRM

While the problem of the creation of a fully fledged EU agency to deal with a European-wide resolution regime has been discussed, this subsection assesses the resolution procedure in the SRM. As discussed earlier, the SRM Regulation does not provide for a European resolution procedure regarding all credit institutions established in participating Member States. Rather, NRAs remain responsible to deal with the resolution procedures as regards 'less significant' non-cross-border institutions and execute resolution measures. This limitation restricts the procedures subject to the SRM Regulation. However, the use of the resolution procedure established in the SRM Regulation will be critical as the resolved institution will be of significant relevance for the euro area and the internal market.

The existing SRM procedural decision-making does not fulfil the objective of achieving an effective resolution. Rather, it may generate a conundrum.[145] This is for a number of reasons. First, the resolution procedure is lengthy and cumbersome. Even if the SRM Regulation sets a strict timing, it does not appear that a resolution decision will be carried out in less than twenty-four hours. The solution found sets several steps that put at risk the urgency of coming up with a fast resolution in a very short time. Second, the procedure involves too many (political) actors. Apart from the Commission, which shall approve, under a silent procedure, the resolution scheme due to the *Meroni* doctrine constraints, the procedure might involve also the Council under specific circumstances. This does not really make the resolution procedure viable for an effective and truly *European* solution as the Council may express its dissent to the adoption of the resolution decision and will reflect, by its very nature, national rather than European interests. It is not excluded that other institutions and national authorities might also be heavily involved in the final resolution decision.

Third, the resolution procedure is highly technical and complex. The resolution scheme may be amended several times, and several bodies and organs will be involved with its drafting at an informal level. This indicates that the resolution procedure may be politically negotiated and result in a political compromise rather than in a purely technical decision. The SRM Regulation is extremely complex and detailed. This hardly contributes to the efficiency of the SRM procedure.

145. *See* Ferran *supra* n. 128, 76.

The assessment of the resolution procedure in the SRM shows that determining and executing the resolution of a big banking group may be difficult to achieve in practice. At present, the existing SRM resolution procedure does not fully support the argument of a strong supranational financial stability framework in Europe and resolution procedure may be burdensome. The final subsection of this part will assess another problematic element of the SRM: resolution funding.

[4] Funding the Resolution in the SRM: How Much Financing Mutualisation for Financial Stability?

The creation of the SRF as the new pan-SRM bank resolution fund is a positive development to provide financial funds to resolution procedures if necessary. This is for a number of reasons. First, the SRF will be placed at European level. It will be a statutory European fund managed by the SRB and may be used to manage bank resolutions if financial resources are needed. The SRF should help ensuring a uniform resolution financing practice and avoiding national obstacles to resolution measures or distortions of competition in the internal market due to divergent national practices. Second, the contributions to the SRF will be based on the progressive mutualisation of financial sources raised from the private sector, which will be progressively mutualised from the national to the European level. The mutualisation process will be achieved over time through resource collection by national authorities into national compartments and the transfer of these national compartments into the SRF. The mutualisation to the collection of such contributions is a very important element to ensure a common euro area approach. Third, the SRF raises its financial sources directly from private entities and not from state resources and, hence, from taxpayers. This means that each bank established in an SRM participating Member States is directly involved in the funding and will provide the required resources to the SRF. Such arrangement will exclude that taxpayers money are involved in the process of funding and that only privately raised resources are used to such purposes.

While these arguments are favourable to a supranational dimension to ensure financial stability in EU law and policy, there are two limitations downsizing the establishment of the SRF.[146] First, the full mutualisation and transfer of resources to the SRF will be phased-in over a very long period – eight years – hence in 2024. The 2013 December Council position was even stricter, as it established the pooling of financial resources over ten years with very small resources from the first year. The final solution pooled 40% of the resources from the first year 2016, while the remaining 60% over the period of eight years. This solution does not appear to be optimal, as the required resources for resolution should have been pooled together and mutualised immediately also to give a strong signal to financial markets. The phased-in mutualisation of resolution funds is at odds with the establishment of a supranational fund as from the day of the full entry into force of the SRM. Furthermore, it is also arguable

146. *See* Federico Fabbrini, *On Banks, Courts and International Law. The Intergovernmental Agreement on the Single Resolution Fund in Context*, 21 Maastricht Journal of European and Comparative Law 444 (2014).

whether the overall amount of financial resources once the SRF is fully mutualised – 55 billion – is sufficient to achieve its purposes. It remains to be seen whether this compromise solution will be successful in guaranteeing that resolutions are funded in a proper manner.

Second, the SRM is based also on the Intergovernmental Agreement that sets the rules for the pooling together of the financial resources from the NRAs to the SRB and for the transfer of these resources from the national compartments to the SRF. This solution shows that a nationally centred dimension has dominated the political comprise leading to the adoption of the SRM Regulation. The Intergovernmental Agreement has partially carved out resolution funding from the EU legal order and has unfairly limited the role of EU legislators in this area. The pooling and mutualisation of financial resources should have taken place within the SRM Regulation, an EU law instrument, and not with an intergovernmental instrument.[147] Article 114 TFEU was a sufficient legal basis for the pooling of financial resources in the SRF. The intergovernmental dimension of the SRF remains a source of uncertainty[148] and runs against supranational financial stability in EU law and policy.

To conclude, the SRF is a welcome development for resolution financing. This is because the Member States have agreed on the creation of a common fund with financial resources levied from credit institutions intended to provide funding to credit institutions under resolution. However, some limitations exist as to its effective structure, legal basis, and use.

§8.05 EU BANKING RECOVERY AND RESOLUTION: FUTURE REGULATORY PROSPECTS

The existing framework of banking recovery and resolution shows that considerable efforts have been taken to develop a European framework for the orderly resolution of credit institutions in Europe. However, the supranational dimension of banking recovery and resolution reveals that some challenges are open to debate and further regulatory improvements and measures should be made in the field. Without being an exhaustive attempt to provide normative prospects, some selective aspects are discussed here: the creation of a common fiscal backstop for the EBU for resolution financing (section [A]); regulatory instruments for harmonising insolvency procedures, a common regime for creditor hierarchy insolvency rules and a regulatory instrument for a moratorium tool at the European level (section [B]). These aspects broadly reflect the Council's conclusions of June 2016 regarding a roadmap to complete the Banking Union and are related to risk sharing and reduction measures.[149]

147. *Ibid.*, 456.
148. *See* Ferran *supra* n. 128, 84–85.
149. Council of the EU, *Council Conclusions on a roadmap to complete the Banking Union*, 17 June 2016 Press Release at http://www.consilium.europa.eu/press-releases-pdf/2016/6/47244642837_en.pdf (accessed 31 December 2016).

[A] Creating a Common Fiscal Backstop in the Euro Area

The creation of a common fiscal backstop in the euro area and the EBU remains an open issue. A common fiscal backstop is considered as being a supranational public intervention assistance measure to provide public funding to enhance the financial capacity of resolution funds.[150] The Commission states that:

> [s]uch a backstop would imply a temporary mutualisation of possible fiscal risk related to bank resolutions across the Banking Union. However, use of the backstop would be fiscally neutral in the medium term, as any public funds used would be reimbursed over time by the banks (via ex-post contributions to the SRF).[151]

These considerations reveal that a common fiscal backstop would serve the purpose to mutualise fiscal risks and to ensure further risk reduction measures. However, at present, in case of financing needs, further financial resources to finance resolution would be taken only through available resolution financing arrangements beyond the SRF, the national financing arrangements or through compatible State aids. At the same time, the problematic set-up of the SRF shows that a pan-euro area and public supranational backstop to finance resolutions beyond the pooling of financial resources raised from private operators is needed in the medium term.

While a common fiscal backstop has not been established yet in Europe, it is argued that the ESM could serve that function.[152] Under the current rules, the ESM may be involved with either an indirect or a direct instrument for bank recapitalisation which may be granted under specific circumstances and which may constitute credit lines to finance resolutions. In this context, the direct recapitalisation ESM instrument Guideline has been adopted in December 2014 for an amount of up to EUR 60 billion.[153] It provides for very strict conditions for activation to recapitalise ailing credit institutions.[154] Thus far, the direct recapitalisation instrument has never been used. Notwithstanding the limitations of the ESM direct recapitalisation tool, Member States could agree on making the ESM a viable public backstop for resolution financing while making it fiscally neutral via an *ex post* contribution of the banks to the SRF. The ESM

---

150. *See* European Commission, *Towards the completion of the Banking Union* COM(2015) 587, 5.
151. *Ibid.*
152. For an analysis of the ESM *see* Chapter 5.
153. ESM, *Guideline on Financial Assistance for the Direct Recapitalisation of Institutions* at http://www.esm.europa.eu/pdf/20141208%20Guideline%20on%20Financial%20Assistance%20for%20the%20Direct%20Recapitalisation%20of%20Institutions.pdf (last accessed 31 December 2016).
154. The ESM Guidelines set outs the following conditions to benefit from a direct recapitalisation: the benefiting entity shall be (or likely to be in the near future) unable to meet the capital requirements established by the ECB in its capacity as supervisor and that it would have to be unable to obtain sufficient capital from private sources; the beneficiary institution in question must also be of systemic relevance or pose serious threat to the financial stability of the euro area; the benefiting institution shall be established in a euro area Member State which would have to be unable to provide financial assistance to the beneficiary institution without very serious effects on its own fiscal sustainability and that the ESM financial assistance would have to be considered indispensable to safeguard the financial stability of the euro area as a whole or of its Member States.

Treaty envisages the possibility of establishing new lending instruments by reviewing the list of financial instruments provided in it.[155] This option could be used to link the ESM to the SRF for resolution purposes and establish a common fiscal backstop in the euro area.

Having the ESM as the public fiscal backstop would grant further credibility to the EBU for the safeguard of credit institutions, should the resolution tools at disposal not be sufficient. Furthermore, the recognition of the ESM as the public fiscal backstop in the euro area would contribute to justify the progressive integration of the ESM into the EU legal order. However, at present, there has not yet been a political agreement on establishing a common fiscal backstop in the euro area. This should be established in the medium-term as a key tool to complete the EBU.

[B] Harmonising Insolvency Rules, Revising MREL and Setting a Moratorium Tool

The second ground of proposals relate to fine-tuning the bank recovery and resolution regime in Europe or to extend the scope of EU law and policy in other resolution or insolvency fields. The adoption of a Directive or even a Regulation harmonising insolvency rules, or setting the creditor hierarchy in banking insolvency as well as a provision establishing a moratorium tool at European level would be important developments in order to strengthen the supranational dimension of financial stability in EU law and policy. In November 2016, the Commission has presented a new package of measures partially aimed at reforming the bank recovery and resolution regime and proposing a harmonisation directive on restructuring and insolvency regimes.[156]

At present, the BRRD and the SRM Regulation do not harmonise insolvency rules for banks, but establish a European framework for orderly resolution. Directive 2001/24/EC sets out rules of mutual recognition of rules related to the winding-down of credit institutions. The recast Regulation 2015/848 harmonises only rules on jurisdiction, recognition and applicable law in insolvency proceedings.[157] However, they do not set harmonising rules on insolvency regimes for credit institutions in Europe.[158] Although the European framework shall take into account national insolvency laws in some cases, the adoption of the BRRD shows two exceptions to this.

155. ESM Treaty, Art. 19.

156. The European Commission proposed three instruments in the field in November 2016: Proposal for a directive amending Directive 2014/59/EU as regards the ranking of unsecured debt instruments in insolvency hierarchy, COM(2016) 853 final; Proposal for a Directive of the European Parliament and of the Council amending Directive 2014/59/EU on loss-absorbing and recapitalisation capacity of credit institutions and investment firms and amending Directive 98/26/EC, Directive 2002/47/EC, Directive 2012/30/EU, Directive 2011/35/EU, Directive 2005/56/EC, Directive 2004/25/EC and Directive 2007/36/EC, COM(2016) 852 final; and the Proposal for a Directive of the European Parliament and of the Council on preventive restructuring frameworks, second chance and measures to increase the efficiency of restructuring, insolvency and discharge procedures and amending Directive 2012/30/EU, COM(2016) 723 final.

157. Regulation (EC) 1346/2000 of 29 May 2000 on insolvency proceedings, O.J. 2000, L 160/1; the Recast Regulation on Insolvency 2015/848 will apply, in principle, as of 26 June 2017.

158. *See* Case C-526/14 *Kotnik*, para. 104.

First, the BRRD and the SRM Regulation set an instrument outside the resolution tools, the write-down and conversion of capital instruments.[159] The features and the basic principles are very similar to the bail-in tool. However, there are two main differences: the write down and conversion instrument covers only AT1 and Tier 2 capital instruments. Furthermore, the instrument can be applied also independently from resolution actions and even before the conditions for resolution are met.[160] This instrument suggests that resolution authorities can also exercise their power outside the resolution using this instrument. It may be argued that this instrument goes beyond the resolution framework as an independent instrument to avoid the liquidation of a credit institution without using resolution tools. However, this instrument does not harmonise insolvency regimes and rules in Europe. Insolvency proceedings remain regulated under national law. A new harmonising EU instrument on banking insolvency and restructuring proceedings should be developed in future.

Second, the BRRD under Article 108 harmonises partially the order of priority of claims in insolvency proceedings.[161] This provision requires that the part of eligible deposits from natural persons and micro enterprises and SMEs exceeding EUR 100,000 and that deposits which would be eligible deposits from natural persons, micro enterprises and SMEs have the same priority ranking, which is higher than the ranking provided for the claims of ordinary unsecured, non-preferred creditors. Similarly, covered deposits and DGSs subrogating to the rights and obligations of covered depositors in insolvency shall have the same priority ranking, to be higher than the ranking for the claims mentioned before. This is a welcome regulatory development, which, however, does not harmonise generally creditor hierarchy in insolvency. However, having to determine the creditor hierarchies in all Member States and ascertain whether the 'no creditor worse off' principle is complied with remains a big challenge for the SRB in the EBU.[162] The Council's conclusions in June 2016 suggested that the Commission proposes a common approach to the bank creditor hierarchy. This would be a welcome development to reduce risks to the possible resolution of cross-border banks and to provide certainty for issuers and investors.[163] In November 2016, the Commission has proposed to harmonise further Article 108 of the BRRD as related to bank creditors' insolvency ranking. The changes in the BRRD would enable banks to 'issue debt in a new statutory category of unsecured debt available in all EU Member States ranking below the most senior debt and other senior liabilities for the purposes of resolution, while still being part of the senior unsecured debt category'.[164] This change would reduce the uncertainty of the treatment of debt instruments and the costs of compliance by the credit institutions with the subordination requirement.

159. SRM Regulation, Art. 21 and BRRD Arts 59–62.
160. Wojcik *supra* n. 58, 112.
161. *See Ibid.*, 125.
162. *See Ibid.*
163. *See*, Jim Brunsden, *Brussels to intervene on bailing in bank bondholders*, Financial Times, 21 June 2016 at https://www.ft.com/content/eddafd5a-37ab-11e6-9a05-82a9b15a8ee7 (accessed 31 December 2016).
164. European Commission, *Frequently Asked Questions: Capital requirements (CRR/CRD IV) and resolution framework (BRRD/SRM) amendments* at http://europa.eu/rapid/press-release_MEMO-16-3840_en.htm (accessed 31 December 2016).

As a second ground of reforms, the absence of a harmonised framework for insolvency proceedings at the European level is a big challenge for a truly European recovery and resolution framework. Normal insolvency proceedings have a 'supporting' role within the framework of banking recovery and resolution. This extends to other issues that are not or only incompletely regulated by the BRRD and SRM, such as transaction avoidance, the treatment of secured creditors, a claims procedure and, most importantly, the ranking of different classes of creditors in general. Moreover, the 'no creditor worse off' principle requires a liquidation analysis based on national insolvency law. In light of this challenge, the EU institutions should take steps to set at least some minimum harmonisation rules in insolvency proceedings beyond the banking sector. In this respect, in June 2016, the Council has suggested the creation of a minimum harmonisation framework in insolvency for companies, justified also by the need to tackle the high level of non-performing loans in some Member States.[165] In November 2016, the Commission has proposed a new Directive harmonising restructuring framework, second chance and certain aspects insolvency proceedings. As stated by the Commission, the proposed Directive includes new rules to restructure business which aim to

> reduce barriers to cross-border investment related to differences between the Member States' restructuring and second chance frameworks, and reduce the number of unnecessary liquidations of viable companies, maximising value for creditors, owners and the economy as a whole, and increase the possibilities of cross-border restructurings'.[166]

The proposed Directive is a welcome development to harmonise restructuring processes and insolvency rules. Its adoption will be an important step to reduce insolvency filings in the EU and to harmonise national rules in the field as well as to attain a supranational dimension of financial stability in EU law and policy.

Furthermore, the adoption of the MREL at European level required that certain liabilities are 'bail-inable' instruments in order to ensure that losses are absorbed and credit institutions are recapitalised if they get into financial difficulties and are subsequently placed in a resolution. The MREL has to be consistent with any standards developed in the international fora. The FSB adopted the TLAC standard applying only to global systemically important institutions. Therefore, the MREL should be aligned with this international standard. In November 2016, the Commission has proposed revised rules on MREL to reflect the TLAC requirements.[167] These establish a system of MREL requirements higher for globally systemically important institutions on top of the MREL requirements for all credit institutions. This is a Pillar 2 add-on MREL

165. Council of the EU, *Council Conclusions on a roadmap to complete the Banking Union*, 17 June 2016 Press Release at http://www.consilium.europa.eu/press-releases-pdf/2016/6/47244642837_en.pdf (accessed 31 December 2016).
166. European Commission, *Proposal for a directive on Insolvency, Restructuring and Second Chance*, Fact Sheet, 22 November 2016 at http://europa.eu/rapid/press-release_MEMO-16-3803_en.htm (accessed 31 December 2016)
167. European Commission, *Frequently Asked Questions: Capital requirements (CRR/CRD IV) and resolution framework (BRRD/SRM) amendments*.

requirement. Furthermore, resolution authorities may introduce additional MREL guidance to credit institutions.

Finally, the introduction of a moratorium tool at European level would ensure that competent authorities have an adequate instrument to intervene and avoid the trigger of resolution. Moratorium tools are intended to 'freeze transfers out of a failing bank to prevent it haemorrhaging cash before authorities can intervene'.[168] In other words, a moratorium tool is a regulatory power to stop the payments to be made by an ailing institution under specific circumstances and with specific exceptions in cases of major risks to financial stability. The BRRD introduces the possibility for the resolution authority to suspend certain obligations when an entity is under resolution.[169] However, it remains unclear whether such instrument can be used also before the resolution. Introducing a European-wide moratorium tool, also *before* a resolution is triggered, would contribute to manage shocks and risks that could jeopardise supranational financial stability. Determining when the moratorium tool can be triggered and what consequences it may have for the creditor to whom the payments were originally addressed are essential questions to be addressed. In November 2016, the Commission has proposed to establish a moratorium tool in the BRRD. This is conferred both to the competent supervisory authority and to the resolution authority and allows the suspension of certain contractual obligations for a short period of time, with specific exceptions such as covered deposits. The design of this tool is highly important as a tool for supranational financial stability in EU law and policy. The tool would stabilise the situation of the ailing institution and ensure that the institution does not face turbulences that could affect financial stability.

§8.06 CONCLUSION

This chapter has examined the newly adopted reforms to establish a new European framework for bank resolution in Europe and has attempted to discuss them in light of the debate of supranational financial stability in EU law and policy. The creation of a European-wide substantive and institutional framework for the resolution of credit institutions is an important evolution in EU law and policy. The BRRD and the SRM frameworks are clearly an expression of financial stability as a supranational objective in EU law and policy. The use of supranational regulation, the introduction of statutory burden-sharing arrangements for banks and the establishment of a privately raised fund for resolution financing are all clear examples of normative instruments developed in this book for the attainment of supranational financial stability in EU law and policy.

The BRRD sets a new regime in banking crisis management as it provides new statutory resolution tools to address privately ailing credit institutions in Europe. As Constâncio indicates, the BRRD:

168. Jim Brunsden, *EU weighs guillotine powers to freeze transfers*, Financial Times, 15 May 2016 https://www.ft.com/content/fe11824e-1914-11e6-bb7d-ee563a5a1cc1 (accessed 31 December 2016).

169. BRRD, Art. 69.

> is (...) the most crucial regulatory change in Europe in relation to breaking the bank-sovereign nexus. It represents a true paradigm change, ending the culture of bail-out and ushering in a culture of bail-in.[170]

The establishment of a recovery and resolution framework marks a new era for in banking legislation as recovery is aimed at preventing risks and shocks in the banking system while resolution aims to break the vicious circle between the sovereign and the banks and to avoid taxpayers' bailouts. Furthermore, after fierce negotiations among key political players the SRM has been established. The institutional structure for bank recovery and resolution is a welcome development in European banking regulation as it sets a supranational regime for the orderly resolution of credit institutions in participating Member States. The SRM will hopefully establish 'a credible mechanism to proceed swiftly, orderly and efficiently in the resolution of banks that have attained the point of non-viability'.[171] This may be achieved in a system where the four main constituents are present: '(a) a single system, (b) a single authority with efficient decision-making procedures, (c) a single fund and (d) a backstop facility for bridge financing'.[172] Many questions are still open to debate as regards this new European framework. Future practice will tell whether the BRRD will be effective in addressing the orderly resolution of credit institutions from a European perspective. Furthermore, future will show whether the SRM will work as a centralised and swift system for the resolution of credit institutions in participating Member States. As demonstrated in this chapter, some key challenges are present in the new European recovery and resolution framework and some regulatory reforms are needed to reinforce the resolution regime for credit institutions in Europe. However, the establishment of the BRRD and the SRM remains an evolutionary cornerstone of reform for the post-crisis regulatory framework in Europe, in light of attaining the objective of supranational financial stability. Having assessed the new recovery and resolution framework in Europe, the book will proceed with some conclusions.

170. Vitor Constâncio, *Banking Union: Meaning and Implications for the Future of Banking*, 24 April 2014 at https://www.ecb.europa.eu/press/key/date/2014/html/sp140424_1.en.html (accessed 31 December 2016).
171. *Ibid.*
172. *Ibid.*

CHAPTER 9
General Conclusions

§9.01 THE FINANCIAL CRISIS AND FINANCIAL STABILITY IN EU LAW AND POLICY

The starting point and recurrent theme of this study has been to analyse whether the objective of financial stability has increasingly acquired a foundational role in EU law and policy under the impact of the global and European financial crisis. The study attempted to provide a legal framework for assessing what this development implies. The conclusions are that, through the extensive crisis-related reforms undertaken in Europe, financial stability has substantially acquired the de facto role of a foundational supranational objective in EU law and policy.

This study has aimed to contribute to a clearer understanding as regards two aspects. First, the role of financial stability has been explored in the context of the reformed EMU framework. This is in particular the case for the new regulatory measures aimed at reaching a renewed dimension for fiscal surveillance of Member States' finances and for the creation of financial assistance mechanisms to distressed Member States. Second, the study has shown the evolving regulatory, supervisory and resolution framework for credit institutions in Europe by assessing in particular to what extent the project to establish the EBU contributes to achieving financial stability and to safeguard the financial system in Europe.

The study presented the concept of financial stability as an evolutionary public good objective as demonstrated in other social science disciplines. It was also explored the renewed IFA as driven by financial stability and showed to what extent at present the objective of financial stability in international law has not yet substantially restructured the international economic order.

Subsequently, the study has explained why the concept of financial stability is difficult to define and argued that it may be considered as a new foundational objective in EU law and policy. Despite the inherently difficult determination of what financial stability is, the study has demonstrated that financial stability is composed of certain normative instruments at European level deemed essential to provide legitimacy to the concept of supranational financial stability. Such instruments are supranational regulation, micro- and macro-economic supervision/surveillance, burden-sharing measures and last resort/rescue measures. These play an essential role in contributing to the attainment of financial stability as a foundational objective in EU law and policy.

§9.02 THE ROLE OF FINANCIAL STABILITY AS A FOUNDATIONAL OBJECTIVE IN EU LAW AND POLICY: MISSION ACCOMPLISHED?

The role of financial stability as a foundational objective in EU law and policy should be seen as an essential component on the trend towards the shape of a renewed EU legal order. As shown in this book, financial stability is not yet a scholarly developed legal concept that can straightforwardly drive regulators and policy-makers. This research has aimed to bring together the main aspects of financial stability in order to examine how financial stability has contributed to the development of unprecedented constitutional mutations of the EU legal order as well as to supranational developments in regulation, supervision and resolution of credit institutions in Europe.

Three main transversal arguments have been examined in this study in order to sustain the foundational role of financial stability in EU law and policy: the major EU constitutional changes in the EMU, the conferral of supranational tasks to EU institutions and agencies, the substantive solutions found to reinforce the existing EU legal framework.

[A] EU Constitutional Changes and Financial Stability

This book has shown that the increasing importance of financial stability as a founding objective of EU and policy has produced many important constitutional changes that have reshaped the EU legal order. In this vein, the study has demonstrated that financial stability is at the centre of the EU constitutional system together with other more traditional objectives or values of the EU legal order. The constitutional reforms promoted after the outbreak of the financial crisis in light of the objective of financial stability have revealed that both *la méthode communautaire* and intergovernmentalism have played a considerable role to achieve financial stability. Some concluding statements can be made.

First, the study has demonstrated that the Member States as masters of the EU Treaties have not made use of the amendment procedures provided in the EU Treaties, with the exception of the introduction of Article 136(3) TFEU, to change the provisions of the EU Treaties and to 'constitutionalise' a financial stability policy in EU law and policy. While the EU Treaties still provide for the use of some special provisions to extend powers beyond the existing Treaty rules such as using the flexibility clause or the enhanced cooperation framework, Member States have been reluctant to amend EU primary law and have preferred to rely extensively on secondary legislation in order to achieve some degree of supranational financial stability.

Second, it was demonstrated that secondary legislation has played a major role to reinforce the current economic surveillance system of Member States' economic policies. It has been highlighted that this is especially true for the euro area Member States where secondary legislation has reinforced the rules on surveillance of euro area Member States' finances - through Article 136(2) TFEU in particular – and reformed the SGP. Similarly, the project to establish the EBU, and in more general banking regulation, has essentially relied on secondary law in the adoption of new EU legal acts to reinforce regulation and supervision of credit institutions in Europe. This has taken place mainly by stretching the existing EU legal basis to harmonise the internal market (Article 114 TFEU) or using unprecedented legal bases (Article 127(6) TFEU).

Third, the need to achieve financial stability without opening cumbersome Treaty amendment procedures and contesting national interests has contributed to the emergence of crisis-related reforms going beyond EU law through the use of a *sui generis* intergovernmentalism. The intergovernmental solution is problematic from a truly supranational perspective on financial stability, but is seen as necessary complementation to the lack of Treaty provisions and specific legal basis to attain supranational financial stability at present. At the same time, intergovernmentalism was motivated by the absence of rules in the EU Treaties to reduce risks and shocks and to shape an EU policy on financial stability. For instance, the book has shown that the TSCG is a clear example of the use of international agreements to strengthen fiscal discipline for a group of Member States without the use of the amendment procedures in the EU Treaties. Similarly, most financial assistance mechanisms have been established outside the EU legal order. This is exemplified by the adoption of the ESMT as a new international public institution to provide financial assistance to euro area Member States and credit institutions in distress. The ESM, which is founded on the objective of financial stability of euro area Member States, is the most important instrument adopted intergovernmentalism to achieve financial stability in EU law and policy. The ECJ in *Pringle* held that the ESM complies with EU primary law, and in particular the no-bailout clause under Article 125 TFEU. It remains to be seen whether the ESM will be integrated to EU law and policy in future. Finally, the mutualisation of the SRF is implemented through a mutualisation system provided in an Intergovernmental Agreement. This choice, motivated more by politically contingencies than by sound legal arguments, illustrates the relevance of intergovernmentalism also within the EBU.

[B] Supranational Tasks and Financial Stability

This study has also demonstrated that EU institutions and agencies have exercised tasks and powers which have pursued supranational financial stability in the EU law and policy. This has been the case of the Commission, the ECB and EU agencies that play an increasingly important role in shaping a 'financially stable' internal market. At the same time, the crisis-related reforms have rebalanced the EU institutional structure with the conferral of considerably important tasks and powers to achieve financial stability since the beginning of the financial crisis. Some concluding remarks can be made.

First, the Member States, and the Council acting on their behalf, have played a predominant role in the European agenda. The Member States as the masters of EU Treaties are the only ones potentially able to amend the EU Treaties in order to introduce financial stability as a foundational objective and a financial stability policy in EU law. In this sense, the Council has shown a very active role in the adoption of both EU legislation and intergovernmental measures throughout the financial crisis and will continue to be a central player in the post-financial crisis era.

Second, in the massive crisis-related reforms intended to pursue financial stability, there remains a concern over the de-legitimation of the European Parliament and democratic values it brings forward in adopting EU law. The role of the European Parliament has not been enhanced by the financial crisis as the urgency of achieving financial stability has prevented the normal use of ordinary legislative procedures or the full involvement of the European Parliament. At the same time, the role of the European Parliament has been – selectively – downgraded to mere legislative controller without the conferral of extensive powers in the law-making process during the financial crisis. Yet in some critical areas, the European Parliament has played a considerable influence to avoid an executive overhaul in decision-making and has effectively played a role in assuring respect of accountability standards as provided in EU law and policy. It remains to be seen whether EU law will enhance democratic legitimacy through a renewed role of the European Parliament in law-making and accountability.

Third, the European financial crisis has revealed that the EU administration and executives – through a reinforced role of the traditionally technocratic EU institutions, agencies and bodies – have played an essential role in pursing financial stability as a foundational objective in EU law and policy. The Commission as proponent of legislation and EU law enforcer as well as EU agencies as executive delegated administrators play a key role to achieve financial stability. In particular, the Commission and EBA in the banking sector have promoted supranational rulemaking and are currently developing an integrated banking market in line with the achievement of supranational financial stability. Furthermore, throughout the financial crisis, the ECB has played a peculiar role in the exercise of its new supervisory functions with a view to contributing to make credit institutions more resilient to financial shocks and risks. The new supervisory tasks of the ECB indicate that a truly supranational dimension for banking supervision can be achieved and can ensure that credit institutions comply with regulatory and supervisory requirements in an integrated banking market.

Fourth, the European judiciary has confirmed that the new financial crisis-related rules comply with the values of the EU legal order. The ECJ has confirmed that many unconventional law-making solutions are respectful to the EU law rules. As shown in this study, three recent judgments, among other ones, show the ECJ judicial activism in constitutionalising financial stability as a foundational objective in EU law and policy. The *Pringle* case has been an essential pronouncement to confirm that the ESM is compatible with EU primary law and to legitimise intergovernmental financial stability instruments in Europe. The *ESMA* case has provided a constitutional confirmation that the rigidities of the *Meroni* doctrine should not apply, especially in the current crisis-related regulatory environment, and has provided for clarification as to the scope of action of EU agencies pursuing financial stability. The *Kotnik* case has warranted that the Commission policy in State aid to financial institutions is legitimate and that burden-sharing measures may be imposed to credit institutions receiving compatible State aid. The ECJ case law should legitimise further the role of supranational measures intended to achieve supranational financial stability in EU law and policy. This will confirm the legitimacy of crisis-related measures intended to pursue supranational financial stability.

[C] Substantive Solutions and Financial Stability

The substantive dimension of EU rules for the renewed surveillance over Member State finances as well as the new degree of regulation, supervision and resolution of credit institutions in Europe show that the attainment of financial stability is at the centre of reform. Two concluding remarks can be made. First, this book has demonstrated that the substantive dimension for the surveillance of Member State finances and assistance to Member State in financial distress has been strengthened in order to provide better surveillance on Member States' finance as part of their decisions in the exercise of fiscal and budgetary powers. There is still ground for improvement as the renewed European economic governance regime lacks supranational real-teeth powers and the financial assistance measures are yet a prerogative of Member States' decision-making powers. At the same time, the establishment of the ESM as a permanent – still not fully satisfactory – solution to overcome the absence of a 'European Monetary Fund' shows that a new substantial solution for the provision of financial assistance in the euro area has been provided. Conversely, the role of the ECB in exercising its new supervisory tasks and powers on credit institutions suggests that new substantial solutions have been found in order to attain financial stability in EU law and policy.

Second, the new regulatory framework for credit institutions in Europe is a clear substantive evolution to attain a resilient and strong banking system intended to attain supranational financial stability in EU law and policy. The launching of the EBU project is an unprecedented initiative to regulate and supervise better banks. The use of EU legal acts in many areas of banking regulation reinforces the supranational dimension of financial stability. Furthermore, the new supranational resolution regime, which is still criticisable for its political compromises, constitutes an evolutionary development in the absence of EU Treaty changes. In particular, the statutory introduction of the bail-in instrument is a strong regulatory instrument to ensure that burden-sharing is respected and that moral hazard issues are downsized.

§9.03 CONCEIVING THE EU AS A 'STABILITY UNION'

Supranational financial stability in EU law and policy has not yet been achieved in Europe. At the same time, it is expected that financial stability will continue to play an increasingly important role in the EU law and policy in order to avoid financial or banking crises and the regression of the EU project. It has been demonstrated that the recent regulatory efforts to safeguard the unity of euro area Member States as well as to provide the appropriate supranational level of regulation, supervision and resolution for credit institutions are considerable improvements of the European system as compared with the pre-financial crisis framework.

Yet many challenges lie ahead for the Union. Although the crisis-related reforms have provided supranational responses to achieve 'more Europe' as well as to avoid the collapse of the single currency or of the financial system as a whole, the EU is still not a federal state. In particular, the reinforced economic governance regime is still weak in nature and appears dependent on national gesture politics. Financial assistance mechanisms to sovereigns still do not provide for a supranational economic and fiscal policy in the EU legal order. Furthermore, the regulatory framework for credit institutions still contains many grounds for national rules that can fragment the applicability of supranational European rules. Similarly, financial supervision is still not fully centralised at ECB level, EU agencies lack fully-fledged decision-making powers and the new European resolution regime is the result of a political compromise.

Notwithstanding these limitations, this book has demonstrated that Europe has achieved a higher of supranational financial stability than in its recent past. This justifies concluding that the EU has become a 'Stability Union' grounded on the objective of supranational financial stability and its normative instruments.

Selected Bibliography

Articles

Adamski, Dariusz, *National Power Games and Structural Failures in the European Macroeconomic Governance* 49 Common Market Law Review 1336 (2012).

Alexander, Kern, *European Banking Union: A Legal and Institutional Analysis of the Single Supervisory Mechanism and the Single Resolution Mechanism* 40 European Law Review 154 (2015).

Allen, William & Wood, Geoffrey, *Defining and Achieving Financial Stability* 2 Journal of Financial Stability 152 (2006).

Amtenbrink, Fabian & de Haan, Jakob, *Economic Governance in the European Union – Fiscal Policy Discipline Versus Flexibility* 40 Common Market Law Review 1075 (2003).

Anabtawi, Iman & Schwarcz, Steven, *Regulating Ex Post: How Law Can Address the Inevitability of Financial Failure* 92 Texas Law Review 75 (2013).

Andenas, Mads & Chiu, Iris, *Financial Stability and Legal Integration in Financial Regulation* 38 European Law Review 343 (2013).

Armstrong, Kenneth, *The New Governance of EU Fiscal Discipline* 38 European Law Review 613 (2013).

Athanassiou, Phoebus, *Of Past Measures and Future Plans for Europe's Exit from the Sovereign Debt Crisis: What Is Legally Possible (and What Is Not)* 36 European Law Review 572 (2011).

Avgouleas, Emilios & Goodhart, Charles, *Critical Reflections on Bank Bail-ins* 2 Journal of Financial Regulation 3 (2015).

Bator, Francis, *The Anatomy of Market Failure* 72 Quarterly Journal of Economics 351 (1958).

Bast, Jürgen, *New Categories of Acts after the Lisbon Reform: Dynamics of Parlamentarization in EU Law* 49 Common Market Law Review 885 (2012).

Beukers, Thomas, *The New ECB and Its Relationship with the Member States of the Euro Area: Between Central Bank Independence and Central Bank Intervention* 50 Common Market Law Review 1605 (2013).

Bieri, David, *Financial Stability, the Basel Process and the New Geography of Regulation* 2 Cambridge Journal of Regions, Economy and Society 303 (2009).

Black, Julia, *Constructing and Contesting Legitimacy and Accountability in Polycentric Regulatory Regimes* 2 Regulation & Governance 139 (2008).

Black, Julia, *Paradoxes and Failures: 'New Governance' Techniques and the Financial Crisis* 75 Modern Law Review 1037 (2012).

Borger, Vestert, *How the Debt Crisis Exposes the Development of Solidarity in the Euro Area* 9 European Constitutional Law Review 16 (2013).

Borger, Vestert, *The ESM and the European Court's Predicament in Pringle* 14 German Law Journal 113 (2013).

Buiter, Willem & Rahbari, Ebrahim, *The European Central Bank as Lender of Last Resort for Sovereigns in the Eurozone* 50 Journal of Common Market Studies 32 (2012).

Busuioc, Madalina, *Rule Making by the European Financial Supervisory Authorities: Walking a Tight Rope* 19 European Law Journal 117 (2012).

Chiti, Edoardo, *An Important Part of the EU's Institutional Machinery. Features, Problems and Perspectives of European Agencies* 46 Common Market Law Review 1423 (2009).

Chiti, Edoardo & Teixeira, Pedro Gustavo, *The Constitutional Implications of the European Responses to the Financial and Public Debt Crisis* 50 Common Market Law Review 685 (2013).

Craig, Paul, *Delegated Acts, Implementing Acts and the New Comitology Regulation* 36 European Law Review 671 (2011).

Craig, Paul, *The Stability, Coordination and Governance Treaty: Principle, Politics and Pragmatics* 37 European Law Review 232 (2012).

Craig, Paul, *Pringle and Use of EU Institutions Outside the EU Legal Framework* 9 European Constitutional Law Review 263 (2013).

Crockett, David, *The Theory and Practice of Financial Stability* De Economist 532 (1996).

Crockett, Andrew, *The Theory and Practice of Financial Stability* 203 Essays in International Finance 2 (1997).

Dawson, Mark & de Witte, Floris, *Constitutional Balance in the EU after the Euro-Crisis* 76 Modern Law Review 830 (2013).

Deakin, Simon, *Legal Diversity and Regulatory Competition: Which Model for Europe?* 12 European Law Journal 441 (2006).

de Gregorio Merino, Alberto, *Legal Developments in the Economic and Monetary Union During the Debt Crisis: The Mechanisms of Financial Assistance* 49 Common Market Law Review 1630 (2012).

de Witte, Bruno & Beukers, Thomas, *The Court of Justice Approves the Creation of the European Stability Mechanism Outside the EU Legal Order: Pringle* 50 Common Market Law Review 805 (2013).

Dougan, Michael, *Minimum Harmonisation and the Internal Market* 37 Common Market Law Review 860 (2000).

Editorial, *Some Thoughts Concerning the Draft Treaty on a Reinforced Economic Union* 49 Common Market Law Review 1 (2012).

Fabbrini, Federico, *On Banks, Courts and International Law. The Intergovernmental Agreement on the Single Resolution Fund in Context* 21 Maastricht Journal of European and Comparative Law 444 (2014).

Fasone, Cristina, *European Economic Governance and Parliamentary Representation. What Place for the European Parliament?* 20 European Law Journal 164 (2014).

Ferran, Eilis & Alexander, Kern, *Can Soft Law Bodies Be Effective? The Special Case of the European Systemic Risk Board* 35 European Law Review 751 (2010).

Ferran, Eilis & Babis, Valia, *The European Single Supervisory Mechanism* 13 Journal of Corporate Legal Studies 255 (2013).

Gadanecz, Blaise & Jayaram, Kaushik, *Measures of Financial Stability – A Review* 31 IFC Bulletin 365 (2010).

Goodhart, Charles & Schoenmaker, Dirk, *Should the Functions of Monetary Policy and Banking Supervision Be Separated?* 47 Oxford Economic Papers 539 (1995).

Gu, Bin & Liu, Tong, *Enforcing International Financial Regulatory Reforms* 17 Journal of International Economic Law 139 (2014).

Haentjens, Matthias, *Bank Recovery and Resolution: An Overview of International Initiatives* 3 International Insolvency Law Review 255 (2014).

Hagan, Sean, *Enhancing the IMF's Regulatory Authority* 13 Journal of International Economic Law 955.

Hicks, John, *The Foundations of Welfare Economics* 49 The Economic Journal 696 (1939).

Hinarejos, Alicia, *Fiscal Federalism in the European Union: Evolution and Future Choices for EMU* 50 Common Market Law Review 1621 (2013).

Hofmann, Herwig & Morini, Alessandro, *Constitutional Aspects of the Pluralisation of the EU Executive Through 'Agencification'* 37 European Law Review 428 (2012).

Huertas, Michael, *EDIS – The Third-Pillar of the EU's Banking Union: Big, Bold but Can It Be Beautiful?* 31 Journal of International Banking Law and Regulation 587 (2016).

Jacqué, Jean-Paul, *The Principle of Institutional Balance* 41 Common Market Law Review 383 (2004).

Kern, Alexander, *European Banking Union: A Legal and Institutional Analysis of the Single Supervisory Mechanism and the Single Resolution Mechanism* 40 European Law Review 154 (2015).

Lastra, Rosa, *The Governance Structure for Financial Regulation and Supervision in Europe* 10 Columbia Journal of European Law 56 (2003).

Lastra, Rosa & Wood, Geoffrey, *The Crisis of 2007–09: Nature, Causes, and Reactions* 13 Journal of International Economic Law 531 (2010).

Lastra, Rosa, *Systemic Risk, SIFIs and Financial Stability* 11 Capital Markets Law Journal 201 (2011).

Lastra, Rosa & Louis, Jean-Victor, *European Economic and Monetary Union: History, Trends and Prospects* Yearbook of European Law 134 (2013).

Lo Schiavo, Gianni, *The Judicial 'Bail Out' of the European Stability Mechanism: Comment on the Pringle Judgment* 5 Italian Journal of Public Law 188 (2013).

Lo Schiavo, Gianni, *From National Banking Supervision to a Centralized Model of Prudential Supervision in Europe: The Stability Function of the Single Supervisory Mechanism* 21 Maastricht Journal of European and Comparative Law 110 (2014).

Lo Schiavo, Gianni, *State Aids and Credit Institutions in Europe: What Way Forward?* 25 European Business Law Review 427 (2014).

Lo Schiavo, Gianni, *The Development of a New Bank Resolution Regime in Europe: Fit for Purpose?* 29 Journal of International Banking Law and Regulation 68 (2014).

Lo Schiavo, Gianni, *A Judicial Re-thinking on the Delegation of Powers to European Agencies under EU Law? Comment on Case C-270/12 UK v. Council and Parliament* 16 German Law Journal 315 (2015).

Louis, Jean-Victor, *The Review of the Stability and Growth Pact* 43 Common Market Law Review 85 (2006).

Louis, Jean-Victor, *Guest Editorial: The No-Bailout Clause and Rescue Packages* 47 Common Market Law Review 984 (2010).

Lupo Pasini, Federico, *Economic Stability and Economic Governance in the Euro Area: What the European Crisis Can Teach on the Limits of Economic Integration* 16 Journal of International Economic Law 221 (2013).

Masciandaro, Donato & Quintyn, Marc, *Regulating the Regulators: The Changing Face of Financial Supervision Architectures before and after the Crisis* 6 European Company Law 191 (2009).

Messina, Michele, *Strengthening Economic Governance of the European Union Through Enhanced Cooperation: A Still Possible, but Already Missed, Opportunity* 40 European Law Review 404 (2014).

Moloney, Niamh, *EU Financial Market Regulation after the Global Financial Crisis: 'More Europe' or More Risks?* 47 Common Market Law Review 1381 (2010).

Moloney, Niamh, *The European Securities and Markets Authority and Institutional Design for the EU Financial Market – A Tale of Two Competences: Part (1) Rule-Making* 12 European Business Organisation Law Review 49 (2011).

Moloney, Niamh, *European Banking Union: Assessing Its Risks and Resilience* 51 Common Market Law Review 1622 (2014).

Moloney, Niamh, *Capital Markets Union: 'Ever Closer Union' for the EU Financial System?* 41 European Law Review 307 (2016).

Osterloo, Sander & de Haan, Jakob, *Central Banks and Financial Stability: A Survey Journal of Financial Stability* 1 Journal of Financial Stability 257 (2004).

Padoa-Schioppa, Tommaso, *EMU and Banking Supervision* 2 International Finance 307 (1999).

Palmstorfer, Rainer, *To Bail or Not to Bail Out? The Current Framework If Financial Assistance for Euro Area Member States Measured Against the Requirements of EU Primary Law* 38 European Law Review 773 (2012).

Palmstorfer, Rainer, *The Reverse Majority Voting under the 'Six Pack': A Bad Turn for the Union?* 20 European Law Journal 186 (2014).

Payne, Jennifer, *The Reform of Deposit Guarantee Schemes in Europe* 12 European Company Financial Law Review 540 (2015).

Peers, Steve, *The Stability Treaty: Permanent Austerity or Gesture Politics?* 8 European Constitutional Law Review 441 (2012).

Peers, Steve, *Towards a New Form of EU Law? The Use of EU Institutions Outside the Legal Framework* 9 European Constitutional Law Review 37 (2013).

Pipkorn, Jörn, *Legal Arrangements in the Treaty of Maastricht for the Effectiveness of the Economic and Monetary Union* 31 Common Market Law Review 263 (1994).

Prüm, André, *The European Union Crisis Responses and the Efficient Capital Markets Hypothesis* 60 Columbia Journal of European Law 2 (2014).

Quaglia, Lucia, Howarth, David & Liebe, Moritz, *The Political Economy of European Capital Markets Union* 54 Journal of Common Market Studies 185 (2016).

Reinhart, Carmen & Rogoff, Kenneth, *From Financial Crash to Debt Crisis* 101 American Economic Review 1676 (2011).

Rüffert, Matthias, *The European Debt Crisis and European Union Law* 48 Common Market Law Review 1785 (2011).

Samuelson, Paul, *The Pure Theory of Public Expenditure* 36 Review of Economics and Statistics 387 (1954).

Schammo, Pierre, *The European Securities and Markets Authority: Lifting the Veil on the Allocation of Powers* 48 Common Market Law Review 1883 (2011).

Schwarcz, Steven, *Systemic Risk* 97 Georgetown Law Journal 204 (2008).

Schwarz, Michael, *A Memorandum of Misunderstanding – The Doomed Road of the European Stability Mechanism and a Possible Way Out: Enhanced Cooperation* 51 Common Market Law Review 389 (2014).

Schoenmaker, Dirk, *Financial Supervision: From National to European?* Financial and Monetary Studies 10 (2003).

Schütze, Robert, *From Rome to Lisbon: 'Executive Federalism' in the (New) European Union* 47 Common Market Law Review 1399 (2010).

Slot, Piet, *Harmonisation* 21 European Law Review 378 (1996).

Smits, René, *Correspondence* 49 Common Market Law Review 827 (2012).

Steinbach, Armin, *The Lender of Last Resort in the Eurozone* 53 Common Market Law Review 361 (2016).

Trachtman, Joel, *The International Law of Financial Crisis: Spillovers, Subsidiarity, Fragmentation and Cooperation* 13 Journal of International Economic Law 719 (2010).

Walker, George, *European Financial Programme: Content, Structure and Completion* 15 European Business Law Review 305 (2004).

Weatherill, Stephen, *The Limits of Legislative Harmonisation Ten Years after Tobacco Advertising: How the Court's Case Law Has Become a 'Drafting Guide'* 12 German Law Journal 827 (2011).

Wojcik, Karl-Philipp, *Bail in the Banking Union* 53 Common Market Law Review 120 (2016).

Wymeersch, Eddy, *The Future of Financial Regulation and Supervision in Europe* 42 Common Market Law Review 987–988 (2005).

Books

Admati, Anat & Hellwig, Martin, *The Bankers' New Clothes* (Princeton University Press 2013).

Allen, Larry, *The Global Economic Crisis: A Chronology* (Reaktion Books 2013).

Andenas, Mads, *Harmonising and Regulating Financial Markets*, in Andenas, Mads & Andersen, Camilla (eds), *Theory and Practice of Harmonisation* 22 (Edward Elgar 2011).

Andenas, Mads, et al. (eds), *European Economic and Monetary Union: The Institutional Framework* (Kluwer Law International 1997).

Andenas, Mads & Chiu, Iris, *The Foundations and Future of Financial Regulation* (Routledge 2014).

Arendt, Hanna, *Civil Disobedience*, Crisis of the Republic (Penguin Books 1969).

Arner, Douglas, *Financial Stability, Economic Growth and the Role of Law* 51 (Cambridge University Press 2007).

Avgouleas, Emilios, *Governance of Global Financial Markets* (Cambridge University Press 2012).

Baquero Cruz, Julio, *Between Competition and Free Movement. The Economic Constitutional Law of the European Community* (Hart Publishing 2002).

Barnard, Catherine, *The Substantive Law of the EU* 558 (Oxford University Press 2016).

Barth, James, Caprio, Gerard & Levine, Ross, *Rethinking Bank Regulation. Till Angels Govern* 22 (Cambridge University Press 2006).

Baumol, William, *Welfare Economics and the Theory of the State* (Harvard University Press 1952).

Bieber, Roland, *The Allocation of Economic Policy Competences in the European Union*, in Azoulai, Loïc (ed.), *The Question of Competence in the European Union* 92 (Oxford University Press 2015).

Bieri, David, *Regulation and Financial Stability in the Age of Turbulence* in Kob, Robert (ed.), *Lessons from the Financial Crisis* 327 (John Wiley 2010).

Binder, Jens-Hinrich, *Resolution Planning and Structural Bank Reform Within the Banking Union*, in Castañeda, Juan, Mayes, David & Wood, Geoffrey (eds), *European Banking Union* 145 (Routledge 2015).

Blair, Christine, Carns, Frederick & Kushmeider, Rose, *Instituting a Deposit Insurance System: Why? How?*, in Campbell, Andrew, La Brosse, John, Mayes, David & Singh, Dalvinder (eds), *Deposit Insurance* 73 (Palgrave MacMillan 2007).

Brummer, Chris, *Soft Law and the Global Financial System* (Cambridge University Press 2015).

Buckley, Adrian, *Financial Crisis: Causes, Context and Consequences* (Financial Times/Prentice Hall 2011).

Busch, Danny & Ferrarini, Guido (eds), *European Banking Union* (Oxford University Press 2015).

Canals, Jordi, *Universal Banking. International Comparisons and Theoretical Perspectives* (Clarendon Press 1997).

Chamon, Merijn, *EU Agencies: Legal and Political Limits to the Transformation of the EU* (Oxford University Press 2016).

Ciro, Tony, *The Global Financial Crisis* (Ashgate 2016).

Cornes, Richard & Sandler, Todd, *The Theory of Externalities, Public Goods and Club Goods* (Cambridge University Press 1996).

Craig, Paul, *EU Administrative Law* (Oxford University Press 2012).

Craig, Paul, *The Lisbon Treaty, Revised Edition: Law Politics and Treaty* (Oxford University Press 2013).

Crockett, David, *Lessons from the Asian Crisis,* in Bisignano, Joseph, Hunter, William & Kaufman, George (eds), *Global Financial Crises* 7 (Springer 2000).

Davies, Howard & Green, David, *Banking on the Future. The Fall and Rise of Central Banking* (Oxford University Press 2010).

De Grauwe, Paul, *Economics of Monetary Union* (Oxford University Press 2014).

Dewatripont, Mathias & Tirole, Jean, *The Prudential Regulation of Banks* 104 (MIT Press 1994).

Dragomir, Larisa, *European Prudential Banking Regulation and Supervision: The Legal Dimension* (Routledge 2008).

Ellinger, Eliahu, Lomnicka, Eva & Hare, Richard, *Ellinger's Modern Banking Law* (Oxford University Press 2011).

Fabbrini, Federico, *From Fiscal Constraints to Fiscal Capacity,* in Adams, Maurice, Fabbrini, Federico & Larouche, Pierre (eds), *The Constitutionalization of European Budgetary Constraints* 408 (Hart Publishing 2014).

Fabbrini, Federico, *Economic Governance: Comparative Paradoxes. Constitutional Challenges* (Oxford University Press 2016).

Fama, Eugene, *Foundations of Finance: Portfolio Decisions and Securities Prices* (Basic Books 1977).

Ferran, Eilis, *Understanding the New Institutional Architecture of EU Financial Market Supervision,* in Wymeersch, Eddy, Hopt, Klaus & Ferrarini, Guido (eds), *Financial Regulation and Supervision. A Post-Crisis Analysis* 140 (Oxford University Press 2012).

Ferran, Eilis, *European Banking Union: Imperfect but It Can Still Work,* in Busch, Danny & Ferrarini, Guido (eds), *European Banking Union* 79 (Oxford University Press 2015).

Gabor, Barbara, *Regulatory Competition in the Internal Market* (Edward Elgar 2013).

Geitner, Timothy, *Stress Test: Reflections on Financial Crisis* (Broadway Books 2014).

Gianviti, François, *The Objectives of Central Banks,* in Giovanoli, Mario & Devos, Diego (eds), *International Monetary and Financial Law. The Global Crisis* 473 (Oxford University Press 2010).

Giovanoli, Mario, *A New Architecture for the Global Financial Market: Legal Aspects of International Financial Standard Setting,* in Giovanoli, Mario (ed.), *International Monetary Law: Issues for the New Millennium* 25–26 (Oxford University Press 2000).

Giovanoli, Mario, *The International Financial Architecture and Its Reform after the Global Crisis,* in Giovanoli, Mario & Devos, Diego (eds), *International Monetary and Financial Law: The Global Crisis* 3 (Oxford University Press 2010).

Giovanoli, Mario, *The International Monetary and Financial Architecture – Some Institutional Aspects*, in Cottier, Thomas, Lastra, Rosa & Tietje, Christian (eds), *The Rule of Law in Monetary Affairs* 45 (Cambridge University Press 2015).

Goodhart, Charles, *The Basel Committee on Banking Supervision. A History of the Early Years 1974–1997* (Cambridge University Press 2011).

Grünewald, Seraina, *The Resolution of Cross-Border Banking Crises in the European Union* (Kluwer Law International 2014).

Herdegen, Matthias, *Principles of International Economic Law* (Oxford University Press 2016).

Hinnarejos, Alicia, *The Euro Crisis from a Constitutional Perspective* (Oxford University Press 2015).

Hüpkes, Eva & Devos, Diego, *Cross-Border Bank Resolution: A Reform Agenda*, in Giovanoli, Mario & Devos, Diego (eds), *International Monetary and Financial Law* 359 (Oxford University Press 2010).

Kleftouri, Nikoletta, *Deposit Protection and Bank Resolution* (Oxford University Press 2015).

Krugman, Paul, *The Return of Depression Economics and the Crisis of 2008* (Norton Company Limited 2009).

Lastra, Rosa, *International Financial and Monetary Law* (Oxford University Press 2015).

Lenaerts, Koen, Maselis, Ignace & Gutman, Kathleen, *EU Procedural Law* (Oxford University Press 2014).

Maletic, Isidora, *The Law and Policy of Harmonisation in Europe's Internal Market* (Edward Elgar 2013).

Moloney, Niamh, *How to Protect Investors* (Cambridge University Press 2010).

Moloney, Niamh, *EU Securities and Financial Markets Regulation* (Oxford University Press 2014).

Mülbert, Peter, *Managing Risk in the Financial System*, in Moloney, Niamh, Ferran, Eilís & Payne, Jennifer (eds), *The Oxford Handbook of Financial Regulation* 369 (Oxford University Press 2015).

Musgrave, Richard, *Public Goods*, in Brown, Cary & Solow, Robert (eds), *Paul Samuelson and Modern Economic Theory* 141 (McGraw-Hill 1983).

Padoa Schioppa, Tommaso, *Regulating Finance: Balancing Freedom and Risk* (Oxford University Press 2004).

Panourgias, Lazaros, *Banking Regulation and World Trade Law: GATS, EU and Prudential Institution Building* (Hart Publishing 2005).

Pareto, Wilfredo, *Cours d'Economie Politique* (Rouges 1896).

Peters, Georgina, *Developments in the EU* in Lastra, Rosa (ed.), *Cross-Border Bank Insolvency* 128 (Oxford University Press 2011).

Piris, Jean-Claude, *The Lisbon Treaty: A Legal and Political Analysis* (Cambridge University Press 2010).

Piris, Jean-Claude, *The Future of Europe. Towards a Two-Speed EU?* (Cambridge University Press 2011).

Proctor, Charles, *Mann on the Legal Aspect of Money* (Oxford University Press 2013).

Prosser, Tony, *The Economic Constitution* (Oxford University Press 2014).

Puetter, Uwe, *The Eurogroup* (Manchester University Press 2006).

Sauter, Wolf & Schepel, Harm, *State and Market in European Union Law. The Public and Private Spheres of the Internal Market Before the EU Courts* (Cambridge University Press 2009).

Schoenmaker, Dirk, *Central Banks Role in Financial Stability*, in Caprio, Gerard (ed.), *Safeguarding Global Financial Stability: Political, Social, Cultural and Economic Theories and Models* 272 (Elsevier 2013).

Schumpeter, Joseph, *Capitalism, Socialism and Democracy* (Harper 1975).

Senden, Linda, *Soft Law in European Community Law* (Hart Publishing 2004).

Smits, René, *The European Central Bank* (Kluwer Law International 1997).

Snell, Jukka, *The Internal Market and the Philosophies of Market Integration*, in Barnard, Catherine & Peers, Steve (eds), *European Union Law* 315 (Oxford University Press 2014).

Snyder, Francis, *EMU—Integration and Differentiation: Metaphor for European Union*, in Craig, Paul & De Búrca, Grainne (eds), *The Evolution of EU Law* 687 (Oxford University Press 2011).

Tridimas, Takis, *Financial Supervision and Agency Power: Reflections on ESMA*, in Shuibhne, Niamh & Gormley, Laurence (eds), *From Single Market to Economic Union* 72 (Oxford University Press 2012).

Tuori, Kaarlo & Tuori, Klaus, *The Eurozone Crisis. A Constitutional Analysis* (Cambridge University Press 2014).

Viterbo, Annamaria, *International Economic Law and Monetary Measures* (Edward Elgar 2012).

Vos, Ellen, *Agencies and the European Union*, in Verhey, Luc & Zwart, Tom (eds), *Agencies in European and Comparative Perspective* 131 (Intersentia 2003).

Zavvos, George & Kaltsouni, Stella, *The Single Resolution Mechanism in the European Banking Union: Legal Foundation, Governance Structure and Financing*, in Haentjens, Matthias & Wessels, Bob (eds), *Research Handbook on Crisis Management in the Banking Sector* 123 (Edward Elgar 2015).

Zimmermann, Claus, *The Concept of Monetary Sovereignty Revisited* (Cambridge University Press 2013).

Others (Reports, Working Papers, Newspaper Articles, Speeches)

Almunia, Joaquín, *The Economic and Monetary Union, the Euro and the Financial Crisis* Speech 22 October 2012.

Angeloni, Ignazio, *Challenges Facing the Single Supervisory Mechanism* Speech 6 October 2016 https://www.bankingsupervision.europa.eu/press/speeches/date/2016/html/se161006.en.html (accessed 31 December 2016).

Asmussen, Jörg, *The Single Resolution Mechanism and the Limits of Bank-Regulation*, 8 November 2013 at https://www.ecb.europa.eu/press/key/date/2013/html/sp131108_1.en.html (accessed 31 December 2016).

Aspachs, Oriol, et al., *Searching for a Metric for Financial Stability*, 167 Special Paper LSE Financial Markets Group (2006).

Barroso, José, *Commission Proposes New ECB Powers for Banking Supervision as Part of a Banking Union* Press Release IP/12/953, 12 September 2012.

BIS, Central Bank Governance and Financial Stability, *Report by a Study Group* 32 (May 2011).

Bofinger, Peter, et al., *A European Redemption Pact* VoxEU 9 November 2011 http://voxeu.org/index.php?q = node/7253 (accessed 31 December 2016).

Brunsden, Jim, *EU weighs guillotine powers to freeze transfers*, Financial Times, 15 May 2016 https://www.ft.com/content/fe11824e-1914-11e6-bb7d-ee563a5a1cc1 (accessed 31 December 2016).

Brunsden, Jim, *Brussels to intervene on bailing in bank bondholders*, Financial Times, 21 June 2016 at https://www.ft.com/content/eddafd5a-37ab-11e6-9a05-82a9b15a8ee7 (accessed 31 December 2016).

Chant, John, et al., *Essays on Financial Stability* Bank of Canada Technical Report 3 (2003).

Chiti, Edoardo, *In The Aftermath Of The Crisis: The EU Administrative System Between Impediments and Momentum* EUI WP Law 2015/13 5 (2015).

Claessens, Stijn, Mody, Ashoka & Vallée, Shahin, *Paths to Eurobonds* IMF WP 12/72 20 (2012).

Clifford Chance, *Legal Aspects of Bank Bail-ins* (2011) http://www.cliffordchance.com/publicationviews/publications/2011/05/legal_aspects_ofbankbail-ins.htm (accessed 31 December 2016).

Constâncio, Vitor, *Banking Union: Meaning and Implications for the Future of Banking* 24 April 2014 available https://www.ecb.europa.eu/press/key/date/2014/html/sp140424_1.en.html (accessed 31 December 2016).

Constançio, Vitor, *The Role of the Banking Union in Achieving Financial Stability* 26 November 2014 https://www.ecb.europa.eu/press/key/date/2014/html/sp141126.en.html (accessed 31 December 2016).

de Grauwe, Paul & Wim, Moesen, *Gains for All: A Proposal for a Common Euro Bond* 33 *Intereconomics* 132 (2009).

de Larosière, Jacques (chaired, *Report of the High Level Group on Financial Supervision in the EU* (Brussels 2009).

Delpla, Jacques & von Weizsäcker, Jakob, *The Blue Bond Proposal* Bruegel Policy Brief 2010/03 6 (2010).

Draghi, Mario, *Speech* Global Investment Conference in London, 26 July 2012.

Draghi, Mario, *Opening Speech at the European Banking Congress The Future of Europe*, 22 November 2013 at https://www.ecb.europa.eu/press/key/date/2013/html/sp131122.en.html.

Draghi, Mario, *Introductory Statement to the Press Conference (with Q&A)* 21 January 2016 https://www.ecb.europa.eu/press/pressconf/2016/html/is160121.en.html (accessed 31 December 2016).

Ferrarini, Guido & Chiarella, Luigi, *Common Banking Supervision in the Eurozone: Strengths and Weaknesses* ECGI Law Working Paper 54 (2013).

Financial Crisis Enquiry Commission, *The Financial Crisis Enquiry Report: Final Report of the National Commission on the Causes of the Financial and Economic Crisis in the United States* (January 2011) http://fcic.gov/report.

Five Presidents' Report, 22 June 2015 at http://ec.europa.eu/priorities/economic-monetary-union/docs/5-presidents-report_en.pdf.

Four Presidents' Report, 5 December 2012 7 http://www.consilium.europa.eu/uedocs/cms_Data/docs/pressdata/en/ec/134069.pdf (last accessed 31 December 2016).

Goodhart, Charles, *Myths about the Lender of Last Resort* Financial Market Group LSE (1999) http://econpapers.repec.org/scripts/redir.pf?u=http%3A%2F%2Fwww.lse.ac.uk%2Ffmg%2Fdocuments%2FspecialPapers%2F1990s%2Fsp120.pdf;h=repec:fmg:fmgsps:sp120.

Goodhart, Charles & Tsomocos, Dimitrios, *Analysis of Financial Stability*, 173 LSE Financial Markets Group Special Paper (2007).

Goyal, Rishi, et al. *A Banking Union for the Euro Area* IMF Staff Discussion Note 7 (2013).

Groenendijk, Nico, *Enhanced Cooperation under the Lisbon Treaty* Research Meeting on European & International Affairs 3 (2011) http://doc.utwente.nl/80704/ (accessed 31 December 2016).

Hellwig, Christian & Philippon, Thomas, *Eurobills, Not Eurobonds* VoxEU 2 December 2011 http://www.voxeu.org/article/eurobills-not-euro-bonds.

Houben, Aerdt, Kakes, Jan & Schinasi, Garry, *Toward a Framework for Safeguarding Financial Stability*, IMF WP/04/101 11 (2004).

IMF, *Systemic Risk and the Redesign of Financial Regulation* (2010) https://www.imf.org/external/pubs/ft/gfsr/2010/01/pdf/chap2.pdf 10 (accessed 31 December 2016).

IMF, Euro area policies. Selected issues. (2016) https://www.imf.org/external/pubs/ft/scr/2016/cr16220.pdf (accessed 31 December 2016).

International Task Force on Global Public Goods, *Meeting Global Challenges: International Cooperation in the National Interest* 13 (Final Report, 2006).

Issing, Otmar, *Monetary and Financial Stability: Is There a Trade-Off?* (2003) http://www.ecb.int/press/key/date/2003/html/sp030329.en.html (accessed 31 December 2016).

Jones, Claire, *Mario Draghi's Bond-Buying Plan Outstrips Expectations* Financial Times 22 January 2015 https://www.ft.com/content/8f215db8-a256-11e4-9630-00144feab7de (accessed 31 December 2016).

Juncker, Jean-Claude & Tremonti, Giulio, *E-bonds Would End the Crisis*, *Financial Times*, 5 December 2010.

Kaul, Inge, Grunberg, Isabelle & Stern, Marc (eds), *Global Public Goods: International Cooperation in the 21st Century* 9 (OUP 1999)

Lamfalussy, Alexandre, *Final Report of the Committee of Wise Men* (2001) http://ec.europa.eu/internal_market/securities/docs/lamfalussy/wisemen/final-report-wise-men_en.pdf (accessed 31 December 2016).

Lautenschläger, Sabine, *Low Inflation as a Challenge for Monetary Policy and Financial Stability?* ECB Press Release 7 July 2014 http://www.ecb.europa.eu/press/key/date/2014/html/sp140707.en.html (accessed 31 December 2016).

Liikanen, Erkki, *High-Level Expert Group on Reforming the Structure of the EU Banking Sector* 4 (2012).

Padoa-Schioppa, Tommaso, *EMU and Banking Supervision*, Lecture in the London School of Economics, 24 February 1999.

Padoa-Schioppa, Tommaso, *Central Banks and Financial Stability: Exploring a Land in Between* ECB Policy Paper Introductory Paper (2002) https://www.ecb.europa.eu/events/pdf/conferences/tps.pdf.

Pisani-Ferry, Jean, et al., *EU-IMF Assistance to Euro Area Countries: An Early Assessment* Bruegel Report 27 (2013) http://www.bruegel.org/publications/publication-detail/publication/779-eu-imf-assistance-to-euro-area-countries-an-early-assessment/.

Praet, Peter, *Fixing Finance* Panel intervention 18 February 2014 http://www.ecb.europa.eu/press/key/date/2014/html/sp140218.en.html (last accessed 31 December 2016).

Quintyn, Marc & Taylor, Michael, *Regulatory and Supervisory Independence and Financial Stability* IMF WP/02/46 8 (2002).

Schinasi, Garry, *Defining Financial Stability*, 04/187 IMF Working Paper (2004).

Schinasi, Garry, *Safeguarding Financial Stability Theory and Practice*, 77–134 (IMF 2005).

Stiglitz, Joseph (chaired), *Report of the Commission of Experts of the President of the United Nations General Assembly on Reforms of the International Monetary and Financial System* 51 (UN 2009).

Van Rompuy, Hermann, *Euro Area Summit and European Council Statement* 29 June 2012.

Van Rompuy, Hermann, *Towards a Genuine Economic and Monetary Union*, Report by the President of the European Council in close collaboration with the President of the European Commission, the President of the Eurogroup, and the President of the ECB, 5 December 2012 www.consilium.europa.eu/uedocs/cms_data/docs/pressdata/en/ec/134069.pdf (accessed 31 December 2016).

United Nations Conference on Trade and Development (UNCTAD), *The Global Economic Crisis, Systemic Failures and Multilateral Remedies* (2009), available at http://unctad.org/en/Docs/gds20091_en.pdf (accessed 31 December 2016).

Wymeersch, Eddy, *The Single Supervisory Mechanism or 'SSM', Part One of the Banking Union* ECGI WP 1 (2014).

Zhou, Jianping, et al., *From Bail-Out to Bail-In: Mandatory Debt Restructuring of Systemic Financial Institutions Paper on Bail In* IMF SDN/12/03 4 (2012).

Table of Cases

Judgments of the European Court of Justice

Judgments of the General Court

Opinions of Advocates General of the European Court of Justice

View of Advocates General of the European Court of Justice

ECJ Order Forms

Index

E

F

G

H

I

K

L

M

N

O

P

T

EUROPEAN MONOGRAPH SERIES

1. Lammy Betten (ed.), *The Future of European Social Policy,* 1991 (ISBN 90-654-4585-4).
2. Annemarie Loman, Kamiel Mortelmans, Harry H.G. Post & Stewart Watson, *Culture and Common Law: Before and After Maastricht,* 1992 (ISBN 90-654-4638-9).
3. John A.E. Vervaele, *Fraud against the Community: The Need for European Fraud Legislation,* 1994 (ISBN 90-654-4634-6).
4. Philip Raworth, *The Legislative Process in the European Community,* 1993 (ISBN 90-654-4690-7).
5. Jules Stuyck, *Financial and Monetary Integration in the European Economic Community,* 1993 (ISBN 90-654-4718-0).
6. Jules Stuyck & A.J. Vossestein (eds), *State Entrepreneurship, National Monopolies and European Community Law,* 1993 (ISBN 90-654-4773-3).
7. Jules Stuyck & A. Looijestijn-Clearie (eds), *The European Economic Area EC-EFTA,* 1994 (ISBN 90-654-4815-2).
8. Rosita B. Bouterse, *Competition and Integration: What Goals Count?,* 1995 (ISBN 90-654-4816-0).
9. René Barents, *The Agricultural Law of the EC: An Inquiry into the Administrative Law,* 1994 (ISBN 90-654-4867-5).
10. Nicholas Emiliou, *Principles of Proportionality in European Law: A Comparative Study,* 1996 (ISBN 90-411-0866-1).
11. Eivind Smith, *National Parliaments as Cornerstones of European Integration,* 1996 (ISBN 90-411-0898-X).
12. Jan H. Jans, *European Environmental Law,* 1996 (ISBN 90-411-0877-7).
13. Síofra O'Leary, *The Evolving Concept of Community Citizenship: From the Free Movement of Persons to Union Citizenship,* 1997 (ISBN 90-411-0878-5).
14. Laurence W. Gormley (ed.), *Current and Future Perspectives on EC Competition Law,* 1983 (ISBN 90-411-0691-X).
15. Simone White, *Protection of the Financial Interests of the European Communities: The Fight against Fraud and Corruption,* 1998 (ISBN 90-411-9647-1).
16. Morten P. Broberg, *Broberg on the European Commission's Jurisdiction to Scrutinise Mergers,* 4th Edition, 2013 (ISBN 978-90-411-3339-7).
17. Doris Hildebrand, *The Role of Economic Analysis in the EC Competition Rules: The European School,* 2nd Edition, 2002 (ISBN 90-411-1706-7).
18. Christof R.A. Swaak, *European Community Law and the Automobile Industry,* 1999 (ISBN 90-411-1140-9).

19. Dorthe Dahlgaard Dingel, *Public Procurement: A Harmonization of the National Judicial Review of the Application of European Community Law,* 1999 (ISBN 90-411-1161-1).
20. John A.E. Vervaele (ed.), *Compliance and Enforcement of European Community Law,* 1999 (ISBN 90-411-1151-4).
21. Martin Trybus, *European Defence Procurement Law: International and National Procurement Systems as Models for a Liberalized Defence Procurement Market in Europe,* 1999 (ISBN 90-411-1167-0).
22. Helen Staples, *The Legal Status of Third Country Nationals Resident in the European Union,* 1999 (ISBN 90-411-1277-4).
23. Damien Geradin (ed.), *The Liberalization of State Monopolies in the European Union and Beyond,* 1999 (ISBN 90-411-1264-2).
24. Katja Heede, *European Ombudsman: Redress and Control at Union Level,* 2000 (ISBN 90-411-1413-0).
25. Ulf Bernitz & Joakim Nergelius (eds), *General Principles of European Community Law,* 2000 (ISBN 90-411-1402-5).
26. Michaela Drahos, *Convergence of Competition Laws and Policies in the European Community,* 2002 (ISBN 90-411-1562-5).
27. Damien Geradin (ed.), *The Liberalization of Electricity and Natural Gas in the European Union,* 2001 (ISBN 90-411-1560-9).
28. Gisella Gori, *Towards an EU Right to Education,* 2001 (ISBN 90-411-1670-2).
29. Brendan P.G. Smith, *Constitution Building in the European Union,* 2001 (ISBN 90-411-1695-8).
30. Friedl Weiss & Frank Wooldridge, *Free Movement of Persons within the European Community,* 2nd Edition, 2007 (ISBN 978-90-411-2545-3).
31. Ingrid Boccardi, *Europe and Refugees: Towards an EU Asylum Policy,* 2002 (ISBN 90-411-1709-1).
32. John A.E. Vervaele & André Klip (eds), *European Cooperation Between Tax, Customs and Judicial Authorities,* 2001 (ISBN 90-411-1747-4).
33. Wouter P.J. Wils, *The Optimal Enforcement of EC Antitrust Law: Essays in Law and Economics,* 2002 (ISBN 90-411-1757-1).
34. Damien Geradin (ed.), *The Liberalization of Postal Services in the European Union,* 2002 (ISBN 90-411-1780-6).
35. Nick Bernard, *Multilevel Governance in the European Union,* 2002 (ISBN 90-411-1812-8).
36. Jill Wakefield, *Judicial Protection through the Use of Article 288(2) EC,* 2002 (ISBN 90-411-1823-3).
37. Sebastiaan Princen, *EU Regulation and Transatlantic Trade,* 2002 (ISBN 90-411-1871-3).

38. Amaryllis Verhoeven, *The European Union in Search of a Democratic and Constitutional Theory,* 2002 (ISBN 90-411-1872-1).
39. Paul L.C. Torremans, *Cross Border Insolvencies in EU, English and Belgian Law,* 2002 (ISBN 90-411-1888-8).
40. Malcolm Anderson & Joanna Apap (eds), *Police and Justice Cooperation and the New European Borders,* 2002 (ISBN 90-411-1893-4).
41. Christin M. Forstinger, *Takeover Law in EU and USA: A Comparative Analysis,* 2002 (ISBN 90-411-1919-1).
42. Antonio Bavasso, *Communications in EU Antitrust Law: Market Power and Public Interest,* 2003 (ISBN 90-411-1974-4).
43. Fiona G. Wishlade, *Regional State Aid and Competition Policy in the European Union,* 2003 (ISBN 90-411-1975-2).
44. Gareth Davies, *Nationality Discrimination in the European Internal Market,* 2003 (ISBN 90-411-1998-1).
45. René Barents, *The Autonomy of Community Law,* 2003 (ISBN 90-411-2251-6).
46. Gerhard Dannecker & Oswald Jansen (eds), *Competition Law Sanctioning in the European Union,* 2004 (ISBN 90-411-2100-5).
47. Nauta Dutilh (ed.), *Dealing with Dominance: The Experience of National Competition Authorities,* 2004 (ISBN 90-411-2211-7).
48. Stefaan van den Bogaert, *Practical Regulation of the Mobility of Sportsmen in the EU Post Bosman,* 2005 (ISBN 90-411-2327-X).
49. Katalin Judit Cseres, *Competition Law and Consumer Protection,* 2005 (ISBN 90-411-2380-6).
50. Philipp Kiiver, *The National Parliaments in the European Union: A Critical View on EU Constitution Building,* 2006 (ISBN 978-90-411-2452-4).
51. Alexander Turk, *The Concept of Legislation in European Community Law,* 2006 (ISBN 978-90-411-2472-2).
52. Dimitrios Sinaniotis, *The Interim Protection of Individuals before the European and National Courts,* 2006 (ISBN 978-90-411-2498-2).
53. M. Holoubek & D. Damjanovic, M. Traimer (eds), *Regulating Content: The European Regulatory Framework for the Media and Related Creative Sectors,* 2006 (ISBN 978-90-411-2597-2).
54. Anneli Albi & Jacques Ziller (eds), *The European Constitution and National Constitutions: Ratification and Beyond,* 2006 (ISBN 978-90-411-2524-8).
55. Gustavo E. Luengo, *Regulation of Subsidies and State Aids in WTO and EC Law: Conflicts in International Trade Law,* 2007 (ISBN 978-90-411-2547-7).
56. Eniko Horvath, *Mandating Identity: Citizenship, Kinship Laws and Plural Nationality in the European Union,* 2007 (ISBN 978-90-411-2662-7).

57. Rass Holdgaard, *External Relations Law of the European Community: Legal Reasoning and Legal Discourses,* 2007 (ISBN 978-90-411-2604-7).
58. Jill Wakefield, *The Right to Good Administration,* 2007 (ISBN 978-90-411-2697-9).
59. Dimitry Kochenov, *EU Enlargement and the Failure of Conditionality: Pre- accession Conditionality in the Fields of Democracy and the Rule of Law,* 2008 (ISBN 978-90-411-2696-2).
60. Despina Mavromati, *The Law of Payment Services in the EU: The EC Directive on Payment Services in the Internal Market,* 2008 (ISBN 978-90-411-2700-6).
61. Anne Meuwese, *Impact Assessment in EU Lawmaking,* 2008 (ISBN 978-90-411-2720-4).
62. Ulf Bernitz, Joakim Nergelius & Cecilia Cardner (eds), *General Principles of EC Law in a Process of Development,* 2008 (ISBN 978-90-411-2705-1).
63. Johan van de Gronden (ed.), *The EU and WTO Law on Services: Limits to the Realisation of General Interest Policies within the Services Markets?,* 2008 (ISBN 978-90-411-2809-6).
64. Alina Tryfonidou, *Reverse Discrimination in EC Law,* 2009 (ISBN 978-90-411-2751-8).
65. Mikael Berglund, *Cross-Border Enforcement of Claims in the EU: History Present Time and Future,* 2014 (ISBN 978-90-411-4564-2).
66. Theodore Konstadinides, *Division of Powers in European Union Law: The Delimitation of Internal Competence between the EU and the Member States,* 2009 (ISBN 978-90-411-2615-3).
67. Mattias Derlén, *Multilingual Interpretation of European Union Law,* 2009 (ISBN 978-90-411-2853-9).
68. René Barents, *Directory of EU Case Law on the Preliminary Ruling Procedure,* 2009 (ISBN 978-90-411-3150-8).
69. Yan Luo, *Anti-dumping in the WTO, the EU and China: The Rise of Legalization in the Trade Regime and Its Consequences,* 2010 (ISBN 978-90-411-3207-9).
70. Patrick Birkinshaw & Mike Varney (eds), *The European Union Legal Order after Lisbon,* 2010 (ISBN 978-90-411-3152-2).
71. Thomas Gr. Papadopoulos, *EU Law and Harmonization of Takeovers in the Internal Market,* 2010 (ISBN 978-90-411-3340-3).
72. Bas van Bockel, *The* Ne Bis In Idem *Principle in EU Law,* 2010 (ISBN 978-90-411-3156-0).
73. Veljko Milutinović, *The 'Right to Damages' under EU Competition Law: From* Courage v. Crehan *to the White Paper and Beyond,* 2010 (ISBN 978-90-411-3235-2).

74. Amandine Garde, *EU Law and Obesity Prevention*, 2010 (ISBN 978-90-411-2706-8).
75. Leonard Besselink, Frans Pennings & Sacha Prechal (eds), *The Eclipse of the Legality Principle in the European Union*, 2011 (ISBN 978-90-411-3262-8).
76. Sacha Garben, *EU Higher Education Law: The Bologna Process and Harmonization by Stealth*, 2011 (ISBN 978-90-411-3365-6).
77. Dimitry Kochenov (ed.), *EU Law of the Overseas: Outermost Regions, Associated Overseas Countries and Territories, Territories Sui Generis*, 2011 (ISBN 978-90-411-3445-5).
78. Pablo Ibáñez Colomo, *European Communications Law and Technological Convergence: Deregulation, Re-regulation and Regulatory Convergence in Television and Telecommunications*, 2012 (ISBN 978-90-411-3829-3).
79. Elise Muir, *EU Regulation of Access to Labour Markets: A Case Study of EU Constraints on Member State Competences*, 2012 (ISBN 978-90-411-3823-1).
80. Tim Corthaut, *EU Ordre Public*, 2012 (ISBN 978-90-411-3232-1).
81. Oana Ştefan, *Soft Law in Court: Competition Law, State Aid and the Court of Justice of the European Union*, 2013 (ISBN 978-90-411-3997-9).
82. Francesco Rossi dal Pozzo, *Citizenship Rights and Freedom of Movement in the European Union*, 2013 (ISBN 978-90-411-4660-1).
83. Jens Hartig Danielsen, *EU Agricultural Law*, 2013 (ISBN 978-90-411-3280-2).
84. Ulf Bernitz, Xavier Groussot & Felix Schulyok (eds), *General Principles of EU Law and European Private Law*, 2013 (ISBN 978-90-411-4683-0).
85. Michelle Everson, Cosimo Monda & Ellen Vos (eds), *European Agencies in between Institutions and Member States*, 2014 (ISBN 978-90-411-2843-0).
86. Stefan Leible & Matthias Lehmann (eds), *European Contract Law and German Law*, 2014 (ISBN 978-90-411-2588-0).
87. Piero Leanza & Ondrej Pridal, *The Right to a Fair Trial: Article 6 of the European Convention on Human Rights*, 2014 (ISBN 978-90-411-4855-1).
88. Patrick J. Birkinshaw, *European Public Law: The Achievement and the Challenge*, 2014 (ISBN 978-90-411-4744-8).
89. George Cumming, *Expert Evidence Deficiencies in the Judgments of the Courts of the European Union and the European Court of Human Rights*, 2014 (ISBN 978-90-411-4123-1).
90. Vesna Rijavec, Tomaž Keresteš & Tjaša Ivanc (eds), *Simplification of Debt Collection in the EU*, 2014 (ISBN 978-90-411-4854-4).
91. Nina Półtorak, *European Union Rights in National Courts*, 2015 (ISBN 978-90-411-5863-5).
92. Kyriaki-Korina Raptopoulou, *EU Law and Healthcare Services: Normative Approaches to Public Health Systems*, 2015 (ISBN 978-90-411-5013-4).
93. Torsten Frank Koschinka & Piero Leanza, *Preliminary Injunctions: Germany, England/Wales, Italy and France*, 2015 (ISBN 978-90-411-5833-8).

94. Vesna Rijavec, Tomaž Keresteš & Tjaša Ivanc (eds), *Dimensions of Evidence in European Civil Procedure*, 2016 (ISBN 978-90-411-6662-3).
95. Stefan Leible (ed.), *General Principles of European Private International Law*, 2016 (ISBN 978-90-411-5955-7).
96. Patrick J. Birkinshaw & Andrea Biondi (eds), *Britain Alone!: The Implications and Consequences of United Kingdom Exit from the EU*, 2016 (ISBN 978-90-411-5832-1).
97. René Barents, *Remedies and Procedures before the EU Courts*, 2016 (ISBN 978-90-411-6614-2).
98. Luca Prete, *Infringement Proceedings in EU Law*, 2017 (ISBN 978-90-411-6900-6).
99. Robert van den Hoven van Genderen, *Privacy Limitation Clauses: Trojan Horses under the Disguise of Democracy*, 2017 (ISBN 978-90-411-8599-0).
100. Mariusz Krzysztofek, *Post-Reform Personal Data Protection in the European Union:General Data Protection Regulation (EU) 2016/679*, 2017 (ISBN: 978-90-411-6237-3).
101. Gianni Lo Schiavo, *The Role of Financial Stability in EU Law and Policy*, 2017 (ISBN: 978-90-411-8230-2).